CW00547864

1001/ 38
£5

Grand Dukes and Diamonds

By the Same Author

The Fortress
A Hermit Disclosed
The Big Tomato
Princes under the Volcano
The Shadow of Vesuvius
A Pre-Raphaelite Circle
Rome '44
Shades of the Alhambra
The Golden Oriole

Grand Dukes and Diamonds

The Wernhers of Luton Hoo

RALEIGH TREVELYAN

Secker & Warburg
London

First published in Great Britain in 1991
by Martin Secker & Warburg Limited
Michelin House, 81 Fulham Road, London SW3 6RB

Copyright © Raleigh Trevelyan 1991

A CIP catalogue record for this book
is available from the British Library
ISBN 0 436 53404 5

The author has asserted his moral rights

Printed in Great Britain
by St Edmundsbury Press, Bury St Edmunds, Suffolk

Contents

Contents

PART TWO
Fabergé

Mulberry

List of Illustrations

Illustrations are reproduced by kind permission of the following: No. 1, Mrs J. P. M. Niven; 2, 10, Cape Archives; 3, 7, Africana Museum, Johannesburg; 4, Barlow Rand Ltd; 5, 6, Africana Library, Kimberley; 30, 40, English Heritage; 50, Lady Lloyd; 53, 54 Imperial War Museum; 62, C. R. Peacock; 68, Press Association; 70, *Country Life*; 75, Lord Lichfield. All other photographs are reproduced by kind permission of the Wernher family.

Foreword

by H.R.H. The Duke of Edinburgh K.G., K.T.

The story of Julius and Harold Wernher is played out during an exceptionally dramatic period in history. Julius became a leading figure in the European infiltration of Africa and with the rapid development of its very rich resources. As a young army officer, Harold lived through the horrors of the trench warfare in France before he was able to enjoy some of the fruits of his father's financial genius. He then started a successful business career on his own account before being caught up in the higher levels of management of the war effort in the Second World War. He lived on to witness the social, political and industrial upheaval in Europe which followed the havoc of devastating wars and revolutions.

It is now fifty years since the end of the Second World War and there have been some ups and downs, but nothing to compare with the collapse of the nineteenth-century world during the first fifty years of this century. This book follows the events in the lives of two particularly able and enterprising men and the domestic and social fluctuations in the fortunes of their families and friends. It would have been an interesting story of human triumph and disaster in any epoch, but what gives it a special fascination is the cataclysmic scenario in which this group of people had to live out their lives.

Introduction and Acknowledgements

The idea for this book arose when descendants of Sir Harold Wernher decided that the record must be put straight about his role in the Mulberry project, the artificial harbour which had been so crucial to the success of the Normandy landings in June 1944. The family was shocked that he should continue to be unjustly misrepresented by some modern writers. I was intrigued by the possibility of such a book, having recently visited Arromanches and seen the remains of that extraordinary structure, still there after over forty-five years.

There is still no satisfactory complete history of Mulberry. But I knew already that Mountbatten had appointed Sir Harold, a tough and brilliant businessman with a fine record in the First World War, to be his Chief Co-ordinator in Combined Operations, with access to all Cabinet Ministers and Service planners. This had developed into a huge and important job – not least of the problems being the successful maintenance of secrecy. Mountbatten, I discovered, had also been appalled by the lack of recognition for Harold when the war was over. From private papers and documents it became clear that Harold had made too many enemies, especially at the War Office; for he was the sort of man to whom the tag 'did not suffer fools gladly' is inevitably applied, and he found himself faced with a barrier of bureaucracy and jealousies. He had of course been hurt at being overlooked in official citations. Yet in spite of seeming thick-skinned to some observers, he was also to a certain degree modest and never wanted to advertise what must have rankled as a deep grievance.

Even a brief study of Sir Harold's life led me inevitably to his father, Sir Julius Wernher, the most powerful of all the 'Randlords' from South Africa, immensely wealthy and a great philanthropist. And neither of these could be separated from their wives, both of them strong characters in their own right: Sir Julius's wife Alice, who later became Lady Ludlow, and Sir Harold's wife Lady Zia, daughter of Grand Duke Michael of Russia. Thus, within the limits of space available, I have expanded my theme to include both generations. I had twice visited the Collection at the Wernhers' mansion, Luton Hoo, with its grand Belle Epoque interior and semi-Palladian exterior, and had admired Lady Zia's famous Fabergé and the Russian Rooms. Thus I was already aware of her Tsarist background and her descent from the poet Alexander Pushkin. In the racing world Zia had become a household name, and at Luton Hoo I saw the many trophies connected with the Wernhers' celebrated racehorses, notably Brown Jack, considered to be one of the greatest horses in racing history, Meld and Charlottown, the Derby winner. I also had been amazed by the richness and variety of the Collection, with its medieval ivories, Renaissance jewellery and bronzes, Limoges enamels, majolica, tapestries, English porcelain, and paintings by Rubens, Titian, Reynolds and Bermejo. Some of the furniture, silver and other objects, including most of the Dutch paintings, had been acquired by Harold, but the main Collection had been formed by Sir Julius Wernher, reputedly so busy that dealers would have to visit him at breakfast. The English porcelain had been the contribution of Julius's wife, and is regarded as the most important after the royal and the Victoria and Albert collections.

Sir Julius had first made his fortune out of diamonds at Kimberley, which resulted in his becoming a Life-Governor of De Beers. The goldmining companies that he came to control at Johannesburg were collectively known as the Corner House, a symbol throughout the financial world at the time for immense prosperity and rectitude. I certainly was not intending to write a business history, but, as in the case of Harold and Mulberry, I was chiefly interested in his character within the context of his business interests.

Geoffrey Wheatcroft in *The Randlords* remarked that there had never been a biography of Julius, and only an early and unsatisfactory one of his close partner, Alfred Beit, much more then in the public eye, and whom Wheatcroft considered the 'greatest genius of the first generation of magnates'. In his book about the Corner House A. P. Cartwright did, however, fill in some of the gaps. Part of the problem has always been that both Wernher and Beit, like nearly all the other 'goldbugs' and for that matter diamond-bugs, confused their tracks by destroying many of their personal papers. Julius, in spite of his great wealth and prestige, was a retiring man. He was a friend of leading politicians but hated becoming involved in politics, and avoided publicity. He also had few interests outside his business and collecting. His acquisition of Luton Hoo and of Bath House on Piccadilly was probably done to please – as Beatrice Webb unkindly put it – his 'society-loving' wife. Indeed, as I was to discover, with certain important exceptions, especially during a time of prolonged private agony near the end of his life, the few revelations about this determinedly secretive man were embedded in correspondence with his business partners in South Africa.

I confess that I began to worry about tackling Julius when I read a diary entry by Bertrand Russell about meeting him in 1904, and even more so when confronted by Hilaire Belloc's scathing poem, 'Verses to a Lord'. These, coupled with Thomas Pakenham's history of the Boer War, seemed to present Julius as a kind of demon, with 'blood on his hands', in cahoots with Joseph Chamberlain and Lord Milner. But I had already decided that it was not within my scope to delve into the rights and wrongs of the Boer War, in spite of my instinctive antipathy towards Cecil Rhodes. I did of course want to establish Julius's view on the War, and to find out if there was any evidence of his colluding in the Jameson Raid. There was also the question of 'Chinese slavery' in Johannesburg, for which he was undoubtedly one of those responsible and which brought down the Conservative Unionist government in Britain. In fact it became clear to me that the real reason for his success, *pace* Belloc and the frequently bombastic MP Henry Labouchere, was actually due to his being regarded by financiers, investors and mineowners as a person of integrity and honesty – unlike certain of the more flamboyant Randlords. 'Race' in his day generally meant the relationship between those of British and Dutch extractions in South Africa. When gold was discovered on the ridge known as the Witwatersrand in 1886, there were very few black inhabitants in the area. Afterwards, as at Kimberley, migrant black workers flooded in from all over Southern and Central Africa. I do not think that Julius Wernher would have been surprised by the conflicts that have developed in the modern townships outside Johannesburg; but he would certainly have been pained and saddened.

It is hardly necessary to say that the discovery of diamonds and gold completely transformed the economy of South Africa. Diamonds were first discovered in the remote desert-like area known as Griqualand West in 1867. The 'dry diggings' in what became Kimberley were already established by the time Julius Wernher, a German aged twenty-one, came out in 1871 as an employee of Jules Porgès, a Parisian Jewish diamond-dealer. In that harsh landscape there was already a large town of tents and corrugated-iron shacks, with a population of fifty thousand and an atmosphere akin to the Californian gold rush. It was also in 1871 that the British moved in to annex the diamond fields. Six years later they annexed the Transvaal. This was followed by the Zulu War, in which a whole British regiment was annihilated at Isandhlwana. The first Anglo-Boer War broke out in 1880, and in the following year the British were obliged to recognize the independence of the Transvaal once more.

Such were some of the historical events in the background of Julius's life at Kimberley, which he left finally for London in 1884; by then he was a wealthy and respected dealer, and a partner in Jules Porgès & Co., eventually on the retirement of Porgès to turn into the firm of Wernher, Beit, and a giant in the mining industry. Julius visited South Africa only twice thereafter, and then briefly. Nevertheless his contemporaries, in Britain, France and South Africa, were always astounded by his detailed knowledge of the mines, and his views were sought not only by Chamberlain but by Balfour, Rosebery, Asquith, Haldane and even Smuts, all of whom became his friends.

Sidney and Beatrice Webb found themselves approving of

Julius, chiefly because of his enormous financial donations towards their pet 'Charlottenburg Scheme', which developed into the present-day Imperial College of Science and Technology, built behind the Albert Hall and where the busts of Julius Wernher and Alfred Beit can still be seen on each side of the entrance. Of the many institutions that benefited from Julius Wernher's generosity, running into millions of pounds at current values, three in particular can be mentioned, having almost been founded on his money and, in the case of the first especially, Beit's. They are the University of Cape Town, the Imperial College of Science and Technology and Sister Agnes's King Edward VII Hospital for Officers.

Julius Wernher's widow, who was partly of Polish origin, was also known for her public generosity, especially during the First World War. After her brief remarriage to Lord Ludlow, she became one of the leading hostesses of the Twenties and Thirties. Famous for her spectacular jewels and furs, she was also a considerable musician in her own right and gave lavish concert parties at Bath House with performers such as Chaliapin, Grace Moore, Gigli, Sacha Guitry, Tauber and the Menuhins. The behaviour of her beloved eldest son Derrick had probably hastened the death of Julius, and a curious and unresolved episode concerning this young man brought further scandal and pain. Balanced against this was the marriage of Lady Ludlow's second son Harold to Countess Zia de Torby, eldest daughter of Grand Duke Michael of Russia and related to most of the royal families of Europe and the Mountbattens.

In fact the cordial relationship between Lady Ludlow and Lady Zia did not long prosper. Harold, apart from his financial and business flair, in some ways perhaps owed more to his mother's side of the family. He had none of his father's monolithic remoteness, and was determined to enjoy his wealth. Often it is the case that the first generation which makes the money is succeeded by a second that spends it and is ruined. This certainly did not apply to a man who was a driving force in Combined Operations, and who was also for many years Chairman of Electrolux and for a short crucial period of Plessey. He also controlled seven London West End theatres in the thirties, and after the Second World War bought and ran hotels in Bermuda, with great success.

Harold had a marked, if individual, sense of humour (again not so evident in his father) and obviously regarded business as a kind of game. In many ways he was the opposite to his wife, who to most outsiders was a fascinating and occasionally alarming character, 'more royal than the royals', proud of her Russian blood, of immensely high standards and a tremendous organizer, and with a strong social conscience. Harold, like his parents, was generous to institutions, particularly hospitals, and especially the Edward VII. He also, quietly and discreetly, helped many private individuals, including some of Zia's family left destitute after the Russian Revolution. If the standards set by the first generation of Wernhers were not dissipated by the second, neither have they been by the third and fourth, who have notably carried on the tradition of hard work and public service.

The daughters of Sir Harold and Lady Zia Wernher, Mrs Harold Phillips and Lady Butter, and the ten grandchildren have been wonderfully generous with their help, reminiscences and hospitality. Even so they may have been surprised by some of the anecdotes that I gleaned from elsewhere. They asked me to write this book, but have allowed me a free hand. So any judgements and opinions are mine alone.

Of the grandchildren, the Duchess of Abercorn and Mrs Randall Crawley have been particularly helpful, and I am also especially grateful to Mrs James Burnett of Leys. I have written elsewhere in this book about the tragedy of the death of Nicky Phillips. My debt to him is great, and without his help and suggestions my task would have been much more difficult, especially when researching Sir Julius Wernher. He was the owner of Luton Hoo and its archives, and it was he who provided me with most of the material about his grandparents' horses and the stud. The other grandchildren have also given unstinted assistance: the Duchess of Westminster, Mrs William Morrison, Lady Ramsay, Mrs Alexander Galitzine, Mrs Peter Pejacsevich and Charles Butter.

I am grateful to HRH Prince Philip the Duke of Edinburgh,

HRH the Duke of Kent and the Countess Mountbatten of Burma for kindly giving up time for me to visit them, and to Lord Brabourne for giving me access to the Broadlands archives.

The memories of Miss Odile Barbier and Michael Urwick Smith, past Curator at Luton Hoo, have been invaluable. I have also had enthusiastic and important help from the present Curator, Mrs Oonagh Kennedy, and the assistance of Denis Garrod the Administrator and many members of the staff at Luton Hoo.

Sir Alfred and Lady Beit have been most kind, and Sir Alfred introduced me to Mrs Maryna Fraser, Group Archivist at Barlow Rand Ltd, Sandton, Johannesburg, where the papers of H. Eckstein and Co. are preserved – essential to the whole section on Sir Julius Wernher in this book. I must also add that Mrs Fraser herself has been essential to the book; I am immensely grateful to her.

At Johannesburg my thanks go to Mrs J. P. Hill and Mrs Nagelgast of the Africana Museum at Johannesburg Public Library, to Mrs Rosemary Burke at the Chamber of Mines, to Mrs Anna M. Cunningham at the William Cullen Library of the University of Witwatersrand, and also to Chloë Rolfes and Jim Bailey. Harry Oppenheimer greatly facilitated my visit to Kimberley, where Dr M. H. Buys, archivist at De Beers, was most helpful and arranged for a visit to the McGregor Museum, where I received useful assistance. Mrs Lesley Brits of the Africana Library at Kimberley also provided important guidelines.

I must also thank Miss Leonie Twentyman Jones at the Jagger Library of the University of Cape Town, Mr A. Fanaroff at the South African Library, and Mr L. A. Theart at the Cape Archives Depot. It was a privilege indeed to have been a guest of Mrs Cecily Niven, daughter of Sir Percy FitzPatrick and approaching her ninetieth year, at Amanzi. Professor André de Villiers arranged for me to see the FitzPatrick papers at the National Language Museum at Grahamstown, for which I am most grateful.

In connection with my Julius Wernher researches I must thank: Stephen Andrews, Louis Baum, A. S. Bell of Rhodes House, Theo Bull, Sir David Butter, Allen Drury, Comtesse Vital de Gontaut-Biron (granddaughter of Jules Porgès), Mr and Mrs Martin Green (Porgès relatives), Ken and Luna Harvey in Zimbabwe, Mr and Mrs Owen Hunt for some Lionel Phillips papers,

Jim Joel, Mrs Alice Kalman for many Jewish references, J. B. Kettel of Charter Consolidated PLC, Miss Deborah Lavin for valuable help, Mrs D. C. Leith and Dr I. M. Leith, descendants of Francis Oats, Joachim Liebschner for help with German translations, Miss Simone Mace of the Rothschild Archives, Dr A. P. M. Malcomson of the Public Record Office of Northern Ireland, Dr Colin Newbury for much valuable advice, Lady Newman, the Hon. Thomas Pakenham, the Hon. Miriam Rothschild, Dr A. L. Rowse, Anthony Sampson, John Saumarez-Smith, Dr Wilhelm Velten, Willem Wasserman, Carl Udo Wernher, Geoffrey Wheatcroft for much essential groundwork, Mrs June Williams for detailed help concerning Rhodes House archives, Mrs Anita Wolfe-Coote and Dr Edith Woodger.

Raúl Balín has helped me with my researches at every stage. Victor Franco de Baux spent much time and care preparing the family trees. Ken Cooper's unrivalled knowledge of Luton history and lore has been invaluable. Mrs Gwynydd Gosling made available her archives on Russian Grand Dukes. Steve Cox has been through the final typescript with meticulous care and saved me from pitfalls. Dan Franklin has given me essential advice. Mrs Joan Haybittle and Mrs Julie Pearce have typed and retyped many drafts, often at short notice. All these have my special thanks, as has Mark Hamilton. Barley Alison, whose death in 1990 was a blow to so many friends and authors, commissioned this book and encouraged me in her marvellous, inimitable way.

For my researches in Part Two of this book I must also thank the following: Colonel Sir Michael Ansell, Mrs Kerstin Asp-Johnsson, Cultural Attaché at the Swedish Embassy, Nicholas Bagnall, Vere, Lady Birdwood, Peter Bishop for much help concerning Mulberry sources, Vincent Bouvier for his generous assistance concerning Mewès and Davis, Lady Boyd-Rochfort, Allan Braham, Vice-Admiral Sir Ronald Brockman, Mrs Humphrey Brooke, Commander I. K. Brooks of the King Edward VII Hospital, Mrs Avril Broster, Stanley Broughton for details about Electrolux, John Buckledee of the *Luton News*, Martin Bunting for papers of his father Colonel T. B. Bunting, Major-General Sir George Burns, Mrs Ruby Busch, Sir John Carew Pole, Dame Barbara Cartland, Mrs M. Chalk at the Broadlands Archives,

Mrs Effie Chambers, Mrs Lorna Citrom of the Friends of University College Hospital, Sir John Clark, late Chairman of Plessey, Dame Frances Clode, niece of Lady Ludlow, Mrs M. S. Coffey, Mrs Norman Colville, the late Mrs Ronald Cooke, Mrs Josephine Corbin, John Cornforth, Mrs Patricia Cullis, Mrs Elizabeth Cuthbert of the Royal Archives, Windsor Castle, Mrs Alastair Dacre-Lacy for many amusing family stories, Mrs Robin Dalton, Mrs L. G. Dower, Mark Evans, Oliver Everett, Librarian at the Royal Archives, Douglas Fairbanks, Jnr, Bill and Jane de Falbe, Stanley Falconer, R. Fellowes of the Jockey Club, Justin Fenwick, author in 1971 of the dissertation *Architecture of the Entente Cordiale: Messrs Mewès and Davis*, deposited at the Fine Arts Faculty, Cambridge, Frank Field, Lady Forwood, Mrs Enid M. Foster of the British Theatre Association, Mrs Anne French of the Iveagh Bequest, Kenwood House, H. S. Gevers, Lord Glendevon, Brigadier the Hon. Richard Hamilton-Russell, Lieut. Colonel A. F. Harper of the Hurlingham Polo Association, Lieut. Colonel Derrick Hignett, John Hislop, Neil Hughes-Onslow, Mrs Joan Hull, Frank Hurd, Mrs Thomas Hussey for lending me her husband's Combined Operations papers, the Rajmata of Jaipur, Mrs Dorothy Jelley, Geoffrey Jones for help concerning Electrolux, the Hon. Pearl Lawson-Johnston, Miss Jane A. Leggett of the Newarke Houses Museum, Leicester, HE Leif Leifland, late Ambassador of Sweden to the United Kingdom, Richard Leigh, Lady Lloyd, the late Joe Loss, Eric Lown, Lord Luke, late Chairman of Electrolux, Angus and Deirdre McCall, Mrs Nicholas MacGillycuddy, Miss Biddy Marc for many reminiscences of her aunt Lady Ludlow, Mrs Mary Morbey, Dr Janet Morgan, Lt-Col. C. A. Murray-Smith, Bernard Naylor of Southampton University Library, Mrs Hilda Neve, C. R. Peacock, Christopher and Charlotte Petherick, C. J. Pickford of the Bedfordshire County Archives, Mary Princess of Pless, Vincent Poklewski-Koziell, Mrs Geoffrey Probert, another niece of Lady Ludlow, Lieut. Colonel Richard Probert, Mrs Polly Proudlock, Paul Raben, John Redman, Mrs Anthony Rhodes, Prince Alexander Romanov, the Hon. Alfred Shaughnessy, E. N. Sheppard, Geoffrey Smith and Aubrey Stevenson of the Leicestershire Libraries and Information Service, Kenneth Snowman, Robert Spooner for much helpful information about Sir Harold Wernher's business life, Hugo Vickers for extracts from Sir Charles Johnston's diary, L. S. Walton, Dr David Watkin, J. N. P. Watson, Miss Rachel Watson, the Northamptonshire County Archivist, Richard G. Watson, Hon. Secretary of the Fernie Hunt, Richard R. Williams, Archivist at the Imperial College of Science and Technology, Mrs Violet Williams, the late Rachel, Lady Willoughby de Broke, the Hon. Mrs Reginald Winn, Miss Tatiana Wolff for advice concerning Pushkin and much else, Dr C. M. Woolgar of the University of Southampton Library, the Hon. Mrs Wynn, C. M. U. Young, Philip Ziegler, Sir Solly Zuckerman. And my thanks to Tony Raven for the index.

Prologue

In June 1917, one month before the start of the third battle of Ypres, and four months after the abdication of Tsar Nicholas II of Russia, an event was announced which ‘caused quite an excitement’ among London society magazines. This was the engagement of Countess Zia (Anastasia) de Torby, daughter of Grand Duke Michael Mikhailovich of Russia, and Major Harold Augustus Wernher, son of the late Sir Julius Wernher, the great ‘diamond magnate’, reputed on his death to have been the richest man ever recorded by Somerset House.

The Grand Duke, ruined by the Russian Revolution, had already been forced to give up living at Kenwood House in Hampstead, and it was rumoured that he might be offered one of the royal lodges at Windsor. Inevitably there were unkind remarks about a ‘marriage of convenience’; one paper remarked that it was a ‘sign of the increasing democracy of our times’. But both young people were very good-looking. Zia, ‘like a Watteau shepherdess’, with eyes ‘as blue as forget-me-nots’, was described as a young lady of many accomplishments – not only a beautiful dancer, but a good pianist, an expert tennis player and skater, a golfer of parts, and as much at home on the back of a horse as was her fiancé. She was often to be seen at the wheel of her Calthorpe motor car with her cousins Princesses Nina and Xenia of Russia. An ‘open-air girl’, like her younger sister Nada, married to Prince George of Battenberg, she ‘enjoyed the privileges of Royalty and the free and informal existence led by girls of somewhat lesser degree’. Zia was twenty-four years old. She had been working for hospitals and charities, her skill as a driver was much in demand, and 'no-one was a more persuasive seller of programmes at charity matinées'.

Harold was also aged twenty-four. He had a fine record on the Western Front, and had been mentioned three times in dispatches. He was in the 12th Lancers but serving with the Machine Gun Corps. Whilst on leave the previous December he had broken his leg steeplechasing at Windsor, and still walked with a limp. The gossip columnists soon revealed the probable extent of his fortune, which appeared to run into millions, and the fact that he had become his father's heir in place of his elder brother Derrick, who had been 'cut off'. His younger brother Alex had been killed in action the year before. Harold was also heir to Sir Julius's immense art collections at Bath House in Piccadilly, opposite the Ritz Hotel, and at Luton Hoo in Bedfordshire, a building more a palace than a country house, set in a park landscaped originally by Capability Brown.

Harold's mother, Lady Wernher, lived at Bath House and Luton Hoo. She had recently caused a sensation by subscribing £2 million to the War Loan in memory of Alex. Sir Julius Wernher, German in origin, had been created a baronet by Edward VII. He had been co-partner in Wernher, Beit, a diamond, gold and financial firm of worldwide renown, and a Life-Governor of De Beers. A retiring man, he had a reputation, somewhat unusual among the so-called Randlords, for absolute probity, and he had been a spectacular philanthropist. Lady Wernher, née Alice Mankiewicz, was partly Polish and partly English.

Articles were written about Zia's ancestry and the bewildering ramifications of her royal relations. She was descended from Nicholas I of Russia. One of her uncles was married to the Tsar's sister, and her aunt was the Grand Duchess of Mecklenburg-Schwerin, mother of the Queen of Denmark and the Crown Princess of Germany. Her parents' morganatic marriage had caused such outrage in Imperial circles that for many years they were debarred from entering Russia. Her mother, once 'one of the most beautiful women in Europe', had been born Sophie von Merenberg, daughter of Prince Nicholas William of Nassau but not considered royal because her father, who was a half-brother of the Grand Duke of Luxemburg and half-brother of the Queen of Sweden, had also married morganatically. When Sophie von Merenberg married Grand Duke Michael she was given the title of Countess de Torby by her Luxemburg uncle. Thus it was that the name Torby was passed on to her children.

None of the magazines seemed interested in the fact that, through her mother, Zia was also the great-granddaughter of the Russian poet Alexander Pushkin. Instead there were remarks such as this: 'It is so strange to think of a member of the Russian Imperial house marrying into a Jewish family! Who would have conceived it possible a few years ago? But wars and revolutions may work even more extraordinary changes than this before any of us are much older.'

PART ONE

DIAMONDS

I

The Young Julius

The Wernhers were not Jewish but Lutheran, from an 'old and reputable' Palatinate family, though many of Sir Julius Wernher's closest business colleagues and friends were Jewish. A Wernher obtained his baccalaureate in antique law at Heidelberg in 1516, but the first recorded direct ancestor was Warden of the monastery school of Hornbach at the beginning of the seventeenth century. There followed a series of pastors and a book-binder. Julius Wernher's great-grandfather was a Judge and Cabinet Minister at Zweibrücken, until forced to leave on the arrival of the French Revolutionary army. It was his son, Julius's grandfather, who rose to prosperity, as a Privy Councillor and President of the Court of Appeal in the Grand Duchy of Hesse.

Julius's obituaries maintained, in parrotlike fashion, that he was the son of a general. They were mistaken. His father, Friedrich August Wernher, nicknamed Gustel, was an eminent railway engineer. The general in question was a cousin, a member of the elder branch of the family which had vineyards at Nierstein on the Rhine. In his old age Gustel became difficult because of his deafness, which interfered with his great love of music. Nevertheless, so we are told, he was 'in every respect a real man', straightforward, simple in manner, honest, exceptionally conscientious, 'without a trace of conceit', 'strict' at work – attributes that were applied later to Julius himself. He was a keen collector of minerals and had an appreciation of art. As a youth he fell

3

deeply in love with his relative Henriette Bruch,★ who unfortunately was under age, so off went Gustel disconsolately to Paris, to study chemistry and mathematics. On his return her parents denied a request for the hand of Henriette, and he left his home again, tortured with love, this time for England, where he became friendly with the engineers Stephenson and Brunel. Then, at last, in 1834 he was permitted to marry Henriette. Alas, she died during a typhoid epidemic seven years later; there had been four children, but only a boy survived.

Gustel's particular friends were the Zöppritz brothers of Darmstadt, cloth manufacturers. One of them had married a Weidenbusch, daughter of a lawyer, and in 1844 her sister Elise became Gustel's second wife. Clearly there was no grand passion this time. She was his 'helpful companion', a good housewife and stepmother. She too bore him four children, two girls and two boys. One daughter, Maria, was sickly; she spent 'many of the best years of her childhood in bed', and never married. Another, Emilie, did marry and had a family. One son was mentally retarded. The other was marked out from early childhood for a brilliant future, on account of his extraordinary memory and aptitude for learning: this was Julius Carl Wernher, born at Darmstadt on 9 April 1850.

Gustel became director of an ironworks at Darmstadt. In 1848 he was sent to England by the Ministry of Marine to buy warships for the German fleet, with unhappy consequences – but that is another story. His next duties took him to Mainz and then to Frankfurt, where the family settled and where he became chief engineer of the Taunus Railway. Julius was therefore mostly educated in Frankfurt. He had been tempted by a career in engineering but eventually decided against it and served an apprenticeship with a bank. Friends and relatives were in awe of his business acumen even when he was aged eighteen, and would ask his advice on abstruse questions of investments.

Portraits of Julius as a grown man show him to be handsome and regular-featured, bearded and with blue eyes wide apart, typically Teutonic. After his death he was remembered as having

★ The future composer Max Bruch was a family connection.

had a massive frame and great strength. It is a surprise therefore to discover that as a child, like his sister Maria, he was a 'weak and thin mite', and thus constantly fussed over by his mother. He had an aptitude for languages and learnt Spanish. Then, in 1869, he insisted on going to Paris to perfect his French, in spite of his mother's fears that his tendency to overwork would harm his eyes. He did work very hard, again in a bank, Ephrussi Porgès, and preferred studying at night to those 'notorious' temptations of Paris in which some of his German friends indulged. He greatly impressed his employer Théodore Porgès, and this was later to stand him in very good stead, in an unexpected way.

Porgès was Jewish, supposedly of Portuguese Sephardic descent, and had emigrated from Bohemia to Vienna and then to Paris. At that period when anti-Semitism was waxing in Europe, Julius's attitude towards Jews was ambivalent. Obviously he had prejudices, for his mother wrote to him: 'What you say about your new employer is not very pleasant, but he does sound a well-adjusted person. I do hope that as a Jew, and especially as a Jew from Vienna, he does not take honesty light-heartedly and will do business in a fair way.'

Julius persuaded his family to invest in the Zöppritz brothers' new blanket-making firm: this too would have important results for him. The family was missing him in Frankfurt, and seemed a little lost. 'As you know, your father takes offence easily. It was easier for you to humour Papa. You had that light-hearted and happy approach that pleased him.'

Julius had been too unfit for his year of military service, but was called up for the army of occupation during the Franco-Prussian War as a cadet in the Dragoons of the 4th Cavalry Division. It is clear from his letters at that time that he despised both the coarseness of his officers and the wave of imperialist sentiment that was surging through Germany. The devastation after the siege of Paris upset him also. 'The whole of joyous St Cloud is unrecognizable and abandoned by its inhabitants,' he wrote to his mother. 'The castle from which eight months ago the Emperor set out, so full of hope, is in ruins. Below me is a beautiful view of Paris, quiet and serene as if we had done it no harm.'

After the war he went to London. In spite of high recommendations from Porgès he could only find a post first as a bookkeeper in a firm of German druggists and then in a bank. He liked London ('Paris is a village by comparison'), but was depressed. Suddenly, however, his luck changed. On 11 November 1871 he wrote to his obviously worried parents that: 'Mr Jules Porgès, the cousin* of my Paris head, and a leading dealer in diamonds both in Paris and London, has engaged me to go with his partner to the Cape of Good Hope to buy diamonds on the spot.' Jules Porgès, still in his early thirties, wanted him to go out for two years, with a free passage and all costs paid, except for clothes. He would be given £150 for the first year, £180 for the second. 'The offer is so extraordinarily favourable that I did not doubt your permission and accepted it.' After all, he was now twenty-one. Then, with his mother's doubts in mind, he added: 'Mr Porgès is the most charming and kindly man in the world, and behaves as heartily and confidentially as you could wish. He looks upon me as his *helpmeet* and *fellow worker.*'

The partner he was to accompany was French, Charles Mège. Julius wrote again: 'The advantage of the whole affair does not lie alone in the conditions that I have been offered, but also in the fact that in a relatively short time there is a chance of independence.' Charles Mège would be returning from South Africa after two years, and Julius had now decided that he would probably stay on out there, as he would be left in sole charge of the firm's interests. 'One wins nothing without daring, and there are few cases where chance offers itself as it does here. There is always a risk and danger in every business, and that can never be a reason for keeping away from it. What reproaches I would have to make in later life if I let such an opportunity go by.'

Diamonds, including the superb stone known as the 'Star of South Africa', had recently been discovered in the arid, desolate country named Griqualand West, over five hundred miles inland to the north-east of Cape Town. As the Wernher parents were well aware, by the year 1871 the scramble of prospectors was well

---

* It is assumed that this was a mistake, and that Jules Porgès was the brother not cousin of Théodore. In France Porgès always had an accent.

6

and truly on; hundreds of fortune-seekers from Britain, Eastern and Central Europe, America and Australia had made the arduous journey to the banks of the Vaal River and the country around. The British government had also recently decided that the moment had come for annexing the territory.

There was only time for Julius to make a quick dash for goodbyes at Frankfurt and to pay one last visit to his 'beloved' opera house at Covent Garden. Within a month he and Mège were off on the thirty-eight-day sea journey, in the course of which Julius started to teach himself Dutch. The family tradition is that the ship ran into a storm, and that he, being very prone to sea-sickness and therefore on deck, was actually washed overboard but swept back by a wave.

He was not especially impressed by Cape Town, as against its 'stupendous' surroundings, and still less by its inhabitants, whom he found indolent and lazy, at least one-third constantly drunk. By 4 January 1872 they had reached Port Elizabeth, which they admired for its fine buildings and warehouses. 'But one must be very careful here of the people, even of one's dearest friends. It is degrading to have to deal with persons who are friendly to one's face but of whom one knows for certain they want nothing but to make a profit out of you.' Ox carts were assembled in the market square of Port Elizabeth for the transport of goods to the interior. Each could carry eighty tons and would be pulled by sixteen animals. The journey would take up to five weeks. Julius admired the physiques of the 'Kaffirs', as the blacks were known. 'They have such a stature and symmetry of limb, and are so strong and muscular that it is a pleasure to look at these naked Apollos. Of course in the town they have to wear clothes.' As for the English, 'they drink and booze like animals.'

Julius attended auction sales of diamonds, and soon realized how much he could earn privately if he had the capital. He therefore wrote to the Zöppritz brothers asking them to help by standing security for a bank loan in London. He had already, it appears, borrowed money from his half-brother August, a doctor of private means. Then he and his companion were off to the diamond fields of Griqualand West, six people packed like herrings in a two-wheel cart drawn by six galloping horses, which were changed every two or three hours. 'You cannot imagine what one has to suffer, over utterly impossible roads. The whole body is bruised and wounded.' The country through which they passed had been almost stripped of its inhabitants because of the frantic dash northward.

At last, after 'many disagreeable adventures in great heat through the weird Karroo' – it was mid-summer – they reached the place known as Du Toits Pan, where only eighteen months before there had been but a single farmhouse (owned by a man called Du Toit) in a barren waste.* Now there was a population of about a thousand, two-thirds black. Diamonds were being found there up to a depth of sixty feet. The richest mines, however, were about three miles away at a hillock called Colesberg Kopje, appropriately renamed New Rush, and at Old De Beers, once part of a farm owned by two Boer brothers called De Beer; round these places were camped some eighteen hundred people in tents and corrugated-iron shacks. Mines at Bultfontein and, some way off in the Orange Free State, at Jagersfontein were also in operation.

The prospectors were mostly a rough lot, to say the least, though 'democratically minded'. The smells were vile, the dust appalling. Rather than stay long in a 'den of indescribable filthiness', one of the many so-called hotels, Mège and Julius erected a canvas house, sixteen feet by ten, with a double roof to keep off the heat and divided by a green cloth into two rooms, forming a bedroom and an office. There was another tent for the cook, and they had a stable for two horses. They also acquired a little canvas office in New Rush, a town of tents, like 'white antheaps', where they found themselves in frenzied competition with other diamond dealers, already well established, and who did not welcome these new arrivals backed by the rich Mr Porgès of Paris.

Not surprisingly, Julius soon had to reassure his mother about his health. He carefully avoided telling her about the epidemic of camp-fever, which had caused some deaths. There was plenty to laugh at, he said, but did not specify what, unless he meant Mège's snores. He avoided telling about the ruthless greed of

---

* A pan was a reservoir or pond.

prospectors, but concentrated on the sense of adventure and discovery. As for the landscape, he told her that he was living in the midst of a great bare plain, dotted with aloes and distantly bounded by pebbly hills, once inhabited only by a few nomadic tribes and some scattered Boer farming families. In summer there was no grass and the few straggling camel-thorn trees were hardly bigger than bushes. Sometimes you saw skeletons of oxen or mules. 'Now and then a little green and yellow sand is broken by muddy water, and that is everything, everything, that can be said of the place.' The contrast in climate between summer and winter was tremendous, snow being not unknown. In due course he was to write of winter days as being 'like paradise' with a 'purity and translucency of air'. Until two and a half years before, traders had rarely come to the district in order to barter with the Boer peasants – who knew absolutely nothing about the outside world. 'And thus,' he wrote, 'there sprang from these farmer Dutchmen a race of terrific bodily strength, but extraordinarily limited spiritually. Among these peasants cooking is an unknown art, and cleanliness doubtful. They leave their sheep to graze unguarded, and do nothing but sit, laze and smoke pipes. Their women are huge.'

He explained how until a short time back the area had been part of the Orange Free State. Soon it would become a British Crown Colony, separate from Cape Colony, with its own administration. The earliest diamonds had been collected or 'washed out' on the banks of the Vaal River, and it was Joseph B. Robinson, a cantankerous bully 'born with a tombstone in his soul' and later to become famous in the diamond fields, who had shrewdly acquired property there at Hebron. But an Anglo-Irishman, Captain Loftus 'Paddy' Rolleston, whom Julius seemed quite to like, claimed to have been the first to initiate the actual diggings; that was in January 1870. Within three months there had been five thousand prospectors at the Vaal River sites, but after this 'short blossoming' the place had 'sunk to nothing' because of the greater number of diamonds found at Bultfontein and Du Toits Pan some twenty miles to the south. Then there had been the even more exciting diamondiferous discoveries at De Beers and New Rush. All those places were known as the dry diggings, as against the river diggings. In eighteen months, Julius said, New Rush would probably be as desolate as before, leaving only the artificial valleys and heaps of earth and gravel abandoned by the prospectors.

Here he was quite wrong. In spite of disasters and periods of crisis New Rush would turn into the awesome Big Hole of Kimberley, thirty-six acres in area and nearly a quarter of a mile deep, in appearance and size not unlike the crater of Vesuvius, and one of the wonders of the world.

Julius admitted that he was finding life pretty monotonous. Not for this circumspect young man the gambling dens, grog shops or bars like the Spotted Dog or Pig and Whistle:

> During the day I run about on the claims to buy small lots
> of diamonds, and in the evening I sit at my table, read or
> learn Dutch grammar, or think of you. There are any
> amount of Germans everywhere, but not twelve Christians.
> Food is expensive, bad, and the 'restaurants' dirty beyond
> description. Drinks are colossally expensive, a bottle of beer
> costs three shillings, a taste of cognac in water one shilling.
> In this my solitude it consoles me to remember that there are
> at least those at home who worry about my future. But
> there is one thing about which you cannot help me, and that
> is the fleas, which are as numerous here as the sands of the
> sea. I spend a fortune on flea powder, but it is hopeless. Mr
> Mège killed fifty-seven on his body the other day, and yet
> he was practically eaten up the same night.

The Zöppritz brothers had willingly obliged with security for a loan, in spite of an impending slump in Germany. Julius warned his family not to sell any shares just because rumours made the prices low. 'There is so much swindling in Austria.' Then came the news that his father was leaving the 'good old' Taunus Railway for a more important post. He was to be the chief engineer of the Hessische Ludwigs Railway, and in due course was to build the Ruhr-Sieg Railway running from Limburg to Westphalia. The family would therefore be moving to Limburg.

Julius wished his mother would write 'more vivacious' letters. Frau Wernher had been worrying about whom he would marry if he stayed abroad so long. She had always hoped for a German daughter-in-law. Julius admitted that he had been quite fond of a girl at Frankfurt, but had not been *in love* with her. At present he knew of only one person who would always be faithful to him, and that was his mother. In any case his work was all-absorbing. There were such enormous possibilities ahead. 'I am becoming more and more indispensable to my Frenchman.' What was more, he expected to be able to send back yearly sums of money 'towards our inheritance'.

Some wives and children of dealers and prospectors had arrived, but he did not of course reveal in his letters that in 1872 a large proportion of the females around New Rush, white and black, were prostitutes.

2

Life in the Diamond Fields

Julius Wernher's early letters were almost like a diary, though he avoided details of business transactions. They were written in German, but some years after his death his widow had most of them faithfully translated into English. He also left a few sheets of paper headed 'Notes on the Diamond Fields', quaintly expressed at times, written in English and in the third person, but typically concise and careful not to lift veils from the ambiguities behind the strange and to this day secretive world of international diamond trading.

He wrote to his parents in deliberately simple terms, explaining that a claim measured thirty or thirty-one feet square but might be divided into eight, twelve or even more pieces, all owned by separate owners. The results were a question of luck. One claim might yield £10,000 in a month, another nothing at all. Thus a digger needed to have plenty of spare capital, or else he had to join up with other prospectors to form a consortium, sharing the risks. Work at the mines began at sunrise, and earth from the 'immense' chasms would be hauled up in leather buckets. The digging in this moon landscape was usually done by blacks, the sorting by whites. He wrote of the cacophony of noise – shouts, clanging metal, rolling carts, the crack of whips, the rattle of the siftings, creaking horse whims, braying mules, the chanting sing-song of black workers. At night there was no peace; the hideous howling of dogs was followed by the crowing of a thousand roosters.

With the onset of the rains the walls of the claims became

dangerous, and every week there were fatal accidents through landslides. Hail would thunder on the corrugated-iron roofs. He slept with a revolver under his pillow, and after dark carried a long stick because of numerous drunkards always 'in ambush'. No doubt anticipating alarm at home, he quickly added that in any case he usually stayed in of an evening, as he shared a mess with a Frenchman who had an expert cook. Game, such as partridges and buck, improved the menus. As for water, it was rarer than brandy, and had to be carted from the Vaal River. Thus many people were discouraged from washing: not so pleasant. And you had to be on your guard with every single person, especially in business. There was such a lot of 'malodorous rabble' from the goldmines of Australia and California.

He then described the original discovery of diamonds at New Rush the previous August. There really had been a 'rush', a kind of crazy panic – a pathetic exhibition of greed, even desperation. Everything at Du Toits Pan had been abandoned, tents, camp equipment, clothes. People ran, galloped on horses, raced along in carts and carriages, in order to grab a claim, even a half or quarter of a claim, before it was too late. His friend Captain Rolleston had said that it had been like a disordered army in full flight.

In April Julius was writing that the South African mines were proving themselves far richer than anyone had imagined. But this had also meant a tremendous drop in the price of diamonds all over the world, and fortunes were already being lost. The cost of claims was 'skyrocketing', too. Would-be prospectors were still turning up daily, hoping to earn heaps of money quickly, but were all too soon disappointed in that ruthless world. Luckily, however, he and Mège had bought their stock carefully and in not excessive quantities.

He complained about the haphazard postal system. Every evening dozens of registered letters containing diamonds, often of the highest value, were being dispatched. They would be left lying about in the post office, on tables, chairs or the floor. After sorting them the postmaster would go for his meal, leaving the packets 'to look after themselves'. 'It is small wonder that the last European post was stolen!' Volunteers were searching all the bars and blocking exits to the camps. On another occasion, during the rainy season, a whole sack of letters had been swept away in a river.

Now Julius, thanks to his loan, was arranging to import not only German beer but sparkling wine from his Wernher cousins' estate at Nierstein. He might dislike drunkenness, but there was a profit to be had from alcohol. In spite, he wrote, of the lack of general business, new shops were appearing every day, and there was even a Lutheran church in New Rush, though 'alive with fleas'. Indeed the white population of the diamond fields remained more or less constant, the numerous arrivals making up for the constant departures.

Trading was still so slack in June that he admitted that he might be sitting at his desk without a client for a whole hour. It being midwinter, the nights were 'ice cold' and he had to have a sheepskin on his bed. Recently people had been found frozen to death, having gone to bed drunk.

Meanwhile he had had a charming letter from Mr Porgès, advancing him a whole year's salary, 'a very fine proof of trust'.

His parents were curious to have more information about the black workers. He replied that apart from the Hottentots and Bushmen, who were the aborigines, and the Griquas themselves, who had mixed blood, the working blacks were from the east, from Zululand, Natal or Mozambique, and also from districts to the north of the Transvaal Republic.

The whole journey here is done on foot, and takes, according to distance, six weeks to two months. On the way they starve, and often do not eat anything for two or three days; then they eat a little maize, and continue the journey. Usually they come in whole troops of forty to eighty, and are greeted by their comrades on arrival with loud cries, singing and dancing. The first month they are usually ill, and some die. Their feet are wounded and swollen, and as soon as they have found service they are nourished. In the beginning they usually over-fill their stomachs, which have been used to emptiness, so that even the Kaffir or Negro cannot stand it. The usual wage is ten

14

shillings per week with board, an extraordinarily high price, but this is going to be reduced soon to six or eight shillings. They are usually very strong, and can work like no white man, but are dreadfully lazy and waste a lot of time. A kick is supposed to bring them to reason, and on the whole they are generous and naïve. They are very grateful for the smallest gift, but often start thieving and steal a lot of diamonds. If this is found out, they are punished vigorously, but usually the fury of the diggers is so great that the authorities try to hang them at once. By now the conditions of the law are slightly more ordered, though in the beginning there were several kinds of lynch justice. It is forbidden for the whites to buy from the Kaffirs, as the diamonds would probably have been stolen; and if it is found out that a white man has bought from a Kaffir his house is burnt down, and he can only save himself by flight. Luckily now there are numerous policeman, and such excesses have not happened for a long time. Before they were of daily occurrence. The Kaffirs save every penny. When they have enough money they buy a rifle and gunpowder, woollen blankets, tin buckets, iron pots and so on, and go home heavily laden. With these treasures they buy a woman and marry.

The blacks were rather given to drink, the whites not setting a good example, because while the average Englishman in England might drink one glass of brandy, if he could afford it, in Africa he swallowed down quantities with water, trying to quench his thirst. Barkeepers were forbidden by law to sell spirits to a black without the written permission of his master. Often there were some quite fierce and alarming tribal battles.

Those blacks who had come from the Cape spoke good English and became servants, copying their masters in clothes and manners. Julius in his old blue coat looked 'far less noble' than his servant.

The other day I came home from a ride and called to him to take my horse. He was lying in the stable on straw, and replied to my call, 'John is drunk, sir' – then he ordered one of his friends to do what was necessary, and even had the presence of mind to give orders about feeding the animals. Next day he had a sore head, and we hoped that it would have taught him a lesson once and for all, but unfortunately since then he is often tipsy.

Julius wrote a long letter home on 15 June, before setting out on a tour to the Vaal River. The great news of the day, he said, was that the post thief had been arrested in Cape Town. He was an Englishman, and about 2,300 diamonds had been found on him, all mixed up together and hidden in his rifle barrel and powder horn. The fellow had arrived at Cape Town in February, lodged in the Royal Hotel, where he had stolen £100 from the man with whom he shared a room, and had then disappeared to the diamond fields. Afterwards he had had the cheek to return to the Royal. 'His luggage was already on board a ship, but Nemesis stood before the door. The ship was a day late in leaving, and Tuesday evening quite by chance the man from whom he had stolen the money returned to Cape Town and went to the same hotel . . .'

'In my last letter,' Julius went on, 'I wrote a little chapter about the Kaffirs. I shall continue today. Although these people are quite unsophisticated as yet, they are human beings and capable of instruction, and man always remains the most interesting part of Creation.' Their small pleasures charmed him. 'When talking or singing excitedly they move their hands vivaciously. The singing is more a soft humming, always the same melody but not unbeautiful. There are many dialects, but mostly they speak a language with accent, and it seems to be rich in vowels and has many curious tongue sounds, like clicks.' Those who worked in the claims were addressed as 'Boy', whatever their ages. They generally possessed only one woollen blanket or sheepskin against the cold, and when digging wore a small rag as a loin cloth. Any piece of clothing would be a deep 'Isabella' colour, possibly a ragged coat or military uniform. 'Our John is a fop comme il faut. He has at least six hats and two smoking caps, coats and trousers, paper collars, and fourteen ties, high boots etc. In short there are not many like him. All the Kaffirs are dreadfully frightened of the police, who do not behave very delicately towards them. The usual punishment is twenty-five strokes.' He wrote of the Berlin missionary station where women were taught needlework and the men agriculture. He seemed particularly to like the Basutos, who 'could not be equalled' in the making of baskets and mats, but they were not so handsome as the 'strapping' Zulus and warlike Matabeles.

A German Club or Mess had just been started, though other nationalities could be admitted. Of the twenty-one members, he said, he was the only Christian. 'The intention of the Club is the promotion of card playing and dominos. Of course I am only going to play whist, and I do not intend to go there more than twice a week.' At least there would be a stove in the Club, particularly welcome in winter, and German newspapers would also be available. Julius's beer and wine would be on sale. As it happened, he said, because of living with Mège, he was speaking more French than German.

At the end of this long letter there was a terse little postscript: 'I am afraid I cannot worry about catching butterflies for Uncle Wilhelm. If he wants fleas I am ready to send him a thousand from my bed.'

By the end of July 1872 he was finding himself much busier. This was partly because he and Mège now had their own kitchen, and Julius had to supervise the buying of supplies and the cooking. Vegetables, except potatoes, were always scarce. Butter was 'disgusting'. There was tinned fruit from California, but horribly expensive. The Frenchman with whom they had shared a mess had not only taken to drink but had stolen money, so that arrangement was over. Even Mège had learnt to sweep out his own office, saddle his own horse and feed it. 'Yes, when the Kaffirs forget to empty his night pot he empties it himself, which especially pleases me. Excuse these details but they give a picture of our life.'

Some claims had by now been bought up by Mège on behalf of the firm. Julius, always in a great white sombrero, was also making regular visits to the Vaal River sites, partly because of a new, though minor, rush at Waldeck's Plant, where once a huge

stone had been found. He also visited Hebron and its neighbour
Klipdrift, after only two years a substantial and pleasant town.
The diamonds he bought were small but of perfect quality. Julius
thought the countryside pleasantly picturesque, at any rate a relief
from the noise and stink of New Rush. Then there was the benefit
of having a morning bath in a reasonable hotel without having to
pay for the water.

For nearly two months there had been no rain. The dust storms
around New Rush and Du Toits Pan, or Dutoitspan as it was
generally called by now, were so dense, that the sky became dark
and reddish and it was 'literally impossible' to keep one's eyes
open.

Suddenly there seemed to be a disastrous setback to the
business. Once more the post had been stolen; and with it all the
beautiful Vaal River diamonds that Julius had collected with such
pains. He 'felt like weeping'. This time the sack containing the
registered letters had disappeared from the back of the mail cart,
and the driver had not noticed until he had gone sixty miles. 'If
Negroes make the slightest mistake,' Julius wrote, 'they are
punished cruelly, but fellows such as this go free.' Anyway, after
a month the thief was caught, and the diamonds recovered.

Now, in response to his father's request for a description of the
actual mines, Julius launched into several pages, in his neat small
script. Patiently he gave details of the system of sieving the gravel
from the river diggings, and reiterated how the majority of
prospectors were now concentrated on the dry diggings. In the
latter the surface was of a yellowish colour, but below the earth
was hard and blue, and this was where the diamonds were
found.* Removing the earth was the great problem – in effect it
was only possible if there were roads or paths between each claim.
These roads, seven feet wide, were like ridges in a vast honey-
comb which was covered with a web of hauling ropes and running
gear. Enormous hills of debris made the excavations seem even
deeper.

---

* This 'blue ground', or kimberlite, was the matrix of the diamond deposits,
and occurred in cylindrical 'pipes'.

When claims began to reach ninety feet in depth the roads
became ever smaller, and there were constant landslides and
collapses of the reef [containing walls] worse than before.
Daily men, carts and horses hurtled into the depths, and
were dashed to pieces. Carts were then forbidden to use the
roads, and all the earth from the middle of the area had to be
brought out in sacks, which made the cost very much
higher. The claims near the border now use the so-called
tramways, scaffoldings from which wire ropes of up to a
hundred feet are sent into the depths, often stretching over
other claims. With these wires the earth is brought up in
buckets, and it really is an extraordinary sight to see those
buckets hovering in the air, with nearly naked Negroes on
the high scaffolding, turning wheels, some singing, others
screaming directions, while others are busy with
wheelbarrows, or toil, like tiny black crows in the depths far
below.

(These were the wires that Olive Schreiner romantically described
in her novel *The Story of an African Farm* as a 'weird, sheeny,
mistlike veil'.)

At the river it had been a question of digging out gravel. In the
'dry' ground, at New Rush for instance, you first had to excavate
up to sixty feet of yellowish soil or sand. Here you would hope
to find many diamonds, and these were easy to pick up. After
that came the hard bluish substance which many people at first
thought was the end of the diamonds. But after digging into it,
the quantity turned out to be even greater, the darker the ground
the better.

Many prospectors sift with sieves which only stop stones
over one carat, so that all the smaller stones are wasted. In
this way you can at least get much more work done, and
gain in time. It is curious how different in quality diamonds
are from closely situated diggings. At Bultfontein the stones
are of little weight but beautifully white. At Dutoitspan you
have the 'fattest' diamonds, more or less yellow, though
there are also some smaller stones of good colour. These

two are now known as the 'poor man's diggings'. At New Rush and De Beers you usually find fragments, many of enormous weight, some of fifty to sixty carats. The prices are regulated by colour, size, form, purity and structure, and there are as many prices as shades. Some stones are sold at five shillings per carat and others at £40 to £100. Every stone has to be judged individually, and in order to be a real expert you need years of practice. Although I have examined thousands of stones and bought hundreds, I am still a miserable beginner, and admit that up to now I have had more courage and good fortune than knowledge.

The more expert you were, he said, the more particular you became. Good light for assessing stones was essential. Indeed many faults were not visible to the naked eye. Julius admitted that he had made mistakes, but Mège had been extraordinarily gener-ous in such matters, taking the view that errors were inevitable where only two per cent of the diamonds were of the finest quality.

Julius had had another warm letter from Porgès, making it clear that he would be in charge when Mège left in 1873 and that he would be permitted to purchase further groups of claims. Porgès, Julius told his father, had 'earned terrifically' and might even consider retiring in a few years' time. This could have an effect on Julius's career, possibly turning into a dangerous situation – or else it might be a great opportunity. 'However as matters go, I am looking into the future full of trust . . . If I remain in good health and keep my wits about me – and two strong arms – I shall never lack anything. Though of course I shall also still need my good luck.'

3

Turn of the Tide

By 1873 the 'respectable female element' had increased in the diamond fields, as more wives arrived, accompanied sometimes by daughters. Julius appreciated their civilizing effect, and on New Year's Eve even consented to go to a ball, where his Nierstein champagne 'flowed like rivers'. Still, however, preferring to stay at home in the evenings, he wrote to his parents for a supply of books; not novels, but biographies, travel books and histories of art. He particularly wanted a work on Michelangelo, Mommsen's *History of Rome* and Macaulay's *Essays*. He also needed cookery books.

Friends from that period afterwards described him as a born diplomat, calm personified, thoughtful, slow and determined, never in a hurry, never suffering from 'nerves', strong in mind and body, keeping to himself. A fellow diamond dealer was to write:

He was known to be a very just man, upright and strictly honourable in all his dealings, incapable of doing anything shady. In a time when fortunes were easily made, by all sorts of means, and temptations to be crooked very great, it was rare to come across a character like Wernher's. A curious feature about him was that whilst he was slow to act in business affairs, when otherwise occupied he raced. He never rode to the mines, or about the camp, except at a good hard gallop, and in the ballroom he flew across like a heavy dragoon in a charge.

Since Julius complained that the women he had to dance with were too small or fat, and since he was usually described as burly or massive, we may assume his performance on the floor must have been quite a spectacle.

Among his competitors in business were the smaller peripatetic dealers, or kopje wallopers, shady operators and scamps many of them, and some rising to enormous wealth, such as the incomparable Barnett Isaacs, from the East End of London, better known as Barney Barnato. Rivalries lay ahead with Barnato, a long way in the future, but even he would have acknowledged that Julius Wernher was that rare combination, a man of unlimited ambition who was also a man of principle. Other potentially colourful but less controversial dealers of the period such as David Harris, Francis Oats and Sigismund Neumann were to become friends or colleagues.

It was said that Julius was 'not luxurious but liked his comforts', and that he used to 'indulge in a great deal of sarcasm, which although humorous was at times very stinging'. He especially liked to 'chaff' about the Boers and loved to tease his Dutch friend Martin van Beek, who later lived with him, about speaking the local dialect, the Taal. For all that, there is not much intentional humour in his letters, which often seem to have a self-congratulatory tone – though this would have been deliberate, in order to reassure his parents, worrying about his future in a time of financial crisis in Europe.

On occasions he felt obliged to apologize to his mother for sending her his Jewish friends from the diamond fields, and would emphasize their special qualities. He himself appeared to have completely lost whatever anti-Semitic feelings he might once have had. As for the blacks, they still 'greatly intrigued' him, though there were some 'serious problems'. In October 1874 he was writing once more about 'this strong though lazy people', and continued: 'As slavery exists no longer one cannot force them, and there is little to be done with money either. It will take a lifetime before these savage forces can be properly channelled. People are thinking seriously of importing Malays and Indians, of whom there are any amount in town.' But the greatest 'problem' of all was IDB (Illicit Diamond Buying), mainly by the kopje wallopers and to a large extent blamed on pilfering by blacks.

Some claims in mines were owned by blacks, and this was resented by white diggers. Julius did not necessarily share such a prejudice but was convinced that the days of small owners were doomed, as the increasing depth of the mines and the frequent caving in of the reef made the working of their holdings unprofitable. Many of the deeper claims were under water in winter, and little combination existed between the various owners. In any case numbers of claims were mortgaged and coming on the market.

You had to be 'very very careful', he said, about lending money. There were some reckless speculators around. 'It is dreadful how much swindling there is here, particularly in dens for billiards or roulette run by Americans and Irish.' Fortunately, he added, there were still decent people about, and 'matters are not anything like as bad as they were and still are in the Californian Gold Fields.'

Here he was speaking from the heart. Some years later he revealed that he had had a bitter experience in 1873. 'An acquaintance from the war, a German, betrayed me to the tune of £400, the savings of my first year. I had lent him the money so that he could establish himself, but he absconded.

For all that, it is clear that Mège and Julius took advantage of buying up claims at bargain prices. Throughout his business life Julius stuck to the maxim that one should buy when prices are at their lowest.

He wrote again about the importance of purity in diamonds. Mège, for instance, had paid £1,600 for a 38-carat stone that Julius by a lucky chance had found at Waldeck's Plant. They had thought it would cut to 16 carats, but one dealer in London reckoned that it would only make 12½, which would have meant a loss. As it happened, it cut to 18, so there was a 'pleasing profit'. On the other hand a friend had bought a stone for £900, and when it was cut the highest offer was only £256. 'Our enemy remains the London market which last year broke the neck of many a fellow.'

He admitted that he was longing for the day when Mège would

return to Europe. Not that they ever had the slightest quarrel. Mège was well educated and had good manners, but he was a 'heartless egoist', rather too keen on the ladies. Julius obviously on occasion had to stifle irritations, especially in the heat of February. He had been annoyed by Mège's selfish attitude during some torrential rains when the roof of their bathroom fell in. Apart from this, he was in suspense about his own future, being aware that a great deal of private correspondence on the matter was going on with Porgès.

He need not have worried. Both Mège and Porgès thought so highly of him that he was given a year's contract as manager with 25 per cent participation in the profits, all expenses paid. He was allowed to do business on his own account, and thus for a while became manager for two other unconnected firms. Looking ahead to the 'joy of independence', he bought and furnished a small house at Old De Beers, corrugated iron of course, 'charming and very comfortable, even with the luxury of a chest of drawers and a wooden verandah'.

Old De Beers had now become the fashionable area in the diamond fields, especially for the British. Ladies in gigs could be seen calling on one another, or cantering about, 'exquisitely dressed'.

His best friend then was his neighbour August Rothschild the auctioneer, known to all as the Baron, a 'noted card', the 'Beau Brummel of Griqualand West' because of his shiny pomaded locks. Julius described him as a 'generous fellow if a bit affected and uncultured'. This Rothschild had made 'pots of money' and would soon be visiting his family in Munich, bringing with him a present of ostrich feathers for the Wernhers.

Julius had to announce that he had been afflicted with severe haemorrhoids, and put this down to the sedentary life in the hot weather, stuck in his corrugated-iron shack behind a pair of scales. It was not possible to go for walks, the countryside being dull and sandy. 'Ninety out of a hundred people here are plagued with haemorrhoids.' Needless to say, his mother reacted at once with the greatest alarm.

The slump in the diamond fields became worse after Mège's departure.

One cannot see the end of it owing to this idiotic rivalry.
For the last six months diamonds have been more expensive
here than in London, but although there have been colossal
losses people go on speculating madly. New buyers keep on
arriving so this condition can last longer than it might
otherwise have done. In order not to fall into this same trap
one needs the patience of an angel, besides a great deal of
caution. People who once earned thousands of pounds are
now not worth ten.

Julius had consequently decided to suspend shipments for a while
to London.

Gold had meanwhile been discovered in the eastern Transvaal.
Julius was sceptical about prospects there, but several diggers left
to try their luck in this fresh El Dorado. The news of the find
spread quickly round the world, and prospectors were landing
'almost daily' at the nearest port, Delagoa Bay (later Lourenço
Marques), in the Portuguese territory of Mozambique, to find
themselves faced with the long and dangerous journey across the
'thankless veld'. 'Many have perished from exhaustion or disease,
or have been killed by animals.'

By the end of 1874 Julius found his circle of acquaintants
narrowing with so many being lured away to the goldfields.
Apart from Rothschild he saw most of Anton Dunkelsbühler,
popularly known as Dunkels (which name he adopted), perhaps
his chief competitor among the dealers and agent for Mosenthal
of Cape Town, and another dealer, Levy, whose wife was a
highly strung lady, fond of practical jokes. This could have been
the same Levy who was a gun and general merchant, in trouble
with some old hands for selling guns to 'niggers' – an offensive
word which had recently been borrowed from America and was
sometimes adopted by Julius.

He had to apologize for his letters becoming so 'dreadfully
boring', but 'my mind is like leather and full of business'. 'Money
is nothing to me now,' he added somewhat alarmingly. 'But I am
not one of those who make fortunes by genius, lose them and
then win them back. I only walk well-known paths.' He had
almost made up his mind to stay on in Africa for a few more

years, in the hope of eventually becoming a partner in the London end of the business. Such news predictably evoked a wail of anguish from his mother. What about that nice German daughter-in-law she so longed for? His reply, under the circumstances, must have seemed a little odd. 'You need have no fear of my respectability. I am as fresh and well as I could wish, especially in the cooler weather when the days are glorious. The work suits me down to the ground. The only disadvantage is its everlasting sameness. I live as regularly as in a girls' boarding-school.'

New Rush and De Beers had turned into Kimberley, named after the Secretary of State for the Colonies, and the area around Dutoitspan and Bultfontein had been anglicized to Beaconsfield, in honour of the Prime Minister. Discontent among the diggers had been growing ever since the arrival of the new Lieutenant-Governor, Richard Southey, mainly on account of his liberal attitude towards the blacks, and his failure to have them 'disciplined'. The main grievances centred upon IDB, and Southey's support for small-scale producers. In order to prevent IDB, the white diggers wanted blacks and anyone of colour to be banned from owning claims or dealing in diamonds. Other grievances were connected with taxation and relations with landowners, or rather speculators. A Diggers' Protection Association was formed, originally a vigilante group but developing rapidly into full-scale rebellion. Arms were collected and parades held in the market square. As a result troops had to be summoned from Cape Town.

Southey believed that German diamond merchants were the wire-pullers behind the rebellion, which became known as the Black Flag Revolt. The maximum number of claims holdings had been restricted to ten, which was frustrating indeed for those who were convinced that the mines could continue profitably only through consolidation. Nevertheless Julius – who to the end of his life tried to keep out of politics – had stayed very much in the background. In the end it seemed as though the diggers had won. He summed up the event for his parents in a bland and short description:

The ringleaders were acquitted recently by a Jury. Thereupon the Governor and his Secretary were recalled by the

Government. The Governor, as such, was hopeless, but admired in his private life. I knew him from his better side, and was very well acquainted with his son and often went to their house. They were always very hospitable. His post will be taken by an Administrator, as the Province is too small to afford a Governor. Taxes are quite enormous here. A white population of hardly more than five thousand souls has to supply about £70,000, and that for an Administration that does nothing, whose activity is only noticeable in the wrong way. No wonder the situation became heated.

Griqualand West was finally annexed to Cape Colony in 1881. The Black Flag Revolt has been regarded as one of the key events in the history of South African labour relations, even though 'persons of colour' continued to own property in Kimberley. It marked a hardening of racial attitudes, and the abolition of the ten-claim limit was the beginning of the period when the mines would be controlled by organized capital.

About this time also, Julius proposed, because of the IDB 'menace' (no longer a 'problem'), that all employees should be searched when leaving mines. The theory was that no honest man would object to this. The suggestion was not taken up, but when put into practice some years later caused violent protests. Although it affected both whites and blacks, historians have pointed out that it was symptomatic of a growing attitude that all black workers were potential criminals.

The Revolt also resulted in the gradual disappearance of the shareworking system – shareworkers being diggers who received a percentage of profits from owners of claims. Southey's complaint about wire-pullers had in fact chiefly been directed against the Moderate Party, which represented the interests of the diamond merchants, and whose committee included the formidable J. B. Robinson, now a prominent diamond buyer, and Julius's friend Rothschild. The huge sums of interest demanded by moneylenders from diggers, some of whom were thereby bankrupted, had been another element behind the Revolt. Rothschild is recorded as having £5,000 invested in loans. Presumably Julius to some extent was similarly involved, as he had picked up claims for himself in the Dutoitspan and De Beers mines. At any rate 1875 had been a brilliant year for him, as he told his parents, 'really too brilliant'. 'Not one young man out of a hundred thousand has earned what I have earned at the age of twenty-three.'

Even before the lifting of the ten-claims limit he had been urging Porgès to consider purchasing a major section of the Kimberley Mine (New Rush), as a means to secure a regular supply of diamonds. In 1875 Porgès was the largest importer of Cape diamonds in London and had £30,000 invested in the business. Delighted with his protégé, he first tried to make him accept a three-year contract, and then announced that he would have to come to South Africa himself.

Julius accepted the contract if he could have some leave in Europe in 1877. Kimberley hostesses were becoming impressed by this extraordinarily successful and good-looking though reserved young man, and Julius mentioned that he had accepted several invitations to balls during the cool season. At these entertainments he could sometimes be persuaded to sing German folk songs, which a Mrs Stonestreet thought 'passably in tune, rather a joke'.

In spite of business being 'as bad as ever', Julius's personal fortunes continued to increase. Indeed he admitted to having 'earned terrifically again', thanks to his growing clientele, both for the firm and privately. There were also new political problems.

The Boers very stupidly have started a war with Zulu tribes on their frontier, and at a decisive moment distinguished themselves by such cowardice that they would have become the laughing stock of the whole country, if the matter had not been too serious for jesting. Up to now the Kaffirs are victorious everywhere but are limiting themselves to the defensive. We are only suffering insofar as a lot of Kaffirs have had to go back to their chiefs, and there are not enough workers about.

This 'war' was more in the nature of a series of skirmishes. The Transvaal Boers, who were also in financial difficulties, had to appeal to the British for help, and, as a result, in April 1877, duly found themselves annexed, part of the British Empire. The Zulus on the other hand were to find that disputes over possession of lands on the Transvaal border were by no means over.

On 12 December 1876 Julius announced that 'our visitor', Porgès, had arrived. 'I cannot imagine a more agreeable event. In all questions we agree.' He would be returning to Europe with Porgès in the spring. Porgès had therefore brought with him a clerk called Charles Rube, a German from Darmstadt, 'a little quiet but seemingly willing and diligent'.

Sir Charles Warren, who had travelled out on the same ship as Porgès, the SS *Danube*, was to write of the 'magnificent Porgès who knows the value of money though he has plenty of it'. And photographs of Porgès do show an amiable face, with a big moustache and hair parted down the middle. Elegantly dressed always, a man of taste, he had sent Julius an exceedingly expensive Christmas present, not at all suitable for the rough life in Kimberley. This was a Louis XV 'mechanical' travelling cabinet. This rare piece is regarded as having inspired Julius on his return to Europe to become a collector and is still owned by his descendants.

Porgès was only in Kimberley for three months, and his visit was a sensation. Under the circumstances Julius's brief account of this period for the benefit of his parents is a nice understatement: 'We have made a not inconsiderable extension to our business in buying claims, in other words buying part of a mine, and I have had rather a lot to do.' Porgès formed a syndicate, mainly of friends in London and Paris, including Mège, and spent no less than £90,000 on buying claims at depressed prices in the Kimberley Mine, ending with owning 10 per cent of the whole. The result was that the market value of claims in general was driven up steeply. Porgès also decided to invest in the newly invented, and expensive, steam haulage and washing machines.

So in April Julius accompanied him to London, where the syndicate claims were put into a private company with a nominal capital of £400,000, the Griqualand West Diamond Mining Company. In August, after visits in Germany, Julius was in Paris, still full of extravagant praises for his employer: 'Mr Porgès really is an exception,' he wrote, 'resplendent in his happiness. I drive with him in the Bois and am always being invited to dinner. At the theatre I have the best seats. In short I am entirely the *Grand Seigneur*, which does not really suit my simple nature and the quiet life to which I am accustomed. As you realize, my *work* is in London, where as nowhere else the proverb Time is Money is better illustrated.'

He was back in Kimberley in November, as a partner, with instructions to watch out for first-class bargains.

4

'Centre of Important Interests'

Julius had just missed the visit of the famous author Anthony
Trollope. But then he was not likely to have been a reader of the
Barchester novels . . . Trollope had found Kimberley, still almost
entirely corrugated-iron shacks, unimaginably ugly. Its population, he noted, if Dutoitspan and Bultfontein were included, was
about 18,000, thus making it the second largest town in South
Africa. About 10,000 of its inhabitants were black. As he peered
into the 'vast bowl' of the Kimberley Mine, he immediately felt
that it was the 'largest and most complete hole ever built by
human hands'. This sinister scene of so many horrible deaths and
shattered hopes was then twelve acres overall and 260 feet deep,
crisscrossed by the aerial tramways.

Yet he thought that Kimberley was one of the most interesting
places on the face of the earth, and this was because of the speed
with which 'savages' from the heart of Africa were so quickly
adapting themselves to the habits and even laws of Europeans.
And would not these habits lead them eventually to Christianity?
'I have looked down into the Kimberley mine and seen there three
or four thousand of them at work, – although each of them would
willingly have stolen a diamond if occasion came – I have felt I
was looking at three or four thousand Christians.' And at least no
employer was allowed now to flog his men at his own pleasure.

His comments on causes of friction between the races, which
included IDB, the illegal sale of guns, and whether or not people
of colour should be allowed the vote, were all the more relevant
in view of Griqua tribal uprisings the following year. These last

were due to disputes over land ownership and the denial of the rights of chiefs to deal with their own subjects; they were mainly sporadic and directed against isolated white communities. Nevertheless there were fears in Kimberley that there might be links with the Transvaal's troubles with the Zulus. All this took place in a time of great drought and thus affected the price of food.

More alarming was the outbreak of tribal wars some hundred of miles away in the eastern Cape. There was an appeal for volunteers to join the Diamond Fields Horse. Loftus Rolleston, J. B. Robinson and Barnato's colleague Louis Cohen, an amusing and scandalous chatterbox, were among the volunteers. Originally this jolly unit had been the Dutoitspan Hussars. Julius had been asked to join in view of his experience in the Franco-Prussian War, but had declined; after all he was a German. Local casualties were few, but soon Julius reported that in the eastern Cape a thousand blacks had been killed to only seven whites. The blacks had good guns but were short of ammunition, so had to rely on their own weapons, which were only of use in close fighting. Meanwhile the arming of colonists continued.

'Without a telegraph,' Julius said, 'we are dancing on a volcano.' Business was 'monstrously bad', because of uncertainty and the scarcity of workers. For months he had not earned enough to 'pay for a breakfast'. He blamed the troubles on the 'all too humane treatment on the part of the English'. 'Instead of treating half-savages like children, they gave them all sorts of freedom, which of course the Kaffirs do not know how to make use of.' The approach of winter would be an advantage, as fires at night would betray the camps of the enemy.

All the same there was no lack of activity for him, and profits returned when the new steam haulage and washing gear was put in working order. He now employed two hundred people; on occasion, three hundred. The acquisition of good new claims began to 'throw off a good profit'; presumably this was made easier while rivals were away at the wars. He did not mention the rumble of resentment against him and his like that was growing among the smaller claimholders. For Julius was now a director of the Mining Board, quite an honour. The Board had the responsibility of removing fallen debris from the mines, which had developed into a very serious problem. Cash was limited and there were complaints that 'capitalists' like Julius were receiving priorities, and were thus enabled to 'swallow up' claims of lesser fry who had become hopelessly burdened by debt through having to cease operations altogether.

Large firms were now attempting to counter reef falls by sinking perpendicular shafts with tunnels for entering the mines. Trollope had gone down one of these shafts, but had not enjoyed the experience, what with clambering over rubble and the terrific heat.

Socially, Julius was leading a very quiet life. In the hot weather he hardly ever went out in the evenings except to the Levys, where he was almost a 'child of the house'. Mrs Levy would be going to Germany soon. She was the 'happiest, drollest soul you could imagine, if a little sentimental . . . you will like her very much.' Once again he was having to cope with the tedium of his mother's worries about when he would marry. She had decided that a young cousin, Anna Weidenbusch, would be a suitable match, and had obviously been fanning Anna's hopes. Julius and Anna had been corresponding a little, but any 'significance' had been 'far fetched', just brotherly affection. He had found Anna's letters written in an 'atoning Magdalen style', which he said had often made him laugh out loud.

He had to be firm when his sister Emilie wrote: 'Mother told me in tears that she hoped you have not given up your idea about Anna yet.' There had never, he replied, been any question of a declaration of love in his letters. He quoted Schiller: 'He who binds himself for ever should find out whether the heart wants the heart. The madness is short, the repentance is long.' He said he would probably end up an old bachelor. To his relief, within six months Anna had been 'driven into the arms of a parson'. Julius did not reveal that he was having something of a flirtation with a girl called Louisa, the daughter of Mrs Stonestreet.

At least Frau Wernher was to approve of Mrs Levy, 'not a bit like a Jewess'. Julius replied: 'Julia Levy is so good and free, in spite of having been in Africa for years, that everyone loves her. If only she could master this groundless excitement all the time.

Her husband is an indescribably good old animal, with whom I am always quarrelling, but we cannot live without one another.'

The 'Kaffir war' in Griqualand dragged on. On 30 July 1878 he wrote: 'Today good news. Our people, mostly volunteers from town here, killed two hundred and took three thousand oxen, three thousand sheep, two hundred and eighty waggons. How long the affair will last cannot be foreseen as one can never depend on the words of these beasts.' And early in the following year: 'Whilst in our Province peace has been restored more or less with relatively few sacrifices, the war has broken out in our sister Colony, Natal. There have been quite dreadful results right from the beginning. An English Corps consisting mostly of line regiments was cut off by a terrific number of Zulus and slaughtered. Fifty-four officers, among them several I know, personally, and about six hundred men, were killed all in one day.' This was the battle of Isandhlwana, fought on 22 January 1879, when a British regiment was annihilated. The casualties, including black troops, in fact amounted to more than 1,000 killed. Julius put the great defeat down to the commanders' lack of caution, and an underestimation of the 'brave and manly and well trained Zulu people.' 'The excitement is very great,' he added, 'especially as one fears the moral effect on certain chiefs whose neutrality will probably end now.'

Massacres on both sides continued. The 'inept' British leadership was faced with 'unbounded courage and great masses'. The death in battle of the Prince Imperial of France was due to 'terrific carelessness'. Then, at long last, the Zulus were crushed at Ulundi. Their chief Cetewayo fled but was captured.

In Kimberley these events of 1878–9 had the effect of stricter segregation, or the 'localization of natives'. The war depressed business, and Julius was so full of gloom that he had decided to leave Africa for good in 1880. 'I love work for its own sake,' he wrote on 4 May 1879, 'and if I am frightened of anything it is that I shall not find such unbounded activity in Europe. My whole position here is very important and influential, and without stepping outside the bounds of modesty I might say that nothing of importance is done here, at least in the business line, without my being consulted – and my opinion usually has the decisive influence. Yet I seriously want to get out next year to be near you again.'

All his plans for return had to be postponed because of dramatic new developments, namely Porgès's imminent formation in Paris of the Compagnie Française des Mines de Diamants du Cap de Bonne Espérance, with a capital of £560,000. It took place in 1880 and was the first Kimberley-based joint-stock company to be floated in Europe.

The various manoeuvres and manipulations around this period were neatly summarized in that matter-of-fact document written by Julius in the third person, 'Notes on the Diamond Fields', in which he recorded:

Orders for suitable machinery, were given [in 1877], more purchases increased the various blocks [of claims] to a very workable concern, and a limited liability Company was formed in England under the title of the Griqualand West Diamond Company. Profitable work resulted, and it soon became apparent that even now the blocks were hardly big enough and would be too small for future underground working. This led eventually to amalgamation with neighbouring holders, especially the firms of Lewis and Marks, and the various concerns were merged into a Company having its seat in Paris . . . a Company which held the largest blocks of claims in Kimberley Mine. The holdings were at first in different and divided blocks, but all the strategical points were quickly secured, connecting all the principal blocks and placing the Company in such a position that no combination of other holdings could injure it seriously. At that time a great deal of jealousy existed between the various large holders, and in their shortsightedness they overlooked their true interest which was to combine together. The management of the Compagnie Française devolved upon Mr Wernher, as Messrs I. Lewis and S. Marks soon retired from active participation to devote their energies elsewhere. Following above amalgamations several other important combinations took place, such as the Central Diamond Mining Company

35

[Baring-Gould], the Standard Company [J. B. Robinson],
all working in rivalry and trying to kill one another,
working without method or plan.

The formation of the French Company, as it was generally
known, did indeed precipitate cut-throat competition, not only in
the Kimberley Mine. At De Beers, where in April 1880 Cecil
Rhodes floated his De Beers Mining Company, the firm of
Lippert emerged for a while as the largest claimholder. Barney
Barnato and his brother went to London to form Barnato
Brothers, and on their return launched four new companies.

When Julius said that Isaac Lewis and Sammy Marks 'retired',
he meant that they were squeezed out of the French Company.
But they did, as he said, 'devote their energies elsewhere with
notorious success' – in the 1890s in Johannesburg they switched
to producing cheap liquor. Lewis and Marks were originally from
Lithuania, and had come to South Africa as pedlars. After Porgès's
spending spree in 1877 they had invested £20,000 on acquiring
claims in Kimberley Mine, and almost immediately had combined
their holdings with those of Paddon Brothers to form the Kimberley Mining Company, and it was this that in turn was
amalgamated with the French Company.

Mrs Levy returned from Europe in June 1879, and for some
reason had to stay a month or two in Julius's house, 'which I do
not like, for in spite of the veneration in which I hold her she is
much too excitable for daily intercourse'. The house was admittedly larger than the one Julius had bought in 1873, but even so it
must have been cramped, for he was sharing it with three other
bachelors.

Almost at once she embarrassingly began to confide in him that
her husband did not return her love sufficiently. Worse, she
transformed the house into a 'dovecot' for the ladies of Kimberley,
all anxious for a peep into this establishment, 'a perfect specimen
of order and cleanliness' where a German cook 'cursed and
shouted like a trooper from the kitchen'. Obviously primed by
Frau Wernher, Julia Levy nagged him about not being married
yet, and he retorted that he was rich enough not to have to
bother. As it happened, that August, his 'flame', 'whose eyes had

looked very sympathetically into mine', Louisa Stonestreet, married none other than Loftus Rolleston, greeted by all as a hero back from the wars. As Julius wrote later: 'The fault was mine. Had she spoken German all might have been different.' There may have been more to it than that, for Louisa was known to have a hot temper.

The three who shared Julius's house were Charles Rube, the young man whom Porgès had brought out in 1876, Martin van Beek, and Alfred Beit, 'a joyous, lusty fellow of extraordinary goodness of heart and very great business ability, compared to whom we are Philistines'. Beit was not only to become Julius's closest friend but his partner in a firm of world renown that bore their names. Three years younger than Julius, he had been born in Hamburg and, like Porgès, was of Portuguese Sephardic descent. His father imported silk from France. Because of the 'ugly monster of anti-Semitism rearing its head' in Germany, his parents had converted to Lutheranism, to give their children a better chance in life. He had gone to Amsterdam to learn about diamond cutting, had reached Kimberley in 1875 as a representative of his cousins' firm, W. & A. Lippert, and soon afterwards had shared Julius's house at Old De Beers. In 1878 he had returned to Hamburg for a while.

Like Julius, Alfred Beit had a 'horror of publicity' and a reputation for honesty. He also had an amazing memory and an almost uncanny knack of spotting a good diamond. Physically they were quite different. Beit was small, delicate, with bulbous, mild blue eyes and a large head. He was also a bad horseman and bad at practical things; but he was tremendously energetic, walking over the roughest country without showing signs of fatigue. In the ballroom, again unlike Julius, he would invariably choose the tallest woman in the room, and dance round her in a wonderfully comic manner. Both men were shy. Julius was merely reserved, but Beit was highly strung, with a habit of fiddling with his tie and biting his handkerchief. He could never be persuaded to make a speech.

Beit brimmed over with enthusiasms. 'You could not help loving the dear fellow.' It was said that he attracted money like iron filings to a magnet. Borrowing from his family, he bought land at New Rush and erected a row of corrugated-iron sheds for use as shops and dwellings, which soon were earning him £1,800 a month in rents. Later he sold the land for £240,000. The Lippert business connection had not been much of a success and he soon found that there was much more profit in dealing privately. 'In those years of securing properties and organizing them,' Julius wrote in his 'Notes', succinct as ever, it was almost impossible to give full attention to the diamond business itself, hitherto the mainstay of the firm. 'Mr Wernher therefore arranged with several younger men with a good knowledge of the article to operate on joint account, the firm supplying capital for shipment. One of the earliest connections of this kind was Mr Alfred Beit.' And he added: 'The account worked extremely well' – another of his little understatements. Meanwhile Beit – like Julius himself – continued to buy his own claims in the various mines, particularly in De Beers, where he came in contact with Cecil Rhodes, about whom Julius appeared to have personal reservations.

In October 1879 Julia Levy decided it was time for Julius to give a ball. Seventy people were invited. The German cook excelled herself, and there was champagne cup. The dancing ending at 4 a.m. 'But the expense?', he imagined his mother complaining. 'And you say business is bad.' The answer was that he didn't care. The cost was as much as a family holiday on Lake Maggiore, and even six such balls would not ruin him. He told his parents that his personal interest in the Kimberley Mine was now worth £12,500.

He had another shock waiting for his parents. He had determined that on his return to Europe he would live in England. 'In Germany business is a chain of intolerable nuisances. Liberal development is fettered [a reference to anti-Semitism], in a way that is terrible for anyone who has experienced the English way of life.'

Two other bachelors, unnamed but very likely Hermann Eckstein and Rudolph Hinrichsen, came for meals at Julius's house, forming a mess of six. One of them was to remember how they would take turns in organizing the catering. 'Interviews with the woman cook were never much cherished by any of us, and frequently Wernher would be called upon to appease her temper, and it was amusing to see how he could settle the trouble of the menu in no time.' In the end she was so overbearing that she had to be sacked.

The six went on a spree over Christmas. 'At half past nine at night on Christmas Eve we got on our horses and rode to a farm about twelve miles distant. The moonlight on the plain was beautiful. We slept at the farm, and were in the saddle again at half past three in the morning, in order to ride to a little village in the Orange Free State called Boshoff, another twenty miles. At that place there were several ladies we knew who were convalescing, and we spent a very high-spirited day.' Then it was back to Kimberley on Boxing Day, a five hours' ride, to be followed by a ball at Rothschild's. 'In spite of the heat there was a lot of dancing. Mrs Levy forgot that she had sprained her ankle.'

From the letter of 22 January 1880 in which Julius told his parents about the formation of the French Company, it is clear how much he had been the driving force: 'Before I managed to get my friends [in Paris and London] so far as to realize the usefulness of this step, and in the end to accomplish it, I had to write reams of letters, and I only achieved my goal after the greatest difficulties.' But he still had to contend with his parents' outrage over his remarks about Germany. In his reply he hinted at his own hurt feelings when an anonymous critic in Kimberley accused him of being a humbug and 'relentless'.

That one can be happy in Germany only as a German has not become a dogma yet, and at least there is evidence to the contrary. Even if I have changed through living abroad it does not mean that I have lost all sensitivity. If I had remained a little wheel in a huge machine in London it would have been easy to go back to Germany. But early in life I became independent and a moving force – I might say the centre of important interests – and I cannot now shake that off. Thus I belong in everything that means business on the grand scale, in everything that demands the power of man and the sharpness of intellect in a foreign land. It is not in my nature to boast of my position and to explain myself. Therefore rumours are being circulated here. Nevertheless I know that there are other people, some of them complete strangers, who have trusted me beyond bounds, and as I am not without honour or even ambition this trust gives me a higher point of view about my duties than is usual. If that is my crime so be it.

He was even contemplating setting up on his own in London. After all he was now aged thirty. Yet he was torn by his loyalty to Jules Porgès.

After such a resounding manifesto his mother could only suggest that maybe it would be better for his health to come back to Germany. But no: 'Sometimes I laughed as a stupid boy, when Father was running up and down the station platform watch in hand and waiting for the last train. But I am just as bad, and the capital I have to administer is much greater than the late Taunus railway.' He admitted that he had anxieties. For instance, there was the responsibility for the safety of his workers, 'who through braving constant dangers become incredibly careless. Now that we are employing between five and seven hundred men there is a lot of trouble. Luckily I have a very cool head; someone with an excitable nature would be driven mad by my position.'

For the next months he would be 'utterly taken up' with the organization of the new company. Expenses, especially because of reef falls, had been greater than expected. 'It causes me many a sleepless night, as you may imagine, with a concern that needs at present fourteen steam engines, nearly a hundred horses, and very many hundred hands. Our daily expenses are sufficient for you to live in Limburg for the whole year, so you can realize how many diamonds have to be found every day to do some good business.' A shaft was being sunk, already two hundred feet deep, and the earth for the first seventy feet had been so loose that a 'fantastic' amount of wood had to be used to shore it up. At present he did not know how deep the tunnel would have to be. The deepest claim in the mine was 320 feet. The company possessed about a hundred claims, and 'we therefore have at least twenty-three million cubic feet before us, which at the present prices of diamonds and according to the experience of years is worth about three and two thirds million pounds sterling.' A miner earned usually £9 a week, gunpowder cost two shillings a pound, and five hundred pounds might be used in a week.

No letter exists mentioning the rise of the Transvaalers against British rule, sometimes known as the first Anglo–Boer War, and their victory at Majuba Hill, which forced the British to give them back their independence. As the end of the year approached, he was admitting that he might even miss Kimberley.

> I hope I shall have brought everything into sufficient order by the end of the year so that my successor will be able to work on the lines that I have laid down. If the worst happened, I might have to come back again next year, which I dread. The thought of being near you again is alone enough for me to give up Africa, in spite of years of quiet satisfaction, in spite of many dear friends . . . Even if as a merchant I am striving after possessions and affluence, yet I have no insatiable thirst for them . . . In spite of the many unusual chances that get offered to me, I am quite contented with what I have got.

One natural successor was Charles Rube. Paul Keil was selected to represent the firm for the shipping of diamonds. Porgès was trying to persuade Julius to stay on at least for a few more months, but he was determined to leave in November. Looking back over the past nine years, Julius said, he could not thank Fate enough for having led him to such a man as Porgès. The only differences of opinion had been not who should take the greatest part but who should take the smallest. Porgès had written to him: 'As far as I am concerned I shall never leave you.'

In the last weeks his head was 'buzzing', he was so overloaded with work. He kept on thinking of new projects years ahead. In almost his last letter he wrote about the 'very curious feeling' he had at leaving what had been a virgin wilderness, 'where the activity and the creation of the individual is brought into relief much more than in the densely populated countries of Europe.' He went on:

41

I have always tried in spite of all my wealth to keep my needs as modest and small as possible; even if I am always aware of the vicissitudes of life, need or necessity could never be the touchstone of my honour. If tomorrow I lost everything, that indeed would not make me happier, but it would not disturb the peace of my soul. I am not proud of my riches, for I know how much is due to luck. That alone does not make me happy. I am happy because I am trusted, and changing fortune could not destroy that happiness.

On 30 November 1880 he sailed from Cape Town in the *Dunrobin Castle*, a rough and disagreeable voyage.

5

Farewell to Kimberley

If Julius ever seriously considered forming his own company, such an idea was abandoned when Porgès made him manager of the London end of the business. The office was established at the newly built Holborn Viaduct, conveniently close to the diamond dealers of Hatton Garden.

Meantime at Kimberley, during six months of 1881, a great inflated bubble of speculation known as the 'share mania' engulfed the town. It was all very different to the struggles and dreams of the 'Grand Old Days of the Diamond Fields'. The success of the French Company and flotations by other main groups suddenly produced a frantic scramble to form public companies by small claimholders, desperate for capital to offset their debts. A Stock Exchange, the first in South Africa, was established temporarily at an edifice of brick and corrugated iron known as Beit's Building. When the boom began there had been twelve companies, but soon there were seventy-one, in which £8 million had nominally been invested. 'The whole of Kimberley took part in these flotations,' said one writer. 'Regular work came to a stop, interest centred in the share market, life was lived at high pressure, and champagne flowed freely. It was Kimberley's heyday.'

It was a heyday also for the common swindler. The prices of shares rose to absurd heights, and plunged dramatically when banks called in overdrafts. Inevitably many companies had to be liquidated, and there were bankruptcies, including that of Rothschild, who had been a main sharedealer. There were also suicides, one being a friend of the Wernher family.

43

Among the principal players in the complicated struggle for power, J. B. Robinson was to end as a loser, though over a matter of years, and he was to rise up again. Barnato and Rhodes, through some shrewd manipulations, had their positions nicely strengthened. Beit was not yet among the big names, but had steered a brilliant course, and it was then, as a future colleague was to say, that his extraordinary financial genius really came to be recognized. He also generously helped to guide various small firms back from 'insolvency to prosperity'. Even so, one-third of the companies floated in this period had gone bankrupt by 1884.

Beit had a small investment in the De Beers Mining Company, and it was during this time of crisis that, as Julius put it, he came into more intimate contact with Cecil Rhodes. To be more exact, he fell completely under Rhodes's spell. Both men were still under thirty, both more interested in making money than in the opposite sex. Beit, though of course a foreigner by birth, seemed to be mesmerized by Rhodes's grandiose and almost mystic, if jejune, ideas about expanding the British Empire, which included not only enveloping the whole continent of Africa but the 'ultimate recovery of the United States of America'. Rhodes by then had already entered politics. After Griqualand West had been formally incorporated in Cape Colony, he had been elected a Member of Barkly West, and thus had a seat in the Legislative Assembly at Cape Town.

Over the past decade the fortunes of the Kimberley diamond industry had seesawed from euphoria to gloom. By mid-1882 the situation seemed to be at its most critical ever. In his 'Notes' Julius spoke of the cutthroat 'senseless competition of producing'. 'Dividends became the exception, and prices of shares in some cases dropped to four per cent of their former values.' Gradually the richer parts of the mines were covered up by fallen reef. 'It was a time of great hopelessness and improvidence by the owners themselves. The French Company suffered with the rest, but remained in an excellent financial shape. Owing to their having a shaft sunk outside the Mine and thus leading into it, they always managed to get some revenue, and they succeeded in making some purchases of claim properties of high strategical value.'

This 'hard school of experience' had now convinced claimholders that only combinations among themselves could save the industry from ruin. Amalgamations continued to take place. The question was, who would rise to the top of the pile? In the Kimberley Mine the most powerful, for the present, was Baring-Gould's Central Company, and in the De Beers Mine it was Rhodes's Company. Julius was not happy about his representation at Kimberley, and decided that he would have to return. So in December 1882 he left for the Cape. He was away for fifteen months, and during that time Porgès made constant journeys across the Channel to London, at least twice a month, 'returning after dealing with mail and shipments'.

So now the letters to the parents resumed. There was smallpox at Cape Town, and he did not linger there. Luckily, with the improvement of the railway system, the journey from the Cape to Kimberley only took four days. 'Business looks indescribably miserable,' he wrote in February. 'Only a few have ready cash. How most of them live is a riddle to me.' It was not until 6 April 1883 that he could say: 'I am gradually getting a little order out of this terrible mess.' A first priority had been to sack his agent Paul Keil.

Julius was living in the institution known as the Old German Mess, frequented by special friends like Alfred Beit, Martin van Beek, Hermann Eckstein and newcomers such as J. B. (Jim) Taylor and Max Michaelis. 'I do nothing but business, and my social life is limited to this circle.' He got up very early and always first rode to the claims. During the day there were constant meetings, and 'therefore I do not feel inclined to do anything in the evenings except play a hand at cards.' He went to the Levys' about once a week, but the poor things had suffered in the great game of 'share mania'. 'Visits there would not be very pleasant if one did not at once arrange for a game of cards, which cuts off Mrs Levy's moanings.'

All the same, there was some good news to relate. 'I have operated a lot in the diamond business in the last month, and what is more important, very successfully. This gives me a special pleasure, as it is my old business, so to speak. But otherwise it still looks dreadfully bad here, and for many there is no future at all. People are leaving the place in hundreds, which is the best thing they can do.'

At least sanitation in Kimberley had been much improved. Gone were the days when cesspits 'fermented and bubbled up'. Dustcarts removed rubbish daily. It has since been estimated that the death rate at Kimberley during the 1870s had been nearly double the rate per thousand found in Calcutta, regarded as the unhealthiest city in the Empire. Julius, however, did not alarm his parents about the smallpox, which arrived in the autumn of 1883. This was a particularly disgraceful episode, for some employers jibbed at paying for medical care and refused even to acknowledge the disease's existence in case it should discourage the arrival of new black workers, or – worse – involve the shutting down of mines. Only when whites became infected were quarantine measures introduced.

Various claims were bought by Julius in the old 'poor man's diggings', Dutoitspan and Bultfontein, and also in Jagersfontein, as these mines had been less troubled by reef falls. Such 'outside ventures' were managed for the firm by Hermann Eckstein, like Julius a Lutheran, the son of a German pastor from Stuttgart and destined to prove an exceeding lucky choice. Max Michaelis and W. P. Taylor, Jim's brother, were co-opted to deal in diamonds on joint account, along the lines of the arrangement made so successfully with Beit three years before. Most importantly, Beit agreed that when Julius left Africa he would take over the representation of the firm. It appears that Julius was not much tempted to join Beit and Rhodes over their customary glasses of champagne at the Blue Post, for we are told by Jim Taylor (who took the credit of introducing them) that Rhodes still 'had no success' with Julius, although Beit 'had little difficulty in persuading Wernher to agree to most of Rhodes's great schemes'. The great schemes were still in the future. The close camaraderie of the Old German Mess, where 'we had such terrific arguments that nobody could hear his own words', was to remain virtually unbroken over the years, with important consequences for all its members.

Gold discoveries at Barberton and De Kaap in the eastern Transvaal brought some hope of a 'new impulse in the land' –

but, said Julius, 'I doubt it somehow. The general tone is still very depressed.' Levy was now on the verge of bankruptcy, and had been taken on as 'a kind of agent' for the dealers Mosenthal & Co.

Julius meanwhile made some nostalgic trips on horseback, eating 'mostly sardines and biscuits'. He went to Griquatown and found that the old chief, Waterboer, who had been imprisoned after the 1878 uprisings, was getting a substantial subsidy yearly from the British government, 'which he invests in spirits and so is not presentable after 10 a.m.' Going on to Jagersfontein, where he said the diamonds were among the finest though very few, he stayed at an inn on the Modder River.

> It belongs to a man who in 1872 robbed the Post Office which contained £6,000 of ours. He then sat in prison for a few years. His wife looked after the business in the meantime and did not do too badly. There we now slept together in the living room, and the wife – mother of fifteen living children – dished up the evening meal. The man quietly smoked his pipe, and the governess played dance music (on a Sunday!) to cheer us up, and we spent a comfortable evening.

There were still parties at Kimberley. 'People seem to live on their losses. They are so used to their conditions that as soon as there is an opportunity for enjoyment there they are with all their hearts. It is ridiculous, but at my age I still enjoy dancing.' Relieved by the successful reorganization of his team, Julius by September was feeling like a 'fish in the water'. He preferred the warmer weather:

> Firstly because I can get up earlier, secondly because when the days are longer and warmer one can get more work out of the niggers. The hotter it is the better they feel. Instead of getting themselves warm in winter by hard work they stand and squat about, and wind their rags about their bodies to keep the cold off . . . of course in winter wages are just as high or even higher, because there are fewer workers

available . . . The energy of the whites, unfortunately, does
not correspondingly increase, and a greater part of the
labour troubles here are due to this.

For there was serious unemployment among the white labour-
ing class, and wages were actually in the process of being reduced.
Whites were usually employed as overseers in the mines. In
September 1883 white workers as well as blacks were required to
change into special clothes on entering mines and be searched on
leaving them. This so-called 'stripping clause' was considered
degrading by the whites, 'bringing them down to the level of the
niggers', for whom they claimed nakedness was after all a 'state
of nature'. Julius had long ago maintained that some sort of
personal search was necessary in order to combat IDB, but the
resentment boiled over, and there was a strike that lasted for
nearly a week. One of the ringleaders worked for the French
Company.

Far more alarming was the strike in April 1884. During a march
on the Kimberley Mine by white and black workers, six white
men, including one from the French Company, were shot dead
by armed police: the first casualties in industrial unrest in South
Africa. But by this time Julius was already back in London. His
mother had been convinced that he would deliberately look for
new business just to delay his departure, but he assured her that
she was quite wrong, and kept his word, even if he was
'fabulously busy, right up to the last moment'. (In November
1883 there had been the largest reef fall ever in the Kimberley
Mine.) So now, he teased her, he was free to settle down in some
quiet cottage with a nice little wife to care for him.

GOLD

6

'Duties and Cares of the Sterner Sex'

The second half of the 1880s was the most crucial period yet in Julius Wernher's life. It included, among other things, his marriage, the firm's involvement in Cecil Rhodes's amalgamation schemes at Kimberley, and the discovery of gold on the Witwatersrand in the Transvaal.

On his return to England he again took control of the ever-increasing empire of Jules Porgès and Company. He would hold a key position in the London Diamond Syndicate. Often it was rumoured he would be in the office until near midnight, even on Sundays. For, by 1885, the diamond trade was in deep crisis, with prices as low as they had ever been. As always, overproduction and reckless competition between producers were the problem. But the basic mining costs were heavy, and there was conflict between the industrialists and the workers.

The Syndicate was not to be formalized finally for some years, and there were stormy arguments meanwhile with Kimberley over prices, quality and profit sharing. Percy FitzPatrick, a future colleague of Wernher and Beit, summed it up in conveniently simple terms as a 'sort of balancing reservoir which could receive and hold diamonds for a period if the demand and supply did not balance'. But by 1885 only the De Beers Company was showing any reasonable profit, 70 per cent of its output being taken up by some dozen London firms, in particular Porgès and Mosenthal, both of which had directors on the De Beers board.

From the comments of the time one has an impression of Julius sitting in his city fastness like some benign if awesome Buddha,

49

inscrutable, wise, imperturbable. He had gained a reputation for being hard, a man 'who did not suffer fools gladly', but colleagues denied this and said he was always ready with sympathetic advice. To such people he was a 'splendid and loyal friend', whose very strength lay in his stubbornness; once he had made up his mind he could rarely be deflected. When faced with some individual's problems, his particular mannerism was to take out his gold pince-nez, wipe it slowly with a silk handkerchief, and then rise to his feet and lay a hand on a shoulder. 'My dear boy . . .' he would begin, like some old uncle, even though still in his mid-thirties. He detested any form of public speaking, but when forced to take the platform his speeches were witty if terse.

Julius met his future wife very soon after his return to London. Her name was Alice Sedgwick Mankiewicz, known as Birdie. The introduction came through one of the great friends of his Frankfurt boyhood, Alex Marc, living now in England and married to Birdie's sister Daisy. The two young women were remarkably alike, though Birdie was prettier. Born in 1862, she was bright-eyed, fair-haired and small, barely reaching up to Julius's shoulder. Intelligent and musical – she had obtained a diploma in pianoforte from the Royal College of Music – she also spoke German, which helped to please Frau Wernher, who seemed doubtful at first about the liaison. Birdie's father, Jacob James Mankiewicz, had died in 1879, aged forty-nine; his background was obscure, but he originally came from Danzig, the son of Joel Mankiewicz, a merchant, and given the fact that he had a brother called Samuel (who changed his name to Danby), it seems probable that he was of Jewish origin. He had been a stockjobber with Messrs Ansell and Tallermann, who became leading dealers in shares at Kimberley. Evidently Mankiewicz had been reasonably well off, for he could afford to send his two sons, George and Franz, to school at Rugby. Mrs Mankiewicz had been born Ada Susan Pigott. Her family came from Colchester, and she had a brother who was a general. She and Birdie lived in part of a big mid-Victorian house in Bayswater, 15a Pembridge Square.

Julius was living at 56 St James's Street. His correspondence with Birdie began in December 1886, ostensibly in connection with the resetting of some jewellery. But in February she was being elusive, and he wrote that he was 'grieved that you have made up your mind not to see me again'. In any case soon after this letter she caught chickenpox and was perforce invisible. A present of a diamond made all the difference, and after her recovery she invited him to tea tête-à-tête in her boudoir. Julius had to refuse not only this invitation but the succeeding one. His explanation was written at the time of some momentous developments in his business life – developments, it could fairly be said, that affected the future of South Africa.

My dear Miss Birdie, I hardly know how to explain my continued non-appearance at tea, as my reasons though intelligible to even dull men will fail to convince ladies of quite superior intellects, owing to the ease and 'Ungelundenheit' [abandon] with which they dance through life in happy ignorance of the duties and cares of the sterner sex. Now I am in this position: that, as the only partner of my business resident in London, I cannot leave my office until my partner in Paris is here to relieve me . . . When I returned a few years ago from the Cape our office consisted of one room, one clerk and the office boy – now we occupy two floors and there are fourteen in the office, some of them getting thin and pale from overwork. It may be a silly ambition to wish to outdo all one's competitors, but nobody can help nature. I am a most restless spirit . . . With kindest regards, Yours faithfully J. Wernher.

Not long afterwards there was another enforced separation, for a reason that overrode even his partner's absence. On 13 May 1887 Julius's father died from a 'seizure' in Frankfurt. The old man had been complaining of giddiness for some while, and had been increasingly troubled by his deafness. Six years before, on his retirement, the family had moved back to Frankfurt. It was always said that his greatest joy had been his son's success, and fortunately Julius had been at the death-bed. But Julius had been unable to stay long with his family. In that same month the firm was establishing an office in the new township of Johannesburg on the Witwatersrand, while at Kimberley Rhodes was completing the amalgamation of the holdings in the De Beers Mine.

It was not quite the moment for love letters, even if the relationship with Miss Birdie was still on a fairly formal level. Julius did begin to write at greater length, though his sentiments were hardly passionate and usually on mourning paper edged with black. Visits to the boudoir had often to be postponed. Nevertheless Birdie was advised by her brother-in-law Alex Marc that it would be worth her while to be patient, and such advice must have been appreciated when Julius gave her a pearl pendant for her birthday.

In 1885 'Little Alfred', as Beit was usually known, had arranged for two trusted colleagues, Hermann Eckstein and Jim Taylor, to represent both his and the firm's interests in the Barberton and De Kaap goldfields, in which there had been a heavy investment. Taylor sent such a gloomy report that it had brought Porgès speeding out to Africa, and both he and Beit consequently decided to pull out. There was a loss, but they were just in time. The usual cycle of avarice was in progress: rush, boom, soaring shares, disillusion, plummet, bankruptcies. However, before the collapse there had been the sensational discovery of potentially huge deposits of gold on the Witwatersrand ('The Ridge of White Water'), forty miles south of Pretoria. Rumours of the new find had reached Porgès and Beit whilst they were visiting the seat of the Boer government in Pretoria with Rhodes and Sigismund Neumann; but at that time they had been discounted, no doubt to the relief of Julius, to whom risks were an anathema.

Meanwhile Rhodes had been nearing the final stage of mopping up the remaining companies in the De Beers Mine, where he found himself baulked by Francis Oats, a rough-mannered Cornishman in charge of the large and strategically placed Victoria Company. In secret collaboration with Porgès and Co. (in this case Julius Wernher), Rhodes set about acquiring shares in the Victoria on the London Stock Exchange. At last he was triumphantly able to announce victory over Oats, in that he was now the majority shareholder of 60 per cent. As a result of this *coup de main*, Rhodes's reliance on the financial brilliance of Beit became common knowledge. 'Ask Little Alfred' was the standard joke when Rhodes found himself faced with an abstruse problem. The two would be seen walking together in deep discussion: Rhodes striding along, tall and moody-looking, with pale glowering eyes, and the diminutive, bald-headed Beit scampering beside him, trying to keep up. But it was not only the Porgès firm that made a satisfactory profit out of the Victoria deal; Beit did well out of it too, and doubled his personal wealth.

So the battle was set for the greatest prize, the control of the Kimberley Mine.

A main loser as a result of Rhodes's machinations was the notoriously ill-tempered J. B. Robinson, who was facing financial ruin. Forever afterwards he had a fierce hatred of Rhodes. Beit was always said to have a soft heart when old-time rivals were in trouble, so perhaps partly out of pity, or perhaps to calm JBR's fury, but chiefly because he realized that Robinson still had a worthwhile portfolio by way of security, in the summer of 1886 he lent him £20,000 (some said more) of his own money with which to acquire properties on the Rand – in which fortunately he still had a certain faith. A syndicate was therefore set up, Beit to receive a third of the proceeds. Porgès, in consultation with Julius, who knew Robinson's limitations only too well, declined to lend money or at that stage take part in the syndicate. Robinson bought heavily on the Main Reef of the Rand: properties, if he but knew, that would turn out to be some of the richest and most productive goldfields in the world. These included Langlaagte, another known as Langlaagte Block B, Randfontein and Bantjes.

Rhodes felt uneasy about investing in gold, and at the time only obtained a minor stake on the Rand. The reefs were hard to value; he was short of funds and too preoccupied with De Beers, although he later claimed to Lord Rothschild that he had proposed to Beit that they should buy the whole ridge in that first year. To him only diamonds really led to the magic path of glory, which included political power in the Cape and the wherewithal to plant the British flag further in central Africa. 'This I cannot do with your gold reefs,' he told his colleague Sauer. The future site of Johannesburg, already being pegged out, might have a more reasonable climate than Kimberley, being 6,000 feet up, but it seemed no land of Ophir, simply a desolate, snake-ridden waste, the haunt of baboons in eroded, treeless valleys, and the prospect of corrugated-iron shacks, drunks, and ox-wagons churning up the so-called roads, the stench of uncollected refuse and the shortage of water, were enough to sink the heart of anyone who had endured the early days at Kimberley. Not that Rhodes was at all reluctant to rough it if need be; but he did enjoy the comforts of the Kimberley Club.

Rumours of fabulous returns of gold from the outcrops soon precipitated yet another rush. The landlocked republic of the Boers, with its small indigenous population, was faced with an influx of hard-faced foreigners, 'Uitlanders', in a desperate search for yet another El Dorado, and apparently assuming that they were a law unto themselves. Beit visited the Rand and saw at once that it was unwise to leave Robinson in control of the syndicate, in which Porgès and Co., after some adjustments, were by now investing. He also saw scope for other lucrative acquisitions. His enthusiasm alarmed Rhodes. Jim Taylor wrote how Rhodes once woke him in the middle of the night to tell him how important De Beers was, and that Beit must be persuaded to curtail his financial obligations on the Rand. He also wrote a letter to Beit urging that he should retire from Porgès and Co. altogether, or at least should leave the gold side of the business to Porgès and Wernher, and 'simply remain their partner in diamond transactions'. After all, Beit would still have a sufficient number of founder shares in Porgès and Co. Rhodes also suggested that the hard conditions in Johannesburg would be bad for Beit's health.

This last point was worth considering, as Beit was not physically strong. In any case Beit decided to appoint Hermann Eckstein, whom Julius knew well and liked from the days at the Old German Mess, to represent the firm at Johannesburg. Eckstein was ambitious and he realized that this could be a great chance to improve his personal fortune. Even so he needed some persuading, not being altogether convinced about gold after his experience at Barberton. He already had a good job at Kimberley; more important, he was engaged to be married, and he doubted whether conditions at Johannesburg would be suitable for a married woman. He knew all about Robinson's rages and bullying, and certainly after his arrival found it hard to get on with him.

In due course the equally reluctant Taylor was persuaded to join Eckstein. 'So began,' we are told, 'the great adventure of their lives.' And so began, it could be added; the foundation of an enormous fortune for Alfred Beit and Julius Wernher.

But back to Kimberley. The duel between Rhodes and Barnato has often been described in dramatic terms. Who would be the matador and administer the fatal thrust? New evidence has proved that it was not quite a fight to the death, and as the historian Robert Turrell has shown, it was Barnato, not Rhodes, who 'laughed all the way to the bank'. Through a series of manoeuvres and takeovers Barnato – once unable to 'tell a diamond from a glass eye' – was already among the wealthiest shareholders in the diamond fields. In the early stages there was indeed a struggle with Rhodes, due to Barnato's commanding position in the Central Company, managed by the less flamboyant but exceedingly stubborn Francis Baring-Gould, who was essential to either side for victory. The problem was raising enough money to tempt the owners. The French Company had been making a loss, but the number of its claims and its size made it a valuable property.

Here Beit's influence and contacts became paramount for Rhodes. He was able not only to interest Porgès but to provide, indirectly, an introduction to Lord Rothschild of N. M. Rothschild in London. The connection came about in a typical string-pulling, roundabout way.★ Rhodes paid a flying visit to London, and succeeded in charming, or at least convincing, Lord Rothschild, who apparently said: 'Well, Mr Rhodes, you go to Paris and see what you can do [buying the French Company] . . . and

★ Jules Porgès's sister-in-law, Mathilde, the wife of Julius Wernher's first employer, Théodore Porgès, had been born a Weisweiller, related to the wife of Baron Henri de Rothschild, and she in turn was 'Natty' (Lord) Rothschild's niece by marriage. Madame Théodore Porgès's father, Baron de Weisweiller, represented Rothschilds in Madrid. In the great Jewish cousinhood there were other connections through the Ephrussis, the Cohens and the Helberts. The Weisweillers had originally put up money for Théodore Porgès's firm, and perhaps Jules Porgès's diamond business. Mathilde married Théodore in 1876 and died in the famous Bazaar de la Charité fire in Paris. Théodore died, aged sixty-five, in 1907.

in the meantime I shall see if I can raise the million pounds that you require.' Two days later, in Paris, a deal for acquiring the French Company appeared to be virtually complete, and Rhodes's London representative, Philipson-Stow, gleefully said to him: 'We have the Kimberley crowd by the throat.'

In London the diamond world was 'at fever heat'. The French Company's shares soared up in price. Philipson-Stow had warned Rhodes of Porgès's cynicism and his 'impertinent' attitude; Porgès was no special friend of Rhodes. Soon the sum required rose to £1,400,000. Julius's summary in his 'Notes' of an extremely intricate series of deals was as always laconic, avoiding any of his own misgivings. 'The two largest concerns [in the Kimberley Mine], the French Company and the Central, could not come to terms owing to the unreasonable pretensions of the Central. Mr Rhodes boldly bought the French Company, and this in a short time brought the Central people to their knees.'

It was by no means the finish of the story. 'The Central's only hesitation,' he added, 'was caused by the fear of their votes and influence being swamped by the compact vote of the De Beers as the largest holder in an amalgamated company.' So Rhodes actually resold the French Company to the Central, for a large sum in cash and a number of Central shares. 'Now,' continued Julius, 'the old jealousies came to the surface again.' Rhodes, through Porgès and Co., and through Beit, who lent him £250,000 without security, duly set about acquiring yet more shares in the Central, though failing to reach a majority holding. 'Thus,' said Julius, 'the balance of power really lay in the hands of Messrs Barnato, who finally sided with Rhodes and the De Beers [Company]. All the very large financial arrangements were initiated, carried out or assisted by our firm.'

He made it sound so simple. There was a bidding war, with shares oscillating up and down, and moments of near panic on either side. Porgès, Barnato and Rothschild, and also Mosenthal, waited to buy at bottom prices. Barnato now had to be 'squared' by Rhodes, and made a collaborator, and once this had been actually done, he worked on behalf of De Beers, buying or selling Central shares, whichever happened to be more lucrative. In this way he increased his fortune vastly. But the greatest bait was a perpetual income as a Life-Governor of the new De Beers Consolidated. Five Life-Governors were provided for. After a dividend of 36 per cent to shareholders (it was to have been 30, but Lord Rothschild objected), the rest of the profits would be divided between them. As it happened, only four Life-Governors were appointed, and these were Rhodes, Barnato, Beit and Philipson-Stow. By rights the fifth Life-Governor should have been Baring-Gould, but because of his previously obstructionist attitude Rhodes had him excluded.

Rhodes of course became Chairman of De Beers Consolidated. As he told a meeting of shareholders, in his peculiar, high-pitched voice, it was now 'the richest, the greatest, the most powerful Company the world has ever seen'. Barnato owned 6,658 of the shares; the other three Life-Governors 4,439 each. It was essential, Rhodes explained, to have wealthy men as Life-Governors as they would plan for the long term and not merely be interested in short-term profits. After a few years Julius Wernher, already a director, was also to be elected a Life-Governor.

Rhodes had promised to help Barnato to be elected to the Cape Assembly and become a member of the Kimberley Club, where it was subsequently said that there were more millionaires to the square yard than anywhere in the world. Both these came to pass. Turrell makes the point that the De Beers directors deliberately fostered the story about the share struggle to the bitter end, in order to conceal from shareholders the huge debts to the bank and the extent to which Barnato had been bribed. The real point at issue had been to convince Barnato that money from De Beers Consolidated could be used not only for acquiring territories in Central Africa, but also – somewhat alarmingly – to 'govern them and if so desired to maintain a standing army'. The terms of the Trust Deed went even further than that, and included the possibility of engaging in 'any' business enterprises. Barnato needed no reminding of Rhodes's part in obtaining a British protectorate over northern Bechuanaland and his plans for sending a mission to the land of the Zambezi. A meeting between Barnato and Rhodes took place in Dr Jameson's house, with Barnato determined that the income from De Beers should be restricted to diamond mining. The argument continued into the small hours. At last, exhausted, Barnato had to say: 'You have a fancy for building an Empire in the North, and I suppose you must have your way.'

There was, needless to say, the tantalizing factor of possibly finding precious minerals up there, which could far outweigh any reduction in profits for the Life-Governors. Time was short, with the Germans already installed in South West Africa and backed by the Transvaalers under their stubborn old President, Paul Kruger, perennially suspicious of the British, and of Rhodes in particular. Rhodes's 'fancy' was to create a new company with powers that would emulate the East India Company of the Raj. Soon, such were his extraordinary powers of persuasion, he managed to convince the Prime Minister Lord Salisbury and the Foreign Secretary Lord Knutsford (against their better judgement, it may be said) of the necessity for a royal charter for the formation of the British South Africa Company, usually referred to as the Chartered Company. Rhodes's magnetic personality carried the day in all the preliminary discussions and meetings, but by his side would be Beit with his invaluable, 'shrewd grasp of detail'. Rhodes and Beit, and their immediate associates such as Rothschild, held half the authorized capital in the Chartered Company (Beit himself had put in half a million). By 1895 the Empire in the north was designated Rhodesia, and Rhodes now had his eye on taking over Delagoa Bay, the Transvaal's access to the sea.

De Beers Consolidated was registered in Kimberley in March 1888. There was a last-minute hitch when a minority of shareholders objected to the merger of the Central with De Beers, and they went to law. Rhodes's solution to counteract this was for the Central to go into liquidation. On 28 September 1889 a cheque for £5,338,650 was deposited by the Central liquidators for their credit on De Beers Consolidated, and on the same day they drew in favour of De Beers for £5,326,260. This was an historic deal, the largest financial transaction in South African history, and the cheque was framed and hung in the De Beers offices.

A further reason for Rhodes's failure in 1886 to take more interest in the goldfields of the Rand had been the death of his secretary and particular friend Neville Pickering at Kimberley. His tremendous grief and preference for male companionship throughout his life have led to speculation that he was homosexually inclined. It was also a fact that many of his closest friends, Beit included, were not married. Nothing has been proved, or probably will ever be proved, in spite of some quite ridiculous 'evidence' produced by modern psychiatrists. One could argue that Rhodes's drive for power and money was a substitute for sex, in whatever direction. It was said that he enjoyed the company of women 'very much as a moderate drinker enjoyed an occasional glass of good port'. Some of his terrific energy was obviously due to his knowing that he suffered from heart disease and that his life could be short (as indeed it was). It is known that Beit had an illegitimate daughter called Queenie by a Mrs Elizabeth Bennett of Kimberley, and that later he contemplated marrying the sister of his brother Otto's wife. If there is any truth in the suggestion that he also was bisexual, it could also explain the affinity with such a dissimilar character as Rhodes: not for any reason of sexual attraction, but because in the homosexual world, as in any minority group, there is a community of understanding, a kind of instinctive comradeship.

If Rhodes was homosexual it could also explain, in part, why Julius Wernher was prejudiced against him and why men such as Percy FitzPatrick and Hermann Eckstein did not get on with or actually disliked him (and in the latter case the feeling was mutual). The friendship between Wernher and Beit was deep, based originally on their common nationality and appreciation of each other's business abilities, and maybe interest in art. Jim Taylor said of Beit: 'Of all men he ever met in the course of his very active life Rhodes and Julius Wernher were the only two he admired to the point of affection. And of all men with whom he dealt Rhodes was the only one who really knew how warm was Beit's heart and how generous his nature. They were poles apart in upbringing, outlook and habits, yet they were drawn together from the day that they met.' Beit's dual and conflicting loyalties were to prove important. One also speculates whether Wernher, as a German still, did not share the enchantment of Rhodes's expansionist schemes.

Here the often repeated story, not necessarily true, about the beginning of Rhodes's friendship with Beit had better be inserted. Rhodes had called at the Porgès office late one night, and found Beit sitting on a stool in front of his weighing scales. 'Do you never take a rest?' he asked. 'Not often,' was the reply. 'Well, what's your game?' 'I'm going to control the whole diamond business before I am much older.' Rhodes said: 'That's funny. I have made up my mind to do the same. We had better join hands.'

Lionel Phillips said in his autobiography *Some Reminiscences* that Rhodes's relations with Beit were 'those of affectionate comradeship', whereas 'Wernher he respected'. Rhodes's dreams of imperial destiny, his backstairs manoeuvres and social manipulations, and his chasing after the will-o'-the-wisp of gold in Matabeleland are reminiscent of the ambitions of Sir Walter Raleigh in Guiana, but, unlike Raleigh's, it is hard now to appreciate the glamour of Rhodes. Photographs of his flaccid, humourless face in his later years do not help, though the strength and relentless will are obvious. Beit on the other hand looks puckish and it is easy to accept that *he* had charm. Rhodes said that all Beit wanted was to be able to give his mother £1000 pounds a month.

'Without Beit,' Smuts wrote after both had died, 'Rhodes might have been a mere political visionary.' Yet all manner of men fell under the spell of Rhodes, and were carried along by his enthusiasm. Lord Rothschild may have scented useful profits out of the De Beers deal, but he developed into a good friend, and was ready to give gentle advice if Rhodes appeared to be straying from the accepted lines of probity. Beit was a gambler, ready for risks, and had an uncanny gift for turning out to be right. Julius was always cautious, acting as a brake. On a typical occasion when Beit had bought and sold rather too heavily, and had to confess that he had made a mistake, Julius merely replied: 'Yes, I know. I was selling to you all the time. Don't do it again.' It was admitted that without Julius's cooler judgement Beit might have been in some terrible financial trouble.

Both Julius and Beit were to become British subjects. However, in the 1880s Julius had his strong feelings of loyalty towards the country of his birth, in spite of German colonial designs and his earlier remarks about Germany in his letters to his parents. This is shown in his sometimes rather awkwardly phrased letters to Birdie, who must have felt that they read like lectures. Their correspondence continued all during 1887. At least for her birthday she was given another jewel, this time a topaz hatpin set in diamonds. When she told him that she read his letters at least four times, he joked that he would try to make them shorter. On 11 March 1888 he wrote a letter, black-edged as usual, saying that he was looking forward to next Sunday 'and all the quiet you can give me'. He was so weary, he said. Over the past seventeen years he had had plenty of hard work, but the previous three had been the worst.

This last week was again one of extreme tension and excitement. The precarious state of the [German] Emperor's health [the nonagenarian William I] disturbed the business world in all parts of the world, and I was fearfully busy. Then came the expected and dreaded end of our great and justly beloved Kaiser, and if the whole world is full of sympathy it can easily be understood that feeling is intensified with deep sorrow with any German, for he was the creator and maintainer of our country. He taught us again to be proud of the Vaterland. He found the nation without unity and difficult to define . . . and he left it after a short but blessed reign a powerful empire and the most peaceful of all nations but conscious of its strength and ready to defend itself against unjust aggression. So we have every reason to be in mourning, especially as in this case 'Le roi est mort vive le roi' calls forth one's sad thoughts as the new emperor will have to follow soon his august predecessor [Frederick III was dying of cancer] and the state of political uncertainty becomes permanent.

Some readers of the British press would have raised their eyebrows at such an outpouring.

Julius now turned to a eulogy of Porgès, who had been in London and had written approvingly of Birdie – which letter Julius enclosed. 'He gave me his full confidence after the shortest possible acquaintance, and I had the disposal of his whole fortune when only a youngster of twenty-three . . . I don't think there are many partners with friendship such as ours. My only thought was always – how will it suit and benefit him, and he would sooner lose a great deal than see any injury come to me.' Julius was sure that Birdie would also find Porgès a steadfast and 'if need be helpful' friend.

The time came to conclude the letter, in slightly warmer terms: 'So my dear Fräulein, it is your turn again. Off and on I spent half last Sunday in your charming spiritual company [i.e. thinking of you]. I do not wish for better with the important exception or rather addition of your presence, and that combination I hope to have before many days are over. With kindest regards, Yours faithfully J. Wernher.'

But hardly had he posted this, than a letter arrived from Birdie herself, obviously designed to force the pace of this too long-standing romance. He replied at once, and this time he ended: 'Good night, and God bless you, and keep me your love, Ever Yours Julius.'

Three days later, on Sunday, in Birdie's boudoir, they became engaged. Birdie dutifully wrote in German to Frau Wernher at her fiancé's dictation.

Letters were now addressed to 'My dearest Girl' and signed 'Your loving Julius'. She wanted more than that, and artfully asked him if he thought her 'handsome'. His reply could not have been quite as she expected:

I confess I am no connoisseur of what is called 'beauty'. To me a woman must be a woman first. It is the expression and the womanly grace, the beaming eyes and warm heart capable of feeling for others and not always thinking of self, which is my type of beauty, and in that respect I find you perfect.

Did he think her 'stupid'?

I refer you to Mr Porgès's letter. I do not think you stupid that you accepted me, for I love you with all my heart and I was so longing to have somebody to care for and love such as one only loves a good and true wife. In fact even in my selfish bachelor days I found it unbearable to have only to think of myself and be nothing to anybody. So I half adopted a few children of friends with large families and small means. I have had in these days the great gratification to obtain for one who has turned out particularly well a splendid situation in Paris.

Then he gave her the comforting news that his partner Beit would be returning permanently to London during the summer. So in future he would not be quite so oppressed by work.

But business is already of second or third importance, and you are and remain number one. I know a good many people laughed at me, that I have not taken things much more easily for years past, but then I wanted something to occupy my mind and tax my energy to the utmost, and if it served no other purpose I gained at least one object . . . to secure for my future wife a comfortable home and the fulfilment of her every conceivable wish.

Perhaps even then Birdie did not quite appreciate the significance of these last words. The wedding took place on 12 June at Christ Church, Lancaster Gate. There were eight bridesmaids and two hundred guests. Only a few hours before Julius had felt constrained to write to his 'dearest treasured mother', thanking her for her love over the years and promising that 'you will always be to me what you are now and always have been', and that 'Birdie will always be a loving daughter to you.' The tone of this letter was more intense than any of the letters that he had sent to the bride. A reception was held at Mrs Mankiewicz's house at Pembridge Square. All the presents were laid out upstairs, including a silver canteen of 152 pieces from Alfred Beit, who had disappointingly not yet arrived from Africa. The first week of the honeymoon was spent in the Isle of Wight, and then the couple were off to Paris, guests of Porgès.

Birdie later confessed that she was 'dazzled' by the sumptuous houses and art collections of her husband's financial friends, and the smart life of the extremely social and very beautiful Madame Jules Porgès, née Anna Wodianer, of Hungarian descent. It was no doubt Madame Porgès who gave her a taste for Worth dresses. The time would come when people would also be dazzled by Mrs Julius Wernher's style of living.

7

The Politics of Gold

It would indeed have been uncharacteristic of Julius if he had avoided talking business with Porgès, even on his honeymoon. Business was his world, and for years to come Birdie was forced to accept this. In any case Porgès had to plan another visit to Africa. More capital was needed urgently for investing in heavy machinery on the Rand, and here the key figure in Paris to be won over was Rodolphe Kann, now a considerable friend of Julius. Another matter for discussion was Beit's return to Europe as a full partner in the firm, which would involve changes in structure and responsibilities.

Rodolphe Kann and his brother Maurice were originally from Frankfurt. Through them Julius became interested in collecting Italian Renaissance bronzes. Since he also was beginning to acquire Flemish and Dutch paintings, the Kanns suggested that, like Porgès, he should seek the help of Dr Wilhelm von Bode, at that time assistant keeper of the sculpture and paintings department at the Kaiser Friedrich Museum in Berlin and later to be that museum's celebrated director-general. Julius seems to have made a start by actually buying and offering to the museum two very acceptable Flemish pictures, dated about 1500. In his letter to Bode Julius said that although he lived in England 'part of his heart' was still in Germany.

The Wernhers had moved into a pretty mid-Victorian house, which the amused Rodolphe Kann called 'bijou', 38a Porchester Terrace in Bayswater, not far from Birdie's mother. In those rather heavily furnished rooms, with plenty of draperies and curtains, potted palms and ostrich feathers in vases, space for objects of art must have been limited, so it is something of a surprise to learn that in 1890 Julius whilst in Berlin bought the splendid (about three foot six inches high) late fifteenth-century Spanish picture *St Michael and the Dragon*, by Bartolomé Bermejo. This masterpiece, originally from the church at Tous, near Valencia, was to prove one of the most important pictures in his entire collection. No doubt Bode recommended it because of its rarity, and very likely it had been turned down by the museum. The Flemish influence is obvious in the style, and the dragon is certainly bizarre, like something dreamed up by Hieronymus Bosch, but the glowing colours and the gilding, and the richness of the details, including the depiction of jewels, must have appealed strongly to Julius. Even so, the final effect is awesome, and one cannot quite visualize it hanging in Birdie's drawing-room at 38a Porchester Terrace. It was said to have been in a bad condition, and no doubt was thus considered a satisfactory bargain.

Bode meanwhile had been in London and had been introduced by Julius to Beit, who had invited him to stay in his rooms at Ryder Street. He was a shy man and thus obviously felt at ease with Beit. For many years thereafter he helped him and, to a certain extent, Julius in building up their enormous art collections. Beit's first major acquisition was *The Milkmaid* by Nicolas Maes. Bode also acted as a dealer, and in his autobiography claimed that he was able to secure several masterpieces for Beit at specially low prices. The tradition is that he did not charge a commission; even if this were true, which seems unlikely, Beit in his typically generous way would surely have compensated him somehow. Bode admitted frankly that he hoped his clients would support the Kaiser Friedrich, and both Beit and Julius obliged with gifts of money and pictures. But there were grumbles about the Kanns, who bought at auction and would only afterwards consult Bode about values, thus avoiding paying a commission. There were hints that they might instead remember the museum in their wills, but unluckily this never came to pass.

★

Beit's arrival in London from Africa had been delayed, partly because of developments on the Rand, partly because of unrest at Kimberley, where commercial decline and unemployment were being blamed on De Beers Consolidated. Early in June effigies of Rhodes, Beit and Barnato were burnt outside the De Beers offices. This was followed by the horrific disaster of a fire in the De Beers Mine, involving the deaths of a third of the workers.

Kimberley was now far from being a mere frontier outpost. Its gabled and fretworked houses were not unlike Simla in India; it had become a metropolis, 'respectable', what with the arrival at long last of the railway, and the installation of electric street lighting, the first in South Africa. But the amalgamation of the mines had meant redundancies, and white workers were being left destitute. The rich were being tempted away to Johannesburg, which in spite of its discomforts was being systematically planned in bricks and mortar. Shopkeepers and merchants at Kimberley were also feeling the effect of the 'closed compound' system for black workers, once strongly promoted by Julius Wernher among others as a way of combating IDB: workers, when not in the mines, were kept shut in a kind of fortified area with its own shops, baths and eating-houses, from the moment of their arrival until their departure months later. No alcohol was allowed. Blacks were also being subjected to humiliating body searches after work. They were stripped naked, every orifice being probed, even open sores, and their hair, armpits and spaces between the toes minutely examined. Even more unpleasantly, they were purged with castor oil in case diamonds had been swallowed. And it has to be admitted that these last methods did produce some dramatic results. On a yearly average 100,000 carats' worth were recovered until 1901. A certain amount of the De Beers work-force was convict labour: another saving.

The mortality rate in the closed compounds was high. These compounds have been seen as a crucial development in South African labour relationships.

Julius had succeeded in arousing Rodolphe Kann's interest in the Rand, and Jim Taylor was asked to follow this up with a 'seductive' selling letter. 'There can be no doubt,' Taylor therefore wrote to Kann, 'about the ultimate success of the gold industry on the Rand. It is only a question of time, energy, practical mining and the investment of more capital . . . Two years ago not a hole had been made and there was no habitation anywhere on the Main Reef. The district was populated by a few hundred farmers who owned nothing but the land they lived on and who subsisted on the produce they raised from their lands.' Now, he said, there were 3,000 houses and 1,700 inhabitants. (By 1892 the total population of Johannesburg was estimated at 21,715, of which 15,005 were white.) Kann had no need to be told that the mining of gold was quite different to that of diamonds, and that the problem of IDB did not exist.

On their arrival at Johannesburg Eckstein and Taylor had erected a temporary wooden office on the corner of Commissioner and Simmonds streets, but this was to be reconstructed in brick in 1889, and later elaborately faced with ironwork. Whether fortuitously or, more likely, by design, it faced the Stock Exchange, already an imposing structure and designed to be permanent, though, as it happened, much of the dealing was done out of doors in a chained-off area between the two buildings. Known as the Corner House (partly a play on the German meaning of Eckstein's name), it was to become famous in the future city not only as a landmark but as the seat of a great dominion that controlled the world's richest goldmines, and much else besides. In 1904 the Corner House was rebuilt yet again, appropriately the tallest building in Johannesburg.

In spite of occasional glooms there was little doubt about the eventual importance of this ridge in the heart of southern Africa. By 1894 a railway connection had been laid to Pretoria from Delagoa Bay. There was a racecourse at Johannesburg. A fine new clubhouse, the Wanderers, had been built, fit for tycoons and magnates.

'What a future there is before us in South Africa!' wrote the mining engineer Theodore Reunert. 'A vast country waking up, as it were, from the sleep of ages, and realising all at once that it is destined to play a great part in the world. A superb climate, a fertile soil, boundless mineral wealth, and, all round, millions of idle hands waiting to be employed in its extraction.'

To which some could only utter Amen. Flora Shaw, the

brilliant journalist and admirer of Rhodes, thought Johannesburg 'hideous and detestable', without taste or dignity, dusty in the winter, a quagmire in the summer. To Barney Barnato's cousin Lou Cohen it was a place where men smoked like Sheffield and drank like Glasgow, and where the air was perfumed with the odour of barmaids, who knew their prices. The historian A. L. Rowse had two Cornish miner uncles who died at Johannesburg, one crushed to death by a skip let fall by a drunken engine driver. In his childhood Rowse used to hear of the 'raw horror' and the gin palaces of Johannesburg where concertinas provided the favourite music and the dust from the mines clogged the lungs. By 1895 there were ninety-seven brothels in central Johannesburg.

Julius Wernher had been responsible for giving the firm a name for fair play, and Eckstein and Taylor were expected to maintain this at Johannesburg. The Corner House acted as a holding finance company for the mines they floated. Each mine had its own directors and management, but the firm had control over appointments and major decisions. Hermann Eckstein's biographers have described him as human, lovable and dynamic, with a skill in 'frenzied negotiations' while still maintaining an equable temperament. His portraits show a pleasant bearded face and smart, well-cut clothes, and his wife has gone down in history as having been the prettiest girl in Kimberley. But an equable temperament did not help Eckstein's chronic insomnia and other nervous ailments. He was without any doubt an immensely respected figure in the South African financial and mining community, and was given the 'unquestioning support' of his superiors in Europe with virtually unlimited credit. Soon regarded as Johannesburg's First Citizen, he was the natural choice as first President of the Chamber of Mines. The policies of the Chamber of Mines, it need hardly be added, on such matters as the control of wages and the organization and flow of the 'millions of idle hands' came almost to be equated with those of the Corner House.

Julius was three years younger than Eckstein. Their Lutheran upbringing was something in common, but Eckstein's meticulous habits and formidable energy appealed to him far more. Then there was that bond, shared with Beit, of having roughed it together at Kimberley. The Corner House partners kept one-fifth of the profits and were free to invest on their own accounts. The rest of the profits went to London. Every week Eckstein wrote a long letter to 29 Holborn Viaduct, so detailed that business colleagues and rivals were amazed by Julius's intimate knowledge of the topography of the Rand, which of course he had never seen, and its personalities, even its gossip.

Eckstein also strove to keep the firm out of politics, knowing Julius's attitude. He used to say that whenever someone came into the office and talked politics he would see Julius's face on the blotting paper before him.

Originally Porgès and Julius had been nervous of seeming to be too closely allied with the controversial J. B. Robinson, so the Johannesburg office became known simply as 'H. Eckstein'. Taylor was still in his twenties, six feet tall and South African born, regarded as an excellent mixer; 'he knew everybody by their first names.' Eventually he became based in Pretoria when it became important for the firm to be in more direct touch with the government and in particular the wily old President, Paul Kruger, whom Carl Meyer of Rothschilds aptly described as a 'queer old Boer, ugly, badly dressed and ill-mannered, but a splendid type all the same and a very impressive speaker'. Kruger was, unfortunately, a man of very little education, in spite of his intelligence, with a literal belief in the Old Testament, and convinced even that the world was flat.

One of the first companies to be floated by H. Eckstein was the Robinson Gold Mining Company, named – naturally – after the 'steely eyed' J. B. Robinson and registered in February 1888. The Robinson Syndicate owned a half share of claims pegged out by a certain Japie de Villiers. Claims on the Rand were much larger than at Kimberley: 150 by 400 Cape feet, approximately one and a half acres. It was the brilliant young Taylor who had spotted the capabilities of that mine: five to eight ounces out of a ton of crushed banket. Robinson had bought the half share for £1,000 but Villiers wanted £10,000 for the rest, which he did receive, though in shares (later to be bought back by H. Eckstein for £80,000).

Shortly afterwards other companies and syndicates were floated in order to develop holdings, such as the Randfontein Estates Goldmining Company, the Modderfontein and Ferreira Companies, to mention a few of the largest. Then J. B. Robinson was persuaded, without much difficulty, to sell his share of the Robinson Syndicate for what then seemed to be the astonishing sum of £250,000. He moved on to the West Rand, but came to realize that he had made a mistake, and considered that he had been swindled by Beit, who thereupon (with all his partners) was listed as an arch-enemy. It was reckoned that over the years the properties of the former Robinson Syndicate were to earn the firm over £100 million. All the same, J. B. Robinson was to become one of the world's wealthiest men.

In that boom year of 1888 gold production had increased by 10 per cent. The Robinson Mining Company crushed in October 726 tons for 3,551 ounces. In November this total had increased to 4,000 ounces. Eckstein wrote to Julius in October that there was a net profit of £71,000 for the Company 'after very considerable writing off and taking in shares at the lowest prices'. He added: 'We start consequently on a very defined and safe basis, and shall show a very handsome balance at the end of December.' Early in 1889 he wrote to say that the net profit for the whole concern in the previous year was £860,505.6s.6d., which 'will no doubt be considered satisfactory'. 'It could easily have been fixed at over £1,000,000, but I preferred my usual rule by taking everything at what I may term safe values.' An elaborately secret telegraphic code for 'high-priority' deals had perforce to come into operation.

Kann arrived at Johannesburg from Paris and was suitably impressed, so much so that he was able to report favourably to financial associates in Europe, notably the Rothschilds of Germany, Austria and France. 'In fact,' Taylor wrote in his autobiography, 'all those who had made money out of the diamond shares became eager to participate in the gold shares.' This 'broadening of the market' was a vital phase in the expansion of the industry.

Rhodes had successfully floated his own company, Gold Fields of South Africa, with a capital of £250,000. Even if he could not quite compete with Eckstein or Robinson, the company proved extremely lucrative, and he drew for himself one-third of the profits. New properties were acquired and there was some playing around with shares. In 1892 when the company was renamed the Consolidated Gold Fields of South Africa its capital had been increased to £1¼ million.

And now the Johannesburg scene was enlivened by the appearance of Barney Barnato, at last a Member of the Cape Legislative Assembly (he had campaigned in Kimberley from a carriage drawn by four horses in silver harness). Proclaiming that he was in a 'financial Gibraltar', he tried almost desperately to catch up in the buying of properties. 'He is awfully jealous of us,' wrote Eckstein. Soon Barnato's investments were calculated to be in the region of £2 million, and this precipitated an 'orgy' of speculation in South Africa. The telegraph line from the Cape was perpetually jammed with buying orders. Half the male population of Johannesburg, we are told, hung around the Corner House, as if waiting for a pronouncement from an oracle. 'If there is anyone in Johannesburg,' it was said, 'who does not own some scrip in a gold mine he is considered not quite right in the head.'

In the midst of such frantic excitement Porgès came to survey the sources of the huge new addition to his wealth. First he went to Kimberley, where there were matters to be settled concerning the London Diamond Syndicate, mostly Julius's brainchild. An enormous diamond, 428½ carats, had been discovered in the De Beers Mine. It was exhibited at the Paris Exposition of 1889. But Porgès missed a much larger diamond, 969½ carats, which was to be found in the Jagersfontein mine in 1893. Porgès found the population of Kimberley dwindling. De Beers was building a model village called Kenilworth for white employees, a counterpart of a sort to the closed compounds for the blacks and again with its own shops. The output of diamonds was having to be restricted, and racial tensions were increasing. Porgès confessed that he left with a feeling of slight gloom. The vibrant atmosphere of Johannesburg was certainly a contrast. He arrived there at a time when the Randfontein Company was about to be floated, with a capital of £2 million in £1 shares, later to be sold for four times as much, with useful profits all round.

Predictably, collapse and panic were to follow later in the year.

This may have been anticipated by Porgès, who had by then already made the sensational decision to retire from the firm. Perhaps he felt that the empire was becoming altogether too complex and unwieldy. Perhaps, as seems possible, he was worried about his health. Or perhaps, as one would almost prefer to think, he simply decided that he had made enough money and wanted to enjoy it and invest some of it in works of art. Madame Porgès certainly wanted him to build a palace that could compete with the châteaux of the French aristocracy. After all he was still only fifty-one. As it happened, he was to live on well into his eighties, which was much more than could be said of most of his colleagues. He has been regarded as one of the most significant figures in the early development of South Africa's wealth, but even now is thought of as 'shadowy'. Yet it is not quite true that he 'simply disappeared into private life'. He kept up several interests in Africa, and was partner in syndicates with Kann and Michel Ephrussi which co-operated with the Corner House. Meanwhile the firm of Jules Porgès and Company was reconstituted on 1 January 1890 under the name of Wernher, Beit, the partners being Julius Wernher, Alfred Beit, Max Michaelis and Charles Rube.

The handover was no gift though. Porgès took with him £750,000 in cash and £1 million in shares. A further £500,000 was deposited with Wernher, Beit, to be paid over the next two years. Wernher, Beit was left with £1 million in cash, diamonds and non-speculative investments, and around £2 million in shares and interests of a non-speculative nature.

The newly designated firm remained a private company, with no shares issued to the public. Julius Wernher and Alfred Beit were considered the ideal combination, with Julius the necessary brake on his partner's enthusiasms. Beit was intuitive, daring, while Julius made sure that there were always enough funds for an emergency. It was said that Beit never seemed to mind who joined them in new ventures, but that Julius 'viewed some of the new alliances with horror' and was always warning the Corner House not to spread the firm's interests too widely. In many cases Julius proved right, and Beit did get into serious trouble when one of his cousins began forging his signature.

Alfred Beit had no desire for fame – unlike Rhodes. But in spite of the alarmingly long hours he spent in the office, he seemed capable of enjoying social life. After all he was now a very eligible bachelor, and on his first return to Johannesburg he gave a ball for a hundred and fifty people. To Percy FitzPatrick he was the 'ablest financier South Africa has ever known'. As always, his energy was prodigious. He built himself a house in Hamburg, and visited Dr Bode in Berlin. In 1891 he trekked with Rhodes (by then Prime Minister of Cape Province) with Lord Randolph Churchill up to Mashonaland, part of what soon was to be known as Rhodesia. He also accompanied Rhodes to Cairo.

Julius Wernher, so Taylor thought, would have been the perfect Chancellor of the Exchequer. He gave the City confidence and was described as 'blameless'. A stranger entering his office was conscious of being in the seat of power and would be afraid of wasting the great man's time. He also loved his home and read a great deal. Those who were allowed into the family's close circle realized that it was a special privilege. The occasional presence of Beit in London did lessen Julius's load of work, and for the first time in years he took holidays, in Scotland and to Dresden or Nuremberg, for instance, and above all he was able to visit his ailing mother in Frankfurt more frequently. Even so his family life suffered.

So the time had still not come for Birdie to take to entertaining on the grand scale, or to be launched into the longed-for *haut monde*. Sometimes there were dinners at Porchester Terrace for international financiers, such as the Rothschilds, Raphaels, Schroeders, Mosenthals and Lipperts, but Julius would also take them to the new Savoy Hotel restaurant. On 7 June 1889 the Wernhers' first child was born, Derrick Julius. Soon afterwards a great shadow fell on their household, which left Birdie 'exhausted and broken' and was responsible for a miscarriage. This was the death of her much loved sister Daisy Marc, after long and horrible suffering. Mrs Mankiewicz seemed to go into a decline and 'was never happy again'. Observing the family's reactions, Julius wrote to his sister Maria, who was coping with their own mother: 'One is inclined to doubt His goodness when one sees such tragedies.'

But Derrick was always the great consolation. His doting

parents called him Sweetface, and he was indeed beautiful as a baby, chubby with curly, dark hair. As he grew older, he was dressed in Fauntleroy suits, and it was obvious that he had a quick brain. The second son, Harold Augustus, was born on 16 January 1893, and the third and last, Alexander Pigott, on 18 January 1897. But Derrick was the favourite and consequently spoilt. He was to cause his father a lot of pain. Under the circumstances Julius's letter to Birdie about Derrick, written on 29 September 1891, is worth quoting:

> The great fear is how he will turn out, and you know my ideas! I would not like a child of mine to be a useless self-indulgent idler simply because he is left so much a year – my pride would be to have a man as a son who will take his place in the world!

As it happened, the son whom he thought the least intelligent, Harold, was the one who followed most closely in his footsteps as an outstanding man of business.

Julius, on a visit to his mother, missed the State visit of the new German Emperor, William II, but insisted that Birdie should watch the procession. On his way home he went to Paris to buy pictures. It was the centenary of the French Revolution and he climbed the Eiffel Tower. Staying as usual with 'Porgi', as he called Porgès, he reported that his old chief's legs were shaky with rheumatism but was amused to watch him gobble up his food – 'two smacks and the plate is empty'.

A couple of years later Julius and Porgès went on a 'bachelors' holiday' round Italy: Genoa, Florence, Rome ('the longed for spot of every German for centuries past') and Naples. Madame Porgès corresponded by telegram, but Birdie dutifully kept up a flow of letters. 'Porgi shows wonderful endurance,' Julius wrote, a comment which seems to show that there had indeed been some worry about health. 'He is jolly and chatty, never reads anything, although he bought many French novels and Darwin's *Descent of Man*. When it is hot he sits in his salon wearing only his red striped under vest. Anyone coming in by mistake would think an acrobat was lodging there.'

A new crisis hit De Beers, with the discovery in September 1890 of yet another diamond mine only four miles from Kimberley. It was named the Wesselton after the Boer farmer Wessel who had originally owned the site. The secret was kept until February when the place, inevitably, was 'rushed'. It seemed to be a divine answer to the misery of the poor whites of Kimberley, but Rhodes was determined that it should not be proclaimed a public digging, which would mean the end of the De Beers monopoly. At once he started negotiations for purchase. There were angry demonstrations in protest, and some subtle counter-arguments were produced. How long, for instance, would this mine last? A new independent mine would only mean a fall in the price of diamonds, and De Beers would have to restrict its operations, with more men out of work. A foreign syndicate would move in, which would mean 'ruin and disorder'.

By December, therefore, after various jugglings, the mine was safely under the control of De Beers. Not unexpectedly, we read in Julius's 'Notes' that 'the firm [Wernher, Beit] was largely instrumental in bringing about the various deals'.

At Johannesburg there was a lively new addition to the Corner House. This was Lionel Phillips, whose abilities had been spotted by Beit when at Kimberley.★ Jewish, born in London, and described as 'wiry' with 'immense energy and tenacity of purpose', he had hoped once to be the manager of De Beers. But Beit's offer was more tempting: £2,500 a year, expenses paid and 10 per cent of the profits from managing the firm's interests in the Nellmapius Syndicate, which owned nearly 2½ million acres, including possible goldmines, in the Transvaal. Phillips arrived at a hectic moment, with Porgès about to retire and the Johannesburg share market in a state of collapse after potential disaster had been discovered in the mines.

Pyritic ore had been struck some 120 feet down, and this would mean special chlorination plants and heavier machinery, enormously increasing the working costs per ton and possibly in any case to no avail. The reaction was similar to the discovery of the

★ Phillips had arrived at Kimberley in 1875, having walked most of the way there from Cape Town.

blue ground in the Kimberley mines in the seventies. Some 8,000 people packed up and left Johannesburg, believing that it was the end of the gold on the Witwatersrand.

The problem was to some extent solved by a new process involving cyanide which in solution produced gold out of crushed ore. This of course was still expensive. The fact that the Corner House came triumphantly through the crisis was partly due to Phillips but even more to the presence of a team of American mining experts. Rothschilds as major investors had insisted, in the Porgès and Co. days, that those highly qualified engineers and mechanics should be brought over from the El Callao goldmine in Venezuela, in which they had an interest. But as Phillips said to Julius, the 'smash', or slump, was not necessarily an evil. 'The small speculators interfere with legitimate operations', and these small speculators found themselves going bankrupt and forced to sell up holdings on the Main Reef to the Corner House.

'Sell and repent' used to be a favourite watchword of Porgès. When markets collapsed, Julius was always ready to buy. As Phillips wrote to him: 'That there is going to be pots of money here again I have no doubt. South Africa is like a Jack in the Box. You hold down the lid, and everyone wonders how they could ever have been such fools as to look at him. Then you unfasten the lid and up he jumps as spruce and lively as before.'

But, most importantly, the firm – 'acting with great circumspection and secrecy' – bought large blocks of claims to the south of the outcrop, in what became known as the deep-level zone. The great reef of gold did not run horizontally along the ridge but at a steep angle downwards, and it was found that it headed towards the south. Many scoffed at the idea of deep-level mining, J. B. Robinson among them. There were possibilities of geological faults. But the deep levels were responsible for springing the Jack in the Box. Beit, who had arrived looking 'pale and worried', caught the excitement, though he knew Julius would need convincing. 'I shall have to put all this to Wernher in detail,' he said.

It was the insistence of the Americans, J. S. Curtis and Hennen Jennings, that eventually persuaded Julius. As a result, the Corner House stole a march on every other company in Johannesburg. The secret was well kept for many months. It was described as the greatest coup in South African mining history. A borehole on the Village Main Reef property hit the Main Reef leader at a depth of over six hundred feet.

Phillips had also pegged out some deep-level claims for himself; these were eventually the Bonanza Mine, the foundation of his own fortune. His faith in the deep levels enormously increased his reputation in Johannesburg. Through its various purchases the Corner House became the owner of some of the most famous mines on the Rand: the Nourse Deep, the Ferreira Deep, the Jumpers Deep, the Glen Deep, the Crown Deep, the Rose Deep, the Village Deep and the Geldenhuis Deep.

But cash had to be raised for the deep levels. The first idea of a 'parent' holding company, Rand Mines Ltd – a group system among houses with common interests – has been variously attributed to Beit and Hermann Eckstein. To some extent the successful rationalization of the diamond industry at Kimberley had provided the model. In February 1893 the company was floated with a nominal capital of £400,000, with assets including over 1,300 claims and interests in five other companies. The Corner House received just over 200,000 shares by way of 'vendors allotment', and the right to 25 per cent of the profits after sums equal to the total capital of the company had been distributed to the shareholders. Within two years the shares had increased in value by 45 per cent. Other shares were divided among well-wishers and allies, the largest amounts going to Rhodes's Goldfields and to Rothschilds of London and Paris. Among other fortunate recipients were Carl Meyer, Rodolphe Kann, Lord Randolph Churchill, Hennen Jennings and Ernest Cassel, eventual financial adviser to the Prince of Wales. Mining magnates such as George Albu, Abe Bailey, Carl Hanau and Sigismund Neumann also received allotments. Some judicious small amounts of shares were planted with the *Star* newspaper, Kotzé, the Chief Justice of Transvaal, and Leyds, the State Secretary. It has been estimated that the firm would have made £10 million gross profit out of its investment in Rand Mines by 1899.

Lionel Phillips had succeeded Hermann Eckstein in 1892 as President of the Chamber of Mines, that 'clearing-house for grievances'. His wife Florence, or Florrie, was a gifted and ambitious woman with a fiery temperament. She also shared his notoriously extravagant tastes, particularly in the acquisition of houses. Her first arrival in Johannesburg, with its dust, mosquitoes and water shortages, had been a testing time. She and her husband had taken over Hermann Eckstein's house, called Hohenheim and described in the press as a mansion but in reality only four rooms. Now that they were so much richer she had set her heart on a real mansion, also to be called Hohenheim, and chose a spectacular site outside Johannesburg. But gynaecological problems forced her to spend long periods in England while the baronial-style house, known popularly as Phillips's Folly, was being built at the expense of Wernher, Beit.

In London Florrie expected to be treated by the firm as a great lady, and efforts were made to please her. She was fond of Beit, presumably because he was so lenient about her dreams of grandeur, but soon sensed Julius's disapproval. And she did not get on with Birdie, whom she thought 'boorish but civil'. Birdie for her part considered her 'amusing but just a wee bit flashy'. They were never on Florrie and Birdie terms; it was strictly Florence and Alice. But then Julius himself is said to have abhorred first names. Only once was he heard to address Beit as Alf.

Nevertheless in those early days Julius entertained Florrie well, taking her to the Savoy or Berkeley, or to the theatre. Birdie would plead absence, usually because she was 'in the family way'. Julius flattered Florrie and made it clear that he thought very highly of her husband. When Christmas came, she wrote that the Wernhers had sent her a 'very grand basket of fruit and flowers decorated with ribbons'.

The Wernhers had unwisely recommended that Florrie should winter in Bournemouth, pronounced by her 'stupendously dull'. Before leaving London, Florrie had met Hermann Eckstein, who had arrived to take up a partnership in Wernher, Beit – an honour indeed. She thought he looked very 'seedy': 'yellow and bloated-looking and tired'. One day in January 1893 Julius came to see her in Bournemouth by train. It was to break the news that Eckstein had died at his native Stuttgart, aged only forty-four and obviously killed by years of overwork. This was a blow to her personally, but she knew from the very fact that Julius had taken such trouble that her husband's prospects were going to be strengthened. It was lucky that she did not know that Lionel was at that time complaining to the London office that he was 'simply worried and badgered to death'. He was in any case far too ambitious to be able to relax.

In Johannesburg the Stock Exchange closed at the news of Eckstein's death, and flags were flown at half-mast. Shops were closed at the hour of the funeral. Even Kruger was reported upset. In 1903 the firm presented to the people of Johannesburg 200 acres of ground in the afforested plantation of the Sachsenwald, anglicized into Saxonwold, still known as the Hermann Eckstein Park and including the zoo.

The firm of H. Eckstein now had 'and Company' added to it. The partners were Taylor, Phillips, Hermann Eckstein's brother Friedrich ('Friedie'), and a Frenchman, Georges Rouliot, who had been manager of the French Company at Kimberley. Alfred Beit's brother Otto was also an associate.★ Then there was the exuberant Percy FitzPatrick, of Irish descent, the future author of *Jock of the Bushveld*, as Secretary of Rand Mines Ltd and in charge of the firm's interests in some non-mining companies such as Pretoria Light and Water and Pretoria Portland Cement. He and Rouliot had attracted Beit's attention on the journey to Mashonaland with Rhodes and Randolph Churchill, in the fruitless search for new Witwatersrands between the Limpopo and the Zambezi. Soon Phillips would be the senior partner of the Corner House, as Taylor, though only thirty-three, had decided to retire – evidently disillusioned by the corruption and the obstructionist attitude towards Uitlanders of the Boer government. Phillips thus became indisputably the leading figure in the business world of Johannesburg.

Phillips was summoned to London for consultations. Florrie was shocked to learn that meanwhile in Johannesburg he was giving a farewell fancy-dress ball so soon after Eckstein's death. But that did not prevent her from joining Julius Wernher, Alfred

★ The partners at Wernher, Beit & Co. were joined by Ludwig Breitmeyer in 1895.

Beit and Max Michaelis in a gala evening, which included a theatre (*Ma Vie Rosette*), and supper at her 'beloved' Savoy, followed by a masked ball at Covent Garden, lasting until four in the morning. Birdie had again made excuses, as Harold had just been born.

In Frankfurt Frau Wernher was gradually wasting away. Julius visited his mother in June 1893 and found her very changed, pale and thin. On his next visit she could hardly speak. His letters to Birdie, in contrast to the days of courtship, were tender, indeed often quite touching. On 4 January he told her that his 'darling sweet mother' was no more. The funeral was described in detail; a palm leaf had been bought, as from Derrick, and placed in the grave. In a postscript he wrote: 'I don't think Derrick or the nurses should wear mourning, but the man servants should of course. We were much touched by Sweetface's sweet words [quoted in her letter]. Give him a special kiss from his loving pappy.' Among Frau Wernher's papers was a sad little note headed 'To my children', and from this it is clear that Julius's retarded brother Hermann was still alive and entrusted to his care.

Lionel Phillips kept up the tradition of writing long detailed letters every week to Wernher, Beit, often including reports, sketches of shafts etc., and newspaper cuttings. A letter from Julius in reply to one of these expressed delight that the firm was investing outside South Africa and withdrawing capital. Whatever that meant, Taylor in his autobiography vaguely referred to various activities of the firm unconnected with gold, which included banking, ranching, farming, irrigation works, cement and other factories, waterworks, tramways, buildings and selling residential lots, and exploration. Eckstein and Co. owned shares in the *Star* newspaper. It also lent money to the Transvaal Republic, further sums being raised from finance houses in Europe, chiefly on the recommendation of Wernher, Beit. Farms had been acquired outside Johannesburg, Doornfontein and Braamfontein, and land bought in Swaziland, but lists of securities held by Wernher, Beit in 1895–6 also show investments in American railways, German industries and British and foreign government bonds.

According to Samuel Evans, a future partner in Eckstein's, the firm also helped the Boer government to acquire certain concessions in Swaziland. 'They did this at the request of Rhodes [who wanted Kruger's attention diverted from Mashonaland, where gold might be discovered], and they made nothing whatever out of the transaction for themselves. However, it exposed them to calumnious imputations in the Press by detractors and rivals, imputations which could not be refuted at the time without giving away State secrets.'

The smouldering resentment among the Uitlanders against the Transvaal government was mentioned frequently in Phillips's letters, with complaints about its inefficiency, graft and sheer obstructiveness. In particular there was the matter of 'monopoly sharks'. The dynamite monopoly was considered the greatest outrage, costing the industry at least £150,000 a year. Its 'tortured history' dragged on over the years and became an obsession with Phillips. The cyanide monopoly involved the Chamber of Mines in long legal battles. A Netherlands company, in which the Germans had a large interest, was given a monopoly of the railways in the Transvaal, and charged excessive rates of carriage.

There were worries about unskilled black labour. As early as 1892, Phillips was writing that 'our niggers are being paid too much'. Because there was virtually no indigenous population, most of the black workers came from the northern Transvaal and Mozambique. Mine-owners poached from one another, with complete disregard for the consequences, and as a result it was considered that wages were disproportionately high compared to those of white skilled labourers from Cornwall, Australia and elsewhere. The Chamber of Mines was constantly petitioning the government for help in forming 'Kaffir stations', where, as Phillips wrote to London, 'natives could get shelter and be able to buy food . . . and return home with their money unmolested.' Not only were there bandits en route but some 'Dutchmen' were making blacks pay fines for crossing their land, or do work in compensation. The government eventually produced a pass law, which was so inefficiently run that it was virtually useless. The unscrupulous method of recruiting by shady characters was another grievance.

As has so often been pointed out, while the gold of the Witwatersrand is rich in the sense that the extent of the deposits is incalculable, the actual gold content per ton is low, compared, say, with some deposits in the United States, where it can be up to six times as great. Consequently the expense of extracting gold is and was enormous, and wages had to be anxiously watched. Hence Phillips's seemingly heartless, penny-pinching remark about the 'niggers'. The same argument applied to the cost of skilled white labour. It was of course inconceivable at that time that white men should take on heavy or menial jobs.

There were also stories of cruelty by Native Commissioners and of black prisoners dying of scurvy in jail without a trial. Then there was the iniquitous liquor concession. Drunkenness was a scourge among black workers, and was exploited by makers of cheap rotgut at the Hatherley distillery, owned by Sammy Marks (who years before had been squeezed out of the French Company at Kimberley), now one of those who had the ear of Kruger. As a result, the black mineworker could easily finish up with nothing left to bring home to his family.

On 16 June 1894 Phillips wrote a letter to Beit, which would have also been for Julius Wernher's eyes:

The open hostility to the Uitlanders, the clear want of appreciation as to the magnitude of the subjects dealt with and the apparent disposition to snatch as much as possible for the poor burghers at our expense, is enough to frighten anyone. Kruger's nightmare seems to be that foreigners (of whom he regards Rhodes as the head) will gradually buy up the whole country and oust the Boer. He is bent, therefore, so far as I can judge, upon introducing repressive legislation . . . On the whole I see no reason to fear rebellion; anyhow, not for a couple of years . . . but I do not think the vested interests can afford to let things drift with indifference. If you trust Rhodes and cable 'See Rhodes', I will run down. My own feeling is to spend some money in trying to improve the Raad [Legislature] . . . I hope you or Wernher will soon come out . . . Kruger seems to think that too many people and too much capital is coming in here and this must be checked!! I think, seriously, that the old man means mischief.

There is no evidence that Phillips did see Rhodes then, but Beit might well have spoken to him about the letter. Phillips was right about Kruger's obsession with independence. Although the total Boer population of the Transvaal did outnumber the Uitlanders, there were probably more Uitlander males than Boer males. The Uitlanders considered that they should be entitled to vote, but this was disallowed unless they renounced their British passports. After all, it would simply mean a form of revolution through the ballot-box. In his Presidential Address at the Chamber of Mines, Phillips had said that the mining industry contributed nine-tenths of the revenue of the State, 'and we have a right therefore to demand, as we do demand, that the expenditure of state funds shall be well administered.' In that same month of June the Transvaal government called up Uitlanders of British citizenship for military service, in order to crush black rebels in the north. Some refused to enlist and were promptly arrested and sent up to the front. Sir Henry Loch, British Governor at the Cape, came to protest at Pretoria, and was greeted at the station by angry Uitlander demonstrators.

On 7 July Phillips was saying to Julius that he did not believe it was 'necessary to use force'. 'The government has had a fright and knows that the first shot unjustly fired by the burghers will mean English intervention and the loss of the independence of the Republic.' Kann had actually suggested that there should be some sort of mine defence association, to which the larger companies could contribute £1,000 each and the smaller ones in proportion. It really did seem alarming when Loch asked him if in the event of a crisis Johannesburg could hold out for six days. Phillips then began to consider the advisability of buying in weapons.

In fact for some while there had been a National Union, designed to represent the views of the Uitlanders of moderate persuasion opposed to the idea of armed revolution. Not surprisingly, Phillips was feeling very jumpy. He told Julius: 'You preserve a calm that is simply admirable. I wish you could send me a recipe.' Beit on the other hand was suffering from 'nerves' and was frequently unwell. 'I quite agree with you,' Phillips continued, 'that it is absurd to allow one's pecuniary ambition to take any sort of precedence. Health is the first consideration in this life . . . As you say, there are lots of partners to do the business, and it is absurd for Beit to make himself a slave.'

Rhodes in 1894 was considered to be at the zenith of his prestige. With the help of his devoted apostle, Dr Leander Starr Jameson, he had conquered Matabeleland and was recognized internationally as the great statesman of the British Empire. He was about to be sworn in as a Privy Councillor. Queen Victoria admired him. There was no secret about his vision of an enlarged and united South Africa. After a disastrous meeting with Kruger, his last, he decided that the time had come for definitive action against the Transvaal. Kruger was also blatantly flirting with Germany, which already had footholds in South Africa. A speech by Kruger in January 1895 seemed almost to invite the Germans into the Transvaal.

The 'Colossus' also had his enemies, and was blackballed from the Travellers' Club. An American woman artist thought him the 'personification of war' as he paced restlessly before her. 'He is for forcing opposition out of his path,' she said with some truth, 'not for undermining it.' But, sometimes to his undisguised fury, he did not always get his way with the De Beers directors in London, who were not necessarily enamoured of the idea of using profits for development in northern territories, which they now knew were not going to be a second Rand. Nor did he always have an easy time with his management team at Kimberley, efficiently run by another 'giant' of the engineering fraternity, Gardner Williams, likewise more interested in building up a sound profit than in furthering individual ambitions.

Phillips also had a frustrating talk with Kruger about Uitlanders and the vote. This was in January 1895. 'The old gentleman,' he reported, 'insisted that before an Uitlander could be given the franchise he must render active service to the state. Contrary to his usual habit he did not get excited or angry.' Phillips also mentioned that Kotzé, the Chief Justice, owed the Corner House the large sum of £4,289. Writing, as it were, with a straight face, he said: 'We had helped him out of pure good nature, without any ulterior motive.'★ During the election the Corner House also helped members of the Progressive Party, deemed friendly to the Uitlanders, with some expenses, again presumably without ulterior motive.

The exact movements of personalities connected with the dramas of 1895 are difficult to pin down. Beit and Michaelis certainly came to Johannesburg in April, and would have been staying previously with Rhodes at his house Groote Schuur below Table Mountain. Beit at that time had just emerged successfully from an unpleasant lawsuit at Cape Town. He and Michaelis were able to soothe Phillips, who had been complaining of 'little digs' from Julius but now admitted that in his overwrought state he had been 'smelling' captious criticisms where they were not intended. If those digs had been relayed to Florrie Phillips, by then back in Johannesburg and queening it at Hohenheim, they would not have improved her opinion of the Wernhers.

Florrie organized a ball for Beit, and another was given by Mrs Friedie Eckstein. Financially, Johannesburg was in a buoyant mood, for a 'Kaffir boom' in shares was beginning. Much to the approval of Julius, Beit was able to shed some of the firm's less interesting holdings for satisfactory prices.

But the real reason for Beit's visit was the worsening relations with the Transvaal government. Hitherto mine-owners had kept apart from the National Union. Now the political situation was more serious. The huge capital investments in the deep levels were under threat and Phillips was the natural leader among the so-called Reformers. No record has been kept of the discussions during Beit's visit, except for a purposely vague comment in Phillips's book *Some Reminiscences*:

> Beit, although German by birth, was a keen imperialist. To my surprise, I found that he thoroughly shared my opinion that revolution was coming. He told me that Rhodes held the same view and thought we should take a hand to ensure

---

★ Kotzé was, however, to be dismissed as Chief Justice by Kruger in 1898.

success, if possible. Generally speaking, I was invited to cooperate and after Beit's return I went to stay with Rhodes.

Before this invitation to co-operate Beit would have been back at Groote Schuur. The fatal conversation between him and Rhodes, when the great scheme was unveiled for reabsorbing the Transvaal into the British Empire, is always said to have taken place at the end of May. Presumably, by that time Michaelis had returned to England. But whether Phillips actually went to stay with Rhodes so soon is not at all clear.

Before Beit left Johannesburg in April he gave a fancy-dress ball for four hundred people, the most lavish ever in the town. A Götterdämmerung perhaps? Every lady was presented with a diamond weighing at least a carat.

Phillips wrote, significantly perhaps, to Julius Wernher: 'It seems that Beit with his gigantic energy has written about all our doings. He is looking very well indeed.' He added that the first deep-level boreholes were about to be sunk.

The essence of Rhodes's extraordinary and audacious plot was to persuade the British government to hand over the Bechuana-land Protectorate to the Chartered Company. Dr Jameson would be appointed Resident Commissioner, and he would then with a mounted force of perhaps fifteen hundred men cross the border into the Transvaal at the same time as a popular rising broke out in Johannesburg. The rebels would then march on Pretoria and seize the arsenal.

Beit was persuaded to share the cost of buying the necessary arms both for Jameson and the rebels at Johannesburg. The immediate question anyone might ask is where the money was to come from. Was it to be supplied from London, or in the form of unlimited credit from the Corner House? Or was it to come from Beit's own pocket, from some business interest not connected with Wernher, Beit? And, then, how much did Julius Wernher know?

The weapons were to be sent first to De Beers at Kimberley. To commit Wernher, Beit without consulting Julius or even Michaelis about this would have been inconceivable. Julius, at least initially, would have been horrified at the suggestion of a deliberately fomented coup, but may well have approved of secretly sending out arms as a protection for the mines in case the long-threatened revolution did occur. It has been pointed out by later historians that the Wernher–Beit complex controlled twelve of the twenty-four deep-level mining operations begun by 1895.

It was widely thought at that time that Beit was probably the richest man in the world. The *Mining World* for the end of 1895 assessed his shareholdings as being worth £10 million. Julius's were estimated at £6 million, Robinson's at £6 million, Rhodes's at £5 million, and Barnato's at £4 million. The Corner House produced 32 per cent of the gold mined and paid 45 per cent of the dividends. With such vast resources on tap, spending a few thousand pounds on rifles might have seemed insignificant. On 1 February that year Julius had given Rhodes £1,000 for whatever 'public acts' Rhodes chose to spend it on in Cape Colony. He wished him 'continued success' and asked that his name should not in any way be mentioned. This gesture was not connected with politics, but does show good will and that Julius may of late have been revising his opinion of Rhodes, after discussions with Beit.

The fall of the Liberal government in Britain in June 1895 and its replacement by Salisbury's Unionists, with Joseph Chamberlain as its brilliant and (when it suited him) unscrupulous Colonial Secretary, was just what Rhodes had anticipated and needed. For Chamberlain also shared his sense of divine imperial mission. Rhodes asked Beit to try to urge him to hand over Bechuanaland. His letter shows that Chamberlain already had an inkling of what Rhodes had in mind. 'Surely,' he wrote, in his rapid scrawl, 'Chamberlain should see all this. He risks nothing. I risk everything and yet he will not budge an inch to help a big idea which [could] make England dominant in Africa, in fact [would give] England the African Continent.'

All that Chamberlain would allow him was a piece of land known as the Pitsani Strip, which ran between the Protectorate and the Transvaal, enough room for a railway to run north to Matabeleland, and at least a feasible launching-pad for 'Dr Jim'. When he agreed that mounted police should be sent down from Matabeleland, he knew very well for what purpose they were needed.

On 11 August Rhodes wrote to Beit: 'I hope you will arrange to send 2,000 or even 3,000 affairs [rifles]; they will get through all right; they will be supplied with necessary things [ammunition] to fill them. You might say, "Oh yes, wait." But, as you know, we will wait too long, and with its marvellous wealth Johannesburg will make South Africa an independent Republic, which you and I do not want.'

'The market has taken a spurt again,' wrote Phillips. It was the old familiar story. 'Every miner and clerk has his little spec and naturally devotes his thoughts to it instead of to his business. Vast tracts of valueless country are being opened up, money is plentiful and valuable labour therefore frittered away right and left.'

The collapse was not far off. On 1 October Kruger produced a genuine *casus belli*, just what Rhodes needed. Because of the high charges of railway freight in the Transvaal, a system had developed whereby the Cape railways unloaded goods at the Vaal River and then took them across the drifts or fords and on by ox-cart to Johannesburg. Kruger now closed the drifts. Shares tumbled. Bankruptcies were threatened. Tempers boiled. The British government issued a fierce ultimatum, and – unfortunately for Rhodes – Kruger climbed down.

Undeterred, however, Rhodes continued to lay his plans. He held a three-day secret meeting at Groote Schuur. Present were Phillips, Jameson, Rhodes's brother Frank, his American consulting engineer at Gold Fields, John Hays Hammond, and 'one or two others', including presumably Charles Leonard, president of the National Union. It was then decided that about 5,000 rifles and a million rounds of ammunition would have to be smuggled into Johannesburg with the help of De Beers. Jameson's men at Pitsani would need to be 'fully trained and equipped with modern arms field pieces and machine-guns'. The date of the rising was provisionally fixed for 27 December.

An unexpected twist in international politics gave an extra urgency to all this. Britain had found itself in a ludicrous confrontation with Venezuela about an area of British Guiana. President Cleveland of the United States had invoked the Monroe Doctrine and was even threatening the British with war.

Meanwhile poor Florrie Phillips was having trouble once more with her 'infernal regions' and had been forced to return to England. Her husband was frantically worried, but at least it meant that Château Hohenheim became free for secret meetings between the Reformers. She was met on arrival at Southampton by 'Little Alfred' Beit, and 'even the Wernhers' came to see her in hospital.

But the tension of the approaching drama at Johannesburg was affecting Beit. Not only his reputation, but the future of the Corner House, and by association the fate of the investments of the great foreign financial houses, were at stake. Florrie, innocent of the true reason for his collapse, thought he looked 'a wreck' and wondered if he might have a fit or 'something awful'. Julius wrote to Phillips that he feared that Beit's reason might be in danger. There was a time, he said, when Beit used to be so careless about his health, but now he was worried about himself. He had a mysterious pain, and was constantly taking his own temperature.

On 18 November Phillips wrote to Julius saying that he had invited about four hundred people to the opening of the new Chamber of Mines building. 'I intend to speak out plainly and strongly . . . The capitalists can no longer look on silently at the maladministration and the contempt for the wishes of the people. Unless wiser counsels prevail the outlook is indeed black, and with the rapidly increasing population I greatly fear a rumpus.' The white population of Johannesburg was then about 51,000, 40,000 being Uitlanders, with 4,000 Asians and 42,000 Africans.

On 19 November Jameson came to Johannesburg and obtained an undated and dramatically phrased letter signed by the five chief reformers: Leonard, Frank Rhodes, Phillips, Hammond, and George Farrar, another mining magnate. 'Thousands of unarmed men, women and children of our race will be at the mercy of well-armed Boers, while property of enormous value will be in the greatest peril . . .' This was to be used as the excuse for rushing to the rescue of the Uitlanders. All expenses that Jameson might incur were guaranteed. The date fixed for the rising was advanced to 28 December.

On 20 November Phillipps spoke at the Chamber of Mines. It was a great piece of oratory: 'All we want in this country is purity of administration and an equitable share and voice in its affairs . . . Nothing is further from my heart than a desire to see an upheaval . . . which would probably end in the most horrible of all possible endings, in bloodshed . . . This much maligned community consists of a majority of men born of freemen . . .' But he also added: 'It would be terrible to have strife, and everything must be done to avoid it.'

On 22 November Julius Wernher read the speech in *The Times* and wrote complimenting Phillips on his courage. 'It is a thousand pities that people who are only too anxious to be loyal and peaceful citizens must in the end become exasperated and dissatisfied.'

Judging from a letter he had from Kann, both were suspicious about Rhodes's and Phillips's real plans, and might even have known more than Julius let on: 'One can never be absolutely sure that the Colonial office will not let one down in the end. I do not think Rhodes, Phillips etc., are imprudent enough to proceed without securing support.' But 'proceed' in what way?

In London Florrie felt a 'glow of pride', which was not, however, shared by the City of London. South African shares fell disastrously. She was told that everyone was 'going' for her husband. 'If you appeared on the Stock Exchange, even you would be mobbed!'

There was a final meeting of the conspirators at Groote Schuur. By this time many had been let into the secret, and those included the editors of the London *Times* and the Johannesburg *Star*, the journalist Flora Shaw, the British High Commissioner at the Cape, Sir Hercules Robinson, and presumably other directors of the Chartered Company such as the Dukes of Abercorn and Fife. Quite how much Chamberlain was 'in it up to the neck' has always been a matter of speculation. The usual conclusion is that he gave encouragement but avoided listening to details. The telegrams to Rhodes from Rutherfoord Harris and other go-betweens in London, that so mysteriously and outrageously disappeared at the time of the eventual parliamentary inquiry, have in recent years turned up. Even they are not conclusive proof of Chamberlain's complicity, but they are certainly open to damning interpretation.

On his return from the Cape Phillips wrote to Julius about the likelihood of a forthcoming 'row'. Significantly, certain words and a whole page were later erased from a surviving letter-book: 'Had we always preserved our policy of trying to do something behind the scenes, but of practically sitting on the rail in public, we might be the subject of infuriated mobs' attentions some day. If such a thing ever takes place I do not think . . . would have a chance . . . present feeling at home [page missing] . . . Government could not afford to look on.'

'Dr Jim' waited with his men in the fearful heat of Pitsani. The approaching fiasco, even if it was long premeditated and expensively underwritten, revolved in the end almost entirely around his own motives and personality. Rhodes himself said later that Jameson's action would not be understood in his lifetime; perhaps never. Jameson was probably his closest friend. They had lived together at the time of the death of Pickering. As Phillips said, everyone loved the pert little doctor with the big soft eyes; he was 'excellent company and had an adorable disposition', fond of escapades and gambles. He hero-worshipped Rhodes, who in many ways was his opposite.

It was soon clear that the Reformers were finding it hard to stir up enthusiasm for an armed revolt in Johannesburg, especially among outcrop mine-owners not concerned with deep-level investment. Telegrams were sent to Jameson, urging postponement. Rhodes became agitated and cabled to Beit to come to his side at once. He added: 'A. Beit must not consult Phillips who is all right but anxious to do everything himself and he does not wish to play second fiddle.' So on 29 November someone at the London office – probably Julius himself – wrote formally to H. Eckstein & Co:

Mr Beit is leaving by this mail. He has been very seedy lately and unable to attend to business. The doctor advises a long rest and under the circumstances a trip to the Cape was the best solution. He may stay a little in Cape Town to rest and we ask you not to trouble him about business more than you can help.

Julius decided to get away from tensions and spend Christmas in Paris. Before he left he wrote to Phillips that he was constantly being asked for his views. 'I wish I knew! I can only answer that all the people want is a decent and honest government, and peace, but they will not for ever stand to be disregarded and their just claims denied – a feeling which you have strongly expressed in your speech.'

Young Percy FitzPatrick had now been made Secretary of the Reform Committee and was responsible for seeing to the eventual supply and distribution of food when the emergency came. He was also concerned with hiding the rifles and ammunition that had at last arrived.

With Jameson becoming impatient, Rhodes wired his brother Frank in code: 'Advise when you can float.' This was followed by a message from Beit on 23 December: 'Our foreign supporters urge immediate flotation.' And Florrie in her innocence wrote to her husband: 'Is it true that things political are so bad over there? You never tell me anything about these things and I am so interested.' Christmas over, she read in *The Times* a manifesto of grievances, supposedly modelled on the American Bill of Rights and issued by the National Union, virtually summoning the Uitlanders to rise and fight. In high alarm she decided immediately that she must be by her husband's side, and could not be dissuaded by Julius Wernher from booking a passage for 11 January.

But Johannesburg was by no means ready for 'immediate flotation'. It had become clear that Rhodes intended Jameson to march under the Union Jack, which the Reformers feared would at once rally the burghers to the side of their President and alienate not only friends in the Progressive Party, but Americans and Europeans. As the day of reckoning approached, emissaries were sent to both Cape Town and Pitsani to insist on a postponement.

The ensuing flurry of telegrams had no effect on Jameson. His force had dwindled to fewer than five hundred men. On 29 December the malcontents of Johannesburg heard to their utter consternation that he was on his way – and their rifles and ammunition had still not been unpacked. The Reform Committee under Lionel Phillips took over the town. Then news came that

Jameson had surrendered to Boer commandos, who had had plenty of warning of his intentions. He had lost nearly a quarter of his men, including seventy killed, against only four Boer dead.

Rhodes on hearing the news said: 'This is the finish of me.' Indeed, it was a turning-point in his life, and he was forced to resign as Prime Minister of the Cape. Beit had a breakdown and drafted a will leaving £1 million to any who had suffered from the Raid. Julius showed rare emotion. According to his young colleague Samuel Evans, he buried his face in his hands and cried out: 'The patient work of years is destroyed in a day!'

8

Gold into Art

The first reaction to Jameson's Raid by the London firm was an apparently bewildered letter to Phillips from Max Michaelis, dated 4 January 1896. The news had come like a thunderbolt, he said. 'We can hardly see how such a mad proceeding as his could have ended otherwise than in defeat.' They were in an awful state of suspense at the new premises at 120 Bishopsgate,* pestered by callers wanting to know what was really going on (not least by the hysterical Florrie Phillips, 'hammering' on the door). Beit had cabled them on 30 December saying that Jameson had marched into the Transvaal and that every effort had been made to recall him. But apart from a *Times* report, mentioning a letter signed by Johannesburg residents appealing for help, that was all they knew. 'We are not aware who the signatories of the letter are and we disapprove of the course taken, and further disavow any authority for anyone connected with our firm attaching his name to the document.'

As they were soon to discover, Lionel Phillips had himself signed that notorious 'women and children' epistle. And by the time Michaelis's letter had reached Johannesburg, Phillips was already locked up in Pretoria jail along with other leading members of the Reform Committee, including Percy FitzPatrick, who had previously burnt many incriminating papers. As has been remarked by

---

* It had become necessary to hive off the Johannesburg side of the business. The new offices had the appropriate telegraphic address, 'Glittered'. The diamond dealing business stayed at Holborn Viaduct.

an historian of the Corner House, it would thus seem, incredibly, that the firm's left hand did not know what the right was doing. Given the paucity of documents (many were deliberately destroyed), there will probably never be a satisfactory answer to this. Samuel Evans repeated that Julius Wernher was emphatically opposed to 'methods of political force'. Julius's admiration for Rhodes was more discriminating than Beit's, he said. 'He [Julius] was not one who could blindly obey and follow . . . He hoped to break down the Boers' unreasonable attitude towards the Uitlanders by the more peaceful means of commerce and persuasion.'

Whatever Jameson's motives were for launching himself into such an extraordinary reverse, the effects are still felt to this day. For the Boers' faith in British imperial honour and statesmanship had been destroyed, with an impact similar to the effect on the Indians in 1919 of the Amritsar massacre. It has been said that Jameson rode because he felt he was fulfilling Rhodes's unspoken wish – a kind of parallel with the barons of Henry II. Maybe he had it in his head that both he and Rhodes were in some way invincible. Then again, he had been reading Macaulay's *Essays*, and some think he suddenly thought he was the incarnation of Clive. Or perhaps he was simply fed up with the shilly-shallying at Johannesburg, and thought he could push the Reformers and the rest of the citizens into action. This last was the more general view; at the Cape they called Johannesburg 'Judasburg'.

The plain fact was that he had not done his reconnaissance work and was not familiar enough with the lie of the land, and it had not entered his mind that at Christmas time Pretoria would be thronged with burghers up from the country.

Jameson had surrendered on the guarantee that his life and those of his surviving men would be spared. In spite of the clamour for his execution at Pretoria, he was handed over to the British govenment for punishment. But the fate of Phillips and the Reformers was more equivocal.

On 31 January Julius wrote about 'these terrible times' to Georges Rouliot.

We are still without much news to understand the whole position at all. I cannot understand the fatal letter which

anyhow throws a false light and cannot see what right P had
to sign it and thus incur heavy responsibility. It will take a
long time to restore peace of mind and harmony, but if the
'Forgive and Forget' is sincere and wisdom prevails, and
faith in a better administration is turned into a visible reality,
the old vigour will gradually be reestablished . . . [It is]
difficult to get capital to flow into this country . . . People
say all kinds of nasty things about us.

'Forgive and Forget' was hardly likely in Pretoria, but public
opinion in Britain veered in favour of the rebels after the German
Kaiser sent a telegram of congratulation to Kruger. There were
indeed some virulent critics, chief among them being the Radical
MP Henry Labouchere, owner of the newspaper *Truth*.

As for the wretched Florrie Phillips, she wrote an impassioned
letter to *The Times* and never forgave Julius when he told her
afterwards she should have held her tongue. Against her husband's wishes she sailed for South Africa.

Beit and Rhodes returned to London 'to face the music'. Beit
looked ill but Rhodes seemed unperturbed. No doubt Julius was
then enlightened to some extent. On 8 February he told Rouliot
that Beit seemed better in health but 'cannot stand mental strain'.
The Johannesburg office was urging that Julius should come out,
but he refused because of too much work and anxiety about Beit.

As the trials in Pretoria dragged on, Julius heard from a
youthful member of the Corner House, Raymond Schumacher,
who had also been arrested but had had a prison sentence
commuted, that whilst Phillips was 'cheerful and sanguine',
Friedie Eckstein was in a bad state of depression.

He [Eckstein] was taken absolutely by surprise, as you were,
and now he feels inclined to throw everything up as soon as
he honourably can, and go home. I really hope he will
change his mind, because if Mr Phillips has to leave, and
then Mr Eckstein also goes, the firm will lose in prestige
. . . The Reform Committee was as much astounded by the
news of the invasion as any outsider. I was present when the

first telegrams came announcing the fact; the whole game
was up from that very moment . . .

Eckstein did not throw in his hand immediately, but the threat
remained. Then came the dreadful news that Phillips, Francis
Rhodes, Hammond and Farrar had been sentenced to be hanged.
Two days later the death sentence was commuted to fifteen years'
imprisonment, and then later changed again to a fine of £25,000
each, with a signed undertaking that they would not again
interfere in the affairs of the Transvaal Republic, which in effect
meant banishment. FitzPatrick was sentenced to two years'
imprisonment with a fine of £2,000. He was also released soon
afterwards, having undertaken not to engage in politics for three
years. Back in London, Jameson was fêted by his many admirers,
especially female. He was tried and sentenced to fifteen months'
imprisonment. After four months he was released because of
illness.

Some of Phillips's letter-books had been seized by the Transvaal
government and extracts published, which also reflected badly on
the firm. Julius wrote in deep gloom about the future, after
learning about Pretoria's 'act of grace'. 'One sees no light anywhere and I am afraid the industry will go more and more to the
dogs. We are anxious not to shut down but circumstances may
force us and the precious metal market must remain where it is
. . . Of course the mines remain what they are but that is not
sufficient for the investor and under present conditions we cannot
see where a profit is to come from.'

In a period when anti-Semitism was increasing across the Channel
because of the Dreyfus case, the campaign against the Randlords
began to take a more sinister turn, thanks in part to Labouchere's
gibes at 'Herr Beit' and the 'Foreign Jew'. A series of derisive
articles appeared in *Truth*, 'Letters from Moses Moss of Johannesburg to Benjamin Boss, London'. Johannesburg was now nicknamed 'Jewhannesburg'. Hilaire Belloc, at Oxford, wrote
sarcastic poems about international financiers and the iniquities of
imperialism, far removed in theme from the Empire heroics of
novels by Rider Haggard and G. A. Henty.

Many of the new super-rich were building or buying houses in Park Lane or Piccadilly. Barney Barnato, at present renting Spencer House in St James's Place, was building a house in Park Lane. Siggy Neumann lived next to Lord Rothschild in Piccadilly. Alfred Beit's younger brother Otto, however, took over the Duke of Richmond's house in Belgrave Square. When Julius Wernher was asked whether he minded all the mud slung at Wernher, Beit, he made a sour little joke: 'Why should I bear malice? They probably think I am only Beit's Christian name.' Most people did assume that the Wernhers were Jewish.

In 1894 Beit had moved into the strange house built for him by Eustace Balfour at 26 Park Lane. It had two storeys and was described variously as an 'enlarged bungalow' or 'more like an encampment than a solid English house'. The ground belonged to the Duke of Westminster, who had at first been uneasy about allowing an upstart from South Africa to build a house there. After hard bargaining, he had sent a last-minute message to Beit to the effect that he hoped he would spend at least £10,000 on his house. Beit's response was that he would be spending that amount on his stables alone.

Beit's special pride was his winter garden, a kind of conservatory, with a rock garden, ferns, palms, a tessellated pavement and an 'electric fountain'. The upper floor was almost an exact copy of his chambers in Ryder Street. During 1895 and 1896 Bode frequently stayed with him to advise on buying pictures, bronzes, and no doubt oriental carpets, on which he was also an expert. Bode was tactfully to say that collecting was not Beit's 'all engrossing passion', as had been in the case of Sir Richard Wallace and George Salting, the great benefactor of the Victoria and Albert Museum. Bode would therefore tip off Beit when exceptional bargains came on the market – and Beit was prepared to pay higher prices than Julius. No doubt there was many a quid pro quo after Julius made his donations to the Berlin museum, but it does seem that Julius was a more independent collector, and that Beit tended to get the cream of Bode's advice on pictures, some examples of his purchases being *The Letter Writer* by Vermeer (famously stolen from his nephew's house in Ireland in

1984) and six magnificent paintings on the theme of the Prodigal Son by Murillo.

The time has come to turn away from the dramas of South African politics, which were to continue for the rest of the decade and lead relentlessly to war, and to consider Julius as a connoisseur: a more peaceful but integral aspect of his life. A hundred years later the name Wernher was the more likely to be remembered in Britain for the extraordinarily diverse collection of masterpieces that he amassed in so short a time.

He had decided to find grander and more spacious premises to live in. Birdie's mother died on Boxing Day 1895, and this made it easier to think of moving eastwards from Bayswater to Mayfair. The opportunity came very soon with the death of Baron Maurice de Hirsch, financial adviser to the Prince of Wales and friend of Ernest Cassel, and who had made a fortune out of the Orient Express. Hirsch had lived in palatial style at Bath House, on the corner of Piccadilly and Bolton Street, facing Green Park and nearly opposite to where the Ritz Hotel now stands. The outside of Bath House was not particularly impressive, and looked rather like a fortress, with a high yellowish blank wall over Piccadilly. But it had a big courtyard, many stables, an impressive staircase, and a large glass dome over the balustraded central hall. Alexander Baring, first Lord Ashburton, had built it in 1821, on the site of an older house belonging to the Earl of Bath, and the Emperor Alexander I of Russia had stayed there in 1814. Thomas Carlyle and his wife Jane had been friends of successive Lady Ashburtons in the 1850s and 60s, and had known the house well.

All details about the purchase of the leasehold of Bath House and its alterations were destroyed by bombs during the Second World War, as indeed was much of the business archives of the London end of Wernher, Beit. The house itself was pulled down in 1960, to make way for a building with an even less impressive façade. Photographs survive of the interior, showing some splendid French furniture, damask wall hangings, marble fireplaces and huge chandeliers. The plaster and woodwork were in the style of Louis XV, and it seems almost certain that these embellishments were executed for the Wernhers by Georges Hoentschel of Maison Leys, Paris.

Furniture and paintings had to be found for the house, and speedily. Again, apart from one notebook and a few scraps of paper, Julius's records have been mostly destroyed, though certain details about prices, dates and provenances have been gleaned through sales catalogues and research connected with exhibitions. He had of course been buying more pictures since the acquisition of the Bermejo in 1890. A conventional though pleasant view of Eton College by Pyne was bought from Colnaghi for £250 in 1893, possibly as a present for Birdie on Harold's birth, since it hardly accords with Julius's later tastes. However, in 1895 he bought a major work, *La Gamme d'Amour* by Watteau, now in the National Gallery and the only example there of Watteau's work. This had been in the celebrated Mrs Lyne Stephens sale in Paris, and had been acquired from Agnew by Julius for £3,350. In the same year he bought another important picture from Agnew, *Lady Caroline Price* by Reynolds, costing £3,885. Over the next years he collected several other English portraits, including some Hoppners (in particular an attractive one of Henrietta Tracy as a child) from the Paris dealer Sedelmeyer, and a large easel portrait by the miniaturist Cosway.

Like other European *nouveaux riches*, Julius collected a number of eighteenth-century English family portraits. It was a time of agricultural depression and landowners were only too glad to sell their pictures to dealers for ready cash. Lords Carlisle, Brownlow and Ashburnham were noted by Bode as among ready sellers, and some of their pictures were acquired for the museum in Berlin. Dutch interiors and genre pictures were also available and quickly snapped up as being easy to live with. Baron Ferdinand de Rothschild was already a leader in the market, but Americans such as Pierpont Morgan, Henry C. Frick and Isabella Gardner were not yet competitive. Thus, for those with the money, there were plenty of opportunities for building up an art collection of importance.

At least six other pictures were bought by Julius from Agnew, including in 1898 Titian's *Giacomo Doria* (£8,000) and *Rest on the Flight into Egypt* by Filippino Lippi (£3,300), and in 1901 a *Virgin and Child between Two Saints* by Francia (£1,700). From Colnaghi in 1899 he bought a small Rubens, *Diana and her Hounds* (£700), believed to have once belonged to Charles II of Spain.

Beit bought some thirty pictures from Agnew, including a Reynolds for £10,650, a figure that was evidently beyond Julius's limit. In the Agnew sales books one notes other purchases by people like Rodolphe Kann and Lionel Phillips. The Filippino Lippi had once belonged to Kann. Some stray jottings by Julius show that there were several good bargains, for instance, two church interiors by Pieter Neeffs, costing 52 and 18 guineas respectively in 1895, and three Guardi capriccios for £93, £170 and 220 guineas respectively.

Prices of course vary according to fashion or rarity, but they reflect a collector's character. A pound in the early 1890s would be the equivalent of about thirty pounds a hundred years later. It is a pity that we do not know how much Julius paid Sedelmeyer in 1900 for another exceptional work, *Lady and Gentleman at a Harpsichord* by Metsu, with wonderfully contrasting lights and shades. Originally belonging to the Hohenzollern family, it was bought by Sedelmeyer in Dresden for 42,000 francs.

The highest known price paid by Julius for a picture was £8,000 for a full-length portrait by Reynolds of the Countess of Bellamont. Other important pictures included a Dutch interior by Pieter de Hooch, a Wouwermans, at least two van Ostades, a fifteenth-century Annuciation of the Venetian school, and a contemporary copy by Augustin Estève of Goya's portrait of the Duchess of Alba.

A feature of Julius's picture collection that differed from Beit's was a large proportion of paintings of the Virgin and Child, and it has been suggested that it was largely to please Birdie. These include one from the school of Botticelli and a little Hans Memling, bought in 1905 from a private source in Rome and in spite of some over-painting still a beautiful work.

The greatest acquisition of all was *Christ Taking Leave of His Mother* by Altdorfer, also now in the National Gallery. This was bought from Langton Davis in 1904 for an unknown price but certainly a great deal higher than the 23 guineas for which it had been sold at Christie's in 1884. Painted in about 1520, it is one of

Altdorfer's most famous works, full of extraordinary pathos, unique because of Altdorfer's pioneer approach to landscape.

In spite of the Altdorfer and the Bermejo, the Watteau, the Metsu and the two Reynoldses, it is surprising that Julius with his huge and ever-increasing wealth did not attempt to collect yet more major masterpieces in paintings. It is perhaps unfair to compare his collection with that of Rodolphe Kann, the 'premier amateur of France' as he was described in 1903. Kann possessed pictures by Bellini, Ghirlandaio, Bronzino, Tiepolo, Vermeer, Fragonard and Boucher, and no fewer than eleven Rembrandts, many of which through some clever manipulation by Duveen and Berenson found their way to Pierpont Morgan after his death. Jules Porgès also had a fine collection, chiefly of Dutch and eighteenth-century paintings, at his sumptuous mansion in Paris, 18 Avenue Montaigne.

The conclusion is that other aspects of Julius's collection engrossed him more, and indeed it is these that help to make it so individual. Like Beit, he had some remarkable bronzes, early majolica and Hispano-Moresque ceramics, but he also amassed Limoges enamels, Turkish ceramics, German stoneware and silver gilt, Palissy ware, clocks, tapestries and blue Sèvres. Among them were pieces of great importance. But one suspects that his ivories, mostly Byzantine, Carolingian and Romanesque, and his Renaissance jewellery were his chief passion.

It is easy to understand why Julius, who had dealt in diamonds nearly all his working life, should be fascinated by small, meticulously made works of art. His tenth-century ivory triptych of the Virgin and Child with angels and saints became famous among collectors. A relief of St Eustace, probably a book cover, may be even earlier in date. Julius collected around two hundred pieces of jewellery, including cameos, intaglios and finger rings, the majority being Spanish or German. The prize was a sixteenth-century Spanish dragon with enamelled scales and set in emeralds. He also assembled a collection of German enamelled cap-badges and jewelled appliqués or dress ornaments, dated around 1600.

His one surviving notebook was neatly kept, with details of prices and provenances between 1893 and 1897. Although objects were shown as having originated from Beresford-Hope, Baron

Seillière, the Duc de Dino, Prince Soltikoff or Mrs Lyne Stephens, the notebook shows that Julius was in the habit of buying through the trade. Several items refer to the huge Friedrich Spitzer sale in 1893 in Paris where it was hailed as 'la plus grande vente du siècle, and can still be identified at Luton Hoo. No pictures are listed in the notebook. The most expensive piece from the sale was a majolica plate dated 1525 by Giorgio Andredi of Gubbio at 25,050 francs (£1,133.6s.). A Limoges plate signed by Pierre Raymond cost 16,100 francs and a sixteenth-century wax portrait 14,100 francs. He also bought at the sale a fifteenth-century Book of Hours, a German sixteenth-century clock, a baroque enamelled pearl pendant, and a manuscript of Ovid's work ascribed to the 'time of Botticelli' and originally part of Henry III's library.

Most important of all, there appear in the notebook '2 plates with the arms of Este. Castel Durante XVI', apparently costing only £460. It would seem that these originated from the Gatterburg-Morosini Sale at Venice in 1894. At any rate they must refer to two of the greatest treasures of the collection, part of the Este-Gonzaga set made for Isabella d'Este in about 1525 and now attributed to Niccolò da Urbino. Another plate from the service was bought at the Spitzer sale by Beit, for hanging on the wall at his house in Hamburg.

Altogether there are 230 items in the notebook from various sources, and they cost well over £60,000. So taking into account additional furnishings for Bath House, he would have spent at least £100,000 in those few years, not counting the Louis XV doorways and fireplaces which must have been imported from France. The other main dealers listed were Seligman, Bramer, C. Davis, Heckschner and Langton Davis. He bought furniture from Duveen and various bronzes from Bode, at remarkably reasonable prices. Some of the highest prices paid were for a pair of lapis and bronze eighteenth-century candelabra (£3,000) from Seligman and originally belonging to Prince Galitzine, and a fourteenth-century reliquary (£2,600) from Goldschmidt of Frankfurt. Three green Sèvres vases (£2,200) were bought from Sedelmeyer.

One of the most interesting pieces of Sèvres still in the collection, a vase, cost £257.5s., and had been in the Lyne Stephens sale. A Régence bookcase from the same sale cost £616.

The four Louis XV tapestries from Goldschmidt costing £2,000 must surely be the huge Beauvais tapestries, 'Histoire du Roi de Chine', now hanging in the dining-room at Luton Hoo. A lovely emerald, ruby and diamond jewel of a falconer and two dogs, from the same source, cost £1,800. Other treasures that came through Goldschmidt were one of the 'Emperor' tazzas in the collection, made in Augsburg in the sixteenth century for a Cardinal Aldobrandini, and a nautilus mounted in the seventeenth century at Ulm (£1,000). A Gobelin tapestry came from Seligman (£1,040). Bramer sold Julius a Limoges plate in grisaille by Pierre Raymond, depicting the Judgement of Paris, for £750 – a superb example – and a Castel Durante plate, *c.* 1525, of 'Portia Bela', for a mere £70. From Beckschner he bought for only £200 a bronze copy of Michelangelo's *Night* in the Medici Chapel, and a twelfth-century casket from Cologne for £660.

Julius also had several dealings with Lord Carmichael, who was also a friend and for a while a Trustee of the National Gallery. Several years after Julius's death Carmichael wrote to Birdie comparing him to George Salting. He said that whilst it had been impossible for Julius to give as much time to his collections, he considered him more independent, 'relying more on his own judgement and – I think, though this is to a great extent a matter of personal opinion – with better taste'. He added that Julius was 'far more modest than he need have been, or than most people are about their own skill in art matters'.

A legend grew up that Julius was so busy that he could only see dealers over breakfast. A postscript to Carmichael's letter may explain how the story got about: 'He used to chaff me because I thought he was the best judge of breakfast before looking at an object. He said it was because porridge always made one feel that it was well not to be over extravagant.'

Carmichael also appended a long assessment of Julius as a collector: 'Of the collectors of works of art whom I have known Julius Wernher was one of the most remarkable, not only because of what he did collect but because of what he did not collect.' Julius, he said, often refused objects which he admired and which were offered at a reasonable price because he did not feel that they would raise the general level. He never bought things just because they were 'pretty' – but when he did buy:

They were always objects which harmonised with others which he used to refer to as 'splendidly ugly'. Once when riding with him in the Row I remember we discussed the respective merits of three objects which had been offered to him for purchase. He and I agreed that one of these was certainly the cheapest if one looked at them merely from the point of view of money value, and we agreed that it was probably the one which most people would think the most beautiful of the three. He said he felt inclined to buy it, but he also felt that it was a piece which if it were in his collection might lead him to buy other pieces not up to his standard and he did not buy it. We used to congratulate each other because we both liked the 'splendidly ugly'. He said, I think probably with truth, it was because we felt that such had been made by stronger and more thoughtful workers than many objects which appeal by the extreme delicacy and beauty of their finish; all the same he did appreciate delicacy and beauty of finish, and no one knew better than he did how to use it in juxtaposition when arranging his collection.

He commented on the originality of Julius's collection. At an exhibition he knew at once what would appeal to Julius.

He was always willing to listen to anyone in whose knowledge he believed, but I don't think he often took advice unless he was quite convinced himself as to the desirability of an object before he bought it. No one was more generous than he was in allowing persons who as he thought really cared about them to handle and examine and criticise the things he possessed, and he was genuinely pleased to look at even a few fragmentary specimens belonging to another collector of anything which had a relation to specimens which he would himself have liked to acquire.

On the score of originality of taste, and setting aside the English portraits and Pyne's *Eton College*, Julius's collection was essentially Continental. The German emphasis was not surprising, and maybe that included what he called the 'splendidly ugly'. He was not at all interested in, say, Chippendale furniture, or in nineteenth-century art. The French Impressionists probably horrified him. Photographs of his elaborately carved showcases at Bath House show how he loved juxtaposing different types of objects, instead of grouping them together as in a museum. 'Every vitrine must be like a picture,' he once said. He may indeed have bought certain things to please Birdie, but the impression is that the collection was very much his own, with some shrewd bargains, though in the first instance obviously influenced by Porgès and Rodolphe Kann.

9

War Clouds

The shock of the Jameson Raid reinforced Julius's determination that the firm should keep out of what he called high politics. In a letter to Rouliot he made a significant remark, which would not perhaps have appealed to Cecil Rhodes: 'We are all interested to maintain the [Transvaal] Republic because that keeps the land free to all nations.' As early as February 1896, he was even contemplating withdrawing from the Rand, or at least reducing liabilities and risks. In the previous year the Banque Française de l'Afrique du Sud had been founded in Paris with a capital of £2 million, on the initiative of Jacques Siegfried and the much esteemed Baron Jacques de Gunzburg, and it was this bank that Julius felt might take over the responsibilities of Wernher, Beit in the deep levels. 'We want to get out rather than get in,' he told Rouliot. In 1889 investment had been a matter of tens of thousands; now it was a question of finding millions. For a start, to meet this crisis, Rand Mines issued £1 m. 5 per cent bonds, of which Porgès and his associates, and various German banks and Rothschilds took about a third.

As soon as Lionel Phillips reappeared in England, he too suffered the lambastings of Labouchere's *Truth*. Like Beit, he was accused of 'wantonly' plotting the Raid in order to depress the Stock Exchange for his own nefarious financial ends. 'We have nothing to be afraid of,' Julius told Rouliot on 29 May, 'as our case regarding Stock Exchange transactions is almost absurdly good and pure, so good that people can hardly believe we did not act differently.' His hope was that Kruger would 'yield wisely here and there'; otherwise the second-rate mines, which were in the majority, had no chance of survival, due to 'unnecessary taxation'.

But the Raid had polarized attitudes between the white communities and had alienated Boers living in Cape Colony as well as members of the opposition party in the Transvaal, thought once to have been sympathetic to the Uitlander cause. At Johannesburg a great dynamite explosion, causing many deaths, had once more stirred up the outcry against the 'muddle' caused by the Republic's system of doling out monopolies, more especially in dynamite. In Britain the rights and wrongs of the Raid in the popular mind had been confused by the ambitions of the German Kaiser. Intellectuals and Radicals like Wilfrid Scawen Blunt, while not necessarily going all the way with 'Labby' and *Truth*, were almost sorry that Jameson had not been hanged by Kruger, thus putting to an end all filibustering for a good decade; and they were cynical about Chamberlain's pretence of innocence. Margot Asquith wrote that 'with the exception of a few people in Mayfair' everyone in 1896 combined to repudiate an enterprise which 'covered England with ridicule and the friends of Mr Rhodes and Mr Chamberlain with confusion'. When the Matabeles rose in Rhodesia and massacred whites, Blunt wished them 'all possible good fortune' and hoped they would capture Rhodes. In the event they were brutally crushed by Rhodes, who thereby gained some helpful publicity.

Julius was looking for means of diversification outside South Africa, and during the next years he and his partners drew out large capital sums. Already by 1895 the firm held American securities, mainly in railways, and bonds issued in Argentina, Chile, Egypt, India, the Netherlands and Portugal – not to mention interests in Rhodesia and Mozambique. There was a large investment in tramways worldwide. Sometime during 1896 Marconi offered the firm world rights in all his wireless inventions past, present and future, except in Italy, for £50,000. This was turned down, no doubt because of the huge investments that would be required for expansion.

On 17 July the official report on the Raid was published. As Julius put it, the principal blame was on Rhodes, 'Beit next'. 'Dr J. is almost ignored and still he truly upset the applecart –

altogether it was a sickening affair.' By the end of the month the markets were 'quite merry again'.

Beit was still not well, and living quietly. The main work in the firm devolved therefore on Julius. Lionel Phillips had perforce decided to stay permanently in England, and in due course became a junior partner in Wernher, Beit. FitzPatrick, however, remained in Johannesburg. Even though he was under oath not to take part in politics until June 1899, he could barely resist them, and was made head of the Corner House's Intelligence department. Obviously he enjoyed writing his long gossipy reports for London, and not surprisingly tended to be more frank with Beit. He was also beginning to write a book that was to become famous and a bestseller, *The Transvaal from Within*.

Far from 'yielding', Kruger in September issued a provocative order expelling from the Transvaal, which included Johannesburg, all aliens who were a danger to public peace. An act was also passed for controlling immigration. The British in protest sent a naval unit to Delagoa Bay.

1897 was the year of the Queen's Diamond Jubilee. In January Julius was summoned by the Prince of Wales to Marlborough House to discuss arrangements, and no doubt contributions, for the forthcoming celebrations, and also for the Prince's Hospital Fund. Other personalities present were the Lord Mayor, the Chief Rabbi, Lord Rothschild and the banker E. A. Hambro. The Prince was evidently impressed by Julius and invited him – with Beit – to stay at Sandringham in June. First there were races to watch. Julius wrote to Birdie:

9th June 1897 Sandringham
Darling, only a line to tell you that I arrived safely and looked at the horses. We went straight to the Stand, had an excellent lunch in a tent. For choice walked here – 2 miles – had tea, introduced to the lady of the house and then went for a long walk over the most beautiful grounds. Dinner at 8.15. A good many men staying here but hardly any ladies except attendance. Unfortunately there was a great deal of rain.

The next morning he wrote again before breakfast.

We dined all on one long table, the Prince and Princess
[Alexandra] sitting à vis in the middle and two
gentlemen of the household taking the heads at the end of
the table, and the small fry took seats anyhow – without
name cards – wherever they found an empty chair – this
after the royal party was seated. The Duke of York and his
wife, Prince and Princess Christian of Denmark, and
Princess Victoria constitute the Royalties beside the hosts.

After dinner only cigarettes, and join the ladies about ½
hour after they left; then perhaps half hour drawing room
where everybody was, and remained standing – then billiard
room and bowling alley which are all most comfortable and
handy. Dinner excellent and the Prince splendid jolly host
talking to everybody – mixing his own liquor etc. etc.
Servants did not appear any more after we went to billiard
room, and the Duke of Portland pulled his own cork and
offered me a Johannes as I was helping myself to whisky.

I don't know many of the people but one talks to
everybody sans gêne and I suppose I will find out their
names bye and bye. The evening finished by Beit playing in
a bowling match – Lord W. Beresford having backed the
other man for a pound. The whole thing was really a joke as
both men previously had played very badly.

It was amusing how the fact of a match roused the Prince
and he chalked for Beit whilst the Prince of D. chalked for
the other man. I am glad B. won!

Before long Julius and Beit were again guests of the Prince and
Princess, this time at Marlborough House. Presumably Birdie
was not at any of these functions because she had not yet been
presented at Court. However, this was soon put right, her
sponsor being Mrs Euan Smith.

Bath House was not yet known for its lavish parties (soon to
come, however), and for the moment Julius and Birdie did little
formal entertaining. Every Christmas Birdie would give one of
her 'Happy Evenings' for some 150 poor girls, each child receiv-

ing a doll. These dolls were 'dressed by members of the house-hold', in other words by Birdie's 'slave', or secretary-cum-companion, Margaret Pryce, whom she had inherited from her mother. The invaluable Pryce was a key figure in the Wernher household for years to come.

Florrie Phillips, fiery and volatile as ever, obviously felt demoted after leaving Johannesburg. It was rather a case of Mirror, Mirror between her and Birdie, and she was desperate to be presented at Court. She had to wait until 1898, and although flatteringly sponsored by the Duchess of Abercorn (the Duke being President of the Chartered Company in place of Rhodes), she was only presented to Princess Christian instead of the aged Queen Victoria.

Some of the Randlords, past and present, such as Max Michaelis, Jim Taylor and Abe Bailey were branching out into country estates of many hundreds of acres. Siggy Neumann outdid them all by acquiring Invercauld near Balmoral, to which he would sometimes be invited. The Phillipses, with a London house in Grosvenor Square, bought Tylney Hall, a vast mock Tudor mansion near Basingstoke, complete with ballroom, oak panelling and an Italian garden, standing in 2,500 acres. As for the Wernhers, they were content for the time being to rent country houses for the summer. One year they took Kimpton Hoo, in Hertfordshire; another year it was Swallowfield near Reading.

Derrick was still the 'apple' of Julius's eye, almost to the exclusion of the other two children. Aged seven, he had a passion for steam engines. 'He is so full of spirits,' Julius wrote to Birdie, who was on a cure at Marienbad. 'He is a wonderful boy, and it is "Wonne" [bliss] to see his sweet eager face.' His godfather Alfred Beit 'doted' on him, and both Julius and Beit visualized Derrick as their successor in the firm.

The Parliamentary Committee of Inquiry had opened in February and lasted some months. Astonishingly, Chamberlain – who had been opposed to any inquiry whatsoever – sat on it when many thought he should have been the one on trial. Labouchere and Sir William Harcourt, two of the prime antagonists of Rhodes and Beit, also sat on the Committee – Rhodes being now to Labouchere the 'figurehead of a gang of Hebrew financiers' with whom he had shared the profits after manipulating the Stock Exchange. A great number of half-truths, untruths, and even whole truths were uttered on oath, and sometimes Rhodes refused to reply at all. The result was that Rhodes was censured but let off without punishment, and Chamberlain was absolved. Blunt's scathing comment on Chamberlain's attitude towards Rhodes holds good to this day: 'Manage the matter in your own way, but remember I know nothing about it.' Really, it was a case of mutual blackmail. If one of the pair held back, the other would do likewise. Rhodes even remained a Privy Councillor.

Beit was obviously nervous when sent for. His answers were patently evasive at times, but some did at least illuminate certain interesting topics. Asked what he felt as a German citizen about Rhodes's imperialistic schemes, his reply was: 'My views are that the interests of Germany in South Africa are identical with those of England.' Both countries, he maintained, were trying to bring about a better state of affairs in the Transvaal, and were anxious to get rid of an 'incapable and corrupt Government'. (This was a subject on which he and Julius were often questioned.) Why, as a German, should he oppose German intrigues in the Transvaal? Beit's answer was that German political aspirations in Southern Africa were 'mere moonshine'. The best service he could do for his native land was, mixing his metaphors, to 'choke off rainbow-chasing' so that German commerce might flourish under the British flag.

German political aspirations were of course certainly not 'moonshine'. After all, £200,000 had been taken up by the German banks in the Corner House's latest issue.

Beit told the Committee that he had always advised the Uitlanders to proceed constitutionally, but in the end saw that it was hopeless with such an administration in power. He had come to realize that a rising was inevitable. After he had given the money to Phillips he did not discuss how it was to be spent, nor did he know to what use it had been put until some while after the Raid. The money was to 'assist the people of Johannesburg to get their rights and to save the industry from ruin'.

Where, then, did the money come from? 'It came out of the

firm.' Out of his business? 'Yes.' He said that he did not 'intimate' to any of his co-directors the facilities given to Johannesburg. Nor did he even discuss the matter with them.

So one concludes that the money had been in the form of an open credit out of Corner House funds. Nothing was said about how the rifles were paid for in England.

Beit was asked if he was prompted at all by financial consider-ations. 'No, certainly not.' He had had no communication with the Colonial Office. He did, however, have discussions with Ruther-foord Harris and Rochfort Maguire, colleagues of Rhodes, and had various conversations about Johannesburg with Flora Shaw.

When Rhodes had seen Phillips at Groote Schuur, it was agreed that the expenses should be divided equally, £200,000 each. (It was later thought that the Raid had cost Beit £400,000.) Beit spoke about the franchise question and taxation, which if reduced could have helped employment, both black and white. He had wanted the native laws to be in more able hands. 'The natives are very badly treated by the Landdrost [magistrature], and our object was that these laws should be carried out in a more humane way in order to attract more native labour to the fields.'

Then came the expected clash with Labouchere – who had already been forced to withdraw his 'not even honour among thieves' speech in the Commons, but had continued with his 'vile attacks' in *Truth* and even in the Paris paper *Le Gaulois*, referring to 'dangerous and discredited sharks'. As the atmosphere heated up, the Committee's Chairman complained: 'I think this is getting very irregular,' and the room had to be cleared.★ Beit demanded that Labouchere should substantiate his accusations or withdraw them. He declared on oath that it was utterly false that he had made 'bear sales' before the Raid, and offered to give the Committee access to his firm's books.

Later Labouchere attempted to trap Phillips, who admitted that since arriving in Johannesburg he had made a large fortune for himself, and that the firm was now worth many millions. So,

---

★ The ritual of clearing the room was lampooned in the House of Commons: 'This is, I think we may assume,/An incomplete affair;/For whilst they often "clear the room",/They never clear the air.'

said Labouchere, referring to the allegations about discriminating taxation, 'You complain that although millions were made, more millions might have been made.' 'Certainly,' replied Phillips with dignity. 'I was not suffering pecuniarily myself. I did not join the revolution on a money thing.' 'That is a matter of opinion,' retorted Labouchere.

Beit and the rest of the 'gang' were also let off, and Beit was invited to Sandringham. The 'few people in Mayfair' also bombarded him with invitations, and he went to the Duchess of Devonshire's magnificent Jubilee Ball dressed as a seventeenth-century Stadtholder of Nassau. At that period he was far more socially in demand than the Wernhers.

The joke at Westminster was that the Inquiry was a 'Lying-in-State'. Labouchere had not come out well, and was attacked in papers such as the *Critic* (backed financially by Wernher, Beit). Undaunted, he produced his own Alternative Report on the findings of the Committee, claiming that Rhodes and Beit deserved severe punishment. 'These two men, the one a British statesman, the other a financier of German nationality, disgraced the good name of England, which it ought to be the object of all Englishmen to maintain pure and undefiled.'

As it happened, the firm had made money during the boom of 1895, not perhaps quite in the way that Labby had thought, and it was Julius as the partner mainly responsible for the firm's investment policy who had been responsible. Julius told Rouliot that during the boom he had got rid of 'rubbish', or doubtful ventures. On 5 December 1895 he had written to Phillips: 'There is no pleasure in helping to push share values artificially, and I am afraid we have not been quite guiltless in that respect on our side; it is tempting but not worthy of a great firm.'

Labouchere, who himself was not averse to using *Truth* for influencing share prices, was still on the attack three years later, during the Boer War, which many came to see as the inevitable consequence of the Jameson Raid. By then he had gained plenty of sympathizers. But at least it is now clear that the role of the Randlords in 1895 was not 'monolithic'. The mine-owners and capitalists were not united then – Barnato and Robinson, for instance, were not among the plotters, and small mine-owners kept their distance. Moreover, as the historian R. V. Kubrick has since pointed out, the firm of Wernher, Beit–Hermann Eckstein was by far the soundest in Johannesburg,· and thus the least vulnerable to the effects of heavy taxation. They also had the most to lose. In sum, the verdict on Julius Wernher's original involvement in the Raid, and any conscious preparation for it, must surely be 'Not Proven' – though with a qualification, which is according to such evidence as is still available. Beit had regarded Rhodes as a supreme authority in politics, invariably right. His motives for supporting Rhodes before the Raid were complex, in part idealism, in part – absurd as it may seem – mere loyalty, and they probably will always remain a mystery. Indeed they could even have been due less to hard-headed political or personal financial reasons than to his sense of personal responsibility towards foreign investors. Still, one cannot but be surprised that Julius had not been dragged into the Inquiry.

Beit's health continued to suffer. As FitzPatrick wrote in retrospect, the subsequent campaign against this 'nervous, essentially modest man' gave him the reputation of a kind of ogre, the arch-capitalist millionaire who would sacrifice everything to making more and more money. When FitzPatrick said that Beit was 'generous in spirit', with gifts of 'forbearance, forgiveness and all that we arrogantly term the great Christian spirit of kindliness and consideration for others', it was not just whitewash. Such things were repeated many times after Beit's death, and not only in the business world. And, as will be seen, it was Beit, not Labouchere, who won posthumous public gratitude.

Friedrich Eckstein told Lord Rothschild that a chief cause of the mining financiers' unpopularity was the 'unspeakable vulgarity' of the Barnato family. There was a joke, possibly even true, that when a great society hostess in London invited Barnato to come upstairs and look at her Watteau he assumed that she was referring to part of her anatomy. His finances in fact became extremely precarious. He was frequently depressed and took to drink. On 23 July 1897 he committed suicide, throwing himself overboard on a liner not far from Madeira. He remains and was considered at the time one of the most colourful and vivid characters of all the Randlords.

That autumn Beit hired a yacht and took Rhodes, Jameson, Jim Taylor and some others on a Mediterranean cruise and up the Nile. It is said that the subject of the Raid was never mentioned.

Julius's reputation as an international financier had steadily increased. By the end of 1897 he was reckoned probably the most important controller of mines in the world. When Barney Barnato died, that left a vacancy among the Life-Governors of De Beers. In 1898 Philipson-Stow resigned, and Rhodes and Beit invited Julius to take his place as Life-Governor. Isidore Dreyfus was named as Julius's alternate. No other Life-Governors were to be appointed. In that same year Julius and Beit took British nationality.

The first deep levels on the Rand went into production in 1897, and continued during 1898. By the following year about 27 per cent of the world's gold production came from Johannesburg. It was boom time again. That was not to say, as Julius wrote in response to a French newspaper article, that the agitation among Uitlanders had not returned to its 'former channels'. Mistrust had increased between the two races, not helped by further immigration to Johannesburg from Europe. Julius tried to gloss over all this when he wrote:

> It is inevitable that in a new country and in an industry quite new to the great majority of people great mistakes should have been made, and very often hopes were raised which subsequently experience could not justify, but every visitor to Johannesburg is not only astonished at the immense development in so short a time, but also impressed with the seriousness of the people. Surely there must have been some merit in the people who built up this vast industry in so short a time, who organized with very crude material, and often inexperienced workers, an industry producing Frs 25,000,000 per month already and in some instances paying large dividends.

So much for the opinion, privately expressed, of the Commander-in-Chief in South Africa, General Butler, that Johannesburg was 'Monte Carlo superimposed on Sodom and Gomorrah', and that of the anti-Semites that it was a 'hell full of Jews'.

A new Governor of the Cape and High Commissioner for South Africa had arrived. Sir Alfred Milner was a complex character of German birth, born in Hesse-Darmstadt like Julius Wernher, and now the epitome of the perfect English gentleman. He had different ideas about the Uitlanders from General Butler, and has been damned by many a historian as the arch-imperial devil who drove the British into war with the Transvaal. Certainly, selected published extracts from his diaries and dispatches do make that sound pretty conclusive. Wilfred Blunt claimed, probably maliciously, that before departing for South Africa Milner told a woman friend: 'If I come back without having made war I shall consider my mission has failed.' He called him an 'enthusiastic Jingo, who knows nothing of Statesmanship'. But Milner was a 'statesman' and saw the problem of a disunited South Africa as affecting Britain's other imperial interests in the world. He also regarded imperial development as a way to social reform in Britain.

Radical historians have gone further by detecting an unholy alliance between Milner and the Randlords, particularly those connected with the Corner House. The debate continues to this day as more documentation is sifted through, but the viewpoint on the causes of the Boer War has moved away from blaming the mere greed of a few crafty individuals. In 1941 C. W. de Kiewiet wrote: 'The picture of the capitalists as men with gold in their hands, brass in their tongues, contempt in their faces, and treachery in their hearts is as untrue as the picture of an Empire robbing a petty state of its independence out of envy for its wealth, or the picture of an ignorant and perverse old man leading his State into destruction rather than yield to a modern age.' More recent historians, such as Kubicek, Duminy and Lang, have examined the relevance of the economic background of the mining industry and its importance to British trade in general and the balance of world order. Indeed de Kiewiet has pointed out that the last thing capitalists wanted was a war. Those who enjoy the fun of major rows between academics (in this case over blame for the Raid and the War) should turn to the writings of Professor Blainey (the 'academic terrorist'), Mawby and Denoon.

It must also be said that there were plenty of contemporaries in Britain in the late 1890s who, while not necessarily approving of Labouchere or writers such as Hilaire Belloc, were either 'pro-Boer' or vociferously critical of British government policy and Milner, and these included the rising young politician Lloyd George, the elder statesman John Morley, and members of the Trevelyan family. The author of this book thus finds himself faced with conflicting loyalties. Paradoxically, most modern 'pro-Boer' writers have found themselves opposed to traditional Afrikaner policies.

As it happened, while tensions increased, Julius Wernher throughout 1898 and well into 1899 was constantly urging his partners at the Corner House to work for peace and stability. He well knew the consequences of war after his experiences in France in 1871. In some degree there was a division of opinion within the firm. Rouliot and Friedrich Eckstein shared Julius's views, whereas others such as FitzPatrick and the new arrival Samuel Evans were for the harder line. The positions of Phillips and Beit were more ambiguous. Both necessarily found it expedient to lie low, and in any case Beit was often seedy, but not surprisingly they still had strong feelings about the 'plight' of the Uitlanders.

FitzPatrick and his family had now moved into Florrie Phillips's beloved Hohenheim at Johannesburg. Politics obsessed him, to an extent beyond even the interests of the mining community. In any case mine-owners, disillusioned with the British government, were still far from united, and several broke away from the Chamber of Mines. The question of the franchise and unfair monopolies still remained the main grievance, and it was reckoned that many mines were working at a loss. Meanwhile Kruger had been constructing forts near Pretoria. FitzPatrick had been to see him in March 1897, and reported back to Beit that the old man had said: 'They don't want reforms. They want my country and, while I live, I mean to prevent them!'

In February 1898 FitzPatrick went to see Milner and on 4 March he excitedly told Beit of the results, which he was to consider crucial in his own career, and as the beginning of a long and close relationship with Milner. He had discovered, he said, that they had an amazing community of interests. And when he had remarked that he wondered whether the Transvaal would ever in fact yield to the most vital points, Milner had said: 'It's absurd to discuss that. There is only one possible settlement – war! It has got to come.'

In that same month Milner wrote to Chamberlain that the 'day of reckoning must be hurried on', and that there was 'no way out of the political troubles of South Africa except reform in the Transvaal or war'. This, however, evoked a response of great concern: 'Nothing but a most flagrant offence would justify the use of force.'

Two murders at Johannesburg helped to exacerbate Uitlander feelings. The most spectacular was when a German who called himself Baron von Veltheim shot dead Barney Barnato's nephew Woolf Joel in his office. The other case was the shooting, again fatally, of an Uitlander by a 'Zarp', a Transvaal policeman. In both cases the assailants were acquitted in Republican courts.

In June another important and formidable figure, with a background very different from Kruger's, appeared on this ever more sombre scene. It was the young and brilliant J. C. Smuts, who had been educated at Cambridge and was now State Attorney. FitzPatrick and Smuts had many discussions and formed a kind of respect for one another. Even so, Smuts's plain speaking made FitzPatrick realize by the end of 1898 that war was now a 'dismal certainty'. FitzPatrick was still under oath not to 'interfere' in politics until June 1899, but Smuts became convinced (not surprisedly) that he was 'at the bottom of all this trouble'. 'I shall catch you,' he said, 'and when I do you can take it I'll hang you, and personal relations will not count.'

Rouliot was now President of the Chamber of Mines. At the meeting in January he was able to announce that the Transvaal was now in 'the proud position of being the first gold producer in the world'. He also was constrained once more to protest against the government's extortionate practices, and in so doing reflected the new relationship with Chamberlain, who had protested to Pretoria that the dynamite monopoly was affecting British trade.

Predictably, the response was that this interference in domestic matters was unacceptable.

Not only Eckstein but Rouliot too had become deeply unhappy in Africa. Eckstein wrote to Julius of the 'incessant worry and strain on one's nerves' on top of the '*very* trying climate'. At that same meeting of the Chamber of Mines he announced his decision to retire. Rouliot as chief official spokesman for the industry felt himself trapped in the nightmare of Johannesburg, and indeed the story of the next months' intrigues, *double entendres*, stonewalling and pretended concessions on both sides is worthy of the pen of a Franz Kafka.

Needless to say, Rhodes, still with his vision of a greater united Southern Africa, was fully on the side of Milner. 'There has got to be a separation of the sheep from the goats in this sub-continent,' he told him. He was determined to regain the premiership, and this involved much bitter, vote-catching strife in the Cape. After the Raid Kruger had demanded £1 million in compensation; but the argument was continuing, and Rhodes and Beit had said that they would reimburse the British government with whatever sum was eventually agreed (in the event nothing was paid). Wernher, Beit contributed funds for Rhodes's railways in Rhodesia, a preliminary to his ambitious scheme for the Cape-to-Cairo link. Nevertheless in February both Julius Wernher and Beit had decided it was not expedient to meet him when he came to London; as Duminy has remarked, this was an interesting example of capitalist disunity in that crucial year.

Julius meanwhile was having his relaxation. In the summer of 1899 he took the boys to the Scottish moors, and later in the year the family had a spell on the French Riviera. Then in March he and Birdie went to Biarritz: this was the fashionable month when the Prince of Wales would be present. Among the many grand personages they met was Grand Duke Michael of Russia and his morganatic and beautiful wife, Countess Sophie de Torby, a granddaughter of Pushkin, but whether they became particular friends at this time is uncertain.

The Boer War, or Second Anglo-Boer War, has been described as the Randlords' War, and Thomas Pakenham in his classic work on it has said that Beit, Wernher and FitzPatrick were encouraging

Milner's belligerence, which is not fair to Julius, or even Beit. Pakenham does say that Julius had originally hoped that war could be avoided. It was increasingly difficult for him to keep away from 'high politics', especially when his opinion was constantly sought by Chamberlain, Selborne the Under-Secretary, Salisbury and others. In a letter written on 16 June 1899, he also said that Beit, because of illness, had been in the office for only four weeks since the previous October. 'You may imagine,' he wrote to Rouliot, 'how little he is troubled about politics in his state of health.'

Nevertheless the crisis, which many historians believe was worked up by Milner, had indeed developed a 'Jingoism' in Britain such as was not shared by the more educated classes outside the financial world, let alone by the government. The Assistant Under-Secretary at the War Office, G. Fleetwood-Wilson, warned Milner on 22 June that: 'Over and above all is a rooted dislike, and flat refusal, to risk men and money for the "dirty, stock exchange jew lot". There is a feeling of resentment against the Beits, the Barnatos et hoc genus omnes.'

Julius of course was completely aware that the Corner House was supporting the pro-imperial English language press in Johannesburg: something which the Transvaal government objected to strongly. Yet even if he sympathized with the grievances of the Uitlanders, he knew that his financial strategy could not be furthered by armed conflict – and the Banque Française was beginning to be frightened off by the undertones of war.

When the Transvaal government put out a kind of olive branch, known as the Great Deal, the proposals were considered in London by a committee of financiers which actually included Beit. Milner was impressed by the efficiency with which agreement on replies was reached both in London and Johannesburg, and told Chamberlain that this was largely due to the efforts of Wernher and Beit, and of Rouliot in Johannesburg. He said that he had found a 'new and astonishing kind of millionaire: men with some higher conception than the piling up of money'. Pakenham has shown that in July Julius had a two-hour talk with Philip Gell, Milner's intermediary. Nevertheless phrases that have been quoted from Julius's letters in July and August – such as the financiers being 'quite prepared for war', and 'the situation must be terminated *now*' – are not as sinister as they might seem. For 'prepared for', for instance, read 'resigned to'. By then there was already a virtually uncontrollable slide to war. On 13 May Julius was still saying that independence for the Transvaal was a necessity and that war was 'uncalled for'. As he so often remarked, and was to repeat, by yielding to demands for reform, Kruger could only better his position. This, though, was what Salisbury described to Lord Lansdowne as a moral field prepared by Milner and his 'jingo supporters'. War was approaching, and considerable military effort, 'all for people whom we despise, and for territory which will bring no profit and no power to England'.

At the end of May, apparently at FitzPatrick's suggestion, there was a conference between Milner, Kruger and President Steyn of the Orange Free State, with Smuts also present. It turned out to be a disaster. Julius, waiting for details, told Rouliot: 'A real concession on the franchise question would have a marked effect on public sacrifices.' He also added significantly: 'I am glad that I enjoy such a peaceful reputation in Pretoria,' and went on to say: 'I know there is no evil intention here [in England] and they want to deal fairly and leave the country independent' – a comment which might still make some historians smile.

Then on 7 July he wrote again, complaining about contradictory reports from Africa. 'Nobody wants war for which however preparations are officially made (vide *Times* today). The whole thing is beastly unsettling and political talk and interviews fill the day . . . The market remains hopeful . . . On the Continent particularly people fail to see the seriousness of the situation.'

The ban on FitzPatrick's involving himself in politics had expired, to his great relief. He sent Julius his polemical manuscript on the Transvaal, and Julius advised publication but only after 'all hope of peace had disappeared'. Milner had also, it seems, recommended that it should be published, so maybe FitzPatrick had envisaged the book as a preparation for war. In August he arrived in London.

Meanwhile, against a background of rumours, and with the Transvaal and the Free State building up their military strength, Kruger did suggest some concessions which for a while made it seem as if the crisis was over. Milner confessed in his diary that this gave him a 'very great feeling of depression' and that British public opinion was going to be 'befooled'. He need not have worried, for Her Majesty's Government quibbled, and preparations for an ultimatum were made. Now Eckstein, Rouliot, Schumacher and most of the staff of the Corner House moved to Cape Town, leaving Samuel Evans as caretaker in Johannesburg. The Republican government issued a warrant for the arrest of the editor of the *Star*, K. W. Moneypenny, but he managed to escape. Smuts urged Kruger to arrest all the leading agitators in Johannesburg, and warrants were drawn up. Evans was convinced that when war came the Corner House building would be destroyed. He arranged for all the Company books to be removed to various banks. Then he himself 'bolted'.

Certain phrases in Julius's letter of 15 September have been quoted in evidence against him, so it should therefore be transcribed in full. Pakenham sees it as an 'apology' for the delay in sending out troops, as if Julius had the power to do such a thing. But the letter was written when war was virtually certain: a war which Julius dreaded, and now understandably hoped, if it came, would be over quickly and decisively.

My dear Rouliot, I received yours of the 14th and 21st August since [when] you are a fugitive from the land you hate so thoroughly – I hope not for long as the present situation is, at last, fast coming to an end. If it has lasted for so long it was for political reasons on this side as knowledge in the [British] public was absent and no sympathy. But gradually matters are understood, *all* admit that something must be done and nearly all agree that Chamberlain is not asking anything unfairly [the franchise issue]. Of course this delay, necessary to give the Government force and the right to act was painfully felt on your side and leads to great hardship but that could not be helped [the 'apology']. The fact that the military arrangements are far backward proves that the thought of war was not seriously entertained here until quite lately – still it seems incredible [*sic*] that an Empire holding half the world should ever be so little ready but this is a cause why delay takes place although not willingly admitted or denied. I believe the 'un-decided answer' of Kruger of which Cape Town cables [another ambiguous offer] will be very acceptable here as hardly any troops are ready to leave this week. You were right about Bathville [a financial matter] and we have informed the other parties. Considering the critical position shares keep up wonderfully. I confess I hardly look at quotations.

There is also a letter dated 21 September from Eckstein to Evans, in which he agrees that war was inevitable and refers to an 'insolent' reply from Steyn to Milner. He enclosed a letter from FitzPatrick which 'I think you had better destroy after perusal as it is certainly very damaging to Joe Chamberlain' – and this is indeed something to raise eyebrows. FitzPatrick was to claim after war broke out that he had been 'in the know', but his opinions and ideas were not necessarily the same as Wernher's and the ailing Beit's. Nor do letters prove that Julius was an 'active partner in the making of war': quite the contrary. It is true that the letter of 15 September does appear to assume that calling Kruger's bluff by sending out troops might yet avert war.

FitzPatrick on arrival had seen Selborne and had told him that there would be no franchise reform until Kruger 'looked down the cannon's mouth'. He also saw various newspaper editors. It cannot be claimed that he had any influence on the British government during those last crucial weeks. Beit did invite him to dinner to meet Rhodes and the Duke of Abercorn, when the possibility of war was discussed. His book *The Transvaal from Within* was published in October, and, being so well timed, it helped enormously to swing public opinion behind the government.

FitzPatrick's most recent biographers believe it possible that he had given up hope for peaceful change as early as in February 1899 after he had met Smuts, and that more than anyone else on the British side in Johannesburg he might have worked to 'see things through'. He was, however, out of touch with Milner after leaving Cape Town, and when it became evident that the Boers were ready to fight the British Empire. He could not have been surprised that it was Smuts who persuaded the Executive Council to draw up an ultimatum demanding that Britain should withdraw its troops from the Transvaal's frontiers.

On 11 October it was the Transvaal, not Britain, that declared war.

Within a week Julius was interviewed by a journalist of the *Daily Chronicle*, and an article was published on 20 October under the title 'Mr Julius Wernher on the Situation'. Julius wrote a letter afterwards saying that it was full of inaccuracies, but did not specify what they were, and much of it does read as if it were his authentic voice.

'When you talk about Boer Government,' he was quoted as saying, 'let me tell you that there is no Boer Government beyond Mr Kruger. Kruger holds absolute despotic power . . . Kruger has inoculated his subjects (for I can call them nothing else) with the idea that the English represent the Philistines of old, and they themselves are the Chosen People.' The Boers, he said, had never forgotten Majuba Hill and fully believed that the Lord would intervene in like manner. Then: 'Kruger is a typical Boer, entêté comme un mulet. He is intensely jealous of the enormous fortunes made by Uitlanders in the goldmining industry . . . I believe out of sheer spite he would, if he could, make an end of all the gold in the country sooner than the "Philistine" should profit.'

He was gloomy about the future effects of the war. There had been so many intermarriages between Boers and settlers that it was practically a family quarrel. The effects would be as far-reaching as those caused by the Franco-Prussian War. Therefore, most certainly, every possible effort to ward off the struggle, so far as this was consonant with British honour, was warmly to be commended. But now there could be no drawing back until victory. 'It is futile to imagine that the matter will be a mere walkover . . . Man to man, physically speaking, the Boer is quite a match for the Englishman . . . It is notorious that the Boer is a superb marksman, and he is very mole-like in his proclivities.'

He thought it would be the toughest struggle for England since the Crimea, 'and I do not believe for a moment that it will only be a matter of a month or so, as we so often hear.' The Boer nation might be thought uncouth and uncivilized in its social customs, but it was civilized in point of warlike equipment, being furnished with German artillery and German artillery officers. Asked whether the Boers would stick it out if they met with crushing defeats, he replied: 'It is said that the Boer is a bad loser, but as is already evident, he intends to avoid a pitched battle as long as possible, and a series of crushing defeats would therefore be difficult to inflict.'

It was indeed a new kind of war for the British Army: a mounted rifleman's war. The Boers thrust into Natal, defeating the British in two humiliating battles. Ladysmith, Mafeking and Kimberley were besieged. At Johannesburg the Republican government took over the control of the goldmining industry and appointed its own State Board.

There had been a stampede of Uitlanders to get away from Johannesburg towards the end of September, and nearly all the mines were shut down, though pumps had to be kept going to prevent them from flooding. Black workers escaped to their kraals. Seven thousand Zulus and other Africans from Natal were, however, left on the verge of starvation, and had to be mobilized by J. S. Marwick of the Native Affairs Department, who bravely led them out on foot for over two hundred miles through the battle lines.

By November nine mines were back in operation. To the disgust of Milner some hundreds of Uitlanders who had opted to remain behind had taken up employment again. The gold they produced helped to pay for the war. Supplies and ammunition were also paid for with confiscated unrefined gold.

The dreary news from Africa did not deter the Wernhers from some entertaining at Bath House. Birdie gave a party for the Schumachers on their arrival from the Cape. Alfred Beit was there. It was reported in a society paper that Mrs Wernher looked regal in a white brocade gown, amid a 'revelry of carnations arranged in graceful crystal and gold receptacles'. The drawing-room looked 'enchantingly lovely', hung with crimson brocade, and the electric light 'set off every object in the room to brilliant advantage'. The Misses Constance and Eva Langton sang 'pretty German and vivacious Spanish duets'.

★

FitzPatrick, because of *The Transvaal from Within*, was regarded as an oracle, and as the war went on his views were published in all the national papers in Britain. He was also frequently consulted by Chamberlain and Rosebery. Not, as he told Friedie Eckstein, that he had a high opinion of the government, which he considered to be 'wobbly, nervous, cumbersome and unmanageable'. 'However,' he added, 'we can hush them up and stick pins in their bottoms,' especially in the matter of supporting Milner. This, he felt, was the 'mood of the great bulk of the public and press'.

But he exaggerated the power of the Corner House over the government.

As Christmas approached, Julius for once tried to look on the bright side. He wrote to Rouliot:

> Things look black, but by no means hopeless and we shall look to ultimate success of a just cause and no sacrifice will be too great to obtain it. Of course the unexpected has created a certain amount of panic in spite of the apparent calm but one cannot contemplate for a moment that England will give way to a dishonourable peace . . . We cannot blame the Govt. so much when we under-estimated the strength of the Boers so much ourselves . . . there is a tough job ahead of us, but the resources of a great Empire are inexhaustable [*sic*].

In the summer of that year the Wernhers had taken a lease on the huge and splendid mansion of Luton Hoo in Bedfordshire, outside the town of Luton. They paid £3,000 a year for this. And here another digression from the main narrative becomes necessary.

The house had been designed by Robert Adam for Lord Bute, the unpopular Prime Minister, in grounds laid out by Capability Brown and on the site of a manor house originally owned by the ancestors of Anne Boleyn and later by the Napiers of Exeter and Merchistoun. There had been an outcry that Bute used public funds to build a palace to rival that of Diocletian at Spalato. Ceilings were decorated by Cipriani, and the magnificent library, 144 feet long, had 25,000 volumes. Dr Johnson was impressed:

'This is one of the places I do not regret having come to see. It is a very stately place indeed; in the House, magnificence is not sacrificed to convenience, nor convenience to magnificence. The library is very splendid, the dignity of the rooms very great, and the quantity of pictures is beyond expectation, beyond hope.' Adam himself described it as his *chef-d'œuvre* 'both in point of elegance and contrivance'. Below the house the large serpentine lake, designed by Capability Brown, who had dammed the River Lea, meandered through the park among woods and plantations.

Many of Adam's plans are now in the Soane Museum. He left the house unfinished, and it was completed by Sir Robert Smirke, the architect of the British Museum, who seems to have made a number of adjustments. The west or entrance front was given a huge portico with six Ionic columns, instead of Adam's elegant colonnade of Corinthian columns with niches for statues between the two bays. In 1843 there was a disastrous fire, gutting most of the interior, although some books and pictures (cut out of their frames by the housekeeper with a carving knife) were saved. Five years later the shell was sold to John Shaw Leigh, a rich Liverpool solicitor who had made a fortune out of speculative building, and he had the house rebuilt, possibly with the help of Smirke. The façade was not altered, since it had been shored up after the fire. In 1872 Leigh's son, John Gerard Leigh, married an intriguing lady, born Eleanor Lucy (known as Louisa) Hawkes, whose first husband had been the Hon. Humble Dudley Ward, son of Lord Dudley. But he died in 1875, leaving Luton Hoo to his widow for her lifetime – and a lot of money. In 1883 Mrs Leigh married Christian de Falbe, the Danish ambassador and friend of the Princess of Wales. The following year they celebrated with a sensational ball, the ballroom being lit by electricity and with forty batteries installed for the purpose.

It was said that Louisa had married once for position, once for money and once for love. Luton Hoo and her house in Grosvenor Square became the scenes of several more brilliant entertainments with royalty often present. According to Sir Horace Rumbold, ambassador in Berlin, the de Falbes were the 'handsomest couple, though no longer young', but contrasting in character, she being autocratic, he quiet and gentle. Both households were perfectly organized and packed with *objets d'art*, often picked up at Christie's. 'Seldom,' said Sir Horace, 'have great riches ministered with so much intelligence to the refined luxuries of life.' A magnificent conservatory had been built at Luton Hoo, carpeted with Persian rugs and full of rare scented plants and singing birds in silver and gold cages: 'giving the illusion of fairyland' according to Lady Airlie in *Thatched with Gold*. There was a special railway station with a covered entrance for royal visitors. Many guests complained about the overheating in the house, and one of these was Princess May of Teck. There were also games of baccarat with 'unpleasantly heavy losses'.

It was at Luton Hoo in 1891 that Princess May became engaged to the Duke of Clarence, the heir to the throne. 'To my great surprise,' she wrote, 'Eddy proposed to me in Madame de Falbe's boudoir – of course I said yes.' She was so thrilled that she danced round and round in her bedroom. But Eddy died a few months later.

Christian de Falbe fell from grace with the Danish government when Britain sold Heligoland to Germany. He died in 1896. By then the increasingly eccentric Louisa was becoming frail, and so it was that Luton Hoo became available to the Wernhers for their 'weekend retreat', stirring up a few caustic comments in papers such as *Truth*. She died after a stroke on 16 December 1899, and the estate reverted to Gerard Leigh's nephew, who himself died very shortly afterwards. The new owner was only a child, and because Louisa had spent so much of the family fortune the Wernhers were permitted to continue renting the house.

It was at Luton Hoo, on 15 March 1900, that Birdie gave a children's fancy-dress party to celebrate the relief of Kimberley the month before. Cecil Rhodes had been at Kimberley throughout the siege, taking a man's part in the town's defence, so it was reported. But he emerged with broken health, and had not long to live.

10

Forward to La Belle Epoque

Johannesburg was at last reached by British forces under Lord Roberts on 30 May 1900. Samuel Evans had been 'borrowed' from Eckstein's as an Intelligence Officer, and it was he who was sent first into the town under a white flag to negotiate the surrender. Later he was appointed Civil Commissioner.

Pretoria was occupied in June, and in October Kruger fled to Europe. It was hoped that the war would soon be over, but the success of the Boer guerrillas, or Commandos, took many by surprise, though not perhaps Julius Wernher, who had almost predicted it in his interview for the *Daily Chronicle*. Arms and ammunition also reached the Boers from German sources, as Evans had noted when on a spying mission at Lourenço Marques.

Meanwhile FitzPatrick had returned to South Africa as confidential adviser to Milner at Cape Town. Thus two of the firm's representatives were conveniently placed in the seats of power. Whatever FitzPatrick's feelings about the necessity for the war, realities had been cruelly brought home when his brother George was killed in the Imperial Light Horse, the first of the volunteer defence organizations, which had been subsidized by the firm with a cheque signed by Julius to the tune of £50,000. Then when he arrived at Cape Town in June, he was informed that a mining colleague, Louis Seymour, had been shot dead whilst repairing a railway line. When the news reached Julius, he wrote from London: 'It has fairly knocked us down, and made us sick at heart.'

The war was arousing strong emotions against the British not only in Europe but in the United States, which had successfully wrested Cuba and the Philippines from another imperial power, Spain, in 1898. The Commandos' bravery impressed people in Britain, and it was admitted that the Boers had military leaders of genius. Even Beit wrote how one of them, De Wet, had 'outclassed our generals'. 'One cannot help admiring the man,' he said. But as the fighting dragged on and casualties mounted, revulsion against the war began to grow and questions were asked as to why it had been necessary to fight at all. Lord Rothschild warned Rhodes not to draw too much attention to himself. By the following year he was writing: 'Feeling in the country runs very high at the moment over everything connected with the war, and there is considerable inclination, on both sides of the house, to lay the blame for what has happened on the shoulders of the capitalists and those interested in African mining.'

Beit seemed to have become alarmingly ill. It was said that a 'sort of madness overtook him', and that he got it into his head that Kruger would take over all the gold and Britain would lose the supremacy of the seas. This may well have been malicious chatter, for Julius made no reference to a breakdown in his letters to FitzPatrick, though they were full of pessimism and discouragement. He told FitzPatrick he was absolutely against the suggestion that the capital of the Transvaal should be moved to Johannesburg from Pretoria, which had a 'quieter atmosphere'. In any case he was 'not for rapid change', a phrase that almost could have been his watchword throughout his life. Milner was anxious to redress the balance of the white races through large-scale immigration from Britain after the war, especially men of yeoman stock. But Julius, observing how in the Lowlands of Scotland agricultural workers and farmers drifted to the towns, foresaw difficulties. The 'real agriculturalists' would want to go to 'better countries'. 'Until America is full Africa has little chance.' Perhaps ex-soldiers could be tempted to stay on after the war.

He worried that too few troops might be available for the Boxer insurrection in China, which might threaten the firm's investments both there and in Korean gold. He fully accepted that the firm had its financial obligations in helping the Relief Fund for refugees returning to Johannesburg. 'Give Milner assurance we shall have to give and willingly the lion's share.' But advantages were soon taken of this show of generosity, and Julius had to emphasize that the actual process of settlement must be the government's responsibility. Too many promoters of the scheme were trying to 'gain laurels at our expense'. 'I don't object,' he told FitzPatrick, 'if good comes out of it for the general welfare of South Africa and quite independent of Imperial favours – I don't look for these and we will not even get a "thank you" for the immense nay foolish risks we have run for the English cause . . . I have this dull feeling that having made a lot of money out of South Africa I am quite prepared to do something about it.'

Soon Eckstein's found itself forced to guarantee the purchase of fifteen large railway engines and two hundred coal trucks, costing about £150,000. FitzPatrick was particularly resentful about this, and thought that having to finance the richest government in the world was 'absolute rot'.

But it was Beit personally who was bombarded with requests for financial aid. Letters sometimes came in at the rate of five hundred a day, asking for help for widows or wounded soldiers, even for shirts for Tommies and military equipment. 'Whenever he felt the cause was a worthy one he helped.' His donations were thought to have run to hundreds of thousands of pounds, though to be truthful, and unknown to the public at large, quite a large proportion came from the firm's coffers, judiciously sanctioned by Julius Wernher.

The mines were intact but 'in mothballs'. During August Julius wrote that the 'stock of gold in the Bank of England is lower than it has been for many years past'. It had been reported to him that Kruger and Smuts among others had originally been 'strongly in favour of the destruction of mines and the burning of houses of certain people', such as Hohenheim no doubt. 'Smuts had particularly urged the war with all his might,' having, like most Boers, a contempt for the British Army. As it turned out, Smuts was one of the most daring of the Commando leaders. In December 1900 attacks were made on the Modderfontein and New Kleinfontein mines on the East Rand by Commando units of up to 350 men. Plants and buildings were destroyed. A Mine Guard of former mine employees was hurriedly formed, but meanwhile the main electric power supply for the mines was damaged, and some mills were burnt down. Again Eckstein's had to bear the brunt of the cost of the Guard, estimated at £136,540. After all, a capital investment for the mining companies of £173 million was at risk. It was not until May 1901 that the military authorities allowed some crushing to go ahead.

Milner, now ennobled, and Governor of the Transvaal (though still High Commissioner for South Africa), needed a new base. He could not abide the thought of stifling summers in the Pretoria 'hole' and wanted a house in Johannesburg. So FitzPatrick arranged for him to be installed – where else? – in a Corner House property, Sunnyside, where once the ace American engineer Hennen Jennings had lived. FitzPatrick had earlier come to Johannesburg to see Lord Roberts's successor, Kitchener, about the men of the Imperial Light Horse, who were aggrieved about their lack of recognition. He was suffering not only from incipient diabetes but a stomach ulcer, both of which appear to have been made much worse by his reception. He found Kitchener as 'hard as the hinges of hell', and contemptuously dismissing him as 'one of Milner's men'. FitzPatrick was also distressed by the burning of Boer farmhouses. As he told Beit: 'Women and children cowering in an out-house watching their smoking homestead is not a kind of sight that is easily forgotten, nor one that [we want] people to remember.' Not surprisingly, his doctor ordered him back to England for a year's rest.

Friedrich Eckstein was also returning to London, and Max Michaelis was giving up his partnership at Wernher, Beit for reasons of health. Alfred Beit was still having his 'ups and downs'. Georges Rouliot, back in Johannesburg as President of the Chamber of Mines, was determined to return to France as soon as the war was over. To meet this crisis, Julius arranged for Louis Reyersbach, an ambitious and somewhat pushy character who had been managing the firm's affairs at Kimberley, to be trans-ferred to Johannesburg, where in 1902 he became a partner in Eckstein's. Raymond Schumacher (who later changed his name to ffennell) was also given a partnership.

March 1901 saw the beginning of what came to be known in the firm as the Markham Case. The new Liberal MP for Mansfield, Arthur Markham, rose in the House of Commons to deliver a speech described in *The Times* as almost incoherent, and in the course of which he denounced Wernher, Beit as being 'nothing more than a gang of common thieves and swindlers'. This was not so much in connection with the prosecution of the war – although he claimed to be a 'pro-Boer of the most advanced sort' – as with the alleged manipulation of shares. He rashly went on to say that he was ready to repeat these words away from the privilege of the House and to 'stand an action in the law courts before a jury of my own countrymen'.

On 7 May Markham addressed his constituents at Mansfield, mentioning the Jameson Raid, 'which as you know was engineered and financed by Mr Beit'. He added: 'But of that criminal proceeding, which has brought misery to thousands of homes throughout the Empire, I say nothing because it is well-known to all.' He continued with his personal attack on Beit, who 'commenced his career as a clerk and has now in a comparatively short time amassed millions'. Markham said that for many years he had been observing the various concerns with which Beit had been connected. This time he coupled Eckstein with Beit as thieves and swindlers. 'I am judging them,' he said, 'by the high code of morality which is followed in this country, and which is essential to public life. If Mr Beit wishes to commence an action against me he will now be able to do so.'

A writ promptly followed, but in the name of Wernher, Beit. The long-drawn-out case received enormous publicity, and Markham was represented by the formidable Rufus Isaacs, later Lord Reading and a Viceroy of India (thus at least ensuring that anti-Semitism would be avoided). Beit took it all very lightly on the surface, but Julius found himself involved with a 'fearful amount of work'. As he told Rouliot on 10 September: 'We wish to throw out political matters which cannot possibly be connected with the charge, but which are "le fond du tout".' Everyone at the London end of the firm, he said, felt absolutely confident about the result, 'knowing one and all that in spite of errors we have never acted from dishonest motives or with dishonourable intention, and there is not a man in our employ who was ever asked to do anything shady or inconsistent with his self-respect'. The firm's counsel was also an eminent QC, Sir Edward Clarke, who had defended Jameson in 1896.

It was revealed that Markham had been an investor in the Rand during the previous ten years, and had once been an ardent supporter of Jameson. A private grievance was suspected. Judgement was delivered against him on 5 December, and he was forced to apologize publicly and to admit that he had no personal knowledge to justify his statements. Wernher, Beit did not ask for damages, and it has been suggested that Beit himself paid Markham's legal costs – though if he did Markham did not show much gratitude.

The whole affair was symptomatic of the rising antagonism towards the Randlords and Johannesburg itself. Wernher, Beit's gifts to charities were crudely described as 'blood money': £5,000 to the Red Cross, £3,000 to the Mansion House fund for widows and children, and later £5,000 to the Coronation Hospital fund. But both Julius and Beit gave large sums to charities that were never publicized.

A future Prime Minister of the Cape, J. X. Merriman, made a speech at Birmingham Town Hall blaming the war on the 'base ends' of those capitalists who had been behind the Raid, i.e. Rhodes and Beit. Olive Schreiner, the famous author, had once admired Rhodes, but now she wrote: 'If there had been 100 honest, honourable, *cultured* English gentlemen in Johannesburg they would have risen up to protest against the Rhodes-Eckstein gang.'

Radicals were agitating for the recall of Milner, but Julius was contemptuous: 'We live in an age of weak men, and acts are too entirely shaped by what people may think of them, not whether they are good or bad.' The torch of anti-Semitism and anti-imperialism was kept alight by Hilaire Belloc and by G. K. Chesterton's brother Cecil in the *Daily News* and elsewhere, and – most notably – by J. A. Hobson in the *Manchester Guardian*. In the House of Commons the labour leader John Burns spoke of the British Army in South Africa having become a 'janissary of the Jews'.

Florrie Phillips and Birdie Wernher several times found themselves working in tandem, organizing committees and fund-raising. It cannot have been an easy experience, for Florrie at that period was described as shrewish. It is also recorded that, whilst Florrie was devoted to 'Little Alfred', with Julius Wernher 'there was no longer cordiality'. Birdie also arranged charity subscription concerts at Bath House. When the CIVs, the City Imperial Volunteers, raised by the Lord Mayor mainly from members of the Stock Exchange, returned from a year of service and paraded down Piccadilly, few houses were as gorgeously decked with bunting and flags as Bath House.

Anxieties about the war did not prevent the Randlords from taking holidays abroad. Those who had interests in diamonds were perhaps less concerned about a drop in income. Biarritz and Cannes remained favourite watering-places. Beit and the Phillipses preferred Monte Carlo. The Wernhers went in for more serious travel: to Oberammergau, Venice, Cairo. At the end of August the family went as usual for the grouse and picnics in the heather, Julius adopting the Sherlock Holmes style of dress. Guests included 'Dr Jim', the Reyersbachs, and the Friedie Ecksteins, but photographs show Beit looking rather miserable in his City clothes.

Luton Hoo was still in the category of a 'retreat', being only thirty miles north of London, though Birdie and the boys seem to have spent rather more time there than Julius. Fancy-dress parties were still a great favourite. Negotiations to buy the house must already have been under way, as Julius was taking an interest in the maintenance of old Madame de Falbe's flock of Southdown sheep. Fitzpatrick was impressed by his efforts and reported to Rhodes that Julius's improvements to the Luton Hoo pastorage had been quite 'dramatic'.

During the 1890s, and particularly in the years preceding the war, Rhodes had become interested in improving the agriculture of Cape Colony, and indeed his efforts were revolutionary and far-reaching, of immense importance to the future of South Africa's economy. He introduced breeds of cattle from other parts of the world to strengthen existing strains. He also launched experimental fruit farms: citrus groves, orchards and vineyards. Needless to say, Beit (or the firm) responded to a request for

1. Sir Julius Wernher at Kimberley.
Photograph inscribed for Sir Percy FitzPatrick.

2. Haulage bucket, Kimberley, late 1870s.

3. Rothschild's sale in Dutoitspan Road, Kimberley, 1875.

4. Julius Wernher's first home, Kimberley, 1873.

5. The first rotary washing machine, Kimberley, 1874.

6. The offices of Beit and Porgès in the Diamond Market, Kimberley,
c. 1888.

7. The second Corner House, Johannesburg, *c.* 1890, without its iron
railings.

8. Alice Mankiewicz (Birdie) and Julius Wernher: the engagement photograph, March 1888.

9. Alfred Beit, dressed as Stadtholder Frederick Henry of Nassau, at the Devonshire House Jubilee Ball in 1887.

10. 'Malcontents at Johannesburg in 1895'. Identified as Alfred Beit, W.A. Walton, Lionel Phillips, Frank Rhodes, George Farrar and Abe Bailey.

11. One of Julius Wernher's most prized acquisitions: a tenth-century Byzantine ivory triptych with Virgin and Child and Saints. Now in the British Museum.

12. *St Michael and the Dragon* by Bartolomé Bermejo, Spanish, late fifteenth century. Bought in 1890.

13. *John the Baptist* by Andrea Sansovino (d. 1529), Florentine. Bequeathed to Julius Wernher by Alfred Beit.

14. Self-portrait in mirror by Julius Wernher and Margaret Pryce, taken in the Blue Hall at Luton Hoo, *c.* 1906, with Ch'ien Lung vase and Mewès and Davis console table.

15. Julius Wernher's sixteenth-century collection in the Red Room at Bath House, *c.* 1902. The Bermejo is in the far corner. Most objects (e.g. Limoges and Este-Gonzaga plates) are still identifiable at Luton Hoo.

16. Luton Hoo, showing the attic floor added by Mewès and Davis.

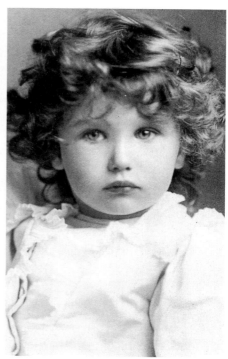

17. Derrick, Birdie and Harold,
1895.

18. Derrick in 1891.

19. Kyllachy, North Berwick, 1901, including Maria Wernher (left), Julius
with Harold over his knee, Derrick blowing trumpet and Franz Mankiewicz
(right).

20. The De Beers
travelling car,
taken by Birdie
with the title
'Julius steps out'.
February 1909.

21. 'In the
Chinese com-
pound, Johannes-
burg', taken by
Julius, March
1909.

22. The Premier
Mine. Taken by
Julius, March
1909.

23. Alex, Derrick
and Harold, 1910.

24. Julius with Sister Agnes, 1908.

25. Birdie as Lady Wernher, 1905.

26. Countess Natalia von Merenberg, daughter of Alexander Pushkin.

27. Countess Sophie de Torby, 1891.

28. Count George von Merenberg and his wife, Princess Olga Yurievsky, daughter of Tsar Alexander II by his morganatic second wife.

29. The Empress Maria Feodorovna with her son the Tsarevich, the future Nicholas II.

30. Grand Duke Michael with Zia, Boy and Nada at Kenwood.

31. From Sophie de Torby's album: a house party at Keele Hall, 1907.

32. Sophie de Torby
and Zia, 1896.

33. Tableau vivant at Cannes.
Left to right: May Van Loon,
Sir Sidney Herbert, Zia,
Count Siegfried Raben.

34. The three Torby children
at Cannes Golf Club, 1905.

35. Derrick, first term at Eton, 1901.   36. Harold on leave, Luton, 1916.

37. 'Derrick in motor costume, Bayreuth, August 1904'.

38. Tennis at Kenwood.
Left: Nada. *Centre*: Zia, Nada, George of Greece. *Right*: Zia.

39. Promenade at Cannes. Zia and Mary Howe.

financial help and appears to have contributed £53,000 by the end of 1900.

Cold storage depots were also built both in the Cape and at Kimberley. Rhodes set about tackling the scourge of cattle disease, rinderpest. In the mid-1890s, in order to combat the Transvaal government's and the Swedish Nobel Trust's monopolies, he had taken the bold action of producing dynamite. Once more De Beers and, after long hesitation, Wernher, Beit, were co-opted. Despite local fears about security and labour problems, and Beit's increasing nervousness over the escalating costs, the enterprise was a success – though again not in Rhodes's lifetime. De Beers also had investments in coal, trams and railways both in South Africa and Rhodesia.

The first peace negotiations began in February 1901 but soon came to naught, and what Julius described as the discouraging endlessness of it all continued, 'though the feeling to continue the war until complete submission is stronger than ever.' However, Kitchener's blockhouses and his lamentable concentration camps had their effect, and in January 1902 Kitchener felt secure enough to authorize the restarting of more mines, to the joy of the London Stock Exchange. A great problem was the scarcity of labour and the need to entice Africans to return to the mines, for wages that had to be substantially less than what they were before the war started. On 23 March Boer representatives arrived in Pretoria to discuss peace terms again.

Three days later Rhodes died, aged forty-nine, at his cottage by the sea at Muizenberg in the Cape. His last words have become famous: 'So much to be done, so little time.'

Rhodes had been visibly failing for some time. FitzPatrick had returned on the same ship to Cape Town the previous month, and had found him breathless and not always coherent. Beit never recovered from the shock of his death. He, with Lords Milner, Rosebery and Grey, were trustees of the extraordinary will, the last in a long series of wills and codicils; but it was on Beit that the main load of work devolved. Among the few personal bequests was £6,000 to Rodolphe Kann, to whom Rhodes and Wernher, Beit had been so much indebted. Rhodes also left £100,000 to his old college in Oxford, Oriel. Groote Schuur was left to the government as the residence of a future prime minister of a federal South Africa.

In its generosity Cecil Rhodes's will was a magnificent document, and the provision of the Rhodes scholarships at Oxford has ensured and will ensure his immortality, long after the name of Rhodesia has faded from memories. It was an inspiration to Beit when drawing up his own will, which was also to cause a sensation and in some degree a reassessment of his character, and indirectly it was to affect Julius Wernher. One can smile at the provisions of clause 23, stipulating that the students must not be mere 'bookworms' but keen on outdoor sports and with 'instincts to lead', Empire-builders in fact, and at the sentiments behind the restrictions of the scholarships to certain British dominions and America. Women were excluded. But at least he laid down that no one should be debarred for reasons of race or religion – even if he was thinking of Boers and Britons rather than black and white. He also provided for five German scholarships to be chosen personally by the Kaiser, in order that 'an understanding between the three great Powers will render war impossible and educational relations make the strongest tie'. As Lord Rothschild, always his staunch supporter, noted on the day following his death, the fortune would be increased on Beit's death when his interests connected with Rhodes reverted to the trustees.

Alfred Beit and Julius Wernher were the only remaining Life-Governors of De Beers. They now decided to commute their interests in the Company's profits, but in return received 160,000 deferred shares, non-transferable until 30 June 1906.

FitzPatrick consulted Julius about going back to South Africa as Milner's adviser, and seems to have been given a somewhat grudging blessing. Eventually he was awarded a knighthood for his work during the war. He became President of the Chamber of Mines and moved into Hohenheim, where his lifestyle became almost as extravagant as that of the Phillipses.

On 3 May 1901 peace was at long last declared at Vereeniging, a place optimistically chosen, since the word meant union – and union or federation with the self-governing Cape Colony and Natal were a hoped-for goal.

So the Transvaal, as historians have pointed out, was made safe for the Corner House, and this was true enough; though to say that the Boer War was fought for that purpose is rather sweeping. Certainly, if there had been no gold in the Transvaal there would have been no war, no constitutional crisis, no capitalists. The peace also made the Transvaal safe for Consolidated Gold Fields, and for J. B. Robinson, the Barnato Group and George Farrar (also knighted), who had all made money out of speculators and promoters; and safe for G. Albu, A. Goerz, S. Neumann, Lewis and Marks, and Abe Bailey. The losses for mine-owners had been huge, however. Malicious gossips said that J. B. Robinson had been near to tears when he learnt that he was worth now only £6 million instead of £10 million.

The whole of South Africa now seemed within the net of the British Empire. The Kaiser's ambitions had been blocked. Arguments among historians about blame and responsibilities will continue, but out of the complexity of the events before 1899, and out of the maze of conflicting personalities, ineptitude, deviousness and clumsiness, it can safely be said that Julius Wernher had never welcomed the possibility of war. Like everyone else on the Rand, he had hoped, when war had been declared by the Boers, that it would be short; and of course if it had been short the already colossally rich capitalists would have become colossally richer. As it turned out, it was a long war, and as in most long wars the bloodshed, misery and destruction were frightful, and the capitalists became deeply unpopular.

On 3 April 1902 Rouliot made his farewell speech at the Chamber of Mines before handing over to FitzPatrick. He estimated the mines' losses at not less than £3,400,000 in cash disbursements. Later the figure was put at £6,667,442, not including loss of profits. Rouliot was a Frenchman who had genuinely worked hard for peace between Boers and Britons, so his remarks in defence of the capitalists were all the more apposite. He emphasized that whereas the Chamber of Mines had always avoided politics, capitalists had involved themselves as individuals, and he could see no harm in that. He spoke of the vast sums sunk already in machinery and works. Would it have been sane reasoning for the capitalists to risk the loss of all that? There were also many properties awaiting development, needing enormous amounts of money to open them up. Would it have been in the mine-owners' interests to 'spread mistrust, frighten capital and possibly run the risk of losing all that had already been done?' He then went on to the sneers about manipulation of shares. 'This, to my mind, is the most untenable argument of all. I have never heard of a capitalist, unless he was mad, that would spend all his time and energies in trying to surely damage nine-tenths of what he owns so that he may or may not pull off a doubtful coup on the remaining tenth!'

Setting aside the loss of life and property, there is another reason why some later liberals have even come round to thinking that it could have been better if the Jameson Raid had succeeded. Among the articles of peace at the settlement was the proviso that the question of native franchise would not be considered until the introduction of self-government for the former Republics of the Transvaal and Orange Free State. In the Cape the professed lack of colour prejudice had once been a matter of pride. When self-government did arrive, this proviso was conveniently forgotten. Milner himself, writing to FitzPatrick in November 1899, had spoken of his eventual objective of a self-governing white community under the Union Jack and 'supported by *well-treated* and *justly governed* black labour from Cape Town to the Zambezi'. Admittedly, 'justly governed' does not mean enfranchised.

Later Milner regretted that he was unable to extend the franchise to blacks before self-government was achieved, and this has to be admitted as a mark in his favour. The Boer delegates at the peace conference had described the blacks as 'getting out of hand'. It was in 1905 that the Native Affairs Commission rejected political equality between the races and recommended segregation.

The years 1902–3 brought a severe shortfall in black labour in the Rand, even when wages were increased. In 1899 the black labour force had numbered about 110,000. Now it was reckoned that 160,000 would be needed. Engineering experts were visualizing deep levels having to reach 6–12,000 feet. This (and other aspects) would require a labour force of 300,000. But by 1903 only about 55,000 blacks had been recruited. The crisis was affecting not only the mine-owners but the whole economy of the Transvaal, so dependent upon gold.

The employment of unskilled white labour was considered. Julius went to see the Italian ambassador who, he reported, thought that three or four hundred thousand Italians were ready to emigrate. There was also emigration from Britain to the Dominions and the United States: 51,000 in September 1903. Could not some future emigrants be diverted to South Africa as unskilled miners? But the idea had to be turned down, because unskilled whites could not be paid such low wages as unskilled blacks, and in any case there was bound to be trouble with trade unions. So there arose the great controversy as to whether Chinese labour could be imported. Many Boers – and other whites – were horrified by the suggestion of yet another racial complication in South Africa. But Julius, representing the firm which was the chief employer of labour on the Rand, was all in favour of trying this out. The Chinese 'coolies' could be brought over on a three-year contract. They were hard workers, accustomed to low wages, less prone to drunkenness, and of course there ought to be no desertions. Julius's support for this scheme at last convinced Milner, who gave his sanction. The British government wavered.

The unpopularity of the Randlords had a personification used in cartoons and satirical journalism, a rapacious exploiter called Hoggenheimer. The name originally appeared in a musical comedy called *The Girl from Kays*, and was seized upon with glee by the Boer and poor white press in South Africa. Julius and Beit were at first fairly amused; but the word continued as a taunt for many years ahead.

Some years later a Tory peer said in the House of Lords that those who had opposed the Boer War had 'confused soldiers with money-grubbers'. This inspired Belloc to write his savagely sarcastic 'Verses to a Lord':

> You thought because we held, my lord,
>   An ancient cause and strong,
> That therefore we maligned the sword:
>   My lord, you did us wrong.

We also know the sacred height
  Up on Tugela side,
Where those three hundred fought with Beit
  And fair young Wernher died.

The daybreak on the failing force,
  The final sabres drawn:
Tall Goltman, silent on his horse,
  Superb against the dawn.

The little mound where Eckstein stood
  And gallant Albu fell,
And Oppenheim, half blind with blood
Went fording through the rising flood –
  My Lord, we know them well.

The little empty homes forlorn,
The ruined synagogues that mourn,
  In Frankfort and Berlin;
We know them where the peace was torn –
We of a nobler lineage born –
And now by all the gods of scorn
  We mean to rub them in.

Twenty years later Belloc was still writing that the war had been 'openly and undeniably provoked by the Jewish interest in South Africa'. But he did also say, with some truth, that there was no antagonism towards 'ordinary' Jews among average citizens in Britain, only an interest, a curiosity. All the same, the anti-Semitism that he and others provoked did affect the public attitude towards the Randlords, Gentile or Semite, throughout the Edwardian period, even if envy and snobbery played a part.

Joseph Chamberlain visited the Transvaal in January 1903 and took a tough line with the wealthiest firms of Johannesburg. There was to be no compensation for losses. Instead the firms were told that they had the patriotic duty to help in postwar reconstruction. On top of a 10 per cent tax on mining profits, he asked for a loan of £35 million. After argument this was reduced, thanks to FitzPatrick, to £30 million, the first third being guaranteed by members of the Chamber of Mines (J. B. Robinson excepted). Wernher, Beit would put up £1 million, as did the other big names: Barnato Brothers, S. Neumann & Co., Consolidated Gold Fields, G. & L. Albu, A. Goerz & Co. The Compagnie Française would provide £100,000.

There was also to be an imperial loan of £35 million. Chamberlain failed to persuade Smuts and other former Boer Commando generals to join an enlarged Legislature, but FitzPatrick became a member of it, as did his successor at the Chamber of Mines, George Farrar, both men whom Milner knew could be relied upon to serve imperial interests – but then, as Julius Wernher was to say: 'What is good for the country is good for us.' Privately Julius was not so pleased about this development in FitzPatrick's career, and remarked that he could not understand why such a decent fellow should want to get himself mixed up in politics.

Julius had already offered personal loans of £5,000–£7,000 cash to the three Boer leaders whom he felt the firm had to thank for the preservation of the mines: Botha, De La Rey and Lucas Meyer. As it happened, the £30 million loan was never raised, because of the continuance of the economic depression. This was, needless to say, a fine piece of ammunition for enemies of Wernher, Beit, when it came to be noticed that huge sums were being spent on building schemes, both for the firm and privately. In the City, near Finsbury Circus, a seven-storey headquarters for all the Wernher, Beit interests was erected, covering an acre of the most expensive land in the world and in a 'bold and handsome Italian Renaissance style'. It cost £400,000, and the proud address was No. 1, London Wall, ready for occupation in June 1903. In Johannesburg the Corner House was magnificently rebuilt and in effect finished by the end of 1904. It had six storeys and was the biggest office block to date in all South Africa, built on a steel frame 'in the American style' and costing £218,000, not counting the Waring and Gillow furniture and such luxuries as Bokhara carpets. Two sensational features were its lifts, five of them, and its own electric power supply. The ambition of every child in Johannesburg was to have a ride in these lifts.

FitzPatrick and other tycoons such as Abe Bailey had motor cars: another sensation. FitzPatrick had also bought a 5,000-acre country estate, which, however, was small compared to colleagues' acquisitions in England and Scotland, where Michaelis had bought the Tandridge Court estate and the Phillipses were spending 'hundreds of thousands' on improving Tylney Hall. Solly Joel and his brother Jack were launching out into huge racing establishments, and between them were to win practically every classic event – the Oaks, Two Thousand Guineas, Derby and Gold Cup. Solly also had a steam yacht. Beit moved into Tewin Water, near Welwyn, a large Regency house with Victorian additions and 7,000 acres, and a few miles away Julius Wernher at last bought Luton Hoo, with 5,218 acres.

Beit had been advised by doctors to slow down, and was noticeably turning to a more bohemian circle of friends, some of whom such as the scandalous boaster Frank Harris were abhorrent to Julius. He was friendly with stage celebrities like Herbert Tree and Lena Ashwell, and kept a box at the opera which was always at the disposal of friends. He often visited his mother in Hamburg, and still relied on the advice of Dr Bode of Berlin for his art collection. Generous as ever, if not more so, he would hire a ship for family and friends at the Naval Review at Portsmouth, and a house at Ascot for the races. He was far more in the public eye than Julius. According to Jim Taylor's autobiography, he once was featured in an American paper as the 'bachelor Diamond King'. 'Now watch the next mail,' Beit told him. 'You will see that I shall receive hundreds of offers of marriage from all sorts and descriptions of women, to say nothing of begging letters of all kinds.' And sure enough, wrote Taylor, 26 Park Lane was snowed up with letters, 'black and white women offering themselves by the hundred'. Yet the memory of Rhodes dominated Beit's remaining years, and he was obsessed by the need to help and develop Rhodesia, which strangely had been neglected in the will. His offer to rejoin the board of the Chartered Company was accepted, and he became Vice-President. The Chartered Company was given offices at No. 1, London Wall.

Most people assumed that he had bought Tewin Water, but it was only a furnished lease. It had belonged to a colleague who was in financial trouble and had a good collection of Italian old masters, majolica and Hispano-Moresque ware. Once Beit, whilst staying with his friend at Tewin Water, had asked his host after dinner if he would let him have the house. 'Yes, at a price,' was the answer. 'I want everything,' Beit said. 'Furniture, servants, horses and all.' A bargain was struck, said to be at £100,000, and only an easel portrait of the owner's wife was allowed to be removed. Beit loved the place, and after his death most of the art collection was bought by his family, a pair of portraits by the Flemish artist Heemskerk finding their way to the National Museum of Wales in Cardiff. His brother Otto bought the freehold after his death.

Birdie Wernher's impressive charity concerts, bazaars and balls during the war had evidently given her the taste for entertaining on the grand scale, and Florrie Phillips found it difficult to compete. At Bath House the Wernhers, among their innumerable treasures, 'set a standard hard to attain, let alone surpass'. During Coronation year, 1902, London's grandees came there to 'suppers' which were really banquets, and guests had £1 million worth of pictures and *objets d'art* to admire. Florrie comforted herself with believing that her own houses showed better taste, not to mention charm and comfort. If the Wernhers, like the conventional English rich, had themselves painted by Sargent, she and Lionel were painted by the more avant-garde Boldini. But it was the age of the Belle Epoque, and the Wernhers, who 'popped over' to Paris whenever possible, rightly felt in the heart of it. Under the circumstances it might seem strange that they were attracted by the formality of Luton Hoo's architecture, let alone by its Victorianized interior. However, they had plans for the total transformation of the latter.

Julius had offered £200,000 for the property, but the eventual price was £250,000. Virtually all the Leigh and De Falbe contents were sold during a three-week auction, though there had to be a lawsuit, which the Wernhers lost, as to whether some Gobelin tapestries which filled panels in a reception room were fixtures.

The plan at first was to reconstruct the entire interior in Louis XVI style, using the French architect Charles Frédéric Mewès, who had designed the Paris Ritz, triumphantly opened on 1 June 1898. Now a London Ritz was being planned only a hundred

yards or so along Piccadilly from Bath House. Russian Grand
Dukes, Marcel Proust and exotic figures such as Calouste Gulben-
kian had been at the Paris opening, and so had Jules Porgès, who
with Wernher, Beit had been part of the syndicate that had put up
the money for César Ritz to launch his international chain of
hotels. Very likely the Wernhers had also been present.

Like all the very rich, including the French financiers and
Edward VII when Prince of Wales, and beauties such as Lillie
Langtry and Lady de Grey, Julius had been a frequenter of the
Savoy Hotel in London when managed by César Ritz, with the
legendary Escoffier as chef. No doubt it was the socially
ambitious Madame Porgès who had had the idea of employing
Mewès to build a gigantic château at Rochefort-en-Yvelines
outside Paris. For the Porgèses were moving into the aristocracy,
their only daughter and child having married the Marquis de la
Ferté-Meun; a niece married a Prince Borghese of Rome, and
other nieces a French Count and a Belgian Viscount respectively.
This extraordinary building was inspired by the Palais de la
Légion d'Honneur, with a peristyle and a cupola, and was
perched above a waterfall that tumbled through a terraced
garden. It is now a golf club.*

At any rate the Wernhers, after seeing the plans for the Porgès
château and other work by Mewès at the houses of Lucien Guitry
and W. K. Vanderbilt in Paris, had been 'totally seduced' by the
opulent style of the Belle Epoque. They also planned to add
another attic floor for staff at Luton Hoo with about thirty-odd
rooms. Madame de Falbe's overheated conservatory would be
scrapped, but her Gothic-cum-Byzantine chapel, created by G. E.
Street in 1874 when she was Mrs Gerard Leigh, would probably
be retained.

The completion date for the purchase was 13 June 1903. Within
months the work of reconstruction had begun, drawing, as usual,
sarcastic comments from the Radical anti-Hoggenheimer press.
One such comment appeared in the *Clarion*:

---

* Jules Porgès lost some of his fortune as a result of the First World War,
having deposited it in Viennese banks. This meant selling the château and *objets
d'art*. He died in 1921, aged eighty-three.

South African gold mines are not paying so well as formerly, but the patriotic Anglo-Saxon-cum-Semitic millionaires manage to make ends meet. At Luton Hoo a quarter of a million is to be spent on the work. It is not true, however, that Mr Wernher is going to turn the mansion into a retreat for maimed and out of work soldiers who fought for him and his brother-plutocrats in South Africa.

11

South Africa Again: Metamorphosis at Luton Hoo

Nikolaus Pevsner in the 1960s thought the interior of Luton Hoo the finest work of its date and style anywhere in England. Certainly there are few grand houses that so perfectly evoke the sumptuous taste of Edwardian new wealth with its festoons, gilded ribbons, rich panelling and almost overwhelming marble fireplaces. Inevitably some of the house's original furnishings have disappeared, partly as a result of the vicissitudes of the Second World War, when Luton Hoo became the headquarters of Eastern Command, but the vision and cosmopolitan taste of the Julius Wernhers are still much in evidence.

The favourite style of Mewès and his English partner Arthur Davis was Louis XVI, but at Luton Hoo one also detects the influence of Jacques-Ange Gabriel, the creator of the Petit Trianon. Mewès, originally from Strasbourg and of Baltic Jewish extraction, had been one of the architects of the 1900 Paris Exhibition. He has been described as having had a 'magnetic' personality, and was known in the architectural world as 'Le Patron'. His debut in London had been the decorating of the interior of the Carlton Hotel, where New Zealand House now stands, and this gorgeous affair so impressed Albert Ballin of the Hamburg-Amerika shipping line that he was forthwith commissioned to design and decorate those great 'floating palaces', the *Imperator*, the *Amerika*, the *Vaterland* and the *Kaiserin Augusta-Viktoria*. Mewès, having been awarded the Légion d'honneur, quickly built up an international reputation, with representatives in Germany, Spain and South America, as well as in England. Arthur Davis ('*bon viveur*, elegant') had been associated with Mewès since 1898, when he was aged only twenty. He too was Jewish, and had been a prize-winning student at the École des Beaux-Arts. Later he was to design the interiors of the *Queen Mary*, the *Aquitania* and the *Franconia*.

Plans for the Ritz in London and another in Madrid were under discussion when work began at Luton Hoo at the end of 1903. At Luton Hoo the original exterior was to be mostly retained, but in the case of the London Ritz an entire new building had to be designed and erected, Parisian in style with a mansard roof and a pedestrian arcade like the Rue de Rivoli. As with the Corner House in Johannesburg, a steel frame was to be used, the first in London. Mewès and Davis's next important building was for the *Morning Post*, at the Strand end of the Aldwych: Inveresk House is still in existence, though spoilt by later additions and alterations.

Luton Hoo was the firm's first major private project in England. In due course it made alterations for a score or more houses in Mayfair and Belgravia, notably 88 Brook Street for Mrs Henry Coventry, 16 Charles Street for Mrs Ronald Greville, later to become the Guards Club, 38 Hill Street for Carl Meyer of Rothschilds, and 49 Belgrave Square for Otto Beit. It also put on extensions to the Cavalry Club in Piccadilly (not considered a great success), and alterations were made to country houses such as Polesden Lacey, Leeds Castle, Combe Court, Norbury Park and possibly Tewin Water. Mewès's work for Hamburg-Amerika led to commissions from Cunard. One of the firm's most spectacular remaining monuments in London is the Royal Automobile Club in Pall Mall, completed in 1911, with a medley of styles (not improved since by overpainting), and including in the basement a magnificent swimming-pool, supposedly 'Byzantine' in conception, but reminiscent of sets for the great Hollywood epics and vying with the 'Pompeian' pool on the *Imperator*.

The building firm used by Mewès and Davis at Luton Hoo was George Trollope and Son, but much of the main and most elaborate decorative work was to be done by Hoentschel of Paris, who had previously been employed at Bath House. Under the circumstances it could seem odd that Julius Wernher should decide to undertake a four-month journey to South Africa just as reconstruction at the house was about to begin. But he had urgent and worrying decisions ahead, with huge fortunes at stake.

A slight market recovery had inevitably followed the war, but as Julius himself told Samuel Evans towards the close of 1902, people were already losing 'pots of money'. This applied particularly in France, where small investors had had their hopes mercilessly raised about prospects on the Rand by Johannesburg operators. Then there were the worries about black African labour. Wages had been raised, but made little difference towards attracting more workers, and the controversy about importing Chinese labour had become increasingly strident. The London partners were also becoming uneasy about the state of management at the Corner House; as Julius put it, there was not enough 'pulling together'. Percy FitzPatrick, of whom he was fond, was often suffering from his ulcer, and much preoccupied by public work. Evans and Schumacher had 'no sense of vision'. There were complaints about Reyersbach's tactlessness, put down in Julius's words to his 'not being a gentleman'. It was of course acknowledged that pressure of work in the Corner House was immense, and that periods of rest for partners were vital, not to mention occasional 'refresher' trips to London. The trouble was that there were simply not enough competent people to hold the fort during these absences.

Worst of all, Beit had had a stroke and for a while had been partially paralysed. This had actually happened at Johannesburg in January 1903 – some people unkindly saying that it was because of the shock of seeing Thomas Cullinan's rival new diamond mine near Pretoria. Others blamed the great heat, which seems just as probable. Luckily, 'Dr Jim' had been to hand to look after Beit.

Rumours about the Premier had suggested that its potential was far greater than anything at Kimberley, but Francis Oats, on behalf of De Beers, and Reyersbach had been sceptical, believing that the mine had been 'salted' – that diamonds had been fraudulently introduced from elsewhere. Beit evidently thought quite the opposite, and according to FitzPatrick actually lost his temper, a rare event. 'He burst out with: "Do not talk damn nonsense . . . Look here, Oats, you always were a damn fool. You are a damn fool now."'

The Premier certainly was not salted, and Oats's attitude was to prove an expensive mistake, for – as a joint enterprise with the Transvaal government – it was to prove an unfriendly rival to De Beers for many years, with its own selling organization in London. Blue ground was discovered in April 1903. The diamonds tended to be small, with at least one notable exception, namely the famous Cullinan diamond of 3,025¾ carats, the largest ever, which was found in 1905 and later presented to Edward VII, two of the largest gems from it forming part of the Imperial State Crown and the Royal Sceptre.

Beit never quite recovered from the stroke. On 20 February Friedrich Eckstein wrote to Samuel Evans to say that Beit had, 'thank God', left for Hamburg. 'If he had stayed much longer he would have been dead in a fortnight.' On Beit's return Julius found him markedly less interested in the business, and knew that his own load of work would thus be increased. Julius now was suffering from indigestion and had developed eczema, which involved having to take an 'oil treatment' and was to recur for the rest of his life.

However much Julius was determined to keep out of politics, he was frequently consulted by the major politicians of the day, Conservative Unionist and Liberal, many of whom became his friends. He also saw Milner when in London, but was sceptical about the results of his promoting agriculture in the northern states. On the question of colour, he was fairly open-minded. On 13 May he wrote to Evans, making one of his rare comments on the subject:

Our struggle and difficulty are in the present and near future, and I think with you that the ever-increasing Kaffir population will present many difficulties. But surely the best way to prepare for them is to get them to work in good time and settled with regular wants. I consider the Chinese necessary as a stopgap to be got rid of when it suits. I cannot understand the objections to a trial at least. We all feel [that] for some years to come we must have outside help and the problem has to be faced. If we go on as at present topheavy, in every respect, there must be a fall and as we and others have been the channel to convey millions [of pounds] to South Africa we cannot stand by and see the confidence go because the agitators object.

On 4 July Julius told Evans that Chamberlain had denied any possibility of an election that year. 'A change of government might lead to unrest re South Africa, and first and foremost the resignation of H. E. [Milner].' Here he was primarily referring to the great new topic in Britain, that of Tariff Reform and Imperial Preference, proposed by Chamberlain on 15 May at Birmingham in what has been described as one of the most sensational speeches in modern politics. To question the efficacy of Free Trade was to many Britons like disputing a religion. Julius was to be strongly in favour of Tariff Reform during the debates of 1904 and 1905, and it was the one political subject on which he felt he could not keep his silence.

In October he launched his £2 million African Ventures Syndicate, 'with a view to steadying the market and regaining the confidence of the Transvaal mines'. Old friends subscribed – Porgès, Kann, Carl Meyer, the Rothschilds, Max Michaelis, Ernest Cassel, Jim Taylor – as did members of the Diamond Syndicate in London and various Swiss, German and French banks, including the new Banque Rouvier, which had absorbed the Banque Française after it had got into difficulties as a result of the Anglo-Boer War. The president of the new bank, Maurice Rouvier, was a politician as well as banker, and soon left the post to become Minister of Finance in the French government: a useful contact for all concerned. Wernher, Beit also arranged for stock options to be made available to twenty-two leading French journals, 'on the understanding that they must write first of all in favour of the importation of unskilled Asiatic labour being allowed in the Transvaal'. Other 'Goldbugs' on the Rand, such as the Albus, Neumann, and the directors of Gold Fields, followed suit with subsidies to these papers.

The African Ventures Syndicate having been satisfactorily put in motion, Julius sailed from Madeira for Cape Town in the Union Castle steamship *Gaika*, leaving behind on the island a disconsolate Birdie. It was to be his first visit to South Africa in twenty years. As a Life-Governor of De Beers, Chairman of Rand Mines, and the greatest financial power in the mining industry, his advent caused tremendous excitement. A. P. Cartwright in his history of the Corner House wrote: 'Everywhere the word went round: "Julius Wernher is on his way", and offices and mines were tidied up as warships are prepared for an admiral's inspection.' Hopes were also raised on the London and Paris Stock Exchange. Had some great new goldmine been discovered? Was yet another new company about to be launched? In fact Julius's main purpose was to assess how much capital would be needed for future large-scale operations.

Julius was travelling with one Schmidt, associated with De Beers and Rand Mines, large and jolly, fond of his food and especially drink. 'Schmidt hardly ever reads,' Julius told Birdie, 'but takes such an interest in all that surrounds him that he is never like a Hoggenheimer and is full of fun.' It was the Wernhers' first separation since their marriage, but as Julius explained: 'The places will be too new to me and I have to concentrate my wits not to appear too ignorant and I have to see lots of things and people morning and night and absolute freedom of any ties even such sweet ones allows me to do what I think I have to do in the short time.'

Birdie's first letter to her 'Dearest Juli' was full of anxieties. Their separation was the 'first cruel thing' he had done to her in fifteen years. She had not liked the colour of his face when in Madeira, and ought to have insisted on that oil treatment (an enema?) as soon as he got on board. He must avoid his favourite tripe and onions, as well as curry and any tinned food, and have plenty of rest, etc. etc. 'If only your health had been what it was some years back this journey would not have been so terrible for me.' She signed herself 'Your Liebchen'.

There was a royal welcome waiting for Julius on the quay at Cape Town, and he stayed at Groote Schuur (where else?). Abe Bailey's motor car was made available: rather too bumpy and narrow, with facing seats ('All the time my knee in Schmidt's tummy'). Julius reassured Birdie that on these journeys he wore his heavy overcoat and put cotton wool in his ears. His first visit was to the Dynamite Works: 'They cost nearly a million and are probably the biggest in the world – they really are much too big and would ruin any private firm . . . but Rhodes could do nothing small and De Beers is fortunately very rich, so the money is squandered.' Then off to inspect tramways and nearby estates, in both of which 'we are largely interested – on the whole I was well pleased.' He visited the printing works of the *Cape Times*, again 'in which we are largely interested', though 'the newspaper is only part of the business as we have the Government contract and private business, printing and bookbinding.' Next, off to the Fruit Farms. 'Nearly all have beautiful old Dutch Farm Houses built in 1774 to 1823 . . . I have personally one sixth interest, Beit the same, Rhodes Trust and De Beers one third each. We go in for scientific fruit farming and wine growing. We shall have finally 45,000 vines and 150,000 fruit trees of which 40,000 pear trees of the finest variety.'

In spite of a week of what he called gluttonness, he was able to console Birdie that he was back to simple food. 'Digestion glorious.'

He arrived at Kimberley on 15 November, travelling by train in a special saloon car with Schmidt, Oats and Gardner Williams. 'I was really excited to see the old place again,' he wrote, 'but hardly recognize where we lived. It used to be bare veld and is now covered with smart residences with pretty gardens . . . Everywhere you see the genius of one man, Rhodes, and his devoted followers. With the exception of a few buildings in the inner town the whole place is rebuilt, splendid streets and parks . . .' He thought the model village of Kenilworth 'nothing short of marvellous', with its avenues of trees, and wild animals such as zebras and giraffes grazing in special enclosures. 'In another part there is a stud farm where we breed horses and mules.'

He also attended the De Beers annual general meeting, making what has been described as a 'picturesque appearance', because of his massive size no doubt. 'I got a very hearty welcome and many a shrivelled face that I had known young came up to shake hands.'

One of the fresher faces present was the young Ernest Oppenheimer, then attached to the diamond-buying firm of Dunkelsbühler.
'To my astonishment,' Julius wrote, 'I was called upon at a
minute's notice to second the Report and had to improvise a
speech.' But it was a very long speech, without notes, and
everyone present was amazed by his grasp of the Company's
affairs, even quoting the number of carats produced at Kimberley
when he left in 1883 (2,413,953) and the yield (£2,742,521, or '£1.
2s. 8d per carat'), which was only half the amount that had been
received for about the same amount of carats in 1903. At the close
of the meeting a subsidy of £10,000 by the Company was agreed
towards higher education in Cape Colony, in keeping with Cecil
Rhodes's ideals.

The Diamond Syndicate now took the whole of the De Beers
output. When approximately 50,000 carats had been mined, the
stones would be taken to the Syndicate office, which worked on
the first floor of Wernher, Beit's own offices. Here the diamonds
would be sorted and graded into eleven categories and classes,
according to size, quality and colour. The firms of the Syndicate
had fixed percentage allocations, and the diamonds would then be
divided up, parcelled and sent to Dunkelsbühler in London, where
they would again be sorted under the supervision of Louis
Oppenheimer, Ernest's elder brother.

Diamonds still remained Julius's 'first love after you', as he told
Birdie. He could not resist 'taking a hand' in the sorting one day.
People had expected to find him alarming, but this 'big actor in
haute finance' turned out to be simple and kindly – 'rather a dear',
one lady said. All the same, Kimberley was beginning to pall on
him a little. He was finding society very confined with 'only three
ladies of my day and half a dozen new ones'. At every dinner you
met the same people and he was getting 'a bit pumped'. Reluc-
tantly he put in an appearance at the races, a waste of his time he
thought. He hated having to have a mosquito net, which was 'not
necessary in my day'.

After Kimberley he had to visit Jagersfontein, where he was a
director of the mine. He shared a compartment overnight in the
train with Schmidt, 'a terror in bed – woodsawing all night!' As
on the journey from Cape Town, where he had seen the remains

of trenches and Lord Roberts's blockhouses, so now he was confronted by more evidence of the war: roofless houses, frameless windows, vines and fruit trees dead from neglect.

> The Boers hardly ever destroyed houses, they looted simply. When they left the neighbourhood of Kimberley for instance after the siege they had done very little harm except loot, and the houses, fences etc. were in good order. One of the mines, Kampfers Dam, where a Long Tom had been [the famous gun], did not suffer in the least. But the Tommies smashed everything partly because they wanted the wood in the houses to cook or for heating, partly as a punitive measure and partly no doubt from wanton desire. If you see these endless waterless plains one looking like the other, the difficulties of the war become more apparent . . .

And he added: 'The graveyards large and small tell a tale.'

Then it was Government House at Bloemfontein. Once again he had to send reassurances about his health; the doctor had said he could stand the altitude at Johannesburg but he was advised to drop his whisky.

Obviously, however, he did feel tired. The first days at Johannesburg were spent quietly, in the house of the Reyersbachs ('a butler, 3 housemaids, another maid and some Kaffir boys'), bracing himself no doubt for what has been described as the 'most calamitous time in the town's history'. *African World* even maintained that the 'financial thermometer' was 'down to zero'. At least the rains had come, and a long drought was over. Julius described for Birdie the town's broad streets with its horse trams and the avenues lined with trees, with buildings worthy of London alongside some very modest early 'erections' that were still in existence. The new Corner House was not yet ready. But 'people are not happy here,' he said, though he found them intelligent and hard-working. 'I suppose the climate and the high altitude make them irritable, and the bad business inclines them to "grouse". There is still a great deal of agitation against Asiatic labour, but in most cases the objection is a political cry and an attack on capital.' Life was certainly expensive, but Johannesburgers of all classes liked to spend money, so much so that often 'if the breadwinner dies there is absolutely nothing in the till'.

'Agitation' about the importation of Chinese was an understatement. Arguments for and against were reaching fever pitch, and splitting the English-speaking community.

Meanwhile Julius was worrying about Luton Hoo. Birdie had sent him a cable about Mewès's estimate, which was £50,000 more than expected. He was not at all pleased: 'The old game.' Luton Hoo was going to cost more than No. 1 London Wall. 'The total expense will be something frightful in these very bad times.' He asked her to seek the help of Lionel Phillips: not the best of advice, one might think, in view of Florrie Phillips's extravagance at Tylney Hall.

His next letter, begun on 7 December, covered nearly a week. He told Birdie how he had now 'started work' in earnest. He had first been driven in a motor car, over deep muddy ruts, to the 'dense forest' of Sachsenwald, 'all our own plantations', destined, he said, to be parcelled up into residential lots, and part in due course to become the Hermann Eckstein memorial park. Percy FitzPatrick showed him Hohenheim – 'really a beauty . . . not a square block, but a kind of odd building with plenty of projections, gables etc. . . . a grotto with ferns, swimming bath, fine stables . . . glorious view'. A fashionable quarter had grown up around it, 'all our own estate', with water and electric light supplied by the firm, which had also created several miles of roads.

He worried about finding jobs for several young men. It was not easy, as 'we still work only half force'.

> For instance in the Ferreira we could do with 2,500 natives
> and only have 900 – the number of niggers determines the
> number of whites who really are more overseers than
> workers, of course with exceptions – but no white man
> works except with black assistance. The noise of the stamps
> is deafening – the Company has 120 each weighing 1,250
> pounds and going up and down rapidly, stamping the ore to
> pulp and you cannot understand a word spoken – some

mines have 200, even up to 300. It takes some time to get the noise out of the head again.

After visiting the Ferreira, one of the oldest and richest of the mines, he motored to the surface works of some of the biggest mines, Glen Deep, Rose Deep, Geldenhuis Deep and Jumpers Deep. As in the old days, when he was at Kimberley and writing to his parents, he tried to explain the technicalities in the simplest terms, avoiding too much detail. The mines, he said, all dated from 1892 and 1893.

But it took 4 or 5 years before production work started & so we had not really much out of them as since the war we had to work on only limited output owing to the shortness [*sic*] of labour. They are the first row of what is called deep levels and have been one of our great successes and promise well.

At each of the mines he astounded the managers and senior officials with his intimate knowledge of the various properties. As A. P. Cartwright was to write, Julius in the past might have behaved as the commanding general in many of the financial operations on the Rand, but for him the battlefield had existed simply as a series of maps and diagrams on the walls of his London office.

He explained to Birdie how Johannesburg was the centre of more than forty miles of Reef, and sketched in a picture very different from the Johannesburg of today with its vast stretches of white suburbs to the north and the huge black townships to the south:

Along the whole length Company after Company follows, with their many shafts, buildings, native compounds and habitations for the whites. At the Geldenhuis the arrangements for the whites are very good, a splendid club house with concert hall, 2 billiard, reading & several small rooms & a big verandah. Our married people have 75 children & generally 2 or 3 Mines have a school. The railway runs all along the Reef & there are about 14 trains each way daily. It is indeed a unique sight – a continuous road of industry & settlement, say from London to Bedford or further.

Meanwhile he had to cope with the exhausting social round. People left their cards at the Reyersbachs', but Julius knew that as soon as he responded there would be invitations, 'which I dislike'. On 12 December he went down the Crown Deep. 'Although I told the Manager to make it "gnädig" [gentle] it took us over 2½ hours. It was warm but never stifling, the ventilation being excellent. I took my shirt off and had a change of underclothing.' Some of the passages underground were only two and a half to three feet wide, and mostly at a steep slant, as the gold-bearing veins were rarely perpendicular. Then he was back for a good rest before visiting yet another mine. That night the Reyersbachs gave a dinner party for eighteen.

Next morning he was up early for an hour's ride before breakfast. There was a mass of callers that day. 'I am getting in the thick now.' He was also longing to get home, and planning to sail back by way of the east coast in a German ship. As at Kimberley, he was meeting more or less the same people all the time; 'although kind and friendly', they were 'far from amusing'. He signed this letter, as so often, 'Ever thine loving and devoted'.

By contrast, his letter of 21 December was brief: 'I have had a busy week, being absent for 3 days – a very interesting trip – in the Pretoria district. I wish I had more time for description.' And indeed it is a pity he could not have explained more, because he had been to see the new Premier diamond mine, now in full open-cast production and arch-rival of De Beers and the London Diamond Syndicate. Unlike Beit, he had taken calmly to this potentially very damaging challenge to their erstwhile monopoly, and was confident that yields would eventually drop – as indeed was to be the case. But he also observed that the new up-to-date machinery at the mine could result in some millions of loads being washed and hauled every year: again true.

Actually the very existence of the Premier, thanks to subtle manoeuvring on the part of FitzPatrick, was in some ways a benefit to the gold industry. FitzPatrick had helped to convince Milner that the discovery of the mine afforded the ideal alternative for paying off the war debt, an unexpected bonanza, a 'nice nest egg'. Thus, old outdated Transvaal legislation from Kruger's day had swiftly to be invoked, and by the time of Julius Wernher's visit the State itself was a co-partner in the Premier, receiving two-thirds of the profits.

Amalgamations and expansions; new farms bought; discussions with Sammy Marks about coalmines; the introduction of tube mills, making possible a finer grinding of gold. On top of all these great decisions there was more bad news about the cost of Luton Hoo, presumably in the form of another cable from Birdie. 'Bother,' Julius this time somewhat mildly wrote, 'the kitchen was always the sore point & a decided step back from the old plan . . . Mewès's rough estimate was £100,000. I reckoned knowing what rogues they are £150,000 & now you make it £250,000. A fine pickle. Oh the old humbug. You must settle as best you can. Have as little done in France as possible.' He added: 'Sorry you have to bear it all alone but it's a good lesson.'

It was a lesson well learnt, for Birdie was to develop into a very capable businesswoman.

Christmas was dominated by the excitement of the Chinese Question. On 2 December the Chamber of Mines had declared its support for the importation of Chinese labour, and on 28 December there was to be a debate in the Legislative Council in Pretoria. On the 27th Julius dined with Milner, recently returned from England where he had spent four hours in discussion with the partners at London Wall. The following morning he and other notabilities left by special train for Pretoria. As he told Birdie, the debate would be crucial to the firm: '*We* alone in our Mines are 18,000 men short compared to 1899, this only for *producing* Mines with hardly any new developments going on – and taking these into consideration *we* would require quite 30,000 more in 2 or 3 years. It is quite a desperate case for owners as millions [of pounds] bear no interest at all at present . . . Nothing can replace hand labour in the all important work of breaking the rock.' Another problem was the fact that there was now so much more cultivation in the country, 'and that is all done by Kaffirs, they prefer that work naturally & even a Kaffir cannot be in two places at the same time.'

On the other hand, he explained, the cost of labour on the Rand was a 'desperate matter' and had to be kept in check. The price of diamonds was fixed by supply and demand. There was an internationally fixed price in gold. Rand gold ore was low-grade, and the only way to make this pay was to reduce labour costs. This was why the use of more white and therefore expensive labour had been out of the question.

The speeches ran on for so long – Sir George Farrar, the new President of the Chamber of Mines, spoke for four and a half hours – that the debate lasted two days instead of one. At last the motion was carried, by twenty-six votes to four, and the government was to pass its Labour Importation Ordinance seven weeks later.

Birdie would have been horrified to read that the special train returned to Johannesburg at 1.30 a.m. and that her Julius chose to sleep on the floor. She had, however, secretly been in correspondence with Lady FitzPatrick about Julius's eczema, and he and Schmidt were now persuaded to join the latter's party for a week on the Natal coast. Mrs Reyersbach gave a 'brilliant' farewell ball, 'beautifully organised', for a hundred and fifty people, which he much enjoyed – he was dancing until 3 a.m.

Two nights on the way to the coast were spent at Ladysmith. They all stayed at the Royal Hotel, whose 'principal asset' was 'a number of holes made by a shell perforating the house and killing a doctor on the "stoep" or verandah – the holes are under glass frames.' He also toured many of the sights of the great siege: 'Useless sacrifices, monuments, graves, nobody can understand the selection of Ladysmith or anything else – a hollow surrounded by hills 3 or 4 miles distant – equal wonder that the Boers did not take it.' But 'independent of the historical interest', he found the countryside exceedingly pretty, with the far view of the 'picturesque almost bizarre massif of the Drakensberg'.

At last letters from home were reaching him. There was one from Derrick, now at Eton, which Julius found a 'little artificial'. Nor could he resist making another comment – significant in view of the troubles that the boy was soon to cause his parents. 'Of course he never was robbed of those precious banknotes. He lost them.' (Or spent them?) But at present, to Birdie, 'Sweetface' could do no wrong. And his school report was very good. From her letters it becomes clear that Derrick was also known as Detty. Harold was Hacky, and Alex Dindle.

Birdie's handwriting was very different from Julius's, sprawling but firm. A letter – one of the few he kept and therefore to survive in that period – dated 2 December helped to explain her cables, and to some extent exonerated Mewès. She had realized, she said, that it was 'absurd and useless' to worry Julius about the awful dramas at Luton Hoo, but she just could not avoid it. She had gone out there by motor – 'in pouring rain!' – for an appointment with Mewès, Davis, Trollope and the surveyor.

> Having discussed prices at length with stupid old Trollope & he keeping on saying 'what I want, Mrs Wernher, is that you should have confidence in us' & all that sort of talk, which I rather sneered at (considering his terms, which are more like the confidence *trick* I think!!) we all proceeded to the house – or what is left of it!! I never saw such a sight & never expected it – devastation & ruins everywhere, there seems scarcely anything left once you get *inside*. I confess my heart sank to me boots at the magnitude of the job we have set going.

The real trouble was the shoddy job that had been done by the Victorian builders during the time of the Leighs. 'Whatever Mr Leigh filled in is cheap, bad work, & it's a wonder it has lasted as long as it has! The whole of the south side is actually leaning over . . .'

All credit at least to Robert Adam in the first instance. The Victorian walls were a 'sham', and instead of being solid brick were filled up with 'rubbish, dust & things like that!!'. It was quite amazing, she said, that there had never been a fire. She was convinced that she had already beaten down Mewès by £7,000. Obviously she was in full command and enjoying the bargaining, the sacking and hiring of gardeners and staff.

Then in contrast came a rather anxious, pleading note:

What I feel very strongly in the matter is that you bought
the place under protest (I persuaded you), you alter it under
greater protest (again I persuaded you) therefore you are
naturally less inclined to spend large sums on it than if you
had been keen on it yourself or than a man who longed for
his own country place &, having got it, did not mind what
he spent so that it was perfect. I know *I* shall love Luton
Hoo, & feel it more my *home* than Bath House, but you may
not and this perhaps is what Lionel Phillips would not
understand.

Julius – ominously maybe – decided to avoid making comments
on this letter. He knew how desperately she longed to be the
great hostess. Instead he wrote of the charms of the Natal
countryside and the orderliness of Durban; also about his companions, the no-nonsense Lady FitzPatrick stuffing fowls in the
kitchen and Schmidt forever hot and thirsty. He was impressed
by the Indian 'coolies', about 100,000 of them in Natal, working
in plantations, on the railways or as waiters, 'very smart, quick
and docile', and particularly by their beautiful children, 'invariably
called Samy'. For eight happy days the word *business* was not
mentioned. Thanks to the sea air, 'my digestion is particularly
good'.

  More letters from the family were waiting at Johannesburg,
some thanking Julius for Christmas presents. Birdie had been the
lucky one. 'The diamond is *too* exquisite and of course you knew
I should love it, though perhaps not quite to such an extent – the
colour and the purity and the *shape* – I *love pear*-shaped stones –
and that sumptuous sable rug!! I *was* glad to have it – I have
always coveted one but thought it rather beyond what I dare ask
you for!'

  How delightful to be married to one of the richest men in the
world, even in such hard times! The diamond was valued in 1937
by Boucheron at £30,000. It was used as the centrepiece of the
largest of Birdie's tiaras.

  But Harold's school report had not pleased his father. He was a
'dear boy, everybody likes him', but 'I have written a little
severely to Hacky, telling him that I would have to reconsider his

going to Eton unless he did more work; perhaps he will wake up yet but he is far behind his brothers in mental condition.'

The plan now was to leave for Lourenço Marques on 14 February, calling at Beira and Zanzibar. He would disembark at Naples, and meet Birdie in the South of France. In spite of continued worries about the labour shortage on the Rand and the future management at the Corner House, he was enjoying himself. 'You have no idea what an interesting and inspiring field this is.' He had come to recognize Reyersbach as the ablest member of the firm after Beit and Lionel Phillips, improving all the while, but he 'acts up rough on small matters'. FitzPatrick, 'dear fellow, a real patriot', had a collapse about once a week from his ulcer and hardly ever came to the office; in any case Julius dreaded his leaving politics in case 'some rotter' took his place.

Slightly misquoting Rhodes's last words, Julius wrote: 'So little done, so much to do,' and added: 'If one could only be 20 years younger, mais je ne suis plus de la même force & my brains are less productive.'

FitzPatrick did indeed become very ill. In March he had to take a year's leave, and it was during that time that he wrote his classic story *Jock of the Bushveld*.

At last, not long before his final departure from Johannesburg, Julius reacted, and sternly, to all the 'distressing news' about Luton Hoo. Among other things, and luckily for posterity, he vetoed any work on the chapel. 'The expense is now double what I thought, and very heavy at a time when it is inconvenient to withdraw cash from the business. Rather than do that I have sold private stocks at a bad moment. You must not forget that for over four years our investments here have on the average brought in little or nothing . . . I dare say better times will come along but crippled as we are in partners I do not feel the strength and spirit to take over.' But Birdie perhaps was not too worried by his next words: 'You need not fear that the great expense will worry me in the future. If the boys have to work tant mieux for them.'

Julius pointed out that the popular belief in South Africa, and shared by Milner, that great prosperity would follow the war had now been proved sadly wrong. Then – horrors, something that would surely have alarmed Birdie – he suggested that she might cut down on buying new dresses in Paris this year. But he was only teasing.

On his last day in Johannesburg a crowd of friends and colleagues gave a rousing cheer as he arrived at the railway station. Needless to say, a special saloon coach was waiting for him. Then at Lourenço Marques there was the 'usual stream' of telegrams wishing him *bon voyage*.

The sea journey in the *Kronprinz* was uneventful if very hot, aggravating his eczema. Both Julius and Schmidt enjoyed their 'quenchers' of good German beer. Birdie brought Dindle (Alex) to welcome him at Cannes. She was hoping they might have a 'nice rest' together, but Julius – already well enough rested – was impatient to get back to England because of 'this Chinese business', now being attacked as 'slavery' by the anti-imperialists, outraged by the spectacle of the Unionist government treating human labour as if it were a commodity. He also wanted to do battle with Mewès and Davis.

To his astonishment, on his return to London, he learnt that a ship had already been chartered for the first Chinese contingent. He was pained when Campbell-Bannerman, leader of the Liberal opposition, moved an unsuccessful motion of censure on the government. This was followed by a demonstration by 80,000 trade unionists in Hyde Park (the issue being confounded with the fear of sweated labour in London and Northern England from Eastern Europe). However, he still viewed the uproar about these 'Celestials', as some called them, as a manoeuvre for getting rid of the government, which he (rightly) guessed would survive at least another year. 1,055 Chinese sailed from Hong Kong on 25 May.

After visiting Luton Hoo, Julius's opinions about both Mewès and Davis were mollified. He managed to get Mewès to reduce his estimate by some 8 per cent, through certain 'réductions et suppressions', to Birdie's regret, though Mewès utterly refused to replace some of the marble work with stucco, even though it would save £2,000. The final bill, presented on 3 December 1906, came to nearly £147,000. This included architects' fees of £8,786; Trollope's construction work came to £94,207; Hoentschel's and others in Paris to £43,915. Mewès had charged three guineas a time for his visits; Davis two guineas for his 102 visits. There was an additional bill for £12,310 from Trollope's, who laid the carpets and did the upholstery, including the materials, and supplied bedroom furniture and suchlike.

So the figure was still well below that appearing in the 'scurrilous' *Clarion*. But then it did not include the making of the Italian garden, with terraces, Palladian summer-houses and fountain, by the popular landscapers of the period, Romaine-Walker and Besant, based on Mewès's designs, or the draining and cleaning of Capability Brown's sixty-acre lake, one of the most beautiful features of the estate, and its restocking with 11,000 trout (many of which were to be devoured by pike).

A vast tented encampment for the workers was spread among the cedars of Lebanon in front of the mansion. The Wernhers on their visits had to make do with staying in the farm manager's house in the woods, known as the Hermitage. What had been the site of Lord Bute's famous library was to be the Wernhers' gold and white Louis XIV style ballroom, on the south side of the building and opening on to the Italian garden. This was one of the rooms where, mercifully, no economies were to be made. The design of the great dining-room, large enough for a table to seat twenty-four people, was arranged around the three Beauvais tapestries of the 'Histoire du Roi de Chine', which Julius had bought in the 1890s – and which in fact had originally been woven for the Comte de Toulouse, son of Louis XIV and Madame de Maintenon, for the Château de Rambouillet. This room, with its great windows looking out on the lawn, sweeping down to the lake, and its marbles, gilding and crystal chandeliers, is the epitome of belle époque taste in an Edwardian country house, and one can indeed appreciate Mewès's alarm at the idea of mixing his lovely marbles with stucco.

The huge entrance hall in the centre of the house, with its columns and glass roof, now known as the Blue Hall, led into the dining-room through double doors. It was set off by five Gobelin tapestries, four of them a set – 'Les Mois Grotesques' – and possibly the subject of the lawsuit after the purchase of the house. The oval white marble hall at the foot of the staircases was designed as a complete contrast, and was Louis XVI in style: 'Beaux Arts at its most convincing and indeed most splendid,' said Pevsner. The staircase itself, black wrought iron in a 'dashing sweep', was grander and more elegant than the one in the London Ritz, to which it has some similarity, and was perhaps copied later in Paris by Count Moïse de Camondo, who seems to have been one of the subscribers to Julius's African Venture Syndicate. In the centre of this hall was placed one of the major objects acquired at the de Falbe sale: a life-size marble group by Borgonzoli of Cupid and Psyche. Two alcoves had groups, again life-size, specially made by Faivre of Paris, another big expense. As it happened, some work was done in the Chapel, but Street's work was carefully preserved. The old organ, on which Sir Arthur Sullivan used to play for Madame de Falbe's guests, was, however, replaced with another by Norman and Beard.

In spite of all those huge sums, Julius at the end of 1904 acquired the greatest masterpiece of his collection: Altdorfer's *Christ Taking Leave of His Mother*. Judging by the dealer's excited letter, one assumes that whatever was asked must have been far higher than anything he had bought hitherto: 'This picture is . . . one of the most important works in the whole range of German painting . . . You will be the first collector to see it.' Believed to have been painted around 1520, it had once belonged to the Prince-Abbot of Ratisbon. But on reaching England in the nineteenth century, it had been far less appreciated. In 1884 it was sold at Christie's for twenty-three guineas. (Somebody was making a nice profit?) When sold for death duties to the National Gallery in 1981, the price was said to have been the highest ever paid to that date for a work of art. £900,000 was contributed by the National Heritage Fund, the National Arts Collections Fund and the Pilgrim Trust. It was thought in the press that the sum paid was in the region of £3 million.

At last the Chinese arrived in South Africa. In the face of such unremitting hostility Milner was probably already deciding that his position as High Commissioner was no longer tenable. His policy of anglicizing the Transvaal had also failed – the Boer population was actually increasing. Julius was sorry. On 9 July he was writing: 'I confess I am still an ardent Milnerite, which does not blind me to his mistakes, but if we have to take sides there can be no question as to which we are on.' And later: 'With all his faults he has in the past listened to us. He will in future be the great authority [on South Africa] in England.' It would be a pity to lose his confidence and faith in Wernher, Beit, even if he complained that the partners took too narrow a view. 'Changes will and must be slow. *We* are not the only people to consult. Without Milner we would have lost the Chinese battle.'

Which does show how closely Milner had been relying on the advice of the Wernher, Beit–Eckstein group.

Julius was still unrepentant in the face of 'Chinese slavery'. In Johannesburg a trade union leader attacked the mine-owners as 'wading through slaughter to a throne'. 'They have shut the gate of mercy on mankind.' But Julius was determined that 'we must push the importation of 30 or 40,000 more Chinese with all our might.' 'If,' he said, 'an Election takes place the Chinese cry will be loud and effective and all sorts of pledges will have to be given to interfere with the supply.' He assumed that the opposition would not be able to 'touch what we already have'. Even if the Chinese 'deplaced Kaffirs' in the mines, he argued, their labour would be set free for other work, and 'would show the Boers how beneficial importation was'.

The coming of the Chinese did in fact provide immediate results. In 1904 production of gold increased from 1,859,482 ounces the previous year by nearly 800,000 ounces. In all 63,695 Chinese labourers were imported between June 1904 and November 1906, about a third employed by Wernher, Beit and its associates, and by 1907 output had increased by two and a half million ounces. The actual cost of labour per head turned out to be rather more than expected, taking into account accommodation and food. And this accommodation was poor and cramped. There were strict penalties for offences that affected productive output. Passes were for forty-eight hours only. When outside their compounds without passes the Chinese were 'outlaws'. Such things were, however, not the only reasons for discontent and disturbances. Some Chinese escaped (in 1905–6 there were 1,700 cases of desertion), and there were robberies, even an occasional murder. Gambling and opium smoking were rife. But at least their record of health was relatively good, better than that of the 'Kaffirs'.

It was a 'painful surprise' for Julius to learn that Percy Fitz-Patrick had diabetes. Then came the news that Lionel Phillips had decided to stand for Parliament in England. This was another blow, as Julius obviously had him in mind for taking over the management of the partnership in Johannesburg. Having discussed the matter with Beit, he decided to write him a stern letter: if he went into Parliament he would have to leave the firm. In his letter Julius also made an interesting historical point:

> When I asked you to join us after the Raid my principal
> motive was to show to you and to the world that we fully
> shared the part taken by you in political matters and that
> you were not the scapegoat – I don't know whether you
> ever appreciated this. The question of work was then not
> half as important as it is today because we were still
> vigorous and also stronger in numbers.

Phillips's reply was stiff: 'My recollection of the circumstances under which I joined the firm in London after the Raid entirely disagrees with yours but that is past history and of no great consequence at the moment.' So he was not to be deterred.

In the end Phillips did change his mind. The cost of his extravagant lifestyle was too high even for a man of his considerable wealth, and Florrie, once the Queen of Johannesburg, was happy to return to their kingdom.

12

Pinnacle of Achievement

It comes as something of a surprise to discover that Julius Wernher was a friend of those two formidable Fabians, Sidney and Beatrice Webb.

The introduction came through R. B. (later Lord) Haldane, Liberal member for East Lothian, in connection with what they called the Charlottenburg scheme. By 1902 Sidney had joined Haldane in a plan to create a college of higher technical and scientific training, as part of London University and similar to the Charlottenburg Institute at Berlin. According to Haldane in his autobiography, the Prince Consort had originally wanted to use the Great Exhibition site for some such project, and the idea had been taken up by the Prince of Wales – even more enthusiastically when he became King. A grant had at last been extracted from the Treasury, but it was insufficient. So Haldane decided to approach Julius, whom he knew of only as a 'public-spirited man of German origin, impressed with the idea of German scientific training'. At the office of Wernher, Beit he had also met Beit, whom he found so 'highly appreciative' that there was an immediate offer of £100,000. Through Beit, Haldane met Cecil Rhodes, presumably just before his death, and this led to promises of help from Lord Rothschild and other 'South African friends', as well as Sir Ernest Cassel. Julius became a member of the Haldane committee. In a time of growing rivalry with Germany, and the necessity of enlarging the fleet, such a project seemed all the more urgent. There was also a growing demand for metals of many kinds, several of which, needless to say, were produced by or financed under the wing of Wernher, Beit. As Julius himself put it, British youth in mining camps of whatever sort throughout the world must have no handicap in competition with Germans.

On 7 February 1905 the Webbs gave a dinner party for Sir Oliver Lodge, the distinguished physicist, Principal of Birmingham University. Their guests included A. J. Balfour the Prime Minister, Bertrand Russell and his wife Alys, the Fabian 'Lion' Phillimore, the handsome actor-producer Harley Granville-Barker, who was putting on Shaw's plays, and H. J. Mackinder, Director of the London School of Economics; and, as Bertrand Russell wrote to a friend:

> Greatest of all Werner [*sic*] of Werner Beit and Co, the chief
> of all the South African millionaires; a fat, good-natured,
> eupeptic German with an equally fat gold watch-chain and a
> strong German accent (characteristic of all the finest types of
> British Imperialists), bearing very lightly the load of blood,
> of nations destroyed and hatreds generated, of Chinese
> slavery and English corruption, which, by all the old rules,
> ought to weigh upon him like a cope of lead. It was an
> amusing occasion. When everyone had come except Balfour
> and Werner, Mrs Webb observed that we should see which
> of them thought himself the bigger swell, by which came
> last. Sure enough, Werner came last: for though Balfour
> governs the Empire, Werner governs Balfour.

Beatrice Webb placed Balfour and Russell next to one another, and felt that they got on famously – though Russell thought Balfour weak, if kindly and not at all *tête montée*. She 'sacrificed' herself to the 'millionaire', Julius. In her typically sharp way she noticed the 'subtle antipathy' of Balfour towards Mackinder and Julius, 'mere philistine materialist administrators he would feel'. After Julius's death, some obituaries listed Balfour (along with Chamberlain, Rosebery, Asquith and Haldane) as among his friends, so perhaps the friendship with Balfour developed later. Or maybe, with the threat of an imminent General Election, mostly because of those sins imputed by Russell to Julius's kind, there was a certain passing unease at such a confrontation.

Julius would have been less worried. In his own words he was a 'wobbler' in politics, siding in his own mind one day with the Conservatives, the next day with the Liberals. In any case, as he admitted to Samuel Evans in Johannesburg, the Liberals needed cultivating. 'We cannot be without friends in a Liberal government. Personally we know the probable leaders almost more intimately than members of the present Government and they would always be prepared to listen [to us].'

Beatrice noticed that Julius and Mackinder 'chummed up' and that they 'walked away together'. It took a little time for the Webbs' own appreciation of Julius to mature. Perhaps it was a case of knowing on which side the bread was buttered. In October 1905 she gave another party, and wrote in her diary:

> On Tuesday there dined with us Wernher, the South African capitalist, a heavy, good-natured, public-spirited and scientific-minded millionaire, Lord Lytton, Bernard Shaw and Mrs Prothero (the mates of these three were ill) – a somewhat crooked party that was only straightened out, by sheer energy on my part, into a comfortable affair. Wernher stumbled heavily along in his broken German, GBS scintillated, Mrs Prothero [wife of the co-editor of the *Cambridge Modern History*] listened with Irish scepticism of Irish wit, Lord Lytton hung on GBS's words looking the beautiful, fastidious young artist and aristocrat – a party of interesting 'types' but not mixing well.

It was not until May 1906 that the Webbs accepted an invitation from the Julius Wernhers at Bath House. As Beatrice said in her diary, this was partly because of Charlottenburg, but also because they were curious to see the inside of such an establishment, and because 'we like and respect the man'. 'He is a German giant, not unduly self-indulgent, and a real drudger at his business.' She went on to say approvingly that he was not only public-spirited but noted for his generosity and the sense of responsibility he showed for the South African commercial world, 'perpetually carrying the weaker men on his back'. 'He is good, that is to say, to his own community.' He was, moreover, unconcerned with social ambition and had no desire to push himself by his wealth. 'I have no time,' he actually told her, 'even to know that I am wealthy: the only result of my millions is to make me dread being introduced to a new person lest they should begin to beg from me. The really happy person is the man with £10,000 a year, reputed to have £2,000.'

Also in May, Julius wrote to Sidney and Beatrice, offering them the use of the house known as the Hermitage within his Luton Hoo estate, for as long as they cared to stay. It is a splendid irony that in these surroundings of luxury they wrote their famous minority report for the Royal Commission on the Poor Law. The excuse of course was Julius's commitment to the Charlottenburg scheme. Some months back Sidney had been invited by Julius to an important dinner for thirty men, mainly concerned with Charlottenburg but with some financiers added. Present had been Haldane; Sydney Holland, later Lord Knutsford, the hospital reformer; Mowatt, the Permanent Secretary to the Treasury; Morant, the Permanent Secretary to the Board of Education; Siemens the electrical engineer; and Sir Felix Schuster the banker. Not surprisingly Sidney Webb had come around to thinking that Julius was the 'best of fellows according to his own lights'. 'Hence,' wrote Beatrice, 'we felt free to accept his hospitality.'

She could not resist little niggles in her diary. The Wernhers only went to Luton Hoo on occasional Sundays and for a few months in the autumn. To keep the place going, there were fifty-four gardeners, ten electricians, twenty or thirty house servants and quantities of labourers, 'to nobody's benefit, except that it furnishes dishonest pickings to all concerned'. (According to the *Luton News*, there were 4,000 potted carnations in the conservatories.) Beatrice wrote:

> The great mansion stood closed and silent – no one coming
> or going except the retinue of servants, the only noises the
> perpetual whirring and calling of the thousands of pheasants,
> ducks and other game that were fattening ready for the
> autumn slaughter. At the gates of the park, a bare half-mile
> distant, lay the crowded town of Luton – drunken, sensual,
> disorderly – crowded in mean streets, with a terrific infant

mortality. The contrast was oppressively unpleasant, and haunted our thoughts as we sat under the glorious trees and roamed through wood and garden, used their carriages, enjoyed their fruit, flowers and vegetables, and lived for a brief interval in close contact with an expenditure of thirty thousand a year on a country house alone.

Their thoughts haunted or not, Sidney and Beatrice were back at the Hermitage three years later, 'toiling at our book on destitution'. Luton Hoo, they found, was conveniently close to the Bernard Shaws, and Beatrice also recorded that they were visited by George Lansbury, future leader of the Labour Party and at that time MP for Bow and Bromley. The Webbs, however, missed the excitement of the visit of Ford Madox Ford (then known as Hueffer) and Douglas Goldring to the Joseph Conrads at Someries Farm, across the park, that resulted in the birth of *The English Review* in December 1908.

To Beatrice, Luton Hoo had been bought by Julius to please his 'society-loving wife', and one has to admit that she was not entirely wrong in this. When she had first met Birdie she found her a 'hard, vainglorious woman, talkative and badly bred', if 'not otherwise objectionable'. Later she revised her opinion a little, and found her 'not a bad sort, an able woman with a clever tongue, direct and good-natured by disposition', though a slave to the consciousness of her wealth, which made her restless, rushing from place to place. Lady Wernher's thoughts, Beatrice considered, were centred in the admiration of others for her millions. 'Consequently, both in person and manners and speed she was essentially ugly: her dress crude in colour and outré in form, covered with extravagant and ill-assorted jewels, her talk of nothing else but herself and her possessions, and her expression a curious mingling of boldness and uneasiness.'

To be fair to Birdie, a quite different assessment of her character appeared in the *African World*, admittedly a journal that had good reason to be sycophantic towards the Randlords. In an article published that same year there was a reference to her 'sweet womanly benevolence', a benevolence 'whose recipients are the flotsam and jetsam of our civilization, the children of our mean streets'. She tried, as she herself said, 'to pull my weight' in the town of Luton and sponsored several good works. She opened the new secondary school and contributed to new wards at the hospital. She showed an interest in the straw-plaiting industry, for which Luton was renowned, and made her sons wear straw hats whenever they drove through the town. Julius as the new Lord of the Manor at once gave up some of his medieval rights, and he also sold the freehold of the Corn Exchange to the town. He spared time to make speeches at the Court Leet dinners, where his jokes seem to have been suitably appreciated.

(The straw-plaiters had been introduced to Luton by James I. They had originally been brought from Lorraine by his mother Mary Queen of Scots, and the King had sent them to Luton because Bedfordshire was a good straw and wheat country. The Luton Hoo farms provided some of the straw.)

The population of Luton was close on 50,000. In mid-Victorian times the town had remained something of a backwater because of a quarrel with Stephenson over the construction of the railway, local vested interests having prevented its development. After the First and Second World Wars there would be vast changes in its industrial development, some of them, arguably, thanks to the inherited wealth and the energy of Julius Wernher's descendants.

Part of the Luton Hoo estate included the ruins of Someries Castle, a late medieval fortified manor house. In the eighteenth century its bricks were used to build Someries Farm nearby, and it was here that from September 1907 until March 1909 Joseph Conrad lived (probably unknown to the Wernhers) rather gloomily with his family when writing *Under Western Eyes*.

During the summer of 1904 Birdie was unwell and had to spend a great deal of time taking the cure at Wiesbaden. She was delighted with her Italian garden at Luton Hoo. The upper terrace was carpet-bedded with annual flowers, while the lower had herbaceous plants and patterned beds surrounded by box hedges with topiary work. Much of Capability Brown's careful arrangement of avenues of trees and woodland coppices still existed, and some of the Leighs' more exotic trees, such as the Californian madroñas, the tulip trees and the Himalayan juniper, had reached maturity. Birdie added specimens of her favourite pink-flowered chestnut. As a surprise for her return from Wiesbaden, Julius had a large rock garden constructed in a dell some way from the house, with ponds full of waterlilies surrounded by ferns, irises and conifers. It was a great success: a quiet, cool oasis, contrasting with the sweeping grandeur of the lakes and landscaped park without.

Also by the time of her return enough work had been done to make Luton Hoo 'habitable'. It was now ready for her weekend house parties. She gave a fancy-dress ball. And, had she lived long enough, she would have been proud of some other comments on Luton Hoo in Nikolaus Pevsner's Penguin *Buildings of Britain series*. No one, Pevsner said admiringly, could have been capable of such a creation after the First World War. He described Luton Hoo as a perfect example of Edwardian riches and exacting French training of the very highest quality.

One of the first guests at a weekend house party at the refurbished Luton Hoo was Agnes Keyser, the founder of the King Edward VII Hospital for Officers. This tiny figure, 'known for her perfect toilettes', was a friend of the King, indeed 'idolized' him, and was the daughter of a stockbroker. She had originally turned her house, 17 Grosvenor Crescent, off Belgrave Square, into a hospital during the war, treating 250 patients, but afterwards had been persuaded by the King to keep it going. 'This hospital,' he told her, 'must not close as there is such a need in time of peace for officers who serve in so many climates over the world.' It was he who suggested she should call herself Sister Agnes, by which name she was known forever after (and to this day). Patients were treated free (though after a while there was a small charge). Many royal and banking friends rallied round with financial support. The Prince of Wales became President. But by 1904 more was needed and the 'South Africans' were approached. 'Friedie' Eckstein donated £1,000, provided that it was kept 'absolutely private'. Shortly afterwards Julius Wernher and Alfred Beit, both at that time abroad, authorized a further payment of £8,000, some in cash, some in Lisbon and Mexican Tramways Debentures. Lionel Phillips gave £500. Times were difficult, he said, but if the hospital was still in straits he would 'harden' his heart and send another £500.

The Hospital moved to 9 Grosvenor Gardens, nearer to Buckingham Palace, and convenient for informal visits by the King.

After such munificence towards two pet royal projects, the decision by His Majesty to confer a baronetcy on Julius in the 1905 birthday honours was not surprising. The news came in a letter from Balfour himself. Julius wrote at once to his brother-in-law Franz Mankiewicz: 'Knowing your democratic tendencies I fear the shock will be great to you. I could refuse but considering the social relations we have and other reasons connected with many political points which touch our firm it would have appeared rude and unwise to refuse what was entirely unsought on my part and what no doubt is intended to be a great compliment.' He had not mentioned it to anybody else. Birdie was much less 'elated' than he had expected. 'It is something,' he added, 'to have escaped the Knight.'

Julius's baronetcy was the first of several conferred on the South African magnates, and was received with 'pleasurable surprise' in the City, but not by the readers of *Truth*.

But there was trouble in the family, to do with Derrick. On 30 May 1905 Julius had to tell Birdie: 'Of course I am in many ways proud of our Detty, but I cannot help feeling that he is not really about anything and may not rise above the ordinary Dutzend Mensch [conventional people].' This was followed by another letter on 14 June, written in Julius's special style: 'The enclosed from D after what passed it is a bit strong. He treats everything as nil and not affecting him and gives you betting tips. He seems to feel absolutely nothing in the whole matter, no sense of shame or mortification; he has no blush left. I don't want to take things too tragic but everything confirms his want of character and even his want of discernment of what is right or wrong.'

Then two days later: 'Enclosed came yesterday evening. It is not pleasant reading and I feel very uneasy about it, and I am sure you will be likewise. The boy seems in a bad way . . . I only hope there is nothing disgraceful. I think I should see Dyer [Eton housemaster] at once.'

These mysterious references are to some extent clarified by a letter from Dyer over a year later, after his retirement. It concerned boys in his house having been involved in betting transactions with a tailor's assistant called Trotman, 'resulting in the dismissal and ruin of the man'. It was Trotman's wife, working as a servant, who had revealed to her employer that the boy at the centre of the scandal was called Wernher. Julius no doubt recompensed Trotman at once. And one can be sure that Derrick, with his usual charm, swore that there never would be a recurrence, and that his mother believed it.

Harold, it seems, continued to have indifferent reports from school, but was still destined to go to Eton in the autumn of 1907. Conscious that his parents regarded him as the least promising of the trio, he became close to his mother's secretary, Margie Pryce. He loved horses and was easily the most athletic of the brothers. When Derrick began to put on weight, and lost some of his good looks, it meant that Harold was now the best-looking. He was also beginning to show an interest in the theatre. Harold was still very young, of course, but his father had long ago sensed a complete indifference to anything to do with South Africa.

There was no doubt that the youngest Wernher boy, Alex, was brilliant. And he did work hard at school. He was the favourite of his uncle Franz, who also was fond of Harold. The great worry was his poor eyesight. But Julius wrote to Birdie: 'I have less fear for Dindle than any of our boys.'

Like all fashionable ladies, Alice, Lady Wernher was painted by Sargent. The portrait was hung in the pillared hall at Luton Hoo. 1905 was the year in which Julius bought, from Langton Davis, the portrait of the Countess of Bellamont by Reynolds, also hung at Luton Hoo. By and large many of the religious pictures, such as the Altdorfer, the Bermejo and the Filippino Lippi, were kept at Bath House, along with most of the Hoppners and Reynolds's *Lady Caroline Price*. Birdie seems to have had a 'private' collection of more modern pictures in her boudoir at Bath House, namely some Leightons, a Frith and a J. J. Shannon: not her husband's taste, she admitted.

Rodolphe Kann died in 1905, and the hungry vultures who immediately gathered round his vast and fabulous art collection in the Avenue d'Iéna included the Duveen father and sons, Bernard Berenson and Nathan Wildenstein. The trouble was that to some extent it was combined with the collection of Kann's brother Maurice. Dr Bode of Berlin was commissioned to make a catalogue. Then, fortunately for the dealers, Maurice died, and they were able to snap up the whole lot for the bargain price of $4.2 million. Pierpont Morgan was allowed first pick, and Julius is believed to have secured an object or two among the scrapings, though details have been lost.

In Cannes that spring Julius and Birdie became friends with Grand Duke Michael of Russia and Countess Torby, who were concerning themselves with caring for Russian officers wounded during the Russo-Japanese War. Grand Duke Michael had also founded the Cannes Golf Club, of which he was President and which Birdie patronized. But the main bond seems to have been between Harold and Alex and the very good-looking Torby children, as they were known: Zia (Anastasia), the eldest, was born on 9 September 1892; Nada (Nadejda) was born in 1896, and Michael, known as Boy, in 1898.

The eventual link between the two families has been revealed in the Prologue to this book, and more will be said later about Grand Duke Michael Mikhailovich ('Micha'; Michel' or 'Miche-Miche') and the beautiful Countess Sophie de Torby, whom he had dared to marry morganatically, causing him to be banished not only from the Imperial court but from Russia. In any case Russia was in a state of revolution, 1905 being the year of 'Bloody Sunday' and 'Battleship Potemkin' – not that it much affected the behaviour and style of living of the numerous grand dukes, including Grand Duke Michael's brothers, in the South of France. Lloyd George was amazed at the recklessness of their gambling at the tables 'at the very darkest hour of their country's troubles'. Grand Duke Serge 'threw away' hundreds of pounds, putting on bets of £30 or £40 at a time, but Grand Duke Nicholas was even more extravagant. Grand Duke Michael kept up a palatial establishment at Cannes, the Villa Kazbeck, and for at least a quarter of the year he lived in the great neo-Elizabethan pile Keele Hall in Staffordshire, where he entertained his cousin Edward VII and Mrs Keppel. So he may, because of the Russo-Japanese War, have been worried about funds forthcoming from St Petersburg and have had some sort of promise of backing from Julius Wernher.

Grand Duke Michael and his wife were invited to Luton Hoo for a weekend in December 1906. There was a pheasant shoot, with a bag of 451 birds (at the first shoot of the season 1,276 pheasants were killed). A photograph shows that it was an extremely cold weekend, with snow. Other guests were the Siggy Neumanns, Baron von Strumm and Lord Alwyn Compton. According to a society paper, the *Onlooker*, Countess Torby left for the weekend looking 'radiantly handsome, wearing a wonderful hat seemingly worked with diamonds and rubies'.

The Luton Hoo visitors' book mentions that other weekend guests that winter included Prince Albert of Schleswig-Holstein, members of Sir Ernest Cassel's family, the distinguished soldier General Sir Arthur Paget, Lord Farquhar, Master of the King's Household, Major Vigant de Falbe, related by marriage to Madame de Falbe, and the Marquise d'Hautpane.

The wonder is that Julius Wernher ever had any time for social life. Most of his real friends were to do with business or his art collection. He played a little golf, shot the Luton Hoo pheasants, and occasionally spent two or three days with Birdie on the Riviera. He never now went to the theatre or opera, and if he had any leisure preferred to read books.

Lionel Phillips had been having second thoughts about a career in politics, and to Julius's relief had decided to return to Johannesburg on a so-called flying visit before making up his mind. He soon appreciated Julius's disquiet about the 'rudderless' Corner House. Added to this there were anxieties arising from the voluntary departure in 1905 of Lord Milner, who realized that his grand design had failed and that his presence only added to the unrest.

It had been noted in the City that Julius had been making frequent trips to Paris, and there were thus excited rumours that some great new financial deal was afoot. Such rumours had their foundation. Under the circumstances his own visits to Cannes must have been very brief. So it was up to Birdie to concentrate on keeping up the Grand Ducal connections: tea at Rumpelmayer's with Countess Torby and receptions at the Club Nautique.

After returning from Johannesburg, Julius had discussed with

Beit the urgent need for much larger quantities of capital for deep levels, new machinery and fresh amalgamation schemes. With gold shares in their depressed state there were unique opportunities for acquiring bargains. The plan was to build upon the African Ventures Syndicate, with French support, and to raise £6 million in capital. The new company, registered on 9 May 1905, was called the Central Mining and Investment Corporation. It caused a sensation. As A. P. Cartwright said in his book, Pierpont Morgan himself could never have flown so high.

But the strain and excitement gave Beit another collapse. On 5 May Julius told Phillips that Beit had been taken ill with kidney trouble and 'catarrh of the big bowel'. With FitzPatrick and now Schumacher also ill, Julius was desperate for Phillips to stay with the firm. 'If you leave us we shall be miserably short.'

Half the capital of £6 million went to members of the African Ventures Syndicate, which meant that Wernher, Beit itself owned £1,200,000. Wernher, Beit had retained for itself 15 per cent of the profits from the African Ventures Syndicate. Since they were managers of Central Mining they would now receive 25 per cent of the surplus profits after payments to shareholders. In return Central Mining was to receive a 30 per cent interest in all new business undertaken by Wernher, Beit and had to offer the firm a 30 per cent participation in any new capital raised for the mines it controlled.

Thus Central Mining was a partner in Wernher, Beit, which was a partner in Central Mining, and this included all Wernher, Beit's interests worldwide, not simply in gold mining. Shares were not made available to the public, but were reserved for 'new interests', nearly all in France. The first directors were Julius Wernher, Alfred Beit and Friedrich Eckstein, and in France their colleague Georges Rouliot and Count Isaac de Camondo.

Again to quote A. P. Cartwright, the creation of Central Mining marked the pinnacle of Julius as a financier. 'The City of London raised its hat to him and henceforth spoke of him with the respect that it normally reserved for the Rothschilds.'*

The enormous success of this flotation was soon to have some

* See Kubiceck for analysis of the biggest trust of its kind the Rand or even London and Paris had ever seen.

nasty setbacks. The Moroccan crisis and Kaiser William II's belligerence, followed by the fall in American stocks, had their repercussions throughout the world. Then in December Balfour resigned and a new government was formed by Campbell-Bannerman, followed by a landslide election victory for the Liberals. The main issues had been tariff reform and Chinese slavery. In the latter case the Liberal press was splashed with headlines such as 'Terror on the Rand' and 'Horrible Cruelties'; and indeed the details of conditions under which the Chinese worked made horrific reading: deep drilling ten hours a day, six days a week, two shillings a day, subjected to flogging with no access to courts of law. Favourite electoral gimmicks were parades of men dressed as Chinamen in chains, accompanied by slave-drivers with whips. Tories were taunted as 'pigtails'.

Haldane became Secretary of State for War, and the young Winston Churchill was Under-Secretary for the Colonies and thus – Lord Elgin being the Secretary – chief spokesman in the Commons. But gold shares, having previously recovered a little, began to slide.

The Liberals had pledged to end the 'Chinese coolie system', but – as Julius Wernher had planned – they found it impossible to do this for legal reasons. Not only were 50,000 Chinese already working in the mines under contract,* but another 14,000 were on their way and there were contracts for yet more to come. Although Churchill did propose a form of assisted repatriation, few coolies took advantage of it.

Hostility to Chinese labour was by no means confined to Britain. Moneypenny, the editor of the Johannesburg *Star*, had resigned. White labourers, including the Cornish 'Cousin Jacks', were fearful that they would be displaced. A new Boer party, Het Volk ('The People'), had been formed in the Transvaal, led by Louis Botha and Jan Smuts, who had seen the chance of drawing some of their discontented former foes into the fold. On the other hand the British government's decision to introduce responsible government in the Transvaal was viewed with apprehension by

---

* In March 1905 Glen Deep (a Rand Mines property) employed 1,752 Chinese as against 23 Africans.

many of the leaders in the mining community – though rather less so by Wernher and Beit.

But at least Lionel Phillips had finally decided to abandon politics and to return permanently to Johannesburg. No doubt his own personal finances and his wife's extravagant tastes were part of the consideration. Perhaps even then he realized that Het Volk's real aim was to avenge defeat and to destroy the dream of a British South Africa. At any rate his energy and enthusiasm were much needed at the Corner House. Florrie returned to the scene of her triumphs in February.

That old friend and supporter of Wernher, Beit, Maurice Rouvier, was now Prime Minister of France. So in November Beit, recovered somewhat, went to see him in Paris and seems to have picked up the idea that war with Germany was likely by the end of February. Then came a surprise invitation to visit the Kaiser. It appears that the ostensible reason was to invest Beit with the Order of the Red Eagle for his generosity towards the Berlin museum. Apparently Bode had passed on a message that the Kaiser was complaining that Beit was doing so much for the London National Gallery but too little for Berlin. Beit had therefore obliged by buying some pictures, including a Van Dyck, that Bode had particularly wanted.

As Beit was now a British subject, he was able to decline the offer of an Order without offence. The Kaiser had evidently confused him with Sir Ernest Cassel, describing him afterwards to his Chancellor Bülow as 'the speculator of Edward VII' and his 'notorious Stock Exchange crony'. The question of Morocco and tariff reform dominated the meeting. When Beit said that tariff reform was best for Britain, the Kaiser was menacing: 'If England builds tariff walls round her Empire, I shall have to decide whether England should be allowed to retain her colonies.' The Kaiser also wanted to know if the British were ready to land 100,000 men in Schleswig-Holstein, but Beit said this was nonsense. He also accused the British of spending vast sums in the Paris press on anti-German articles, which seems to have been true.

Beit is said to have maintained an independent point of view (and one hopes a straight face) in this peculiar and apparently somewhat naïve interview, but the whole affair can be looked upon as a measure not only of his own personal renown internationally but of the reputation of the firm. He told Julius that he thought the Kaiser did mean peace, and was surprised at how well informed he was. On his return Lord Esher was sent round to Beit by the King to find out exactly what had happened.

Wernher was now able to report to Phillips that Beit was 'wonderfully well and jolly'. 'He drops in almost daily.' But this was not to last.

The City was ever more pessimistic, Julius said, following the 'abject defeat' of Conservative Unionists and the 'tremendous headway' of the new element, the Labour Party, which could have far-reaching effects on South African affairs. He and Beit had been pleased by a surprise visit from Smuts, and in writing to FitzPatrick, now back in Johannesburg and leader of the Progressive Party, Julius said that they had encouraged him to speak his mind. The gist was that Smuts had hinted that the capitalists should come to a private arrangement with Het Volk, the price being a more lenient attitude towards Chinese labour. This suggestion was rejected, but because the hullaballoo about the Chinese was increasing rather than diminishing, they began to find the bait a little more tempting. They had been impressed by Smuts as someone 'to do business with'. 'I believe he has a somewhat open mind,' Julius told Phillips, 'and might give help – he is open to be talked to, otherwise he would not have seen us.'

After a few weeks Beit wrote a strong letter to FitzPatrick – one of the last of his life, as it happened – spelling out their revised opinions, and specifically ruling out the idea of a Progressive government headed by FitzPatrick himself. Even if Fitz left the firm, he would always be associated with it in the public mind. Beit and Wernher favoured Sir Richard Solomon as leader of the party, as a man absolutely independent of mining interests. This was a bitter blow to FitzPatrick, who did not in any case like Solomon. It was in effect a demand that he should abandon his much cherished political ambition of the past few years.

Julius's gloomy mood as share values continued to drop is shown in a letter he wrote to Phillips on 15 February 1906:

The feeling against Chinese is very strong, genuine or not genuine . . . Do not forget what fearful sacrifices we have made and the enormous responsibility resting on us – many people cling to us as their last hope . . . Our losses are terrific . . . We are looked upon as fools by one section and as knaves by the other – the majority does not care a straw what happens as long as they have nothing to pay and no bother, added with the malicious joy of the capitalist losing his money . . . If we have to shut up mines the calamity will be fearful. Without many more people of British descent the position is lost . . . You talk of Lord Milner seeing people but he has hardly anybody to talk to. As he says himself he had better not attempt it as it might do more harm than good . . . We came in for a great deal of blame. It does get on one's nerves. Beit seems to suffer ever more and he gets into states of collapse.

And then later: 'We have had a beastly week. One does not know what financial calamity may happen . . . the losses are terrible.' He even spoke of panic. 'We are prepared for almost everything. The political position is very despairing [a favourite word]. I feel all our sacrifices have been in vain. Most people will lose or have lost everything and are completely ruined without hope of recovery. Where we are to blame, perhaps, is that we ever allowed things to get to such a mad height.' He mentioned a jobber who had sold for £21,000 what he had bought for £82,000. As A. P. Cartwright remarked, Central Mining was going through its baptism of fire.

He cheered up a little when Churchill made an 'extremely clever' speech in the Commons, attempting to balance sympathy for the Chinese with imperial obligations: a speech in which the phrase 'terminological inexactitude' was first used, in connection with that dread word *slavery*. But soon afterwards Churchill caused outrage over his attitude towards Milner, when a motion of censure was proposed concerning the authorized flogging of Chinese. 'Milner is treated quite shamefully,' said Julius. 'It seems the fate of all great [public] servants.' Others used stronger language about Churchill: 'utterly mean and contemptible', 'calculated to offend everyone'.

Julius kept in constant touch with Milner at this period, sending him copies of FitzPatrick's long gossipy letters from Johannesburg.

The Chinese situation was not helped by murders and marauding gangs roaming the countryside. Then there was the shock of the revelation of 'unnatural vices' being practised on a large scale in the compounds, since wives and families had not accompanied the workers. Venereal disease was rife. Churchill upset people by using another word that until then was unknown in the House: *catamite*. Voluntary repatriation had failed. Now there was a case for enforced repatriation of the many 'professionals'.

On 26 March Julius had some very bad news for Phillips: '*Quite privately* Beit has had another stroke.' The left side was paralysed, and nobody before had ever seen Beit so apathetic and depressed. 'The despairing fact is that B is a hopeless creature, he cannot be without people around him . . . his house in Park Lane is open to everybody. You never go there in the evening without meeting 2 or 3 brokers etc. etc. It is unspeakably sad more so as one is quite helpless . . . When he feels well he will commit no end of indiscretions etc.'

About this time there was an article in the *New York Press* contrasting Alfred Beit with his more 'sprightly' younger brother Otto, who was 'on terms of personal intimacy with King and Prince of Wales' – his house in Belgrave Square was 'one of the few in London where His Majesty visits to have a hand at cards and a game of billiards'. It also included a piece about Julius Wernher, described as one of the most modest men of wealth in London:

He dresses more like a poor grocer than like a man of many millions. When he does not walk all the way, his travelling expenses to his office and back home never cost him more than ten cents daily. He stands on the doorstep of his mansion in Piccadilly almost every morning to wait for an omnibus that carries him to the door of his office in the City. Like his partner he is punctual to the extent of being

almost eccentric. If anything occurred in his home that
might delay him in the morning beyond his usual time he
would not go to the office at all that day. 'The only way,' he
will say, 'to encourage punctuality is to punish your staff as
you punish yourself.' Eight solid hours' work at his office is
his usual day. Frequently he does not go out to lunch, and
then the office boys are heard to giggle among themselves
that the governor must have brought sandwiches in his
pocket that morning. Away from business, he enjoys life
mostly as other men do. He smokes, drinks, likes a modest
gamble and plays a good game of billiards. In the latter
connection it is said that he has the most luxuriously fitted
billiard-table in Europe.

On 30 May 1906 Julius was writing that the news about Beit
was again very serious. There was an 'unusual accumulation of
dangerous symptoms', and his life was 'held by a thread'. There
followed a remarkable recovery, though, alas, brief. Beit had
been in Wiesbaden, and had returned, bringing his doctor, because
he wanted to die at his country house, Tewin Water. Julius was
one of the few allowed to visit him.

'With a heavy heart', Julius recorded that he had to be host at a
reception at Bath House for an official visit by members of the
German press. An account was published in the *Anglo-German
Courier*, accompanied by a photograph of Birdie, now fully
confident as a leading member of society and wearing her
magnificent pearl choker and ostrich feather cape. The article
reported:

At midnight, many of the editors proceeded to the residence
of Sir Julius and Lady Wernher, who were 'At home' to
their friends. Bath House, Piccadilly, though not designed
on the big, palatial lines of the Stafford mansion, lends itself
readily to entertainments of the kind given on this occasion,
which was characterised by the homely kindliness and
courtesy of the hosts. It, therefore, was no surprise to see
within its hospitable portals an almost ceaseless stream of
visitors from 11 p.m. to 1 a.m. Lady Wernher, dressed, as

always, gracefully, wore a chic pale blue satin gown, and looked at her best when she received her guests, who included, besides many well-known South Africans, a host of London celebrities in politics, art, literature, and the drama.

On 6 July Julius was struck down with a severe attack of shingles. He was still very ill when Beit died on the 16th of that month, and therefore could not attend 'our dear dear friend's funeral.'

The obituaries were many and varied. As FitzPatrick said, only a few intimates knew the real 'Little Alfred'. Beit, to Fitz, was a man never known to do an unkind act or say an injurious word, the exact antithesis of the popular view of the Randlord as being a 'sordid and vulgar Hoggenheimer'. And there is no reason to dispute this. The journalist W. T. Stead made a much quoted remark to Fitz at the funeral: 'There was something Christlike about Alfred Beit. They are afraid to say so but you know it.' But for some people, especially Radicals, the Jameson Raid had given Beit an indelible label. The *Daily News* wrote sarcastically how 'Mr Beit played an inglorious part in one of the most inglorious episodes in modern times and afterwards confined himself to the futile task of heaping up millions and the still more futile task of spending them.' To the Radical MP John Burns he was 'a vampire, an octopus drawing out the life-blood of South Africa'.

Beit on his death was still popularly believed to have been the richest man in the world, though William Rockefeller and George Westinghouse in the United States may have had greater fortunes. But the assets of the partners of Wernher, Beit were thought to be worth at least £100 million. Officially Beit left about £8 million in shares, which were then of course at 'rock bottom'. Much was made of the successful combination of the two different characters of Beit and Wernher, the founders of the firm: the one excitable, intuitive, quick in decision, optimistic, boyish; the other cautious, difficult to convince, clear-visioned, stolid, wise. Both avoided publicity, and both had the German gift of thoroughness.

The *New York Press* said that, like Rhodes, Beit had the capacity for 'thinking in continents'. As for Julius Wernher, 'when it comes to looking at things imperially', as Joseph Chamberlain used to say, he was 'rather at sea'. Julius was more of a disciplinarian than a 'hustler', unlike Abe Bailey and Rhodes's friend Rochefort Maguire, for instance.

The final sentences in Beit's entry in the *Dictionary of National Biography* are perhaps the best epitaph. 'An active sympathy with every form of suffering and an ardent belief in great causes led him to distribute vast sums of money, and his benefactions were always made privately with rare self-effacement. The terms of the will give the true measure of his character.' It was a sensational will, which made many ill-wishers think differently of him. Its benefits are still being felt to this day in southern and central Africa.

On Beit's tombstone at Tewin are the words: 'Write me as one who loved his fellow men.'

13

Alone without Beit

'So we have lost and buried him,' Julius wrote to Phillips. 'Although I felt his days were numbered, the end came surprisingly quick, and I had the mortification to be ill and useless at the time, and am only now slowly recovering . . . I have been v. seedy and knocked up.' A small private memorial service was held in Luton Hoo chapel. Soon afterwards Julius wrote of Beit's 'intense love' for South Africa, where he had spent the happiest days of his life. 'There was no more fervent believer in the future of South Africa than Mr Beit.' A letter of condolence had been received from Smuts.

Julius told Phillips later that he would be sending him a copy of the will. 'Some of the dispositions rather astonish me but there it is.' Beit's capital would have to be withdrawn gradually from the firm. Julius was one of the three executors, the other two being Otto Beit and the Beits' cousin Franz Voeklin, who had also been Alfred Beit's secretary.

About £650,000 had been left to individual legatees, in addition to bequests of property and *objets d'art*, and about £2 million to charities. A large piece of land – woods and pleasure-grounds – was left to the City of Hamburg, and the splendid Este-Gonzaga plate from the Spitzer sale was left to the Hamburg Museum. Only the year before he had given £100,000 to Hamburg University. Now he also left £20,000 for Hamburg charities. Six paintings, including two Reynoldses and a Gainsborough, were bequeathed to the National Gallery in London, and another Reynolds and a bronze statuette of Hercules by Pollaiuolo went to the Berlin Museum. Julius was left a bronze statuette of John the Baptist by Sansovino 'as a mark of my esteem and friendship', and this is still to be seen at Luton Hoo. Dr Jameson, who had been Prime Minister of Cape Colony since 1904 (only seven years after the Raid), was left £25,000, and Beit's two godchildren, Derrick Wernher and Carl Michaelis, had £1,000 each 'to purchase a memento of me'. The residuary estate, which included the remainder of his art collection, went to Otto Beit.

It had been a surprise to many that Cecil Rhodes had not provided money for the development of Rhodesia, but it would seem that he had come to an agreement with Beit about their respective wills: Rhodes's money would go to the Scholarship plan, whereas Beit's would fill some of the needs of Rhodesia. Beit, however, did leave £200,000 for educational and charitable purposes in Rhodesia North and South and 'other territories within the field of the British South Africa Company'. His most important legacy was the huge sum of £1,200,000 for the establishment of a 'Railway Fund', the object of which was to construct and further generally all types of communication, such as railways, and telegraph and telephone systems, for the benefit of inhabitants 'whether native or immigrant', not only in the Rhodesias but in the Portuguese colonies and German East Africa. In particular he had in mind completing Rhodes's dream of a Cape-to-Cairo railway and telegraph system. Julius and Otto Beit again were nominated as trustees. The other was Bourchier Hawksley, who had been Rhodes's financial adviser.[*]

Beit left £200,000 for the establishment of a university at Johannesburg on land at Frankenwald that he had already donated for this purpose in 1905, then valued at £80,000 and comprising some 950 acres. In his typical way he had originally bought Frankenwald to help a friend, and had spent a lot of money in turning this piece of veld into forest, orchards and plantations. After realizing that he was losing money, he had asked Julius to visit the place and to give his advice. It had been Lionel Phillips

---

[*] The will allowed for the proceeds of the Railway Fund to be used eventually, if need be, for 'educational public or charitable purposes' in the Rhodesias. The Beit Trust is still in operation in Zambia and Zimbabwe.

who had arranged the official transfer of the property to Johannesburg. As will be shown later, this great gift was to result in considerable controversy – which has never been quite forgotten.

Beit left £25,000 to Rhodes University, Grahamstown, £10,000 to the Rhodes Memorial Fund, and £15,000 each to the Transvaal, Kimberley and Cape Colony for charitable and educational purposes. He left £10,000 to the Union Jack Club in London, £20,000 each to the King Edward VII and Guy's Hospitals, £25,000 to the Institute of Medical Science, London University, and £20,000 for general charities in London. £50,000 and a number of his shares in De Beers were left to the proposed 'college of higher technical and scientific training', i.e. the 'Charlottenburg Scheme', the shares realizing some £150,000; in his will he specifically mentioned Lord Rosebery and Julius Wernher as having agreed already to be trustees of the College and added that the sum was to be irrespective of the fact that he had recently doubled its grant from £100,000 to £200,000. Before his death Beit had founded a chair in Colonial History and an assistant lectureship at Oxford University.

Otto Beit had been working in a stockbroking firm after leaving Wernher, Beit in the late 1890s. He now resigned from that firm and devoted his time to running his brother's Trust. But it was to take many years before any major projects could be put under way. Meanwhile the capital was well invested and the value more than doubled. The first great enterprise was the Beit Bridge over the Limpopo. There followed other bridges across the Luangwa, Kafue, Sabie, Zambezi and Chinsali. Without help from the Beit Trust the rapid development of the railway and telegraph systems in the Rhodesias would not have been possible. The Trust bought rolling stock and contributed to the cost of the Victoria Falls Hotel. After many years the Trust's money began to be used more for education, and in the provision of scholarships, bursaries and training grants, and as such it is still very much in existence to this day under the trusteeship of Beit's nephew, Sir Alfred Beit, Bt.

Julius's great grief and all the anxieties resulting from the will had a severe effect on his already declining health. It was obvious that he was ageing, although he was still only fifty-six. His family and close colleagues had become exceedingly disturbed by his depression. He referred often to the possibility of his own death, in which case the firm would be forced into liquidation and his wife would have to take charge of his affairs. Most of Beit's capital would probably have to be withdrawn by the end of 1906. Julius of course had the major share of the remainder of the capital. Friedie Eckstein and Ludwig Breitmeyer also had sizeable portions, but the other partners had very little, if any, and most were in debt. He therefore felt a solution had to be found urgently, to 'give full protection to all who are working for the firm's success'.

Many of his worries were unloaded on Phillips, who naturally could not but agree about this idea of 'protection'. Julius told him that he had decided that the firm ought to be turned into a limited liability company, and that a start should be made with Eckstein's in Johannesburg (an idea that was scotched, temporarily at least, by the partners). It was plain that he was being worn down by the increasing unpopularity of the capitalists, 'the hatred of the masses and the enmity of the Liberals'. Then there was the perennial difficulty about FitzPatrick, who obviously would prefer politics 'pure and simple' if only he could afford it; 'but he can't, and the difficulty is that there is really no fund from which to pay him – it is curious that neither Rhodes nor Beit left any money to pay men like Jameson or Fitz to carry on ideas which were so dear to them'. He had become very fond of FitzPatrick, who had often stayed at Luton Hoo, but the man was such a 'free spender'.

Julius was also now sceptical about the possibility of founding a university at Frankenwald, even though in the first instance he had been responsible for promoting it. The 'inspiration' had been FitzPatrick's, he said, but as time went on he had come to the conclusion that a scheme akin to Rhodes's would have been more practicable. It would be better for young Afrikaners to come to England to study. 'They [would] get in new surroundings, mix with all conditions of men, and get the best teaching and see a little of the world.'

Then there was the tricky subject of the Phillipses' own extravagant tastes. Lionel and Florrie Phillips had been allocated an admittedly attractive house, traditional gabled Dutch colonial in style, called Villa Arcadia, another Corner House property. But Florrie seemed to be wanting something larger, suitable for entertaining on a grander scale. 'I am against building new houses,' Julius wrote on 15 August, continuing with his occasional quaint choice of words: 'I know we don't agree on what is reasonable or necessary re hospitality. No doubt my having lived in modest Kimberley accounts for my inferiority. I only wish Joh [Johannesburg] people had followed the simple genial Kimberley example which made life delightful – now most have the disagreeable task to withdraw back.'

Florrie might have commented that the Wernhers' standard of entertaining was hardly modest or inferior. However, her husband, although plainly irritated, felt at this crucial period in the firm's progress that it was not worth making the matter an issue: 'About the house,' he wrote, 'why do you harp every mail upon it? We can make it do *quite well* . . . I may be over-sensitive or overworked, but there is a *tone* in your letter that I do not understand.'

In October Julius was 'literally pushed off' on a cruise to Egypt. At Gibraltar he posted a letter to Birdie that disturbed her 'deeply':

> I try to keep my mind away from City matters, but I have realized very profoundly in the last month or two what it is to be without Beit. There is nobody to take his place and when he was still there a talk with him would throw a mass of light on any subject. I had the check of another mind, things could be settled and dismissed from one's own mind. E [Eckstein] is excellent in purely job matters. My pleasure in business is certainly gone without Beit but the load remains.

It was curious, as Julius admitted, that in spite of his closeness to Beit there had never been any discussions about the Railway Trust and other large bequests in his will.

Something else was weighing heavily on Julius, which he had to face up to on his return. This was what came to be known in

France as L'Affaire Lemoine. It was to linger on for some years, and it proved a bitter personal humiliation for Julius.

In 1905 an engineer, Henri Lemoine, son of the French consul in Trieste, had been in touch with Beit, claiming that he had a secret formula for mass-producing gem-sized diamonds. The possibility of producing diamonds chemically by subjecting carbon to intense heat had for long haunted the trade. Beit had duly visited Lemoine's forge in Paris, and was amazed and alarmed to be handed a stone of flawless quality. Even the rumour of such an invention could cause a selling panic among De Beers investors. Somewhat impetuously, therefore, he signed a document certifying that this diamond was the real thing. Julius was more dubious about its authenticity, but being the only surviving Life-Governor of De Beers he agreed that they should secure the exclusive rights to the formula 'to save the industry'.

This sorry affair, which so delighted ill-wishers, will be dealt with at length in a future chapter.

Back in Johannesburg it was reckoned that the firm of Wernher, Beit now effectively controlled 52 per cent of the gold industry. Julius was still strongly in favour of retaining Chinese labour. To do without the Chinese, he said, would be 'suicide'. As he put it: 'South Africa is highly mineralised. The Rand is only a small spot on the map, and we have other chances to look forward to. What is its value if we have to rely upon the South African labour supply?'

In yet another long pessimistic letter, written on New Year's Day, 1907, he told Phillips he would really prefer to 'get out and take the rest of my life easy'. According to Julius, Friedie Eckstein was also being driven to his limit and probably killing himself, while Breitmeyer was 'too negative a character'. 'But I go on from a sense of duty and love for the firm . . . I like to keep up the business for one or two of my boys or sons of partners as I do not approve of the usual style that if a father has made a fortune the sons should become idlers or worse still. Two of my boys [i.e. Derrick and Alex] are promising for business, unfortunately too young, but in 3 years time Derrick will have made up his mind and I would like to see him take to the City.' Derrick – now as tall as his father and running to fat – would soon be at Balliol.

Harold, the 'least intelligent one, inclined to be lazy', would soon be at Eton. 'I hope Derrick will know how to take care of himself. The danger is that there are so many fellows [at Oxford] with no real object in life except sport and enjoyment.'

He ended: 'Poor South Africa. Few people have a good word for it now.'

At long last the alterations at Luton Hoo had been completed. The house was therefore ready for a royal visit, and the appropriate arrangements were made through Lord Farquhar. The King would come to lunch on Sunday 18 February.

(Actually, very soon after that date, dry rot was discovered on two floors, and the builders had to be called in again. This additional work lasted until 1909.)

The King, accompanied by Lord Farquhar, duly set out by motor car. But, as the press reported, on the way to Luton Hoo he had an 'unpleasant experience'. 'About a mile outside Harpenden the sound of a burst caused the chauffeur to pull up, and it was discovered that one of the back tyres had come to grief through running over a rough flint.' The King and his friends smoked their cigars while the tyre was being replaced. Meanwhile a whip of the Hertfordshire Hunt who happened to be passing was dispatched to find a carriage. Then one of the King's staff telephoned from the Railway Hotel at Harpenden to Buckingham Palace for a relief car, as the 'engineer' had decided that the wheel was not quite safe. 'His Majesty proceeded to stroll about Harpenden Common, smoking still and chatting.'

'Meanwhile Sir Julius Wernher, growing anxious at his Royal visitor's non-arrival, dispatched a motor along the St Albans road. His car and the carriage from Harpenden arrived about the same time, and the King with the remark, "I'm beginning to feel hungry", mounted his host's car.' His Majesty thus arrived at Luton Hoo 'quite ready for a good lunch', being two hours late. 'The relief car from Buckingham Palace came up later at a furious pace. A Harpenden policeman was seriously disturbed by its speed, and carefully noted its number.' Then a second car was seen tearing along, drawing up sharply outside the Railway Hotel.

This one had no number whatsoever! 'The chauffeur was about to be arrested, when the policeman noticed the Royal arms.

The King had to return to London at 4 p.m., immediately after lunch. A correspondent for the *New York American* may, or may not, have decided that the story needed embroidering, in an undated cutting kept by Birdie. He described how the 'merry monarch' would receive 'many a good tip on the South African market from Sir Julius Wernher', and greatly enjoyed his quiet Sunday lunches with him 'to learn of what was doing or likely to be done on the Rand'. On the way to one such 'functionette' the royal car broke down (yet again?) and Julius had to send his own to fetch the 'stranded monarch' (from Buckingham Palace – only half a mile away?). As the King was already late, he told Julius's chauffeur to 'put on the power'.

The Wernher car went scorching along, and was just entering Piccadilly when a policeman, seeing the vehicle coming at a tearing rate, jumped in the middle of the street and held up a warning hand.

King and policeman both cried 'Stop!', and the car was brought to a sudden halt. 'You're going at an illegal speed,' said the policeman, taking out his notebook. 'I must take your name and number.' 'My name is Wernher,' said the King. 'The number you can see on the car, and my address is Bath House, Piccadilly.'

'Very sorry, sir,' replied the policeman, 'but I shall have to summon you to appear at the police court tomorrow morning. Go on, but keep down your speed.' The King leaned back in his car, convulsed with laughter, and when Bath House was reached told Sir Julius that he could get ready to pay a fine for scorching on Sunday. But the policeman must have learned one or two things that afternoon, for the summons never came.

No doubt, during that other, and too brief, luncheon at Luton Hoo, there had been little time for tips on the South African market, let alone for a discussion on the effects of the impending

general election in the Transvaal, which were to be more important than perhaps the King realized.

Not surprisingly, the big issues in the election were Chinese
labour and British domination. Percy FitzPatrick was standing as
a candidate for the Progressive Party and horrified Julius by
suddenly asking if he could make use of the private letter that
Julius had written after his meeting with Smuts the year before in
London. Smuts had been making particularly vicious attacks on
the mining houses, as had FitzPatrick's great rival, Richard
Solomon, and Fitz felt that Julius's letter would show up the
hollowness of their accusations.

Julius reacted sternly. It has always been his principle, he said,
not to disclose private communications. 'If a good many people
have in the past shown confidence in me, it has been no doubt
due to the fact that they felt sure of my discretion and knew that
there would be no abuse of their confidence.' He also, rather
woundingly, told Fitz that in any case the Progressives had little
chance of winning. 'As I told Smuts then, and as I repeat now, if
the popular vote does not see fit to give us a majority under our
system of election ["one vote one value"], we can hardly complain, and must do the best we can as a minority. As such a fate is
possibly awaiting us, it seems to me of the highest importance
not to embitter future relations.'

FitzPatrick was elected, but Het Volk swept in with a clear
majority, under Botha and Smuts. FitzPatrick told Smuts they
would survive only five years. To which Smuts replied, almost
fiercely – and, nearly eighty years on, one might think propheti-
cally: 'Not five years! Fifty years! For ever!'

At least Botha and Smuts had agreed to retain the British flag.
FitzPatrick wrote to say that he had telegrams of congratulation
from the people he most admired: Wernher, Milner and Kipling.
Be that as it may, it did not stop Julius carrying on with his usual
deflating grumbles about keeping the firm out of politics. He had
now definitely made up his mind that Fitz must be eased out of
the firm; on no account must it appear that he was still being
financed by the Corner House. So a solution was found whereby
a trust fund was created to buy a farm for Fitz and provide him
with an annual income, and this would be out of money that had

once been set aside for 'public and political purposes' by Rhodes, Beit and Julius from their De Beers Governorships. It was not an entirely happy conclusion for FitzPatrick, who continued to suffer from financial anxieties over many years.

1907 was another year of deep depression in the stock markets, with a financial crisis in the United States. 'It will be come time before the public regains confidence in American management and honesty,' wrote Phillips. There was a long strike of white workers in the Rand mines. The diamond market all but collapsed, resulting in cuts in directors' fees. Cullinan's Premier Mine had been forced to reconsider its independent selling policy, and had come to an arrangement with the London Diamond Syndicate, headed by Julius. This arrangement, however, had to be suspended, so the 'war' with the De Beers flared up once more.

Some young Afrikaners were actually being lured into the goldmines. And the new Transvaal government had to call in the British garrison to disperse the strikers. As Lionel Phillips wrote to Julius: 'The whole position is really getting topsy-turvy; a Boer Government calling out British troops to keep English miners in order while the Dutchmen are replacing them in the mines . . . You may rest assured that we are taking every advantage of the strike to reduce working costs as far as possible.'

Florrie Phillips was back in London, wanting Julius to contribute to her excellent scheme for an art gallery in Johannesburg. Perhaps she was not quite so much of a virago as hitherto, and she certainly had developed an interesting taste both in art and decoration. It was not surprising that Smuts was to describe her as 'no ordinary woman'. But she still had an antipathy towards the Wernhers, which must have been embarrassing at times for her husband. 'Cold and laconic', 'nothing in common', even 'odious', were her comments on Julius. The snag was that in him she was faced with a stronger and apparently impenetrable, character; and it was he who held the purse-strings. She did admit to Lionel that she had been invited to lunch by Julius, who had been extremely kind to her. 'They asked me to dinner but luckily I was not able to accept. Our interview passed off without any breezes as we were both on our best behaviour.'

Encouraged by Julius, Lionel Phillips tried hard – with success – to keep on good terms with Botha and Smuts, who were invited to Villa Arcadia. Florrie was a considerable help in charming them, as Julius was forced to concede. So once more there were hints about the inadequacy of the size of the house.

On 8 August 1907 Julius presided over the second annual general meeting of Central Mining, held at No. 1 London Wall. He had to tell the shareholders that the value of forty-four of the leading South African securities had dropped by an appalling £20 million, down to £65 million between January and June, compared to £154,500,000 in December 1904. While attacking the behaviour of Winston Churchill, whom he described as the 'enfant terrible of South Africa',[*] he said he was really hopeful about the rulers of the new self-governing Transvaal, who he felt had the 'very best intentions'. He spoke next of the 'Chinese experiment', which he claimed had never had a fair trial and was saving the mining industry. Even General Botha had said to him: 'Proceed slowly, and don't let them [the Chinese] go until you are sure of substitutes.'

Dealing with the white strikers, he said that the cry had been that the Chinese would take their place. But of course the Chinese were only permitted to do *unskilled* labour, and they would all be returning to China after the expiration of their contracts. 'No, I take it that this agitation is directed against the natives, many of whom have become very efficient. You may restrict the Chinese, who leave shortly, but can you prevent the Kaffir, the son of the soil, from rising to a higher plane?'

This pronouncement was slightly marred by his next remark: 'The black man cannot be eliminated; South Africa will always be a white man's country, three quarters black.'

Throughout the year Julius had been pressing the point of the firm's inevitable collapse if he were to die suddenly. So at last it

[*] In March Schumacher had written to Julius: 'It would be a great thing for us if we could go for Winston Churchill and *break* him; and this might be possible if he could be taunted into making the charges outside the pale of privilege. I cannot help thinking that many of the sober members of the Liberal party must be realizing that an unscrupulous and dishonest politician of the Churchill class is sure to do the party harm in the long run.'

was agreed that the assets of Wernher, Beit and Co. and H. Eckstein and Co. should be taken over by Central Mining and Investments. The exception would be the diamond company at Holborn Viaduct. This would be formed into a separate company, in which all the partners would have an interest. It was typical of Julius that he should write to Phillips: 'What keeps me going is a sense of responsibility, a desire to give my partners a chance, consideration for our boys [Phillips also had a son at Eton].' As usual, he was against making gambles over new ventures, such as investing in some 'fiddling' goldmine in Rhodesia. 'Although in good health and with renewed force, I feel I am getting older and I have nothing of my life except work and worry.' He also saw far too little of his family. 'I am inclined to slow down, reduce as much as possible and leave the younger partners to decide a few years hence. I know it is only a dream, I am destined to work to the last atom of my strength and shall never get out of it.'

He still had hopes that Derrick might in some way succeed him. But this 'end of an era', the liquidation of the 'old firm', could not be hurried through. It would have to be delayed until 1910, by which time it was hoped that the value of the firm's assets would have improved. 'Yet three years run off with frightful speed, and we have to think beyond it.'

In November 1907 'all had to be put to one side', because of the visit of the German Kaiser. Julius was one of those on whom was bestowed the Order of the Crown (Third Class). He tried to decline this honour, but only half-heartedly, it would seem, for in 1911 he received a letter from Buckingham Palace granting him permission to wear the insignia.

Back in August, Julius had been able to take time off with his family, and as in past years they had all gone off to North Berwick 'for the grouse'. The Grand Duke Michaels had also gone to Scotland, though 'for the golf'. Birdie had hoped that the Torby girls might be inveigled over to Killachy, but there was a polite though firm refusal. In any case Zia was off to Wiesbaden, her birthplace, to stay with her widowed grandmother, Countess Natalia von Merenberg, daughter of the great Russian poet

Alexander Pushkin. It was in Wiesbaden that she had been christened, carried into the Orthodox Church on a white satin cushion.

Later in the year, to Birdie's undisguised delight, Countess Torby had invited Julius and Birdie (but not their sons) for a weekend at Keele Hall. The ubiquitous Lord Farquhar would be a fellow guest.

Keele Hall belonged to Ralph Sneyd, and had been leased to the Grand Duke for several years from 1901. Baroness de Stoeckl, a family friend of the Michaels and known to the children as Aunty Ag, has written of the beautiful park being 'very smutty as it was near Newcastle [-under-Lyme] and surrounded by coal mines'. 'If one touched a leaf one's hand was black.'

No doubt the Wernhers' weekend was a success, at any rate for Birdie, whom the Michaels knew as Alice. Regular visitors at Keele included Daisy, Princess of Pless, the George Keppels, Constance, Duchess of Westminster, King Manoel of Portugal, Lady Randolph ('Jennie') Churchill, Prince Francis of Teck, the Maharajahs of Patiala and Putacola, and Lady Maude Warrender; any of these might have been co-guests. Croquet was always the great entertainment. Ladies played in their 'long dresses, elaborate coiffures, and large shady hats held on by numerous hatpins'. The Grand Duke had also created his own eighteen-hole golf course. Being so tall, he had to have specially made clubs. He was very proud of having been made High Steward of Newcastle-under-Lyme, even if the mayor and corporation (so it was wickedly suggested) had their eyes on the pecuniary advantage.

He had a long, pale and at times almost expressionless face – 'inscrutable'. At the time of the Russo-Japanese War he decided to shave off his 'Grecian' beard and stop dyeing his hair. George Cornwallis-West, another frequent guest at Keele, described him as a born autocrat, at times an absolute child. 'If he got an idea into his head, no matter how wrong it was, nothing in the world would get it out.' This did not make things easy for the children, especially Boy. He was also a stickler for protocol. Ladies had to curtsy on arrival, and he always led his wife first into dinner, instead of last which was the social custom. Winston Churchill refused to take much notice of etiquette at Keele, let alone manners. Baroness de Stoeckl was aghast to find him lounging on a sofa with a leg over one arm, not bothering to get up. One cannot help assuming that the Grand Duke and Julius Wernher had few subjects of conversation in common, except perhaps money.

Sophie Torby was considered a great beauty, with – according to *The Lady's Realm* – a 'delicately moulded face and exquisitely pencilled eyebrows'. She was a 'born hostess' and very popular as such, 'always laughing'. Her figure was generally considered 'fine if rather full'; later she became extremely stout.

When the King visited Keele he came by special train. Mrs Keppel would invariably be invited too, and would have to be his partner at croquet. The King hated to lose at croquet, but then so did the Grand Duke . . .

14

Imperial Interlude

Grand Duke Michael Mikhailovich was born on 16 October 1861 at the royal palace of Peterhof outside St Petersburg, the second son of Grand Duke Michael Nikolaievich, youngest son of Tsar Nicholas I, and Cécile, daughter of the Grand Duke of Baden and known after her marriage as the Grand Duchess Olga Feodorovna. He had five brothers, like him all over six feet, and one sister. The eldest brother was Nicholas, born in 1859, known as Bimbo, an historian with a profound knowledge of French culture, probably the most talented intellectually of all the Romanovs, but also radically inclined and socially unostentatious, moody but witty; he remained a bachelor, because of his undying love for his first cousin Victoria of Baden, who became Queen of Sweden. Then came George, born in 1863, known as Gogi, a general (also a numismatist), and married to Marie, or Minnie, daughter of George I of Greece. Next there was Alexander, or Sandro, born in 1866, the best-looking, cantankerous at times, and married to the Grand Duchess Xenia, sister of Tsar Nicholas II; he was made honorary colonel of the Kerinsky Infantry Regiment within twenty-four hours of his birth. Serge, born in 1869, had a mathematical bent and was an intimate friend of Nicholas II; Inspector-General of the Russian Artillery, he too was a bachelor, with a famous mistress who had also been mistress of the Tsar when he was Tsarevich: she was Mathilde Kscheshinka, the prima ballerina assoluta at the Marynka Theatre, ranking in greatness with Pavlova and Karsavina, and instructress-to-be of Margot Fonteyn. The youngest, Alexis, was born in 1875 but died of typhoid aged twenty.

The sister, Anastasia, or Stassie, at an early age married Grand Duke Frederick Francis III of Mecklenburg-Schwerin, and was said as a girl to have looked like 'an ivory statue, delicate but transparent', very Russian with green eyes. She was the centre of many scandals in Cannes, where she lived after her husband committed suicide by jumping out of a window. Alas, in middle age she lost her looks, about which Baroness D'Orczy made some very rude remarks. Some thought she had great charm, but others complained that she was haughty and she was certainly much disliked by the German Kaiser.

The father, Grand Duke Michael senior, was able and intelligent, a keen soldier and a great disciplinarian. For nineteen years he had been Governor of the Caucasus, where his children were brought up in an extremely Spartan manner, sleeping on iron bedsteads, bathing in cold water, prayers and gymnastics daily, and only allowed to see their sister on Sundays. In spite of the boys understandably feeling lonely, they all loved it there, and Michael the younger's Villa Kazbeck in Cannes was named after the highest mountain in Georgia. The family had a huge estate at Borjom near Tiflis, larger than the whole of Holland, as well as palaces on the Black Sea and near St Petersburg, the last being so enormous that the boys when summoned urgently by Papa would have to bicycle along the corridors.

At an exceedingly tender age young Michael served in the Russo-Turkish War and was soon afterwards made honorary Colonel of the Chasseurs of the Imperial Guard. He was handsome, though even then rather solemn-faced, charming, a good dancer, but lacked some of the intelligence of his brothers. He had an extraordinary, indeed frenetic obsession to find a wife, and built himself a large palace in St Petersburg to that end. ('We must have a decent place to live in,' he used to say.) In 1886 he was a candidate for the hand of Princess May of Teck (the future Queen Mary), but her father said he would not be a party to 'sacrificing his child', and that Russian Grand Dukes made notoriously bad husbands, which was certainly true. In the following year Princess Louise, daughter of the Prince of Wales, wisely turned him down because he said he could never have any feelings of love for her. In any case she knew he had just been rejected by Princess Irene, daughter of the Grand Duke of Hesse. In 1888, after a brief love affair with Princess Walewski, he fell frantically in love with Countess Katya Ignatiev, daughter of the former and somewhat shifty Minister and diplomat who had done much to bring Bulgaria under Russian influence. Any suggestion of his marrying this 'little commoner' was adamantly rejected by both his mother and the Empress. Finally it was decided to send him abroad to let him cool off. Whilst he was away, a delegation arrived at St Petersburg from Bulgaria, with a suggestion that he might become their King. Apparently the Bulgarians had not learnt that the Ignatiev marriage was being disallowed.

In 1891 Michael met Sophie von Merenberg, probably at Biarritz, though there are more romantic stories about his snatching the bridle of her horse as it bolted through the flower market at Nice, or sending his ADC to find out the name of this beautiful girl. They fell instantly in love, and were married secretly at San Remo. When his mother, the Grand Duchess Olga, heard this appalling news at St Petersburg, she collapsed and had to be sent at once by train to the Crimea to recover. On the way she had a heart attack and died in the station waiting-room at Kharkov, before her husband could arrive. The blame was at once laid on Michael, and the whole scandalous story was relayed to Windsor Castle: not that it dismayed the Prince of Wales – quite the contrary. Tsar Alexander III thereupon stripped Michael of his military ranks. Sophie's mother, the Countess von Merenberg, retaliated by refusing to let her son-in-law go to the funeral. Perhaps she was afraid that the marriage would be annulled. Michael was now forbidden by the Tsar to return to Russia at all. As has earlier been mentioned, Sophie was given the title of Countess de Torby by her father's half-brother, the Grand Duke of Luxemburg.

Sophie might not have been purely royal, but her credentials were not too bad, though not good enough for the Russians. Indeed, to most of us today, being the granddaughter of Pushkin would seem a trump card. Her aunt was Queen Sophie of Sweden (wife of Oscar II). Her first cousin Emma married King William

III of the Netherlands, and they were the parents of Queen Wilhelmina. Another cousin, Hélène, married Duke Leopold of Albany, fourth son of Queen Victoria, and they were the parents of the future Countess of Athlone. Her brother, Count George von Merenberg, married Princess Olga Yurievsky, daughter of the second, admittedly morganatic, wife of Tsar Alexander II, and failed in the courts to claim the throne of Luxemburg. Through her Würtemberg grandmother (and the Athlones) she was related to Princess May of Teck. She was also descended from George II of Great Britain.

Sophie's mother, Natalia von Merenberg, was born in 1836, the year before Pushkin was killed in the famous duel. Some research about the undoubtedly lovely Natalia, of the 'divine' shoulders, has revealed some facts which may have contributed to the horror of Grand Duchess Olga. The fact that Pushkin's great-grandfather, Ibrahim Hannibal, had been a dark-skinned Ethiopian was probably bad enough, even if he had been a prince and in the service of Peter the Great. But in 1853 Natalia had married Lieutenant-Colonel Dubel't, by whom she had two daughters and one son. That marriage was not a success, and the miseries involved probably brought on her mother's death. In 1864 Natalia had been granted the right to separate from her husband, but on 1 July 1867 she married Prince Nicholas William of Nassau in London, *before* her divorce proceedings were over. The divorce was not finalized until 18 May 1868. Two days later, on 20 May 1868, Sophie was born. George was born in 1871. Another daughter, Alexandrine, born in 1869, was destined to marry someone rather less blue-blooded: Don Máximo de Elia of Buenos Aires.

In 1899 Sophie and the Grand Duke moved into their Villa Kazbeck at Cannes, a great white terraced structure full of jardinières and with ferns hanging from the walls. It had a splendid garden, full of mimosa, roses and lilac. The staff included five footmen, a butler, a valet, a lady's maid, a governess, a nursery maid and six chefs. Much of Michael's income came from estates near Tiflis, and he was said to have owned a lucrative factory there for bottling mineral water. Sophie set a fashion at dinner parties by twining spring flowers round the candlesticks and then linking them to the chandeliers above. Those were 'crazy days when one only thought of amusements, of flirtations, of admiration', and according to Baroness de Stoeckl, whose husband* was equerry to Michael until they quarrelled, the Grand Duke did not stop falling in love with pretty girls, one after the other, while remaining 'devoted' to Sophie.

At the Golf Club you had to wear a red and white blazer, and no one was allowed to drive off before Grand Duke Michael, even if he was as 'uncertain' a golfer as he was in the many languages he spoke. Nevertheless he always presented 'lovely Fabergé things' such as snuff-boxes and parasol handles set in diamonds as prizes at tournaments. The first chef at the Club, founded in 1891, had been none other than the famous César Ritz. Originally the Club building had been the hunting lodge of the castle at Napoule, and Michael had added spacious stables for visitors' carriages. He also laid foundation stones here and there at Cannes, and was a natural choice to inspect the British fleet when it arrived at Villefranche. He founded the Russian church and even deigned to carry round the plate himself. He was a musician of sorts and composed songs, the most notable being the 'Influenza March'. His sense of humour was unpredictable and clumsy, as for instance at the Café de Paris at Monte Carlo when he spread a napkin on an enormous and delicious-looking soufflé and sat on it.

Sophie Torby's type of humour was quite different, needless to say; more 'refined'. 'Gracious', 'delightful', 'unfailingly kind-hearted' were the epithets generally used when describing her. The Battle of Flowers would not be the same, they said, without her presence.

In 1903 old Grand Duke Michael Nikolaievich had a stroke, and had to be moved to Cannes. 'A helpless giant', he travelled by special train with six coaches, never allowed to exceed more than 24 m.p.h., thus disrupting the entire railway system of Central Europe. At Cannes he quickly 'fell a victim' to the charm of his daughter-in-law Sophie and her children, who in turn loved

---

* It was the father of Baron de Stoeckl who negotiated the sale of Alaska to the United States in 1867, for $7,200,000.

Grandpa with his funny long white beard. Zia was his favourite. He wrote once to Sophie: 'She is délicieuse, si jolie et si naturelle. In general you have charming children, you have brought them up admirably. Votre devoué beau père.'

Everyone agreed that Zia and Nada were growing up into beauties, but they were different both in looks and character. Zia was blonde, blue-eyed; Nada dark-haired, dark-eyed. Zia was more feminine, looking like her Nassau ancestors, with a great sense of fashion in dress. Nada was a tomboy, a tease, 'une vraie Caucasienne', with a skin 'd'une blancheur éblouissante'. Their father also liked Zia best, and would bring her expensive presents – but none, cruelly, for Nada, which made her cry. He would say: 'Quelle idée a le bon Dieu de créer les brunes, alors que les blondes sont si ravissantes?' Baroness de Stoeckl's daughter Zoia was one of their best friends; they also saw a great deal of the two (somewhat older) daughters of their Aunt Stassie, Grand Duchess of Mecklenburg-Schwerin: Cécile, who was to marry the Crown Prince of Germany ('Little Willie') and Alexandrine, or Adini, who became Queen of Denmark. The Grand Duke Alexanders also came frequently to Cannes. They had seven children, the eldest, Irina, marrying Prince Felix Yusupov, who murdered Rasputin.

Judging from a letter to Zia from her mother, it does not seem all that surprising that the girls were not allowed to accept the Wernhers' invitation at North Berwick. She was writing from Gateacre Grange, near Liverpool.

> Your Papa allows you to accept Mrs Hall Walkers' invitation to Gateacre, *as a special case.* You are to travel in your green dresses from Newcastle and your motor bonnets and your green capes. Then you must bring your blue and black striped summer dresses to wear for teatime, and dinner dresses like at Keele . . . You will lunch with us and probably dine upstairs.

There were so many house parties. 'Papa shot three stags today,' Sophie wrote to Zia whilst staying with the Siggy Neumanns at Invercauld. Everywhere Sophie took with her an enormous autograph book, into which photographs of the grand houses were pasted, surrounded by the signatures of fellow guests. They went to Eaton Hall with the Westminsters, Cliveden with the Astors, Rufford Abbey, Stoke Rochford, Chatsworth, Tranby Croft, Ruthven Castle, and on the Continent to Fürstenstein with the Plesses, Ludwigslust, Trachtenberg, Ulrichshausen. But generally the children did not accompany their parents on these visits.

The arrival of Grand Duke Nicholas at Cannes meant that his other four sons also bought or rented houses there. They were nicknamed by fellow Romanovs the Caucasians or the Mikhailovichi. Other cousins – Cyril, Constantine, Dmitri – were familiar figures there. These Grand Dukes considered themselves a race apart, and dominated the gaming tables at Monte Carlo. At the Club Nautique six bottles of vodka were always kept waiting for them on ice. There were plenty of rows and scandals. 'Your uncle Serge is playing tricks on everybody as usual,' Sophie wrote to Zia, 'and annoys your Papa very much, especially about his hair [no longer dyed].' Daisy Pless was often at Villa Kazbeck, and in her diary she described a family dinner where the food was very badly cooked. Grand Duke George 'shouted and yelled' at his sister Stassie, who went very red in the face and had to apologize to Daisy; and Daisy in turn felt constrained to soothe Michael by saying that she far preferred him to his brother George. Later, however, she told her diary: 'Entre nous Michael himself, poor dear, is not anything particular, mais contre son frère there is no comparison.' Of all the brothers she really liked Grand Duke Alexander best.

Edward VII as Prince of Wales stayed at Villa Kazbeck, and it was there that he first met Mrs Keppel, with the well-known consequences. Another visitor was the Empress Eugénie, 'looking ethereal in black', accompanied by the Comtesse de Portalès, known in Cannes as La Cocottedette.

In that exotic atmosphere scandals abounded, and few more than about Stassie, the Grand Duchess of Mecklenburg-Schwerin. When she became pregnant by one of her staff, she pretended that the bulge was due to a tumour. 'Of course,' said Countess Torby, 'we *all* knew the truth. In due course a sweet little bouncing baby boy was seen playing at her villa.' (The boy grew up to become a wine merchant in Paris and was accepted as a relation by the descendants of the Grand Duke Michaels.)

Various brief letters from Edward VII to 'my dear Michi' exist, and are practically illegible, though usually sending love to the 'Circus Torby'. Sophie was always one of his favourites, and at the Coronation she was put in a special box at the Abbey with Mrs Keppel, Daisy Pless and Lady Randolph Churchill. Every year the Grand Duke Michaels stayed at Windsor or Sandringham, and there were regular luncheons at Buckingham Palace.

In 1908 Michael published a novel, entitled *Never Say Die*, the theme being a morganatic marriage. His rather surprising preface ran as follows:

Belonging, as I do, to the Imperial Blood, and being a member of one of the reigning houses, I should like to prove to the world how wrong it is in thinking – as the majority of mankind is apt to do – that we are the happiest beings on this earth. There is no doubt that we are well situated, but is wealth the only happiness in the world? Take also into consideration the many official duties belonging to our position, and how much more we are exposed to public opinion than humbler mortals. Which is the greatest happiness in this world? Surely love for a woman – the choice of our future wife and family life. And even in this we have not the facilities of private individuals. We have less choice, and there is often the question of religion. So it will be easily understood what a terrible lottery marriage in our position is, and why, consequently, there are so few happy unions.

The real reason for writing this novel was his resentment at still not being allowed back in Russia. Edward VII had done his best to get Tsar Nicholas to relent, but to no avail.

The Grand Duke Michaels were favourite patrons of Carl Fabergé. It is recorded that one of the prizes given at the Cannes Golf Club was an entire Fabergé tea set of red enamel and gold.

Fabergé objects were also bought by the Wernhers, but Birdie's taste seems to have been for the heavier green nephrite rather than for the familiar delicate sprays of flowers or cloisonné and enamelled snuff-boxes, or even for the famous Easter eggs. When Fabergé's first representative arrived from Moscow in 1902, Julius was invited to inspect the 'large and interesting assortment of objets d'art and Russian jewelry, suitable for Christmas presents'. By 1906 the London branch of Fabergé was at 48 Dover Street, but one of his best markets was of course at Cannes. On 16 May 1906 Sophie Torby wrote to Zia:

> I was fearfully busy before leaving Cannes and missed your help, especially for the Fabergé things very much. Buy the big light amethyst, which I have marked [on a catalogue]. If price of cross and earrings entirely mounted is £10 you can order them, although it is rather expensive.

Sophie, a lover of rubies, of which she had 'many ropes' and a tiara, was also a great collector of miniature Fabergé elephants. She also wore ruby and diamond elephant brooches, and had an elephant on her book-plate (with these words underneath: 'Cet animal est fort méchant. Quand on l'attaque il se défend'). Comic pictures of elephants adorned her boudoirs at Villa Kazbeck and Keele, some in ruby-studded frames. Writing about her pleasure in these beasts, Fabergé's London partner, H. C. Bainbridge, said with some truth: 'That is the most significant thing I can say about her, because it implies a quiet, undisturbed and jolly humour.'

He also rightly said in his book that the Grand Duke Michaels had 'forged for themselves an unique place in Edwardian Society'. They were considered by the British to be exotic, and their movements would be reported in *The Times*. And in South of France newspapers and journals, their arrival at Cannes would automatically merit a headline. Zia's beauty was often remarked on, and even at the age of sixteen she was regarded as a leader of fashion. She consulted a clairvoyant at Cannes, who predicted that she would 'marry great wealth'.

15

A Couple of Scrapes

In January 1908 Birdie was enjoying the Cannes season (selfishly, Florrie Phillips thought) while her husband was 'stuck' in the Grand Hotel in the Boulevard des Capucines in Paris because of L'Affaire Lemoine.

Before Beit's death it had been settled that Lemoine should be paid for setting up a plant for making his artificial diamonds in, of all places, a remote spot in the High Pyrenees. Julius himself had found the money, and he did pay out some very large sums. Even so he remained uneasy. A price for the formula had yet to be agreed, and this formula had been placed in a sealed envelope in a London bank. Lemoine was insisting on a royalty. Julius was also worrying about what would happen when the time came to market those diamonds; a distinction ought to be made as with real and cultured pearls. Lemoine of course disagreed. This was to be about the only occasion in his life when Julius was fooled – and it proved a painful experience. The irony was that in effect he was carrying the burden of Beit's mistake.

The formidable Francis Oats, who was to become Chairman of De Beers in 1908, was now called in. On 14 December 1906 Julius wrote to Phillips that he had visited Lemoine in Paris with Oats, Breitmeyer and another, again secretly. Only Dr Jameson was in the know. The first test failed, but in the second there was a small result. 'My companions were most suspicious and I am not free of doubt, although we watched like the devil and could not detect foul play . . . It is quite possible that we have been done which would be a blessing in spite of the loss.'

The four men, 'kings of the diamond world', had been seated before the huge glowing furnace while Lemoine had left the room. Lemoine ludicrously returned stark naked, explaining that he did not wish them to suspect any conjuring tricks. Then, like a medieval alchemist, he proceeded to pour some mysterious substances into a crucible, stirring them together. At the second test, after withdrawing the crucible from the fire – abracadabra – he removed some tiny diamonds. Oats demanded yet another repeat. Lemoine obliged and produced no fewer than thirty gem diamonds. Oats remained scornful and thought the diamonds too similar in colour and shape to those found in the Jagersfontein Mine near Kimberley. Nevertheless Julius, backed by Breitmeyer, insisted on continuing with his payments, bringing the total to a staggering £64,000. In return he at least received an option to buy the secret formula.

The completion of Lemoine's diamond factory in the High Pyrenees had been delayed again and yet again, and Julius had become increasingly irritated. But when he heard that a rival banker named Jackson had actually visited the Paris forge, he could stand it no longer and decided to prosecute. Lemoine was arrested on 11 December 1907.

The trial began on 9 January. Lemoine's lawyer was Maître Labori, who had defended Dreyfus. This was enough to make L'Affaire Lemoine a matter of worldwide interest; and the spectacle of such a dignified old financier, one of the greatest names in the business, with his gold pince-nez and butterfly collar, being confronted by such an obvious scamp delighted the French press. Julius himself admitted that sometimes in court there were 'roars of laughter', and he did not like it. The magistrate demanded that the secret formula for making artificial diamonds should be extracted from the London bank where it had been placed under seal, but this was opposed by Labori. Julius in turn refused to agree that Lemoine should be let out on bail. Then it was revealed that Jackson on his visit to the forge had been accompanied by the famous British industrialist and arms manufacturer Lord Armstrong. The next sensation was when two jewellers testified that they had actually sold a number of uncut diamonds to Lemoine's wife. Lemoine retorted that they had been for study and comparative purposes.

Writing to Phillips, Julius said that the 'Lemoine business' was occupying his time to the exclusion of almost all else. 'It seems in the general interest to protract matters and I have a strong suspicion that it suits my lawyers. The rottenness in France is really terrible . . . Lemoine's system now is to introduce side issues having nothing to do with his swindles.' It was also becoming clear that Lemoine had deliberately planned to force down the value of De Beers shares, which he would have then bought up and afterwards sold at a nice profit when the market recovered. The more Julius came in for ridicule, the more he pressed on relentlessly with the prosecution. From the very beginning he had been determined to treat the matter as his own personal liability, and not to involve De Beers, however much Lemoine attempted to implicate them.

L'Affaire Lemoine soon earned its place in literary history. For it caught the imagination of Marcel Proust, who proceeded to publish a series of hilarious parodies of the trial for *Le Figaro* in the styles of Balzac, Flaubert, Edmond de Goncourt, Sainte-Beuve, Renan and others. As his biographer George Painter has said, these pastiches are among the funniest and at the same time most profound in the French language. Take for example this paragraph from the Balzac piece, best quoted in its original Proustian French:

> Bien plus, l'homme qui était alors à la tête de la plus colossale affaire de diamants de l'Angleterre s'appelait Werner [sic], Julius Werner, Werner! ce nom ne vous semble-t-il pas évoquer bizarrement le moyen âge? Rien qu'à l'entendre, ne voyez-vous pas déjà le docteur Faust, penché sur ses creusets, avec ou sans Marguerite? N'implique-t-il pas l'idée de la pierre philosophale? Werner! Julius! Werner! Changez deux lettres et vous avez Werther. Werther est de Goethe.

Faust, the philosopher's stone, Goethe. It was brilliant stuff. Proust also wrote 'à la manière de' Ruskin (in this case best in

English): 'Perhaps you will ask: "How would Giotto have represented L'Affaire Lemoine? It does not seem to me that he would have chosen *this* subject")* and Chateaubriand: 'Il y avait alors à Paris un pauvre diable du nom de Lemoine qui pensait avoir découvert la fabrication du diamant.'

Needless to say, it transpired that Francis Oats had been absolutely right about the stones looking like ones obtained from the Jagersfontein Mine. That was actually where they had come from. The French papers made hay with this revelation. So all those thousands of francs had been paid out for diamonds from Julius Wernher's own mine!

Still the London bank refused to hand over the sealed envelope containing the formula. Still Julius refused to consent to Lemoine's release.

On 29 March he told Birdie that he was having to return to London in order to tackle the bank. He was nervous that while he was away Lemoine might be let out, 'which would be a blow – a moral defeat for me after all these months of fight'. He went on: 'There are extraordinary influences at play, subterranean and uncontrollable, and I am frightfully disgusted with the whole affair which may drag out for months.' He longed to join her. 'Don't be angry – I am the sufferer.'

Considering the precarious state of his health, it does seem surprising that Birdie had not been with him during those trying weeks at the Grand Hotel. Instead Derrick had been there for some of the time. 'He never wanted to leave my side although I offered it when we had our business talks, but he said he was interested. With all his weakness he is a dear lovable boy.' This, unfortunately, was not to be Julius's opinion of his eldest son a few months later.

On 2 April Julius wrote again to Birdie. Just as he had feared, Lemoine had been let out on bail. 'The papers say he wants to pay me an early visit!' Again there were obstructions over getting hold of the formula.

---

* This piece is headed (again translated): 'The blessing of the wild boar. A study of the frescoes of Giotto representing L'Affaire Lemoine for young students at Corpus Christi'.

Meanwhile Lemoine's envelope had at last been released to the French court and Julius hastened back to Paris, confessing to Phillips that he felt 'under constant strain'. When the magistrate began to read the formula out loud, as the *Times* correspondent reported, the audience began to look at one another in amazement. 'The formula was nothing more than a clumsily compiled statement of certain facts of elementary chemistry, such as one taught to children in primary schools. As the reading advanced, the astonishment turned to stupefaction.'

Julius, likewise stupefied, at last was able to make a joke: 'He forgot to say how to cool the crucible.' Nevertheless the magistrate doggedly insisted that an experiment should be carried out according to the instructions in the envelope. So more time was wasted.

The next development was hardly surprising. Lemoine jumped bail, having sold his furniture, and took with him a huge quantity of luggage. He went to Budapest, then to Constantinople, then to Sofia. As Julius said, it was not an unhappy ending, indeed an admission of guilt, though he would have preferred to have him condemned after a proper trial, which would have 'cleared up many false insinuations'. But at least he felt he had a certain peace of mind. Lemoine's trial *in absentia* was to be a formality, mercifully brief, with Julius represented by Counsel.

Lord Rothschild neatly summed up the situation in a letter to a colleague:

People talk a great deal about Sir Julius Wernher, and his friends say that he was anxious to protect the public from being taken in by Lemoine, as he was informed that this unscrupulous character was making use of his name to obtain fresh victims. Everyone has a very high opinion of Wernher's honesty but in this case to say the least he displayed a want of judgement which in ordinary cases might have led to serious misunderstanding, but we are bound to say that here everyone recognizes that whatever fault was committed must be attributed to Wernher as a person and not to the De Beers board and representing the Company.

If Julius had been able to read this, he would have been man enough to accept the verdict on this ridiculous affair.

Julius continued collecting *objets d'art*, but the great days of picture buying seem to have been over. Whilst in Paris he had picked up some pieces, possibly Renaissance jewellery and medieval ivories. He was also being pursued by another collector, who wanted to buy his Watteau, for which he had originally paid £3,500. The offers were gradually increased to £12,000, but Julius was not interested.

In that same month, July 1908, he presided over the Annual General Meeting of Central Mining. His speech was long and mostly optimistic, in spite of the depression, and gave no indication of his having fallen off either in vigour or judgement. He insisted that he still had the fullest confidence in the abilities of the new Transvaal government, which was giving 'constant proofs of its solicitude for the welfare and advancement of the industry' and showing an 'earnest drive to forget and bury the bitterness of the past'.

All very different to pre-Jameson Raid days. Even the word *Uitlander* had been dropped from the vocabulary. 'The clouds have lifted.' It was indeed something of a paradox that the Boer generals had now come to realize that the success of the goldmines could help to win the peace. A certain amount of this spirit of reconciliation was chalked up to the efforts of Lionel Phillips, who later in the year could write to Julius that Botha 'treats me like a colleague of long standing instead of an ally of a day', and that Smuts, for all his 'perfect air of camaraderie and overdone boyish frankness', was even more 'pronouncedly a partner'.

Julius in his speech had to announce that in spite of these improvements, both political and financial, the capital of Central Mining would have to be reduced to £3,600,000 in 300,000 shares of £12 each, from the original £6,000,000. Wernher, Beit's participation in surplus profits, however, would be reduced from 25 to 20 per cent.

Julius also dwelt on the so-called Creswell Commission, whose object had been to find ways of increasing white labour in the mines, in view of the serious unemployment at Johannesburg.

Here his attitude towards the blacks appears ambiguous, and is possibly in part intended as a joke:

> The solution suggested is remarkably simple, namely, abolish Kaffir labour. In a country which contains six or seven times as many blacks as whites, the solution suggested is that you ignore the black man and leave him to his fate – for if you banish him from the mines the logical conclusion is that you remove him gradually from other occupations and substitute white men. It would no doubt be a happier condition if the natives did not exist; but to ignore them, to take away from them the chance to work and to improve their condition is surely no solution and in the end would lead to mischief.

In any case Creswell's recommendations were not accepted by the government.

Birdie was now in Carlsbad, taking a cure. Among her surviving papers there is a fat envelope marked 'Derrick's first scrape'. The first document in the packet is a letter, partly destroyed, from Julius, dated 4 August, which begins: 'I opened by mistake a letter to Derrick in which a bookmaker complains that Derrick has not settled his losses, and that a postdated cheque of his had been *dishonoured*. As D. had received his cheque of £180 [a princely monthly allowance] early in July it revealed a nice state of affairs.' Julius said he had written to Derrick, and had at last had a reply, 'full of the usual soft soap about love etc.', admitting that he had other debts and asking for his next month's allowance in advance. Julius had had to restrain himself. He felt 'more sad than angry'. 'He is no longer the Eton schoolboy – of course he promises Heaven and Earth to remain straight but he has no character, never had and I fear never will have. There are things on which I cannot compromise and what is more will not. I am afraid this is a sad letter but I feel hopeless and miserable.'

After Julius had written to the bookmaker asking for detailed accounts, it was revealed that Derrick had made no fewer than forty-six bets in ten days, twelve in one day alone. Derrick himself had admitted to quite different sums to his father, who had 'never been so disgusted about anything'.

Only the previous November, new Articles of Partnership had been drawn up for the firm of Wernher, Beit (i.e. the diamond business), to last for three years. In these Julius was to receive 65 per cent of the net profits, Lionel Phillips 15, Friedie Eckstein 12½, and Ludwig Breitmeyer 7½. Julius would make provision out of his own share to Charles Rube and another partner in Wernher, Beit, Ludwig Wagner. If he died during the term of partnership, it would be left to Lady Wernher and Derrick to decide on new conditions. If Derrick had reached the age of twenty-one (he was nineteen in June 1908), then he would be admitted as a partner in the firm.

Now all was in ashes. 'Fancy taking such a son into my business.' Derrick of course had been told of this arrangement.

The correspondence with Birdie continued all through August. There would be no Scotland this year. Derrick had even suggested leaving Oxford and 'going into business', a desperate cast to earn more income, as his father must have realized. Margie Pryce, Birdie's secretary-companion, noticing Julius's depression had shrewdly said: 'I am sure it is Derrick.' At this, Julius, 'this most controlled of men', had almost broken down, and the two of them had decided to keep the matter secret. But Julius suddenly became 'very seedy', and a letter to him from the bookmaker, asking for payment of Derrick's debts, was opened in his absence by a clerk at the office and given to Margie, who herself burst into tears.

Birdie sent Julius a telegram, recommending he should take a good dose of castor oil.

Next Julius asked Harold if Derrick owed him money. Harold confessed that he had lent him £25 at 5 per cent interest. 'What,' his father cried, 'are you not ashamed to ask usurer's interest from your brother?' But Derrick had suggested it. 'One thing after another leaks out.'

Birdie suggested that Derrick should join her at Carlsbad for a good talking to, but Julius asked her to wait. He did not want to 'cast him aside'. 'Greater sinners have turned into useful men. The boy has had most frightful temptations. I think the £1,000

Beit bequeathed to him has something to do with it.' He could not forget all the happiness Derrick had given him 'when he was pure'. 'I am so alone in many ways and his warmth and affection were a comfort.'

He begged Birdie not to 'crush all your love' for Derrick. 'You have a way of saying things which make reconciliations difficult.' Evidently he had been confiding in Sister Agnes, who had been counselling restraint. She had stayed at Luton Hoo and, castor oil notwithstanding, the tiny woman and the 'giant' had played forty-five holes of golf together.

Then back he wavered, as Derrick set out for Carlsbad. He would not trust him for a long while. 'Lord Rothschild had to kick his son [Walter, an eccentric, a famous naturalist] out of the firm for getting into the hands of money lenders.' 'If I had not been made a baronet I would refuse it now [Derrick being heir to the title]. I would certainly refuse anything more [a peerage] if offered.' The letters from Eton in 1904 had been in exactly the same vein – 'wish to spare me, God is called to witness etc.' 'He feels a pang at the moment – one day he hopes to get into the money and this is the principal thing with him.'

That Julius Wernher should ever have been unfaithful to his wife seems hardly conceivable. Yet the story persists in the family that in those difficult times he found consolation with Margie Pryce. Later Margie wrote a long letter to Birdie, hardly soothing, and referring to Derrick's lack of grit and manliness:

> I cannot forgive him for taking so much of the joy of life from his father . . . whose children were his all in all, and I always thought his love and tenderness with his big son so beautiful. How could Derrick destroy all that . . . As regards the other boys, I do not think they will ever give you uneasiness. Harold may be a little weak, but not in D's way, and as to Alex I think he will be the living image of his father in every way . . .

Evidently Julius had decided to give Derrick one more chance. In September he told Phillips that while the boy had a head for business there was a 'certain slackness' about him – a useful euphemism. 'He will scarcely ever be the worker we were and are. The young man of today says: "If I have sufficient money why should I work – or anyhow work hard?"' He added ominously: 'I am becoming less concerned with the maintenance of the firm than I used to be.'

So the situation about Derrick rested for a while, but Julius again became ill, with neuritis. This was alarming because he had determined to visit South Africa again in the winter, 'before I die', before the liquidation of the firm, and above all before the birth of the Union of South Africa, which he strongly supported as 'broadening the basis of the economy of the country and settling quarrels of the past'. During 1908 the National Convention had been meeting and was in the throes of producing a draft convention for the Union. There were also problems in the diamond industry, due to the continued hostility of the Premier people and to some extent to the discovery of diamond deposits in South West Africa. The London Diamond Syndicate was having to be restructured.

Many important new developments had taken place at Gold Reef City since Julius's last visit in 1904, and the pendulum was at last swinging back to prosperity. The years of stagnation had driven the mine-owners to consider economies and ways of reducing costs. Drills were replacing hammer boys. Electric power was gradually replacing steam – and this was to lead to the flotation in 1910 of the Victoria Falls Power Company. It was also the era of the great amalgamations, the first being the bringing together of 3,700 claims and six East Rand mining companies under the umbrella of East Rand Proprietary Mines. In 1909 the Corner House was to register Crown Mines Ltd, an amalgamation of a nearly similar amount of claims. Modderfontein B was also floated in 1908.

Nevertheless it has to be said that opportunities were being missed, and some of this has been blamed on Julius's being overburdened, on top of Lemoine and his personal troubles. At any rate Birdie came to the great decision that she must accompany her husband on the grand tour, which would also include Rhodesia.

The Wernhers sailed via Egypt round the east coast of Africa, once more in the *Kronprinz*, 'because of the German beer'. They stopped at Beira, and at Lourenço Marques were transported by rail in the luxurious De Beers Travelling Car (still in existence, custom-built in Chicago and with its own bathroom and wine-store) to Livingstone and the Victoria Falls. Everyone had been warned of Julius's shaky condition and told that he was not to be worried, but he turned out to be 'full of beans', enjoying boat trips on the Zambezi, the birds and the monkeys, and riding on a giant tortoise. They visited Rhodes's grave at Matopos, then went on to Kimberley, Birdie taking 'snaps' all the while, again in the De Beers Car. Adventures at Kimberley included their motor car's sticking in mud during a picnic and visiting the De Beers stud farm.

They arrived in Johannesburg on 10 February 1909, the day after the publication of the draft Constitution, and thus began their stay at the Carlton Hotel in an 'atmosphere of tense excitement and discussion'. Florence Phillips, out of loyalty to her husband, was waiting for them, but then she needed to convince Julius about rebuilding Villa Arcadia and subscribing to her Art Gallery scheme. The following week she was away to England, thankfully no doubt, via Cape Town, hoping to have achieved both objects. Even Julius saw her off at the station, amid a 'throng' of mining and non-mining personalities, including prac-tically the whole of Lord Milner's Kindergarten – the name given to the group of young Oxford intellectuals, such as John Buchan, Lionel Curtis and Geoffrey Dawson, editor of the *Star* and later of the London *Times*, whom he had brought out to help with reconstruction after the war.

Overshadowing the Wernhers' arrival was a recent disaster in the mines when many lives had been lost through flooding. Otherwise it was more like a State visit, and Birdie – who did not much like Johannesburg or its 'miles of cat's cradle mines' – knew what was expected of the wife of this 'giant among men', what with her fine Worth dresses and dazzling jewels. They were guests of honour at the opening by Lord Selborne, the High Com-missioner, of the Transvaal University at Pretoria, and at the opening of Parliament. For Julius there was a 'red carpet' trip to Basutoland, and visits to model farms and irrigation works. He was present when Lionel Phillips, in the Presidential Review at the Chamber of Mines, triumphantly announced that 'never in our history has the outlook been higher'.

On 15 March Birdie gave a 'scintillating' reception for 'hundreds of guests in spite of the depressing weather'. For the occasion she was dressed in a 'charming gown of heliotrope, fish net over white chiffon, adorned with imitation pansies, diamonds and pearls', plus a black picture hat with white ostrich feathers. The papers thought the party a 'welcome lead', 'bidding fair' to sweep aside the 'stigma of Johannesburg's mushroom growth'. Four days later she gave a ball, 'the most brilliant the Rand has ever witnessed', this time with osprey wings in her hair, and wearing a 'princess gown of old gold satin', a magnificent dog collar of pearls, 'many spectacular and varied jewels' including 'an abundance of sapphires', and a corsage 'in loose zouave effect'.

Julius went back to Kimberley for a De Beers board meeting, having first 'sneaked a look' at the dread Premier Mine, which was producing such an enormous quantity of diamonds that it was causing 'havoc and dismay' in the London Diamond Syndicate. Julius told the meeting that he thought the two companies were working under entirely different policies. De Beers was trying to increase prices, whereas Premier was working in the opposite direction. He considered that if Premier found their margin of profit very small they would listen to reason.

It was to be a long while before the invectives ceased between the firms and reason was listened to. By the end of 1909 the crisis was at any rate over for De Beers, and the Diamond Syndicate had been able to return to its original agreement made in 1906, purchasing £450,000 worth of De Beers diamonds a month.

Julius now launched the Alfred Beit Memorial Fund. The aim was to reach £50,000. He himself contributed £10,000, as did Otto Beit and the directors of De Beers. A bronze bust of Beit was to be erected, and the residue of the money would be for the aged and poor of the diamond fields.

Julius was also a little sad that during the years of depression 'my old friend' the Dutoitspan Mine had had to be closed. He felt quite sentimental, he said, about 'dear Kimberley'. Without the help of Birdie, who was staying on at Johannesburg, he now gave a costume ball. 'There has not been a big function since 1906 when the Duke of Connaught was here,' he told her, 'and we sweep in the lot, about 200. It will be a great treat . . . We have thunderstorms every day but the rain does not last long and just helps to keep the air pleasant. It is very quiet after the gay golden city and most of the streets are quite empty but I like dear old Kimby and have allowed plenty of time. I am not rushed but there is lots to discuss with dear old Oats and others.'

The last week of the Wernhers' tour was spent at Groote Schuur as guests of Dr Jameson. They travelled back to England with Phillips. 'Please do not talk too much "shop" with Sir Julius,' Florrie had written to her husband. She had rented Alfred Beit's old house in Park Lane from Otto. 'I did not realize what I was taking on when I asked for the house – unfurnished, dirty and neglected. A positive scandal!'

No sooner had Julius reached London than he had to be off to Paris, once again to face Lemoine, who had been arrested following his decision to return to France from Sofia. He had been spotted there by a friend of Proust who gleefully reported back the sighting to Paris.

'I am so sick of the whole business,' wrote Julius. 'The worst is that there may be the usual adjournments.' Adjournments there were indeed. Lemoine was 'as bold and audacious as usual, and several times got out of hand and was frightfully cheeky.' The case dragged on, until – after some 'beastly days in court' – Lemoine was at last found guilty and sentenced to six years' imprisonment. Then he appealed.

Meanwhile Proust continued with his pastiches, to the delight of his readers and secret distress of Julius.

Julius managed to rush back to London for a coming-out ball given by Florrie for her daughter Edie. 26 Park Lane had not only been tidied up but looked like a 'scene from the Arabian Nights'. All the greatest names in London Society were there, including of course Lady Wernher. 'Diamonds were the rage at the time,' remembered a fellow guest, 'but the wives of the two magnates from South Africa wore pearls.' Lionel's part in smoothing relations in the Transvaal had been widely appreciated, so a committee had been formed under Lord Lovat, and including

Julius, the Dukes of Abercorn and Westminster and Lord Milner, to organize a sumptuous dinner, men only, in Lionel's honour at the Savoy Hotel.

Lionel was also able to tell his wife that during the sea voyage there had been a happy conclusion to the 'Villa Arcadia question'. Julius had agreed that the firm should sell the property to the Phillipses for £10,000; in addition Lionel would receive an allowance of £2,500 a year 'in lieu of the free use of the house as heretofore'.

It had been decided to sell Tylney Hall, Florrie's 'mad extravagance', and many of her treasures would be transported to Africa. She had already engaged Herbert Baker, who as a young man had been employed by Rhodes for Groote Schuur, to design the new Arcadia in the style of a Mediterranean mansion. And very handsome it was to be. The cost was reckoned at £28,000.

Raising money for the art gallery was another great excitement. Few of the rich South African magnates escaped her blandishments, though the generally detested J. B. Robinson was disdained. She returned in November to Johannesburg with promises of more than £20,000 in addition to works of art. Julius gave her £5,000 and was to present four pictures: by Falguière, Géricault, and two by Millais (not his taste, but thought by him to be hers). Otto Beit was more generous and eclectic, and his contributions included works by Monet, Pissarro, Courbet, Boudin and Sisley.

On 20 July Julius received a letter from the Speaker of the House of Commons, James Lowther, about an ominous matter. Julius replied:

To be quite frank I was very glad to hear of your disapproval of our sons going frequently to race meetings as my son thinks me rather old fashioned & I was thankful to be able to add your great authority to mine in trying to persuade him to use his time to greater advantage at Oxford: but in making use of some reported remark of yours I was most concerned to impress upon my son, that naturally parents would throw some blame on him if it were known that he took his friends by the carload several times a week to the races, & to avoid temptation I have prohibited the car for the future.

He was quite agreeable, he continued, that Derrick should have some latitude, but he was most anxious that duty should come before pleasure. He deplored the lack of discipline at Oxford, and would like to see their sons 'united in some common enthusiasm or noble aim'.

Lowther invited him to lunch at Speaker's House, but Julius had to refuse because he again became ill, this time, it would seem, with heart trouble and thrombosis. Birdie took him to Carlsbad for a cure, and afterwards he went alone to a specialist at Wiesbaden. He was away two months, but enjoyed the proximity of his German relations and visited the Wernher *Stammhaus* (family home) and vineyards at Nierstein. The alarming-sounding treatment included 'widening of the lungs' and electric shocks. He worried a little about Harold's bad reports at Eton. The housemaster said the boy was lazy, but intelligent, he just didn't bother to *try*. Alex would also be going to Eton. 'I only hope Hacky will behave towards him.' Alex was so much cleverer, and Julius was afraid that Harold would be jealous. If Derrick was keen on racing, Harold's particular interest still seemed to be the theatre, and his father disapproved of his 'mania' for collecting photographs of music-hall actresses.

Julius was at Luton Hoo in December, with Harold and Alex, but Derrick was staying with the Lowthers. Birdie, feeling the cold, 'abandoned' the family for Cannes. She was there on the 18th when old Grand Duke Michael Nikolaievich died, and watched the procession before the funeral, all the younger Grand Dukes walking behind the horse-drawn catafalque, decorated with black ostrich feathers.

The coffin was afterwards taken by a Russian cruiser to Sevastopol, where it was met by the Grand Duke's great-nephew, the Tsar, with the Tsarina, who had cancelled their visit to Moscow. On arrival at St Petersburg the coffin was transported to the Fortress of St Peter and St Paul for a lying in state. Grand Duke Michael the younger had been granted permission to attend the second funeral ceremony, so at last his exile was over. His wife Countess Torby refused to accompany him, having sworn after the original insult over their marriage never to set foot in Russia again.

Extraordinary police precautions had been taken for the ceremony on 4 January 1910, which began during a thick snowstorm, followed by a thaw which, reported *The Times*, 'only made walking the more uncomfortable for the august personages who followed the coffin of the oldest member of the Russian Imperial family'.

The Emperor, the foreign Princes, and the Grand Dukes marched bareheaded, bravely enduring the inclemency of the weather. The Empress and the Grand Duchesses drove in their carriages. Enormous snowflakes swirled down the Nevsky Prospekt and across the Champs de Mars and the bridge over the Neva, and practically blotted out the gorgeous pageant. The spectators were few, both because of the snowstorm and because thousands of police and gendarmerie, not to speak of troops, occupied all the streets and approaches. The Diplomatic Corps assembled at the Fortress of St Peter and St Paul for the Requiem. Their Majesties returned to Tsarkoe Selo.

There were memorial services in Berlin and Paris. Sophie Torby and her three children attended the Requiem Mass in the church of the Russian Embassy.

16

An Era Ended

Time and again it had been remarked that Julius Wernher abhorred politics. So it caused a sensation in City circles during the General Election of 1910 when he descended from the heights to pronounce – like Lord Rothschild – in favour of tariff reform. He was also moved and heartened on hearing that Derrick had spoken publicly about the subject at Oxford. Even 'little Hacky' was 'mobilising support' at Eton.

Julius had greatly disliked Lloyd George's 'shrill' demagogic tone in his speeches, and had deplored his Budget, which had been thrown out by the House of Lords, which, however, he considered ought to be reformed on a non-hereditary basis. He was against Irish Home Rule, but in favour of female suffrage. As *The Scotsman* rightly predicted, in such a time of 'excitement and anger', his published remarks in addresses to shareholders came in for much abuse on public platforms ('Sir Ludwig Sauerkraut Bart of Sweatem Towers'). 'But abuse is not argument', and he had his captive audiences at the annual lord of the manor and agricultural association dinners at Luton.

Believing that the Conservative Unionists were 'more liberal than the Liberals', he sent £10,000 to their treasurer, Lord Farquhar. Perhaps by now an inkling of how Lord Farquhar was handling party funds, and how titles were thereby procured, had already reached Julius. For he made it clear that this money was 'sans condition'. 'I wish it to be distinctly understood that I ask for nothing and expect nothing.'

A small, unspecified operation prevented him from attending a meeting of the 'Charlottenburg', which since 1907 had become the Imperial College of Science and Technology, whose foundation stone in Prince Consort Road had been laid by the King on 9 July 1909. Julius was a member of the governing body. He presented £10,000 for a new Physical Laboratory for the extension of its metallurgical department, while Otto Beit founded the Beit Memorial Fellowship for Medical and Scientific Research. In the following year Julius was presented with the Gold Medal of the Institute.

His illness caused Birdie to cancel one of her Happy Evenings for poor children, and also some charity concerts at Bath House. She was now quietly beginning to build up an extremely valuable collection of English porcelain, a 'little hobby' begun when she bought two birds which she was told were valuable and thereupon continued because it was something that did not conflict with Julius's interests. It grew into an obsession, gathering momentum until in years to come it came to be recognized as one of the greatest collections of English porcelain after the Royal Collection and the Victoria and Albert Museum. But in the early days her knowledge was not very great, and her purse was the ruling factor. She was far more interested in music.

In March Julius had to face Lemoine again. His presence was not strictly necessary at the Appeal, but it suited him to be in Paris to see 'Porgi', de Camondo, Gunzburg and others. Lemoine was visibly startled to see him entering the court, but quickly recovered and began laughing insolently. Julius reported that his own 'performance' in giving evidence was a 'perfect triumph'. 'I did not notice any marked hostility on the part of the canailles à gauche.' Lemoine attempted unsuccessfully to interrupt him. Next day the 'gloves were off'. The conviction for fraud was upheld. In addition to the sentence of imprisonment Lemoine was banished from France for five years. Julius was awarded £400 in advance of damages to be paid later.

At last the absurd and exhausting saga was over, and diamond shares were booming again. Birdie joined Julius at the Hôtel du Palais, Biarritz, where Edward VII was recovering from the threat of bronchitis. Their friend Lord Farquhar intimated that the King would accept an invitation to dinner at the hotel, but on their submitting a proposed list of guests the grander names were disappointingly turned down, to wit, Lord and Lady Londesborough, Lady Irene Denison and Lord and Lady de Ramsey. The party consisted of twelve people, including the Siggy Neumanns and Mrs Keppel, who sat on the King's left, with Birdie on his right. There were ten courses and the wines included Veuve Clicquot 1900 and Porto Royal 1832.

The Neumanns' unabashed cultivation of Royalty had become a joke. Shortly after the Wernhers' departure Mrs Neumann gave another dinner for the King. Julius was amused to hear that it cost £240, and the flowers £60. Later, she was to declare that Queen Mary was 'too shy'. 'We must all bring her out.'*

Birdie went to Paris. But there was no peace of mind for Julius. It was Derrick again. Birdie had received disturbing news about the boy's being pursued by a French lawyer over unpaid debts. It seemed that Julius, back in London, had already been aware of some 'scheme to entrap D.', and had actually seen Derrick, who of course had 'denied everything'. He told Birdie he was calling on their lawyer, and asked her to suspend judgement meanwhile. Of course it was 'most peculiar if this smoke should arise without *some* substratum', and he had heard that Derrick 'had been to the Grafton ball and had supper with shady people'. 'I still hope that D. is not the consummate liar as he would be if the reports were true and which he denies with apparent frankness and energy.'

These shady people appear to have included the two sons of James Lowther the Speaker: Christopher and Arthur. Lowther was the son of the second Earl of Lonsdale and was to remain Speaker of the House of Commons until 1921, when he was created Viscount Ullswater. Christopher was aged twenty-three and Arthur twenty-one. Derrick would be twenty-one in June.

The whole sordid story emerged on 27 April. Julius had seen both the Speaker and Christopher, and had pieced together a kind of sequence of events. He told Birdie:

---

* Sigismund Neumann was made a baronet in 1912. Other Randlord baronets included or were to include George Albu (1912), Abe Bailey (1919), Friedrich Eckstein (1929), George Farrar (1911), Dr Leander Starr Jameson (1911), Frederick Philipson-Stow (1907), Lionel Phillips (1912), and J. B. Robinson (1908).

D. has put in circulation bills for £25,000, his name does not appear but the two Lowther boys endorsed them and are legally liable for these bills. £7,500 has been paid. D. bought £20,000 of jewellery from Lacloche [of Bond Street, head office in Paris] and pledged them for £8,000 to pay £7,500! No doubt through touts. I have the names of several . . . Old L. *knew* of D's irregular behaviour since Christmas. He wrote to Derrick asking to confess to me and got the reply he could not do it, it would come all right – I was ill and he could not bother me etc. etc.! There the matter remained and all old L. cared for was to save his sons and get their names off the bills and sacrifice D. Oh it is so sickening, these abominable lies and deceptions.

Christopher Lowther had said that the money had all gone in bets, gambling and extravagant living. A bill for £12,500 had been running for a considerable time and had renewals.

Margie had seen him writing this letter, 'almost in tears', she said later. He ended: 'I shall never believe again a word D says. I have to tear him out of my heart but it is very bitter. The Lemoine business is nothing to it for this pain will last for ever and you my dearest so proud of your boy at one time will suffer with me.'

If this were not enough he next heard that the bill of £7,500 which had been returned to the Speaker as paid had been fictitious and simply replaced by another with the same signatures. Such a 'perfect maze of lies' was now made far worse by the 'abominable tone' of Derrick's letter received on 28 April. Julius asked Margie ('so discreet and trustworthy, so devoted to us all') to copy it out for Birdie, and she in her covering letter said: 'Sir Julius has received a blow from which I am sure he will never recover. I should die if I had done anything like that and had to face either of you afterwards. I tremble for Sir Julius's heart. I do indeed.'

Derrick had written from Balliol:

My dear Father, I am afraid my affairs have of late become somewhat involved, and I shall have to ask you to make use of your cheque book to some considerable extent in order to put everything right. I have been exceedingly stupid, and wish I had applied to you before, but things go on and one waits and plays the idiot in a way which you, who have never been in trouble, cannot very well realize. I know that to you money qua amount does not matter, and that this part is quickly solved . . . Will you come down here for the night tomorrow, and we can talk it all over and I promise you there shall be no evasion or concealment . . . I wish to put everything before you myself, and your cheque book can in a short time put the financial part right . . . I am anxious to trust to your fairness and affection in this as in everything else. Your affectionate son.

Not surprisingly, Derrick was ordered to come to Bath House immediately. Meanwhile the Speaker wrote regretting the part his sons had played in the affair. 'There is nothing to be said in their defence except that neither of them received or has ever had any money for their own use or purposes . . . I also blame myself exceedingly for not having gone to you last Christmas . . . I begged and implored your son to inform you fully.' Derrick had told him that he had at last been able to withdraw sufficient money from a (non-existent) syndicate in which he had a large holding.

It became clear that Arthur had been the main accomplice, and Julius was convinced that he had kept some of the money back for himself. The interview with Derrick went off – in a sense – quietly, Derrick behaving in an 'absolutely callous' and supercilious manner, with an Etonian's air of superiority towards his bourgeois parents, and even attempting jokes, coolly asking for a cheque there and then to pay £4,000 to a bookmaker. Money was also owing to the jewellers Lacloche, in Paris (presumably the source of Birdie's 'disturbing rumours'). As for the jewels from Bond Street, Arthur admitted that he had removed half of them from the pawnbroker in Victoria Street and had given these to an accomplice to sell.

The distraught Speaker desperately tried to exonerate both his sons, and finally managed to recover the jewellery from Arthur. He hinted at slander, and then said that Arthur was owed £2,000 by Derrick. Infuriated by this letter, Julius went himself to the pawnbroker and redeemed the rest of the jewellery. He then managed to get Lacloche to take back the whole lot, though meanwhile he had to pay off Arthur's accomplice, who turned out to be one Luigi, of Romano's restaurant in the Strand.

Derrick was made to give up his latchkey to Bath House. 'He is perfectly gay and unconcerned'. But he did not know that his father had given instructions for his name to be removed entirely from his will.

Julius had also written privately to Phillips in Johannesburg, telling him how Derrick had been 'fleeced by bookmakers and moneylenders'.

> The disgusting and disgraceful part is the deceit and the lies . . . The influence of Oxford and Cambridge is baneful. I shall never send another boy there. The matter will have a bearing on my future decisions as I only hung on to the business on Derrick's account. I know you will feel for me. My wife and self are heart-broken and I really could not attend to anything else and cannot for the moment think of anything else. I know you will excuse apparent neglect.

Phillips wrote on this letter: 'Advised drastic punishment but not attitude that past cannot be wiped out.'

Four days later Julius was again writing that: 'The Lemoine business took it out of me considerably but this is a bigger blow . . . Now I have nothing to wait for and I feel extremely tired . . . One cannot detach one's mind, day or night, from this cruel blow and I decided to give it up.'

Those last words meant that he had irrevocably decided about the future of the partnership of Wernher, Beit and H. Eckstein & Company, and that both would be totally merged in the Central Mining and Investment Corporation.

He was writing on the eve of the birth of the Union of South Africa, and could hardly turn his mind to that great event. It took place on 31 May 1910, eight years to the day since the Peace of Vereeniging. Pretoria would be the executive capital, Cape Town the legislative capital and Bloemfontein the judicial capital. A triumph for the Boer negotiators of 1908–9, it was a union of peoples bitterly divided, yet caught in the legacy of history, a legacy of fear and suspicion: whites were faced with an ever-growing population of blacks, coloureds and Indians, biding their time. Whites of British origin were drawing together in opposing their Afrikaner co-citizens. The Afrikaners were themselves divided, some hankering after the days of the old republics.

On 6 May 1910 the King died suddenly – he had been dining quietly the night before with Sister Agnes. The Speaker therefore found the situation about his sons and Derrick all the more embarrassing, because of his official duties and attendances at the Lying in State. Having received another upsetting letter from Julius, he wrote to say that his wife was making herself ill with worry and was unable to rest. Julius agreed to see her.

Birdie, as she had done at Queen Victoria's funeral, arranged for some fifty people, including Prime Minister Asquith's children, to watch the funeral procession of Edward VII from the balcony of Bath House. The King's gun carriage was immediately followed by his fox terrier Caesar, and then by King George V, Kaiser William II of Germany, eight kings, and royal princes such as the Duke of Connaught and Grand Duke Michael.

After a visit from both Derrick and Arthur, Julius had told Derrick that he now had a complete list of debts, amounting to some £35,000, plus a promissory note in Arthur's name from Westbrooke the bookmakers. Of this, £14,000 was owed to Sir Charles Friswell, 'that unmitigated blackguard', and £10,000 to Eric Fitzwilliam, both friends of the Lowthers. All the bills had been endorsed by Arthur, some by Christopher as well.

The next blow was the revelation that Arthur had actually had the audacity to visit Harold at Eton, 'to try to put him against his father', and had even introduced him to a moneylender's tout. The Speaker attempted to soften this by saying that Arthur had only been trying to make peace between the brothers, and that while the conversation was going on, Hayden the 'tout' had pushed himself into the room – presumably hoping that Harold would influence Julius into paying off a debt.

On 22 June Julius had to leave for Germany. He could hardly believe it when Derrick turned up to see him off at the station. His heart 'melted' at once. 'There is such a lot of good stuff in that boy . . . He is quite prepared to put himself into my hands to travel or explore.'

On the very next day the Speaker wrote a letter with yet another shock, which reached Julius at Heidelberg. A writ had been served on Arthur for £10,000 in respect of the Westbrooke promissory note, and the case would come up on 14 October. Lowther said he proposed to put up a defence showing that the whole of this money was owed by Derrick, at that time under age, and that his son was 'not liable for one penny'. He objected when Julius in reply used the word 'threat' – 'an ugly word'. Actually Julius had thought it more like blackmail.

Julius demanded detailed accounts from Arthur. He told Birdie that he was prepared to settle the sum eventually, 'plus interest', but only if he was satisfied that the accounts were genuine. In a pathetic postscript he admitted that he did not want to give up all hope for Derrick. 'I cannot forget how much I loved him once, and what a joy he was to me, so I am loath to drop him entirely. Perhaps he will reform later on.'

He did pay up. A very long and angry draft letter to the Speaker exists and may not have been sent, beginning 'I have been rather expecting to hear from you on having paid the legal obligation of your sons a word of acknowledgement would not appear out of place', and bitterly attacking the 'astute and immaculate Arthur, the chief of the gang, who found my son a willing tool'. But perhaps an acknowledgement did arrive in time, for their subsequent exchange of letters was amicable enough. Julius told Phillips that he wanted to send Derrick round the world to get him out of 'this present rotten milieu'. 'His enormous body has in a sense outgrown his mind.'

Meanwhile Julius had had further thoughts about the firm's future. He would remain Chairman of the 'new amalgam concern' for a few years, and Phillips and Eckstein would be Vice-Chairmen. The liquidation would realize a 'handsome profit above book value' for the directors. On top of that they would receive profits on the shares and income from the 'always acceptable diamond business'.

Then came the surprise. Although remaining Chairman, he would not participate in income from diamonds. It would all go to the other directors, 'as I have enough and am only anxious that those who had co-operated so long and loyally with me and who in a great measure will do the work will also get the full benefit.'

He also made the following generous gesture to Phillips: 'Regarding the demands on your private purse I shall be very glad to assist you as there no doubt are many demands which could not be put down to the firm.' He had already refunded nearly £17,000 to Schumacher and Reyersbach for a debt they had incurred in 1905.

This was all conditional, in effect, on their not launching out into new ventures. The losses made by the Rhodes Fruit Farms, for instance, and all the work that these had entailed, had been a lesson to him. He would really like to devote himself to the Imperial College and the Beit Educational Trust, which was building up interest but 'not fulfilling the intentions of the donor'. He was referring chiefly to Alfred Beit's wish to found a University of Johannesburg at Frankenwald, and the stipulation in the will that the money (£200,000) would revert to the residuary estate if not used for such a purpose within ten years of his death, i.e., before 1916. Hitherto there had been virtually no movement towards creating such a university. And so was sown the seed of what was to become a heated and much argued over issue, long after Julius's own death.

Julius wrote to Phillips:

Otto recognizes that times have changed and he would be quite prepared if the thing was declined to rededicate it say for the creation of a South African University and in such a thing I would like to join in a liberal manner. I would feel to do some permanent good & it would be a nice finish to my more actif [*sic*] S. A. career . . . I think Otto would be prepared to do anything which meets a public want and wish. It is a pity that Natal just lately started a kind of university & voted £1,000,000. It was at one time thought that the University of South Africa would be built outside Capetown on ground left by Rhodes & I see in the *Times* that the idea is revived. I think Otto (who is away) talked to Smuts already as I often discussed my intention with him.

The only objection I see is that the Cape people are such a sleepy and lazy lot no doubt owing to the climate.

The problems about Derrick momentarily settled, Julius took Harold and Alex to Munich, while Birdie was on one of her cures. He was delighted that Alex had won three prizes at school – he would be going to Eton next term. Harold's latest report described him as an 'out and out performer', and added: 'He suffers by imagining he knows a subject before he has really grasped it.' This was a slight improvement on the previous report: 'Works hard but without enthusiasm.'

Julius was able to report from Munich that both boys were 'very dear and jolly', adding, enigmatically: 'I took your advice about Hacky and it makes all the difference.' Then three days later: 'Hacky is wonderfully cheerful & smiling from morning to night.' But Alex was sulky at times and disappointingly less interested in the sights of the city.

It was on this trip that Julius decided that Harold would be his main heir, and that he would be the one most suited to care for the art collection.

Before returning to Eton, Harold was invited to play tennis with Zia and Nada Torby at Ken Wood House, in Hampstead, into which the Grand Duke Michaels had recently moved. According to Baroness de Stoeckl, Michael had become even better off since his father's death, and certainly the superb Ken Wood (now Kenwood), with its famous decorations and furniture by Robert Adam, was more convenient for entertaining royal and imperial relatives when visiting in London, not to mention receiving George V, with whom Michael regularly lunched at Buckingham Palace, sometimes once a week. The house had been leased fully furnished from Lord Mansfield for twenty-one years from 1 March 1910 at a rent of £2,200 a year. 'Boy' would be going to Eton in 1911, but when Harold discovered this fact he was warned by the Grand Duke that it had to be kept absolutely secret.

About this period there was a rumour that Grand Duke Michael had a 'soft spot' for Nancy Astor. If at all true, it must have been an attraction of opposites. A little later he became embarrassingly 'keen' on Zia's great friend and contemporary, Vi de Trafford.

Elections had been held in South Africa. Lionel Phillips had at last managed to persuade Julius that it would be in the firm's best interests if he were to stand for the Unionist Party. The legislature being a thousand miles away, he could not just 'slip over in a motor car and interview ministers when an important issue emerged'. Moreover, the mining industry was still a 'closed book' to many people, who were frankly hostile to it. 'Mine-owner' was a designation usually used in an opprobrious sense, and this, he pointed out, was largely because a few men, 'individuals of poor repute', had amassed large fortunes and were completely devoid of any sense of public spirit. He was, in particular, irked by the remarks of General Hertzog, Cabinet Minister designate and Prime Minister in the 1920s, who lumped the firm together with 'English fortune-hunters with no interest in South Africa apart from getting rich.'

Phillips was elected, and found himself sitting on the Opposition Front Bench with Dr Jameson, the man who 'fifteen years earlier had led the Raid and wrecked the plans of the Reform Committee'. FitzPatrick had not only also been elected but had defeated the Prime Minister elect, General Botha, who thereupon had to seek another seat – confirming Julius Wernher's opinion that politics is a mad business.

Phillips remained in the House of Assembly until 1915, dividing his time with his Corner House business. Looking back on that experience in his book *Some Reminiscences*, he included a passage of which Julius would undoubtedly have approved:

Native questions, naturally of supreme importance, were usually approached [in the House of Assembly] in a spirit of gravity and judicial propriety. But some of the members, usually bearded denizens of the backveld, who still lived in the tradition of the slave days, harboured in their minds the nomenclature of the Transvaal Grondwet which classified the population as mannen, vrouwen, and schepsels (creatures), and would, upon occasions, let loose a flood of wrathful invective if they imagined the sable inhabitants

239

were not being kept in their proper place. Those who had kept in touch with the natives, since the discovery of diamonds signalised the era of industrial development, know what prodigious strides they have made. Watched from day to day, the change has crept along almost imperceptibly, like the sea encroaching upon a line of coast. Looked at over a gap of years, the subtle education has eaten consistently into the savage life and produced a veritable transformation. Where will it end? How will it end?

Otto Beit and Julius had now come to a definite decision about the idea of a national teaching and residential university in Cape Town. If Alfred Beit's legacy of £200,000 could be diverted to such a project, then both Otto and Julius would each be prepared to subscribe another £200,000. They would also increase the total by £100,000 if it were found that £500,000 would be needed. 'The idea of a South African University at Groote Schuur appeals to me very much on sentimental and practical grounds,' Julius wrote to Smuts. He also hoped that Herbert Baker and Edwin Lutyens would be the architects, and that Smuts would support him on this. Later that year De Beers volunteered to add £25,000.

Controversy immediately arose, and it was thought that the existing South African College at Cape Town could form the nucleus. The Victoria College at Stellenbosch, 'the Mecca of the Dutch Reformed Church', had recently received £25,000 from De Beers for a physics laboratory, but it was fearful of losing its identity. And there were other problems, before a Bill accepting these proposals could be considered by the House of Assembly. But the great row lay some years ahead, when Johannesburg came to the conclusion that it did need a university after all and had been cheated of Alfred Beit's bequest.

All these decisions by Julius about the disposal of such huge sums of private capital had been made without referring to Birdie, who was only told about them later.

Notwithstanding the arguments, the Duke of Connaught duly laid a memorial stone for a proposed University Hall★ at the

---

★ Now the Archives building. Julius donated £500 towards it, Otto Beit £100, the Union government £15,000, and Sir Donald Currie £25,000, among others.

Cape, and Baker and Lutyens were asked to put up plans for the main buildings. Lutyens was also to design both Florrie Phillips's art gallery at Johannesburg, for which an impressive collection of paintings had been assembled, and the Rand Regiments Memorial in Eckstein Park, Otto and Julius having each subscribed £1,000 to the latter and the Phillipses £500. The Duke also laid a foundation stone for the Memorial and formally opened the temporarily housed exhibition of paintings. Hugh Lane was the first director of the art gallery, followed shortly afterwards by Robbie Ross, the friend of Oscar Wilde.

The whole drama about Derrick reared up again during October and November. Julius had had to harden himself. He realized now that he and Birdie had brought someone mentally 'unbalanced' into the world. There were also problems with Birdie's nephew Jim Marc, who was turning into a scapegrace, and Birdie was slightly on the defensive about the Mankiewicz 'blood'. Her younger brother Franz was charming, a bachelor, much loved, but, in Julius's view, feckless and he should have helped in influencing Derrick. Her elder brother George had died the year before and had led a notoriously double life, leaving a widow, Emily, née Ranger, of whom Birdie had in any case always disapproved – and this too had caused a coolness between the families.

Derrick's behaviour was typical of a young man being given too much money too soon. Even when he was at Eton his father had put a large number of De Beers shares in his name: all of which Derrick had sold when he came of age. He was obsessed with motor cars. Photographs of him in his goggles inevitably remind one of an outsize Mr Toad.

Birdie had suggested that Julius should buy Derrick a partnership somewhere. It was of course an absurd suggestion. As Julius said, the boy couldn't 'jump in without some apprenticeship and experience'. In any case in all business matters Derrick was a 'perfect mug and victim'. On 16 October Julius had a communication from a banker 'of a sort' in Paris who had been offered 'acceptances by D.' – and Derrick once again had denied their existence. 'The only thing is to get him away somehow.'

It seems from inferences in the correspondence that Derrick

was in the 'clutches' of a baron in Paris called Grundherr, also known to Julius and Birdie. This man appeared to be acting as a kind of double agent, reporting back on Derrick's activities, and at the same time obviously hoping to get money out of Julius. A dubious character named Ginger also cropped up in letters.

Julius arrived in Paris at the Grand Hôtel to find that Derrick had left there without paying the bill. Derrick had been spotted at the races, along with the 'tout' Hayden. He had moved to the Hôtel Meurice, and once again left without paying. 'It is awful to think of the boy swindling wherever he goes.' Julius now put notices in *The Times* and *The Telegraph* and in the Paris and Monte Carlo papers to the effect that he was not responsible for his son's debts. 'Such a disgrace!' And Derrick actually had the effrontery to return to the Meurice, saying that he would be going on to London in a day or two and would send the money from there. 'He dined in a *tweed* suit with the Baron and had champagne,' Julius told Birdie. 'I am now arranging with the Chief of Police to have him watched.' Julius had managed to stop a loan of 500,000 francs, and another of 10,000 marks in Germany.

In a peculiar way Julius was almost enjoying himself. He felt fit and slept well. But Birdie said she was suffering from insomnia. He had heard that Derrick had said that his father always said he would not pay up but would do so in the end. Derrick had moved into the Savoy in London with the Baron, who had claimed that he was 'fascinated' by him. At least he had broken with Hayden, who had 'a sort of mistress called Mrs Chaplin', one of Derrick's friends. Hayden had wanted Derrick to buy a house where all three could live together. Then came another letter from Paris. As Julius said, it was Lacloche all over again.

Harold of course had been told something of what had happened. He had written to his mother from Eton: 'We are both very surprised about D. especially as I have just had a delightful letter from him in Paris saying how he is enjoying himself'; and to his father: 'I read the notice in the *Telegraph*, though I was very upset about it, I cannot but think it was the only thing to be done.' His handwriting was surprisingly mature and self-assured. Now he wrote to Birdie:

I am so furious with D. that I can hardly control my
feelings. I think he is the wickedest person I know and fancy
defying the law again when he knows what the
consequences must be. It makes me absolutely sick to think
of it and I think it is really too tragic that you and Father
should be thus rewarded for all your kindness to him. Pres
[his uncle Franz] could hardly speak of D. he was so
disgusted.

At last Julius had found a friend in the Colonial Service called
McGillivray who would be willing to take Derrick as his assistant
in the Sudan for some months. This would bring him into contact
with 'serious people', and it would be an interesting job, as
negotiations were under way with Egypt about a new constitution
for the Sudan. Later there would be a shooting expedition in East
Africa.

It was left to Birdie to persuade Derrick, who promptly agreed
– to his parents' surprise and relief. By early December therefore
he was in Cairo, and on his way to Zaidal. 'I hope the desert will
purify him,' Julius wrote to Phillips, 'as it did in the days of the
Bible.'

Arthur Lowther had been sent to Ceylon. Now recriminations
flared up again between the Speaker and Julius, furious again, this
time about Lowther's refusal to pay his solicitor's legal costs.
Lowther had long ago said that he could not afford to pay more
than £2,000 to 'save my sons from bankruptcy', and he still
insisted that Derrick owed Arthur £2,000. He took exception to
Julius's remarks about moral responsibilities. 'Before my son
went to Oxford he had never been on a racecourse or made a bet.
Can you say the same of Derrick? I have heard of certain events
at Eton which are not compatible with such a contention.' It was
Derrick who 'by means of his motor car had carried Arthur off to
the racecourse and introduced him to various betting men of
undesirable reputation. Derrick had made use of Arthur, who was
then of age, to raise sums of money and persuaded him 'by untrue
statements as to his future income and prospects to lend his name
and figure as a principal when, in truth, he was little more than a
cat's paw.'

The correspondence seems to have ended with a mutual agreement to discontinue questions of moral responsibility. Although Lowther considered that Julius had been unnecessarily prolonging the involvement of lawyers, he agreed to pay his solicitor's fee, nearly £2,000, and accepted that Derrick's indebtedness to Arthur should be reduced by £700.

Thus it was that because of the stupidity of one spoilt young man the future of a great financial house was decided. Julius made his formal announcement of the absorption of Wernher, Beit and Eckstein's into Central Mining at an Extraordinary General Meeting held on 22 December 1910. A. P. Cartwright in his books gives some financial details. Central Mining's capital was increased from £3,600,000 to £5,100,000 by the creation of 125,000 new shares at a nominal value of £12 each, actual value £15 5s. The agreed valuation of the assets of Wernher, Beit and Eckstein's was £1,154,109 9s. 11d., for which the partners received 75,679 shares. They were also paid £85,522 as their participation in surplus profits. Shares were also issued to Otto Beit and Max Michaelis for interests valued at some £70,000. The total number of shares issued was 80,278. Julius kept a credit balance of £180,000 in Johannesburg, on which he received interest.

Central Mining now owned all the assets of the partnership, but the former partners were in control of Central Mining. Other shareholders did at least have the advantage of participating in the profits of Wernher, Beit, apart from the diamond business. On the day of the meeting the market value of the shares of all the twenty-two Transvaal mining companies to be controlled by Central Mining was given as £69,522,078. Rand Mines and Crown Mines were easily the most valuable, at £15,429,248 and £15,276,722 respectively, followed by Robinson G.M.C. at £5,225,000 and City Deep at £5,156,250. There was also a large holding in East Rand Proprietary Mines, which had an enormous capital value.

As Cartwright says, the group could well have claimed to be the fifth province of South Africa, its budget being bigger than that of Natal or the Orange Free State. It still had interests in De Beers and the Diamond Syndicate, its mining organization was the biggest industry in the country, and it was also the largest landowner. It had big shareholdings in banks and newspapers, and controlled the Braamfontein Company, which was laying out white suburbs. There were interests in Natal coalmines, tramways, cement works, and many others in foreign countries, including as a reserve £3 million in British gilt-edged stocks.

Julius of course was Chairman and Phillips and Eckstein Vice-Chairmen, though it was anticipated that Eckstein might before long retire. The other fortunate directors were Schumacher, who ran the business while Phillips was in Cape Town, Reyersbach, Rube and Wagner, and for the French Rouliot, Octave Homberg, the Vicomte de Breteuil and Count Isaac de Camondo (who soon dropped out). Samuel Evans was not a director but Chairman and Managing Director of Crown Mines.

By 1913 the Rand produced 40 per cent of the world's gold. It used to be said that Johannesburg was fathered by gold and mothered by money.

Julius had not been well after Christmas, with 'rather severe intestinal catarrh'. He was breathing heavily and noticeably walked more slowly. In spite of this he insisted that their annual ball should be held on 11 January 1911, with the servants' ball afterwards. Nada and Boy Torby came to stay. Then Birdie took him to San Remo, where he was taken very ill with an agonizing inflammation of the bladder and a high temperature. He was left exceedingly weak and had to remain at San Remo for two months. Inevitably there were rumours of cancer. Countess Torby at Cannes had recommended the surgeon who was attending him.

In her letter of 11 March 1911 to Lionel Phillips Birdie wrote:

It is all cruelly disappointing and I feel very heartbroken at the way his health is breaking up. He hardly goes 3 months without an illness now and each time something fresh which is worrying.

There is *no doubt* the fearful shock and bitter disappointment Derrick caused him a year ago and the subsequent humiliations and mortifications so bitter to his proud spirit which have been the consequence, have undermined his health permanently and aged him beyond his years.

She said that Derrick was giving 'absolute satisfaction' in the Sudan, but she and her husband could hardly share Mr McGillivray's hopeful views about his future. They knew he still kept racehorses on borrowed money. 'His letters to *me* show no change of ideas or spirit in the essential things and as long as he considers borrowing money when you have no chance of repaying it, so long we can see no improvement or reform . . . I really look on him as "morally insane" in these matters.'

There was not much improvement in his health when Julius returned to England. In June he threw open Luton Hoo park for the coronation of George V, and presented his manorial rights to the town of Luton, 'for the rightful benefit of its inhabitants'. Harold, who had been with him, wrote to his mother: 'I was awfully worried about Father, he does try so hard to be cheerful when one is in the room & it is only when there is a silence that one notices how depressed he really is. I think it is too tragic for words.' Harold had to preside at a reception in the grounds for the Bedfordshire Agricultural Society.

Ever since his last visit to Johannesburg, Julius had been worrying about the mortality and diseases among black mine-workers, resulting in phthisis, scurvy, pneumonia, typhoid and dysentery – also occurring, to a lesser extent, among the whites. He had had much correspondence with Samuel Evans about this. Early in 1911 he wrote to the managers at Central Mining urging them to induce the Chamber of Mines to press for a medical research institute at Johannesburg, subject to the government providing the necessary ground, and proposing that the industry and the government should each bear half the cost of running this institution.

A foundation stone for the medical research institute building, designed by Sir Herbert Baker, was duly laid in 1912.

Julius could no longer go to the office. Papers would be sent to Bath House for him to sign. He was nearly always in pain, but until the autumn kept up his correspondence with Phillips and Schumacher.

In 1908 Lord Curzon had written to Julius, thanking him for a 'noble donation' to Oxford University. Julius had also promised to add 5 per cent to any other private donation up to £2,500. He also sent a further sum on 30 October 1911. Curzon then said how grieved he was to hear of Julius's disappointment in his son. He had spoken to the Master of Balliol, who had declined to believe it.

When Derrick returned from the Sudan he must have gone back to his old habits. On 12 December 1911 a petition was filed for his bankruptcy at the High Court. His address was given as 73 St James's St, Westminster. The petition was to be heard on 18 January, but was delayed when he disappeared to Paris. In the Johannesburg *Star* it was said that this 'fly in the amber' of the Wernher family was being 'publicly discussed with painful freedom'. Derrick's liabilities were £81,865 and assets £225.

By then Julius was too weak to deal in any business. He went to Luton Hoo but asked to be taken back to Bath House to die.

On 31 December 1911 a circular letter announced the voluntary liquidation of Wernher, Beit and Company. Its diamond business, then amounting to 45 per cent of the Syndicate, was taken over by L. Breitmeyer and Company.

Two weeks after Derrick's final appearance in the bankruptcy court, on 21 May 1912, Julius Wernher died, aged sixty-two, in great pain. Birdie kept the messages of condolence from the King and Queen, and some particularly affectionate letters from Princesses Louise and Helena. During his last illness Princess Louise had sent Julius mayflowers 'to remind you of your boyhood days in Germany'.

The obituaries, as when Beit had died, contrasted the characters of the two men: Beit – intuition, dash, imagination, faith; Wernher – sagacity, prudence, accuracy, caution never over-tinged with optimism (the one typically Jewish, the other typically German). They concentrated on Julius's modesty, great aversion to anything in the way of self-advertisement, simplicity, constant good humour, politeness, erudition and love of art; also on his interest in young people and working men, and in the 'fight against corruption'. 'Leonine', 'more like a Cossack general in a frock coat than a modern captain of industry', he was 'one of the great financial geniuses of our time', a man who 'emanated an aura of power and wisdom'. It was also frequently noted that he had not been implicated in the Jameson Raid.

There were a few sneers about the extent of his wealth, and the fact that he had never even lived in Johannesburg, whence his wealth mostly came. Those remarks ceased, however, after his will was published. A 'Liberal statesman' was quoted as saying that 'Wernher's shekels were nothing in value compared to his organising power'.

Before Julius's death, in January 1912, an article in the *African World* mourned the dissolution of Wernher, Beit in terms that could almost have been part of an advance obituary for Julius himself:

> The scale of the firm's enterprise, its energy, the high
> standard of its dealings, the integrity of its name and whole
> reputation – these things throughout the years have given
> the Rand a prestige and place in universal esteem which have
> been an invaluable asset to it in the markets of the world;
> and it is to the [Mining] Houses that remain to maintain the
> high levels. Meantime the noteworthy thing about it all is
> this – that Sir Julius Wernher and Mr Alfred Beit, the
> predominant partners, hailing from the Continent, have all
> these years cheerfully devoted their days and their stout
> labours to the enrichment and advancement of this our
> British Empire, achieving in the process a record of
> citizenship which is for the admiration of men . . .

Julius was buried at East Hyde near Luton Hoo, where now stands a Gothic mausoleum. Birdie was too upset to attend, and Derrick was not there. Harold and Alex were chief mourners. The pall-bearers included Jules Porgès, Otto Beit, Jameson, Eckstein, Michaelis and Sir Algernon West. Although it was an unostentatious funeral, five thousand people from Luton lined the route. The papers published long lists of tributes, headed by Grand Duke Michael of Russia's.

When the estate was provisionally estimated at £11,500,000, it was remarked that the least speculative of all the Rand magnates had ended with the largest fortune. The will was dated 23 December 1911, with a codicil of 15 March 1912. Derrick was in effect disinherited, and Harold was the main heir.

Great fortunes are often made by men who are aggressive or bullies. This was certainly not the case with Julius Wernher. He was taciturn and withdrawn, which put people in awe of him. It is easy to be cynical when the very rich start giving to charities or foundations, or to the needy, but as an early letter to Birdie shows he was being discreetly generous in his Kimberley days, before he became so hugely wealthy. He was generous to her too, but, as she confided to Alex Marc's second wife Florence, in spite of wonderful compensations, it had been hard and sometimes lonely being married to such a man. Probably she had even been a little afraid of him.

PART TWO

17

Legacies, Love, War

Flags flew at half-mast at Kimberley, as they had done after Beit's death, and banks and the stock exchange at Johannesburg were closed. The legacies to charities were predictably huge, but none quite as sensational as Beit's 'Railway Trust'. In his enormously long will Julius made it clear that he had already made substantial capital gifts to relatives and special friends, mentioning in particular Friedrich Eckstein, his closest colleague. He had also passed on some very large sums to his wife, running into millions.

He left £5,000 each to Lionel Phillips and Franz Mankiewicz, £3,000 to Percy FitzPatrick, and £10,000 to Jameson and Margie Pryce, 'as a special mark of devotion'. There were bequests to all his old partners and employees in Wernher, Beit and Eckstein & Co., and at Kimberley, to his domestic servants, coachmen, gardeners, and to other friends and his many German relations. He left a picture by Boilly to Jules Porgès and *La Gamme d'Amour* by Watteau to the National Gallery.

The most talked of legacy was his £250,000 to the Union of South Africa 'to assist in building and if sufficient partly endowing a University at Groote Schuur', provided its constitution was approved in writing by Phillips and Jameson, 'in fulfilment of the promise made to the Honourable J. C. Smuts of Pretoria'. In actual fact Sister Agnes's King Edward VII Hospital was to benefit far more, having been left £25,000 with a share of the residuary estate, reckoned a year later to reach a possible total of £465,000. The *Pall Mall Gazette* wrote in December 1913: 'We hope that the habitual assailants of "Randlords" will make a note of what one of them has done for the abatement of human suffering.'

The Imperial College of Science and Technology also had a share of the residuary estate, but because of a restricting limit only benefited by £145,000 – which, however, meant that the College received £473,000 altogether from Julius, Alfred Beit and their firm. Later the Beit family added further large donations for specific purposes such as the building of hostels. As a result, busts of Julius Wernher and Alfred Beit were placed on each side of the College's main entrance in Prince Consort Road, and are still to be seen there.

£100,000 was left to Trustees for unspecified educational and charitable purposes. Some of this went to the German school at Johannesburg, at Birdie's special wish, and £5,000 – to which Birdie added a like amount – to form the Wernher Laboratory of Metallurgy. There were also legacies to the German Hospital in London, the German Benevolent Society, the Society for Foreigners in Distress, the London Hospital, the Kimberley Hospital, the Bute Hospital at Luton, and the Children's Home at Luton. Money was also left for distribution among charitable and educational institutions in the neighbourhood of Luton.

The Luton Hoo estate went to Birdie for her lifetime and then to Harold. Birdie was left Bath House and the contents of both houses, including horses, carriages, motor cars and wines, but not the art collections, which were in trust for Harold. Birdie also had income from a £1 million trust in favour of Harold and Alex. In addition there were very large trusts for both Harold and Alex, though not fully effective until they reached the age of twenty-six, and with provisions for any descendants. There was a £150,000 trust fund for Derrick (no mean sum by today's standards), with the stipulation that he should not receive more than £1,200 per annum in monthly instalments between the ages of twenty-six and thirty, and not more than £2,400 per annum thereafter, with safeguards for his widow and children should there be debts and another bankruptcy. Three-quarters of the residuary estate was divided equally between Birdie, Harold and Alex. Death duties were estimated at £850,000.

In a short memoir of Julius Wernher written years later by

Charles Rube there is a paragraph which is decidedly disappointing for the author of this book:

> The correspondence between Rhodes and Wernher was
> enormous and was carefully preserved by him, but when
> Wernher felt he was dying he directed his wife to
> immediately destroy it lest it fall into the hands of
> biographers and thus sacred confidences be violated –
> Wernher dealt in the same way with the correspondence
> with Beit and other friends. Thus perished documents which
> would have illuminated one of the most important epochs in
> the history of the British Empire [and, no doubt, Wernher's
> real feelings about Rhodes].

Otto Beit confirmed his gift of £50,000 to the proposed university at Groote Schuur, and a Bill was put forward in Parliament at Cape Town. Arguments and discussions continued, indeed raged, throughout much of 1913. Julius had hoped that such a national institution on the slopes of Table Mountain would bring the white races together, but it proved just the opposite. He and Otto were accused of having wished to control the future of education in South Africa. Worse, they had been trying to enforce 'narrow' British racialist ideas. 'Afrikanerism in Revolt', 'Bilingualism Run Mad', 'Cramping Intolerance of Stellenbosch Ideals', 'Fiasco', were among newspaper headlines. The very idea of founding such a university on land associated with Rhodes was anathema to those on the extreme right, and some remarks were ungracious, not to say hurtful, to Birdie. 'Under no circumstances,' declared *Die Voorloper*, 'must we permit two ignorant capitalists to give a wrong character and direction to our higher education.'

At No. 1 London Wall, as A. P. Cartwright has said, the old name of Wernher, Beit died hard. Everything was judged by the standards that Julius had set. 'The aura of power and financial wisdom' still influenced those who had been his colleagues. For small investors in France, where once the shares of Rand Mines had been regarded with 'something approaching veneration', Central Mining was still associated with the magic of 'Sir Wernher'.

Julius died convinced that the days of great opportunities on the Rand had gone. His pessimism would have increased in 1913, when there was a general strike in Johannesburg, with bloodshed in the streets, and he would have been appalled by the attempt on Lionel Phillips's life. He was too ill in January 1912 to have reacted when some members of the black middle class formed the South African Native National Congress, to defend their political rights and privileges, but he surely would have looked upon this development with appreciation if not support – the organization became the African National Congress in 1923. As for the complicated world of diamond dealing – the Syndicate's relationship with the South-West Diamond Control Board or Régie, the important, indeed crucial, transfer of Solly Joel's holdings in the Premier Mine to De Beers, and other matters – readers are best referred to specialist works such as those by Colin Newbury and Theodore Gregory.

Cartwright, summing up Julius Wernher's achievements, adds this:

> Wernher had played a part in the two greatest discoveries in mining history in the short space of fifteen years. He could not imagine, nor could anyone else, that there were discoveries as great as those yet to be made in South Africa. It would have been impossible to persuade anyone who had visited the Central Rand in 1909 that the gold-mining industry was in its infancy. They gave it a life of twenty, perhaps twenty-five years – and then (they thought) would come the end as mines were worked out. But they were wrong . . . There were to be great discoveries and a vast extension of the goldfield. There were to be new diamond fields, platinum mines and eventually uranium.

Although Florrie Phillips persuaded her husband, as a trustee, to allocate some small sums from Wernher's money for her pet projects in Johannesburg, she obviously shed few tears on hearing of his death. Lionel, on the other hand, was genuinely distressed, and at his own expense commissioned Naoum Aronson of Paris to sculpt an Angel of Peace in his old chief's memory as a finial

to the Rand Regiments Memorial. Florrie noted that it symboli-
cally turned its back on their Villa Arcadia.

Derrick was now Sir Derrick. At least his father was spared
further grief about his conduct. In August 1912 Derrick went to
Paris, where he was at once arrested because two cheques totalling
half a million francs had bounced. He claimed that he had been
persuaded to invest in furniture and pictures for twice this amount
by the so-called Baron Grundherr, who had taken the goods to
Germany, sold them at a profit, and then decamped to England
with the money. To many people's surprise Derrick turned out
to have been telling the truth. Grundherr was arrested and handed
over to the French. Derrick was set free, and went to New York.

So ended the 'first scrape'.

Alex nearly died of appendicitis, and there were grave worries
about his eyesight. His career at Eton was brilliant, and he and his
friend Oliver Stanley scooped most of the prizes. It was said that
they made a deal between themselves as to who should concentrate on which subjects in order to divide the laurels. His
housemaster, A. E. Conybeare, foresaw a good future ahead for
him. 'He rarely agrees with my view of things,' he wrote in 1913,
'but I like him none the worse for that. He is growing older
rapidly and is a social success. He works with remarkable
industry.'

Harold went to the Royal Military College, Sandhurst, from
Eton, having been brought up to believe that he had no head for
business, and passed out as sergeant. He longed to get a commission in the 9th Lancers, so one of his father's trustees, Colonel S.
H. Pollen, wrote off on his behalf to George V's equerry, Sir
Frederick Ponsonby: '. . . He is very keen about soldiering – plays
polo etc – and is a really *nice* boy. The Regiment know him and
are anxious to have him, and had invited him to go with them on
the coming manoeuvres prior to being gazetted.' It was important, he said, for a youth with such great possessions coming to
him to get into a really *good* regiment.

Harold was indeed so keen on polo – and steeplechasing – that
he would have special leave for the day from Sandhurst. Once,
fearing that he would be late, he actually hired a train to get him
back in time. Those were the days, as he used to say.

The matter of his commission was handed over to Lord Stamfordham, the King's private secretary, who found that in fact there were only two vacancies in the regiment, and those were being taken up by people who had passed out above Harold at Sandhurst. Sister Agnes had also been pulling strings and Birdie wrote to thank her from Bad Mannheim, where Alex was recovering in a sanatorium. This letter has found its way into the Royal Archives at Windsor:

> . . . Harold is a dear boy, but *very* immature at present. His common sense is his great asset! The next few years will be the most impressionable of his whole life . . . and I am earnestly hoping for his dear father's sake [his outlook on life and ideas] will be *serious* ones! . . . All I want is that Harold should get into a regiment where the tone is good and healthy, and this awful 'money' is not the god worshipped, and one which does not go to India for some years to come. Now that I stand so alone, without my great Rock to lean on and advise me & alas! without an eldest son (for I can no longer count on D.) I do feel I must keep Harold at home and near me . . . I dread – with a *cruel* dread – going back (I can no longer say going 'home' as it seems no *home* to *me*!) – for the first time in 24 years that his dear face will not be there to greet me at the station, for he never missed meeting me if we had been separated!!

She hoped that some further vacancy could be found in a '*suitable!*' regiment.

It was suggested to Stamfordham by the War Office that Harold should go into the 3rd Hussars. A reply came from Balmoral emphasizing that while the King did not like trying to influence nominations to regiments he did feel that Harold's case was a special one, seeing that his father had been a man so universally respected and who had done so much to help others. The King wanted Harold to go to a regiment where there was no chance of junior officers exploiting his wealth and encouraging extravagant tastes.

The 3rd Hussars has not, I think, a very great reputation
. . . If however there is no chance of a vacancy [in the 9th
Lancers] would it be possible to gazette him to the 11th
Hussars, 16th Lancers, 19th Hussars, preference in that
order. The last named is, as you know, rather a poor man's
regiment . . . The King quite realizes the serious objections
to what you term the 'boycott of certain regiments'; but as I
have tried to explain there are in this case special reasons.

But none of those regiments turned out to have vacancies.
Thanks again to Sister Agnes, Harold was accepted by the 11th
Lancers. Even so the King did not approve of this regiment, and
'requested' that he should be gazetted into the 12th. This was in
effect a command, and had to be obeyed. Within days Harold was
off abroad with the 12th, not to India but to South Africa. At
Windsor there is a letter from his Commanding Officer assuring
Stamfordham that Harold would not be allowed to keep racehorses. Yes, the colonel said, Harold did seem a good boy, 'the
only crab being his great wealth'. At least he was not likely to be
tempted away by a highly paid job on the Rand, as so often
happened with young officers.

Indeed during the whole of his life Harold continued to show
very little interest in South African matters, apart from having
South African shares in his portfolio (which lost him money), and
to the end of his life was remarkably ignorant of the details of the
origins of his fortune. But there was a reason for this. Having
suffered from his father's believing that he was the least intelligent
of the three brothers, he had determined to prove himself in his
own way on his own terms.

The 12th Lancers were back in England after a year, and then
were posted to Ireland, where Harold was able to follow up his
favourite sport, polo. Between whiles he called on Grand Duke
Michael's family at Kenwood, and tried out the golf course,
having borrowed his mother's Rolls for the occasion. Zia saw
him win the United Services Handicap at Newbury. He also won
the Naval and Military Chase at Hawthorne Hill, and the Open
Hunters' Chase at Aldershot.

Residents in the area to the north of Hampstead Heath were

evidently proud of their Imperial neighbours and the succession of royal visitors, as John Betjeman infers in his poem *Summoned by Bells*. The Grand Duke became President of the Hampstead General Hospital, to which he donated an ambulance, the first of its kind outside the City. He was also made President of the Hampstead Art Society; and he erected a high diving-board at Highgate Ponds for Olympic hopefuls.

In private life Michael was becoming notoriously short-tempered. His nephew Prince Felix Yusupov has written how he was a great trial to his wife at times. Guests were sorry for her, and also horrified by Michael's rudeness to servants, especially if they had ugly faces. He was said to have chosen his valet because the man had well-shaped calves. No wonder young people were in awe of him, and no doubt this would have included Harold, even if at that age he was far from being considered shy.

Presumably any possibility of a romance between Harold and Zia, or Nada, was never then contemplated. Both girls, but more especially Zia, were constantly being singled out in London and the Côte d'Azur as 'up and coming stunners', and often Zia would be photographed in her 'ultra fashionable' clothes and hats when promenading with young friends such as Mary Howe and Vi de Trafford along the Boulevard de la Croisette at Cannes. The far less conventional Nada, on the other hand, was more noted for her 'startling colours' in dress; Princess Helen ('Sitta') of Greece called her Orange Legs. In 1912 Jennie Churchill had arranged an exhibition called Shakespeare's England at Earls Court, and this ended with a parade of beauties, Lady Curzon as Queen being carried in under a canopy attended by Zia, Violet Keppel, Diana Manners and Jennie's niece Clare Frewen.

Checking through Countess Torby's guest lists elicits such fashionable names as the Patrick de Bathes (he had been an attaché at St Petersburg), Consuelo Vanderbilt (signing under this name after her separation from the Duke of Marlborough), Leonie Leslie (sister of Jennie Churchill and daughter of Leonard Jerone), the Duke of Alba, the Curzons, Princess Louise, Sir Donald Mackenzie Wallace (groom in waiting to the King), Mrs Keppel, Tom Goff (the harpsichordist), and Victor Cazalet (still a boy, politician to be). Chaliapin came to sing once at Kenwood – the

Grand Duke's valet was quoted as having said that he had a voice like a tree-trunk.

In fact at that time Zia was involved in a flirtation with her relative Prince George of Greece, Sitta's brother, who, it must be said, was very different in character from Harold, being quiet and modest, though in later life – like Harold – not one to tolerate fools. He too was a soldier, and after his first visit to Kenwood in 1911 with his sister Sitta had been sent to train at Potsdam, under the eye of his uncle the Kaiser. He would sign his letters to her 'Yours devotedly', but after a further visit to Kenwood the temperature rose:

> There is really no use your telling me to forget you, because as I said, I have been thinking of you since a whole year without knowing you well and now that we have become good friends (at least I hope so!) I even dream about you. With best love and kisses your devoted Georgie.

All this in spite of having had 'dirty soapy water' poured over him at Kenwood. Zia must have inherited her penchant for practical jokes from her father, for once she gave Harold Epsom salts instead of champagne – though he in retaliation pulled out the black bows in her hair, which Georgie would never have dared to do.

Georgie was recalled to Greece when war broke out against Turkey. His grandfather was assassinated, and his father Constantine became King. As the eldest son, he was now the heir to the throne.

Hints about his correspondence with Zia had reached his mother the Queen, and on 13 April 1913 she wrote to Countess Torby:

> Dear Sophie! Excuse my troubling you with these lines upon a very delicate question. I hear some rumours are going about concerning our son and your daughter Zia, and as this alarms and distresses me I should like to say the following.
>
> It seems so hard and cruel if your daughter has any false

hopes on this question, and [it is] better she should know that there can be no possibility of marriage between them so that she should not suffer unnecessarily under an illusion.

This is a very delicate question. I discover a correspondence is going on between my son and your daughter – which I fear must be *without* your consent, or else it would be impossible. I am awfully sorry if our son has given false hopes to your daughter or shown her too many attentions.

Upon these feelings which one hardly likes to intrude on, I would only like to say, that I regret it, as he knows it cannot possibly end in marriage.

Sophie Torby kept a draft of her tactful if somewhat ironic reply. She was happy, she said, to be able to relieve the Queen's mind. 'To my knowledge there is no serious feeling underlying the friendship with my daughter, with whom I always speak openly on many subjects, and she with me wishes me particularly to mention to you that your son has never in any way led her to believe that he wished to marry her.' She also said that she had read many of George's letters to Zia (*really* true?). Perhaps the Queen did not realize that girls in England were brought up much more informally than on the Continent. 'The only wish Micha and I have, and which is shared by my daughters, is that they may yet get married in England. However at the present moment they are far too happy to think of anything of that kind. I also fear that England with its luxury, interests and pleasures have unfitted them for anything else . . .' Zia and Nada were devoted to all the Greek royal children and only too delighted to see them or hear from them. If the Queen still objected, then of course she would stop the correspondence.

As it happened, the Grand Duke had laid down that he would not allow his daughters to 'marry into Balkan royalty'.

The correspondence did continue, and the young prince wrote to Zia: 'I was even told by somebody I was behaving like a blackguard. You cannot imagine my feelings on hearing all this. Because I really sincerely never dreamt of doing any harm. You cannot imagine how depressed I feel, absolutely in despair about the whole thing.' Maybe unknown at first to him, plans were being hatched for his matrimonial future. Zia wrote to him early in 1914 to tell him that he must come to the great ball that her parents were giving at Kenwood for her and Nada in the summer. Soon afterwards she had a shock. She read in the *Tatler* that he was to marry Princess Elizabeth of Romania.

He therefore replied to her enquiry:

You wanted to know about my engagement. Well there is not a word of truth about it yet. That is I mean to say I am not really engaged at all, only the papers make it an arranged thing. Of course I would have let you know. Sorry you have so little faith in promises. Everyone seems to want this affair to come off, especially the leading politicians of the country. For that reason I was sent to Romania to see the 'Tatler bride'. She really seems to be awfully nice, but still one can't do things in that way, at least *I can't* . . . One can't do these things as if one were sent to buy a horse. We got on *quite well* together, but only as a guest would with his host . . . Your ever devoted friend.

The ball was held in June, and both Prince George and Harold Wernher were there. It was an enormous affair with several hundred guests. 'The beautiful grounds of Ken Wood,' one reads in a society paper, 'were brilliantly illuminated; the drive to the house was outlined with myriads of fairy electric lamps, and the entire suite of rooms was artistically decorated with poinsettias, hydrangeas of varied hues, and other blooms.' First there was a select dinner for twenty-four, including George V, Queen Mary, Anastasia of Mecklenburg-Schwerin and Arthur Balfour, each guest being presented with a Fabergé object. After dinner there was an exhibition of 'à la mode dances', followed by general dancing to Stanislaus Wurm's Viennese Orchestra.

The London season rolled on, in that summer before the dark: Wimbledon and Ascot, Chaliapin singing *Ivan the Terrible*, and the Russian ballet. But none of the balls were as splendid as Kenwood's, which was compared to the Devonshires' in 1897.

Years later Harold was to write: 'In July 1914, after a successful polo season in England, no one had the slightest idea that the next month would involve us in the deadliest war known in history.' He could also have mentioned that in that same month there was a ball at Luton Hoo, to celebrate his coming of age, and a huge party later in the grounds – mainly for tenants and the people of Luton.

On 6 August his regiment mobilized 500 men and 24 officers, and on the 10th it was ready to move. By the 21st it was near Mons. On the 23rd the disheartening withdrawal towards Paris had begun.

Luton Hoo became 3rd Army Headquarters, and Kitchener held a major review of troops outside the house.

Derrick was accepted as a lieutenant in the Royal Army Service Corps. In the early stages of the war he worked mainly with French forces, and was to be awarded the Croix de Guerre, though it seems unlikely that this was for gallantry. In January 1910 he had been commissioned in the Hertfordshire Yeomanry, but had resigned in November 1911.

Grand Duke Michael, on the declaration of war, had impulsively telegraphed the Tsar, 'My dear Niki', to say he was 'burning' to return to Russia at this 'sacred hour'.* Then, somewhat shamefacedly, he had to write backing down, because of his health and not wishing to abandon wife and family. He signed himself 'Ton fidèle Micha, qui t'aime ardemment'. As it happens, it is not likely that his services would have been very welcome at St Petersburg, where for years his unkind nickname in the Imperial family had been 'le sot Michel', 'the fool Michael' – presumably harking back to his romantic escapades and morganatic marriage.

Kenwood was offered as an auxiliary to Hampstead Hospital, and with this in view the daughters trained as nurses and learnt 'invalid cooking'. Michael also launched an appeal for half a million gloves and mittens for the British Expeditionary Force.

---

* Nada was at Lord St Oswald's coming-of-age party, which turned out to be the day of the outbreak of war. She received a telegram from the Grand Duke, 'Come at once. I am off to lead my troops in the Caucasus,' and left in tears, thinking she was never going to see her father again.

'The idea belongs entirely to my daughters, Countesses Zia and Nada, and their friends Miss Violet de Trafford and Miss Bridget Barclay, who had received letters from subaltern friends mentioning men's hands literally frozen to their rifles.' In their social circle the appeal was a 'vast' success, and many grand ladies took up knitting. The four girls organized the sorting and packing.

As for Prince George of Greece, there was a sad little letter of farewell written while he set sail from Tilbury:

My dearest Zia, My whole departure was so awfully hurried that it sort of took me with a rush. This morning on parting from you I had such a lot of things I wanted to tell you and such a lot of people about I could not do anything. Perhaps it was better so, because I might have made a fool of myself and besides I felt more like howling than anything else . . . Who knows when we will meet again and in what circumstances. My thoughts always have been and always are with you. Very best love (and *please* allow it to be a kiss) from your ever devoted friend Georgie.

The story goes that at Kenwood Zia had only allowed him a kiss 'through the door' of her room.

Judging by his next letter, he must have had a stern rebuke: '. . . your horribly cruel threat. If you gave up corresponding I would commit suicide as life would not be worth living.' He told her he had fourteen photographs of her around his bedroom. He signed himself 'y.e.d.f. Georgie', adding: 'My thoughts are all with you.' And y.e.d.f. he remained for years ahead.

Harold was keeping a diary. His soldierly self-control and cool detachment were a contrast to his father's letters home in 1870. But then Julius had never been under fire. Harold was proud of having been part of an attack on Moy on 28 August, 'the first Cavalry charge of the war, and very successful too', with only eight casualties, against sixty-eight Germans killed. 'We had to charge several times as they first held up their hands and then turned and fired on us after we had passed them.' Nor were there any heroics in the diary. 'I had some nasty patrol work during the day, but did not lose any men.' 'We had to retire under a hail of shrapnel. 28 horses out of 100 in the Squadron were hit, but only 3 men. There were many wonderful escapes such as bullets passing through saddles and coats etc.' 'Poor Eustace Crawley had his head blown off yesterday, and is buried behind German lines.' 'A man went mad with cold and ran out of our trench towards the Germans unarmed. He was naturally shot before he got there.'

One night he thought water was dripping on him, but it turned out to be blood from someone killed on the parapet above. He wrote of refugees, rumours of atrocities, and billets: 'The house we live in is getting on everybody's nerves, as it smells horribly of drains, babies and pigwash.' His feet were frostbitten and he had to spend a few days in hospital. One also notes that the fact that the Wernhers were originally German never seemed to occur to him.

Harold had four days' leave at Luton Hoo before Christmas. All was not going well there, judging from a letter from Birdie to Stamfordham dated 28 December. She felt she was being 'misrepresented', 'a guest in her own house', although she had supplied the officers' mess with wine, cigars, flowers, fruit and game. Evidently there were complaints because she kept so many rooms for herself, and had put away for safety works of art, old rugs etc. 'I am utterly disappointed to feel I am hardly welcome here. My main object in remaining is to see that everything is properly carried out . . . I have written to Lord Kitchener as this may be twisted into some charge of want of hospitality. It is a bitter lesson for a woman alone in the world facing criticisms and condemnations no matter how hard she tries.'

A fortnight later Stamfordham wrote from Buckingham Palace to say that the War Office had written that 'all was happily settled and your charming house will be restored to you.'

Later in 1915 Luton Hoo became a convalescent home for Sister Agnes's officers: a far more appreciated arrangement. Margie Pryce was made commandant, and Birdie put £1,000 into running expenses.

Birdie was now coming to terms with her wealth and widowhood. Photographs also show a remarkable improvement in looks. She dyed her hair, but kept a large white streak down the middle, considered very becoming. She caused a stir by wearing men's trousers at tennis. Conscious of her role as Lady of the Manor, she contributed extravagantly to many local war charities. She also restored Someries Chapel in Luton Parish Church in memory of Julius.

Her niece Winifred, daughter of her sister Daisy and Alec Marc, had married a German, so now was cut out of her life for ever. As for George Mankievicz's widow Emily, she married her chauffeur, twenty years younger, and so became a pariah too. Birdie said she did not approve of second marriages (a sentiment soon to be conveniently forgotten). No doubt Emily's marriage was a mistake, for she died of drink.

Birdie during 1915 was also being harassed over the Cape Town University affair, which had been put to one side with the outbreak of war, but now reared up again. She was a member of the South African Hospitals' Comforts Committee, whose head-quarters were at Bath House. She and Otto Beit each contributed £5,000 towards the fund, and other large sums were donated by various Rand personalities. She caused a sensation at a Christie's Red Cross Sale of bric-à-brac for charity through buying Lord Newland's Stradivarius violin for £2,500. 'Be quick!' she cried out afterwards. 'Tell the auctioneer to offer it again.' This was done, and it raised £1,400 second time round. She also bought a manuscript chapter from *The Pickwick Papers* and some pages of Jane Austen's, which she presented to the British Museum.

Alex insisted on leaving Eton when only seventeen in order to join the Army. But because of his poor eyesight* he had to work with the Red Cross. Later he went to Rouen as an interpreter. Finally, in mid-1915 he obtained a commission in the Royal Bucks Hussars.

Throughout most of 1915 Harold's diary was maintained in the same cool style. No wonder he was said to have nerves of iron. He never wore a greatcoat, but covered his feet with thick grease to keep them warm. He visited Ypres, a 'ghastly sight', once a magnificent place but ruined forever. Three times he was told he

---

* Once, when he was playing with a dog, a knife had flown up and hit him in the eye.

had been reported killed in action. 'Our parapets are made of dead men and we cannot dig down for fear of exhuming a corpse.' 'An 8 inch shell burst within 10 yards of me during the night and covered us all with dirt. Luckily only one man was hit.' There were gas attacks and he watched zeppelins heading for England. He then revealed, a year after the declaration of war, that he was the only surviving officer from his original Squadron, two others having been killed, the other four wounded. Obviously, however, by then even he was beginning to feel the effects of the horrors of war. He was ready to transfer to another regiment if he could be adjutant. He also took a course on the Maxim machine-gun. So his brigadier let him have a base job for a while. In the 'exquisite' summer weather he even managed some polo and cricket.

During moments of boredom in the trenches he had occupied himself with adding up columns of figures. When he discovered that he could manage four columns at a time he realized that he had a head for figures after all.

At the end of the year he wrote that Alex was to be sent to East Africa with General Sir Horace Smith-Dorrien as ADC. He himself was off to a less 'cushy' spot.

Tuesday December 28. We are going to the trenches in the neighbourhood of the Hohenzollern redoubt, and I hear it is pretty beastly there. The trenches are only 30 yards apart and bombing and mining goes on all day and all night. It is an odd thing that although everyone knows what this trench business means, yet everyone is quite pleased to go into the trenches, even at the cost of being done in.

Meanwhile at Kenwood a mobile anti-aircraft brigade had been stationed in the palatial stables, which were used as barracks. This brigade usually included seven 75 mm. French auto-cannons, mounted on trailers, and two searchlights. The establishment was run by the Navy, and it is recorded that the barrack routine was 'carried on as on board ship', with 'ratings' sleeping in hammocks that had to be stowed away afterwards. There were several actions against zeppelins. The Grand Duke's cricket pitch and golf-course were available for those off duty, and the commander frequently breakfasted with the family. Grand Duke Michael was intensely interested in the whole operation, and had to be dissuaded from joining sorties into the East End when bombs were being dropped.

He was, at the Tsar's command, president of the Anglo-Russian committee, and he and his family were 'untiring' in their philanthropic work, which included charity concerts of Russian music, one of them in aid of the widow and children of the Spanish composer Granados, who was drowned on the way from New York when the *Sussex* was torpedoed by a German submarine. He kept up his long correspondence with the Tsar, relaying the results of his conversation with Kitchener and 'Georgy', the King. In great excitement he told him of his new 'invention', the idea of which had hit him suddenly early in April 1916. He had been worrying about the ineffectiveness of shrapnel – solid balls contained in an anti-aircraft shell – against zeppelins, after observing them at close hand. Suddenly he had had an idea: why not make these balls explosive? He could not sleep for excitement, and the next day rushed to see Sir Francis Barker, head of Vickers, the armament engineers. Vickers were exceedingly interested. Michael quoted their expert's very words to the Tsar: 'I think your idea grand and I see a great future in it.' Plans were put up to the War Office; Sir Basil Zaharoff 'the munitions king' was even involved; and finally Michael was given a job at Vickers, with a salary – which he needed badly since some of the money inherited from his father was stuck in Berlin.

In July he was able to ask 'Niki' to 'share my joy' at the news that his youngest daughter Nada was engaged to Prince George of Battenberg, eldest son of Prince Louis, later to become Marquess of Milford Haven and change his name to Mountbatten. Prince George's mother was Princess Victoria of Hesse, sister of the Tsarina. He had two sisters: Princess Alice, who was to marry Prince Andrew of Greece, parents of Prince Philip, Duke of Edinburgh; and Princess Louise, who was to marry Gustav VI of Sweden; and a brother, Prince Louis, known as Dickie, who was to become Earl Mountbatten of Burma and marry Edwina Ashley.

Zia telegraphed her faithful 'beau' in Athens about Nada's engagement. They had kept up their correspondence, exchanging photographs and mementoes. She had sent him a St Christopher medal after he had written: 'We are passing through the most critical moments in the whole history of our poor little country.' This was in connection with Greek neutrality and King Constantine's break with his Prime Minister, Venizelos, who at the end of 1916 set up a revolutionary government in Salonika. Georgie wanted to know whether he needed to feel jealous of the attentions of the 'pretty little Buddha', King Manoel of Portugal. 'And what about Lionel Portalington? Has he given up drink for you? (Ahem!)' 'You must be quite extraordinary at tennis this year. One only sees your name in tournaments with the very best of (handsome?) players.' Now he wrote: 'I nearly collapsed with shock about Nada's engagement. I received your wire and didn't notice the first word was Nada. Please don't forget I am *always* ready to do anything in my power to help and be of service to you. You can't imagine how often I think of you.'

And so back to Harold. The catalogue of horrors continued. He was at Béthune, a place now familiar from Robert Graves's *Goodbye to All That*. It was typical that in his diary he should not even say that he had been mentioned in dispatches for bravery. He volunteered to be transferred to the Machine-Gun Corps, and was given the command of the 166th. The French were locked in battle at Verdun, and the news was depressing. 'We also have had a nasty little rebuff.' He was sent on leave, 'the best of my life', because he found Alex there, having returned from Africa when Smith-Dorrien became ill. Alex was to be commissioned in the Welsh Guards: 'he was so amusing and we had a great time.' Harold heard that Derrick had been sent to Salonika: 'I am sure he will emerge with flying colours, and will probably be all right now that he has got away.'

He returned to the 'great silence of suspense' before the big push, the Battle of the Somme, where the Germans were estimated to have lost 500,000 men, the British 410,000 and the French 190,000. It was a little while before he was actually sent to the 'slaughter in the south', and even then he was kept on the move. The sheer, unimaginable ghastliness of the sights he saw are revealed in brief occasional sentences: 'Delville Wood – piles of dead, many of them locked together and bayonetted mutually in the last struggle.' 'Fricourt – trenches full of German dead, which lie about with their mouths open and covered with flies.' And there was worse. 'The odd thing is,' he wrote on 29 July, 'that the longer one waits, as we are doing, to be launched into the attack, the less one minds it. I do not suppose there is a single man here who cares twopence what happens to him.' Most of the men in the Machine-Gun Corps came from deprived back-grounds. He later looked upon his contact with them as a turning-point in his life. His fellow officers in the 12th Lancers had all had private means, which was not now the case with officers in the Corps, who were anxious about jobs for themselves and their men after the war. He understood the privilege of his wealth and realized that it must be his duty to help the less fortunate.

On 7 August he watched the Liverpool Irish preparing to go into the attack. 'Lots of them were shaking hands and saying goodbye. All knew that within 24 hours a good many would be lying out dead or seriously wounded . . . I must say I have seldom realized the horror of it all quite as I did tonight.' He commented on the 'hopeless sacrifice' of so many lives 'just to please G.H.Q.'. 'How can they, 50 or 60 miles from the line know the situation as we do?' On the 9th the show began, the 'perfect hell – I shall never forget the hopelessness of the situation.' Two of his guns were blown up, and the wounded were lying out in the sun all day, crying out for help or moaning.

August 18. A glorious day. In the afternoon went to see Alex, but found he was in the trenches at Beaumont Hamel. *August 31st*. Hope to see Alex tomorrow. Such unnecessary misery I have never known, and the Staff do not seem to care a damn what happens to the men. *September 1st*. To my delight Alex came over in the afternoon. It was ripping to see him again. His sangfroid is wonderful, and he is much too good to be an Infantry subaltern. He felt he had to go into the trenches, and would never be happy until he had. *September 3rd*. Delville Wood. Alex came over and we had a great time. He is quite extraordinary and has become a fatalist, as he does not seem to fear death in the least. He also does not seem to mind the revolting and bestial sights, but is just like a man of 40 in that and many other respects. It is a pity we have not got men of his character to run the Army. *September 11.* Poor old Alex is having a bad time at Ginchy, as the Welsh Guards were three times attacked. *September 15.* Last night Walker got back and told me that the Welsh Guards were going up to the front again. It struck me at the time that something was wrong. In the morning he told me that he happened to be present when Alex was buried at the Citadel, but he wanted to make sure before he told me. The news has fairly bowled me over, though, as a matter of fact, I never expected to see him again after our last meeting. I rode over in the afternoon and saw the grave. It is very nice and tidy and a cross had already been put up . . . He made a stupendous sacrifice, having been thrice refused [a commission] on medical grounds. One begins to think every one of this generation will be killed, and it is merely a matter of time before one's own time comes. *September 16.* I keep on thinking about Alex, and it seems impossible that I shall never see him again, and yet there are probably 2,000 men killed every day, who are all mourned by somebody . . . The whole road near Delville Wood is littered with English dead and horses, all covered in blood, terrible agony on their faces. *September 20.* Walker saw the Colonel of the Welsh Guards yesterday. He said that Alex was originally wounded in the leg, that he was put on a stretcher and was hit in the head by a sniper on the way down to the ambulance.

Actually Alex had been lying in no man's land and was shot when being dragged back. He was nineteen years old. Ginchy had been recaptured from the enemy three times. On that day there had been five German counter-attacks within a few hours, and nearly all the men in Alex's company had been casualties. After the war the cross on his grave was crated up and sent to Lady Wernher at Bath House. It was never taken out of that crate, but put in an attic at Luton Hoo, where for the rest of his life Harold too could not bear to open it.

Murders and Marriages

One of the last recorded letters from Grand Duke Michael to the Tsar was written on 31 October 1916, when he sent him a model of his explosive shrapnel bomb. Soon afterwards he told him that, having just returned from Buckingham Palace, he had learnt from the King that British secret agents in Russia were predicting a revolution in the very near future. The King had been exceedingly upset. 'I sincerely hope, Niki, you will find it possible to satisfy the just demands of our people before it is too late.'

He also said that Nada's wedding would take place on 15 November, first in the Orthodox chapel at the Russian Embassy and then in the Chapel Royal at St James's Palace. George Battenberg was attached to Admiral Beatty, Commander-in-Chief of the Grand Fleet, and Michael had bought them a 'cottage' near Rosyth. He then bemoaned his financial difficulties, caused by the war and now made worse by the expenses of his daughter's marriage. He had never had debts before, and begged Niki to help over transferring some of his money from Russia.

But Niki had other things to think about.

The Battenberg parents themselves were worried about finance. Prince Louis had been First Sea Lord, but after a campaign of vilification because of his German birth had had to resign. He also owed money in Russia, but the rate of exchange for roubles was so bad that he was letting it accumulate. Their property in Germany was of course 'un-get-at-able', as he put it. Taking into account the needs of his other three children, all he could afford to give George for the present was £350 a year.

In spite of the war, and in spite of the Battle of the Somme, the wedding was a spectacular social event. The King and Queen, Queen Alexandra, the Princess Royal and Prince Albert were among the personages present at the Chapel Royal. But only Battenbergs and Russians, including the Ambassador, Count Benckendorff, had been at the Embassy chapel. The bride wore a Russian head-dress. Zia, Princess Louise of Battenberg and Princesses Nina and Xenia of Russia, the daughters of Grand Duke Michael's brother George, were bridesmaids. Afterwards there was a reception for two thousand people at Kenwood. At the luncheon the King proposed the health of bride and bridegroom. The Tsar had sent Nada an aquamarine and diamond pendant.

George Battenberg was considered to be cleverer than his younger brother Louis (Dickie), but had been very lazy at school. He was 'endlessly inventive' and loved gadgets. Both he and Nada enjoyed the good life, and were well suited. Nada rather shocked Zia by telling her that they smoked cigars together after dinner during their honeymoon in Switzerland.

Boy Torby had of course been present at the wedding. He was causing a great deal of anxiety in the family, dating it would seem from an attack of measles whilst at Eton. He was developing into a manic depressive. During most of 1916 he had been having treatment in Switzerland, and he obviously enjoyed being separated from his parents. His letters to Zia, in handwriting sloping to the left, were full of spirited drawings of the latest women's fashions from Paris. As for Zia herself, society papers recorded that this 'admirable conversationalist' had started a new fashion for 'boudoir teas': a Persian jacket over a chiffon and lace slip. She also claimed to prefer amber to diamonds. Her preference for high collars and chokers was noted, but this was really because she had to hide a distressing scar on her neck from a childhood operation.

Meanwhile Harold was back in England, so perhaps he too was at Nada's wedding reception. Whilst at the Front, during a miserably wet and cold September, he had been promoted to Major. 'Drenched like rats,' he had written in his diary. 'Worst since beginning of war. 4 days without washing, 3 without lying down to sleep.' On 23 September there had been an 'awful dose

Drawn by Boy Torby

of gas shells'. Then he had gone back to the mud of Ypres: 'quieter now, gas our only fear'. Suddenly on 14 October he was allowed to leave, and on arrival in England he found he was to have a base job as Chief Instructor at the Uckfield Training Centre.

News was beginning to leak out about Alex's will, though a year was to pass before details were published in the press. He left £50,000 to various charities, and £5,000 each to General Smith-Dorrien and his Colonel in the Welsh Guards. He left £50,000 each to Margie Pryce and Franz Mankiewicz and to two other friends, and £10,000 each to more friends, including his late housemaster at Eton, A. E. Conybeare. Some more friends were to receive £3,000 or £1,000 each, and these included Friedie Eckstein. The residue out of an estate in excess of £1 million went to Harold, to whom Alex's share out of his father's will would also revert.

But this soldier's will had been made when Alex was still under age, and was therefore deemed not to be valid. Legally, it was claimed that his estate should revert to his next of kin, therefore his mother, but Birdie absolutely refused to consider contesting the will. There had to be a court appeal, which was dismissed. By that time (1918) some of the legatees had been killed or had died, including Alex's much loved uncle Franz, or 'Prof'.

At a Red Cross sale at Christie's Birdie caused another sensation by bidding £5,670 for the painting *The Plough* by Frederick Walker, which she thereupon presented to the nation, i.e. the Tate Gallery. Then, much more dramatically, she invested £2 million in War Loan stock in memory of Alex. At another sale she bought a tapestry which she gave to the Victoria and Albert Museum.

The trustees of her husband's will tried not to worry her too much about the revival of the bitter quarrels over the proposed university at Cape Town. The South African government's Parliamentary Commission had decided that the idea of one national university was not practicable, and the whole matter had been shelved until the war was over. But it did not stay shelved, and a great campaign arose, headed by Samuel Evans among others, to divert the Wernher–Beit bequest to a new university in Johannesburg, perhaps even to be known as the Wernher–Beit University. This, it was maintained, was in accordance with the wishes of Julius and Alfred Beit (patently not the case with Julius). The South African College at Cape Town counter-attacked with a demand that it should be the one to receive the legacies and thus be turned into a university. A new University Bill was brought forward in Parliament, and on 7 March 1916, as Florrie Phillips' biographer has written, 'a tired House passed the Bill, without even questioning the allocation of the Wernher–Beit money to the new University of Cape Town.' Birdie was also tired of it all, and quoted to Lionel Phillips a favourite saying by Julius: 'It is a sad thing that one cannot be allowed to give money pleasantly.'

Even half a million pounds was not enough to finance a new university, so most of the money was set aside for building new medical laboratories, and the name Wernher–Beit was given to three chairs in Bacteriology, Pathology and Pharmacology. Faced with what was described in Johannesburg as such 'unconscionable piracy' in Cape Province, a committee on the Rand launched an appeal for a proposed Witwatersrand University, to be situated in Milner Park. Birdie duly subscribed, a trifle wearily, if not resentfully, a sum that has been unrecorded, and Otto Beit sent £8,000. She seemed far more interested in the progress of the Kirstenbosch Botanical Gardens at Cape Town, largely promoted by Lionel Phillips, and the opening of a new gallery in Cape Town for the magnificent collection of Dutch and Flemish pictures presented by Julius's old colleague Max Michaelis.

The events leading up to the abdication of the Tsar and his internment at Tsarskoe Selo had a devastating effect on Grand Duke Michael. 'His Imperial Highness,' he wrote in the third person to Balfour at the Foreign Office, 'is entirely without means for his living requirements and has no capital or money here.' He asked him to arrange with Sir George Buchanan, the British Ambassador at St Petersburg, to have all his securities placed in the name of Drummonds Bank so that a temporary loan could be negotiated.

The answer was a regretful refusal. The Grand Duke had no option but to move out of Kenwood forthwith, and to try to sublet it furnished.

On 4 April there was a letter from Michael's ally 'Fritz', Sir Frederick Ponsonby, at the Privy Purse Office, Buckingham Palace:

Sir, I have had a long talk with the King and Queen, and I repeated a good deal of what your Royal Highness and Countess Torby told me. Their Majesties, who appeared to feel very deeply for you in this cruel situation in which you have been placed, expressed their willingness to help you in every possible way. The Queen was especially anxious to be allowed to join with the King in advancing whatever sum might be necessary.

I told their Majesties that until things settled down in Russia it would be impossible to say how much you would in future receive but that I understood that if £10,000 could be advanced to you, that would suffice to carry you on for the next six months or so. I said that I understood that Countess Torby's jewels which were at the bank were worth £40,000, and if any security was needed that would be ample.

The King and Queen said they did not wish for any security and that they would together send you £5,000 now and £5,000 in July. They did not wish any documents drawn up, or formalities gone through. I however ventured to suggest that perhaps later, when you knew how you stood, something in the nature of an agreement might be drawn up, and in the meantime the jewels might be regarded as a nominal security although I quite understood Their Majesties' dislike of any legal documents.

If you think this satisfactory I will place the sum of £5,000 in Drummonds Bank at once and give instructions for another £5,000 to be paid in July. The King has put every penny he has in the War Loan and has left me little margin . . .

Evidently the Grand Duke wrote at once to thank the King, and Countess Torby wrote to the Queen. The King, signing himself 'Yours very affectionately', wrote back to assure 'Michel' that 'May and I are only too happy to help you and your wife at such a moment as this and thus to prove our friendship to you.' Queen Mary did her best to console Sophie Torby: 'What a grief leaving your beautiful Ken Wood which you made so charming and comfortable, but I hope you will find a small house to your liking and that before long things may improve all round. Poor poor Russia! What a tragedy, I will say no more. My love to you, Micha and Zia . . .'

The family moved into 3 Cambridge Gate, Regent's Park: part of a brown limestone block put up in Edwardian times, thereby spoiling visually the beautiful sweep of Nash terraces, but with modern comforts.

One of the first houses to be sacked in the burgeoning reign of terror at St Petersburg was that of Mathilde Kscheshinka, mistress not only of Grand Duke Serge, Michael's brother, but of another Grand Duke, Andrew Vladimirovich.* The fact that she had had a liaison with the Tsar, and also that she was rumoured to be able to arrange lucrative perks for officials, made her into a kind of Imperial symbol – so wrote the French ambassador, Maurice Paléologue. Paléologue also said that on 23 March Sir George Buchanan had attempted to offer sanctuary to the Tsar and Tsarina. As Kenneth Rose in his biography of George V has indicated, it was the King of England, not Prime Minister Lloyd George, who put a stop to this. The King also refused permission for another of Grand Duke Michael's brothers, George, to come to England, in spite of the fact that George's wife and daughters (Nada's bridesmaids) were living in London.† He had reached the painful conclusion that to invite any member of the Imperial family would cause great public resentment in Britain. In her autobiography, *A Romanov Diary*, Grand Duchess George wrote of her predicament, through having two unpopular royal nationalities, Russian and Greek – Greece being then under blockade by the Allies: 'I was accused of being a spy . . . I was not supposed to be seen in public then with any member of the Royal family, as my poor eldest brother [King Constantine] was dubbed a traitor, as was the Czar.'

The King also refused to allow Boy Torby a commission in the British Army. This was just as well, for one reads in a letter from the father to Zia that Boy was suffering from fits and headaches. On 7 November he went to bed 'howling'.

Michael's eldest brother, Nicholas, because of his radical ideals and professing to be a socialist, had been ordered to leave St Petersburg by the Tsar. After the outbreak of the Revolution he returned to the capital, believing that he would be safe. George was allowed to go to Finland, but foolishly returned after some while to St Petersburg. Serge was also in St Petersburg. The other

---

* According to Alexandre Benois in his Memoirs, Prince Constantine Radziwill said to Kscheshinka: 'Madame, vous devez être fière d'avoir deux grand ducs à vos pieds!' To which she replied: 'Quoi d'étonnant? N'ai-je pas deux pieds?'

† Grand Duchess George was the sister of Prince Andrew of Greece, who married Alice of Battenberg (Mountbatten). Queen Alexandra and the Dowager Empress were her aunts.

brother, Alexander, an admiral, was, as it turned out, the luckiest. He was at Kiev, and later escorted the Dowager Empress, his mother-in-law, to the Crimea.

Perhaps Zia realized or had been told by her father that it was her duty to find a rich husband. Evidently Harold was very much under consideration. In December he had broken his leg whilst steeplechasing in Windsor Park, and Zia had often visited him in hospital (whilst there he had received a second mention in dispatches). On 9 April Nada had written to Zia:

> What about the 'Kapols' boy. *Any* chance? I have an idea
> there would be, if not stick to Harold, don't let the latter slip
> on any account. I'm terrified of M – , because if Lady
> Wernher thinks you don't want him you may be sure she
> will go for her, as she always tells you she likes her. Harold
> is as nice as last time, you will do jolly well & have
> everything you wish for in the world & certainly the nicest
> mother-in-law in the world & she really loves you. Tons of
> love old Creature.

Sometime in May Zia and Harold became engaged. Only Margie Pryce was let into the secret. 'It is so funny our being engaged,' Zia wrote to Harold, now her 'Hacky'. 'Although I have known you for so long I never thought of you in that way.' She had regarded him as an 'awful tease', her earliest memory of him being his sitting on a wall at Kazbeck and spitting on passers-by. Harold used to say later that he had been in love with her since he was fifteen. She had had various proposals of marriage in the past, and been 'a bit of a butterfly'. But now 'the butterfly has landed'. Then, most surprisingly in view of her ideas in later years, she added that she 'absolutely refused to have a horrid wedding'. 'I've always wanted to be married in a registry office. We won't even announce it in the papers, just tell our best friends.' Such sentiments were not at all acceptable to either set of parents, to whom the news was broken on 2 June. Harold's leg would never be right, and he had to have a built-up shoe. Still he was liable to be sent to France again. No time must be wasted. The King and Queen had to be invited. Queen Mary said that they would be available on 20 July, and permission was granted for the wedding to be held at the Chapel Royal. Gossip papers seized on the 'most discussed engagement' between this 'vivacious beauty, a favourite in Society, and an able horsewoman', descended from Catherine the Great and Genghis Khan, and an extremely brave young man who was 'not only a capital sportsman' but – so it was wrongly assumed – 'springing from a Jewish family'. It was agreed that the great wealth of the Wernhers would lift a shadow from the Grand Ducal house.

The whole drama of Derrick's having been disinherited was dragged out. But the great problem was: *What would she be called?* Surely not plain Mrs Wernher? The Grand Duke was much exercised on this matter. There was the precedent of Countess Valda Gleichen, descended from Queen Victoria's half-sister, who had married Mr Percy Machell. She was given the title and precedence of an earl's daughter. At last, to the relief of all concerned, royal assent was obtained. The same precedence would now apply to Zia, and after her marriage she would be known as Lady Zia Wernher. Harold had to pay £140 for this to Garter king at Arms.

A little before this announcement, Prince Louis of Battenberg changed his family name to Mountbatten and was granted the title of Marquess of Milford Haven; thus he was no longer 'Prince'. George had the courtesy title of Earl of Medina. And the royal family name became Windsor.

But what of 'Georgie Greece?' A lack of immediate reaction to Zia's forthcoming marriage was not surprising, seeing that his country had been on the verge of starvation and that the French, 'those dirty pigs', as Georgie called them, as one of the Allied Protecting Powers, had threatened a second bombardment of Athens if the King did not abdicate. When King Constantine did finally abdicate, Georgie was overruled as his successor because he had received his military training in Germany. So his younger brother Alexander became King, and the rest of the Greek royal family went into exile.

As with Nada's wedding, the first ceremony was held at the Russian Embassy. Again Princesses Nina and Xenia were bridesmaids. The King, dressed in khaki, and the Queen, Queen

Alexandra and various other members of the royal family were at the Chapel Royal, as were Grand Duchess George and King Manoel of Portugal. Afterwards the King and Queen came to a small informal reception at Bath House given by Lady Wernher. The young couple had rented a ten-bedroomed house called Boothby Hall near Grantham, but some months afterwards Harold was posted not to France but to the Italian Front.

Kenwood was at last let to Nancy Leeds, a wealthy American widow, said to be worth many millions of dollars; so that may have meant more income for Michael. It was also considered an especially happy arrangement, more or less within the family, because of yet another connection with the Greek royals. For it was well known that Grand Duchess George's youngest brother, Prince Christopher, was in love with Nancy and hoped to marry her (which he did in 1920).* Thus the Wernhers were spared having to support Zia's aunt as well as her parents. As it happened, Harold's main fortune, according to his father's will, was not available to him until he was thirty. He, however, was due to come into a quite considerable sum when he was twenty-six, in two years' time. So at first it was his mother who bore the main expense in supporting Grand Duke Michael and Countess Torby, and she was presented with a very large bill after the wedding. Because there was no marriage settlement, Birdie executed a deed whereby Zia, in the event of Harold's being killed in action, would receive an 'annual sum equivalent to £1,000,000 5% War Loan.' Birdie's sure grasp of finance was becoming noticeable. Friedie Eckstein joked that Lady Wernher would have become a very good chairman of Central Mining if Sir Julius had anticipated this.

When Harold reached the age of twenty-six, he gave his parents-in-law an undisclosed sum of money on behalf of Zia for some of their important Fabergé collection. Queen Mary also bought Countess Torby's sapphire and diamond necklace, which she gave to the Princess Royal as a wedding present.

Zia was pregnant when Harold left for Italy. Nada's first child,

---

* Before their marriage she was received into the Orthodox Church, and her name was changed to Princess Anastasia, a 'Greek princess in her own right', so that the union would not be considered morganatic.

a girl, was born in December 1917. It was said that her birth caused more of a sensation than any subsequent event in her life. The royal family, on receiving a telegram 'Tatiana has arrived' thought that the Tsar's daughter Grand Duchess Tatiana had escaped from the Bolsheviks.

The Tsar and his family were moved to Tobolsk and eventually to Ekaterinburg. In March 1918 there was a decree making obligatory the registration of all men in the house of Romanov in Russia. So those living in and around St Petersburg, or Petrograd as it was now known, were sent into exile. Grand Duke Serge, with three sons of his first cousin Grand Duke Constantine, was sent to Ekaterinburg and later transferred to Alapayevsk, where they were joined by the widowed Grand Duchess Elizabeth Feodorovna, sister of the Tsarina and a Mother Superior in a convent in Moscow.

Grand Dukes Nicholas and George were sent to Vologda, where they were interned in the local prison, soon to be joined by another cousin, Grand Duke Dmitri. The French historian Frédéric Masson tried to have Nicholas released, given his left-wing politics, his well-known criticisms of the Tsarina and his open approval of the murder of Rasputin. Nicholas was a member of the French Academy, and it was often said that he should have been born a Frenchman. He was a friend of Maxim Gorky, who admired his clear mind, modesty and sincerity. Gorky too tried to get him released, but Lenin is reputed to have said: 'The revolution has no need of historians.'

Whilst the Imperial family was at Tobolsk a somewhat madcap scheme was devised to rescue them by a Norwegian called Jonas Lied. The plan was to take them after the thaw by fast motor boat through the Kara Sea. Lied had already raised £500 and in his diary of 20 March 1918 he wrote that he went to see Sir Francis Barker and Grand Duke Michael at Vickers. 'Sir F. listened very interested, then asked me to keep his name out of it. Introduced me to Michael in next office (he was a director at £800). He understood, he said, why I came, but would I keep his name out!' In spite of this damp response it seems that Vickers did volunteer to make a torpedo boat available, and Lied said that George V backed the plan, which fell through because of opposition from

Lloyd George. Perhaps in this instance the King hoped that the Tsar and his family could be planted in some Scandinavian country.

As is well known, the Imperial family was massacred at Ekaterinburg on 16/17 July. About twenty-four hours later the prisoners at Alapayevsk, who included a nun and the secretary of the late husband of the Grand Duchess, were taken to an abandoned mineshaft and thrown into it, alive. It seems probable, though, that Serge may have died beforehand, for at the last minute he apparently gripped one of the assailants by the throat and received a bullet through the head. Grenades were thrown down the pit, possibly killing Romez, the secretary. It took some time before the others died from starvation and wounds. Peasants said they heard the singing of hymns down there.

On 21 July Grand Duke Michael's brothers Nicholas and George, with Dmitri and another cousin Paul, arrived at St Petersburg and were put in cells in a common prison, crammed with officers and their wives and several Jews. George was able to smuggle out letters to his wife, which were of course shown to Michael, and these continued until November. George knew that Gorky and Chaliapin were trying to save them, but felt it was hopeless. They still believed that Serge was imprisoned and alive in Siberia. As for Mathilde Kscheshinka, she waited for three years to be sure of his death, and then married Andrew Vladimirovich. Her house at St Petersburg had become Lenin's headquarters.

The position of the other brother Alexander and the Dowager Empress was from the start more agreeable. They, with others, went first to his estate at Ay Todor in the Crimea. Later they were transferred to Dulber, the estate of another Grand Duke Nicholas, the former commander-in-chief, until temporarily liberated by the advancing Germans.

And Countess Torby wrote to Zia:

I am ashamed beyond words to have forgotten your wedding day! But you know that I have never remembered a date in my life including my own birthday . . . Yesterday your Papa and Auntie Minnie [Grand Duchess George], the

2 girls and I ordered a mass for the poor Czar. I see in the papers that the 'so-called Russian Embassy' has ordered one for tomorrow. I personally am afraid that the children have been murdered too, but we know nothing, everything being carefully kept from us. But bad news always travels somehow, and some day we shall know everything. Most of the Russian generals and officers here have sent wires to your Papa. It would have been more humane to kill him 16 months ago, than to expose him to such tortures. How useful in this world it is to be good, gentle, kind and religious, only to be slandered and betrayed by fools and blackguards. Au revoir darling Zia, Your loving old Mama.

Not surprisingly, many people thought Grand Duke Michael was becoming 'unbalanced'. The situation was not helped by Boy, who was constantly rude to his parents. Harold, in Italy with the Headquarters of XIV Corps, received letters from the Grand Duke which he thought positively 'dotty', and hardly legible.

On 22 August Zia gave birth to a boy, George Michael Alexander, to be known as Alex. Nada sent Zia a telegram: 'Congratulations. Tell Harold he is a good shot.' Margie was a godmother. She was thrilled to be asked, but it seems that Lady Wernher was not pleased, for another godparent was to be George V.

This time Harold did not keep a war diary in Italy, and in any case he remained mostly at Corps Headquarters. At last, as the Armistice approached, he was able to write that 'things have begun to happen'. The Piave had been crossed, and 10,000 prisoners taken. 'It is wonderful to be advancing for the first time in my experience.'

After the Armistice he had a very bad attack of Spanish flu, so severe he could not even walk. He stayed on in Italy until February, restless, longing to be his own master. 'I have never been able to do what I like,' he wrote to Zia. The time had come, he had decided, for her to tell 'Her Ladyship' [Birdie] that they needed a country house of their own and a headquarters in London.

Sheffield Park [near Haywards Heath, grounds laid out by Capability Brown] is the type of place we want, but we must have shooting (4 or 5 days' shoots) & we must have a home farm of 300 or 400 acres at least. We have got Alex's legacy to play with . . . Another thing is that we must be within easy distance of golf links. Tennis courts we can build . . . Don't be shy about telling Her Ladyship as it will do her good & she *might* offer to help us!

The country house they bought in due course, fulfilling most of their requirements, was Thorpe Lubenham Hall – with 300 acres – near Market Harborough, which had the added advantage of being just outside the Fernie Hunt country. Their London headquarters became Scudamore House off Regent's Park and almost next door to 3 Cambridge Gate. It was an eighteenth-century house, including a sunken lily pool and an old mulberry tree, larger than Thorpe Lubenham and with a beautiful garden, admired by Queen Mary, who visited it yearly. Eventually the name was changed to Someries House, after the medieval castle ruins on the Luton Hoo estate.

Before leaving Italy, Harold was also being plagued by letters which were 'not quite begging' from the Grand Duke. On 21 December he wrote to Zia: 'I told him that I was not going to encourage Boy to do nothing by giving him an allowance now. Of course it must be an awful come-down for them to have absolutely nothing after having had so much but I think it is a pity that they talk about it so openly.'

At least there was news that Grand Duke Alexander had managed to get away from the Crimea. He had left on the British warship HMS *Forsythe*, ostensibly to represent the Romanov dynasty, even Russia, at the Paris peace conference. Money was now also his problem, even more so when the remainder of his family escaped. There seems to have been no love lost between him and Michael thereafter. Perhaps he thought that some Werner money should have at once been forthcoming.

Frédéric Masson had a last letter from Grand Duke Nicholas on 24 December, written from Cell 207 and telling him that he had been in prison for six months. Luckily he had access to a library and had been allowed to keep a little white cat. On 27 January 1919 Nicholas was roused and taken from his cell. He thought he was being transferred to Moscow, and so brought his cat with him. He was put in a lorry with his brother George and Grand Duke Dmitri. At 1.20 a.m. they left the prison and were driven to the Peter and Paul fortress, where they were joined by Grand Duke Paul, hardly recognizable, he was so thin. They were made to get out of the lorry and were brutally pushed to their place of execution, where a large ditch had been dug. The Grand Dukes were made to stand in front of the ditch and were told to take off their pelisses and jackets. At this moment, Masson was later told in a letter, Nicholas began to speak. It is not known what he said, but he spoke for a long while, and his calmness impressed the soldiers. The Grand Dukes then embraced one another. Nicholas gave his cat a last caress and handed it to a soldier. They undressed further, and were all killed at one salvo. The bodies were stripped and thrown into the ditch.

It was Countess Torby who had to arrange masses in memory of the Grand Dukes. On 18 April Michael wrote to Zia that he was 'sad and lonely and bored'. 'Never in my life have I had such a dull time as now. I have no car. I long to play golf and tennis. I haven't been to Clubs for five years so have lost relations with men. Dear Mama leaves the house every afternoon at 3.30 and does not return until dinner.'

They had now moved to 8 Cambridge Gate. Gone were the days when Michael was part of a group of 'swells and johnnies', including Sir Ernest Shackleton and Lord Derby, who around midnight would disturb neighbours with their 'carousals' at a cabmen's shelter near the Ritz, nicknamed the Junior Turf Club. At least he was invited to visit the Dowager Empress when she arrived in London, after her rescue with eighty others from the Crimea on a British warship, to stay with her sister Queen Alexandra at Marlborough House; he also went to see Grand Duchess Alexander at Buckingham Palace.

He was becoming edgy and cantankerous, and took to railing against other surviving members of the Imperial family. Countess Torby by now was very fat, and reputedly could not see her feet over her bosom. When she laughed her necklaces would bounce up and down.

After the signing of the Peace Treaty on 28 June 1919, town councils and other organizations all over the country in Britain made plans for celebrations. Lady Wernher presented eleven acres to the town of Luton in memory of her son Alex, and contributed a large sum to the new hospital. Meanwhile Luton Council arranged festivities for 19 July. There would be a procession, including floats and bands, a children's entertainment and a banquet for the Mayor, Corporation and selected guests.

Birdie now found herself unexpectedly involved in an ugly situation. There was resentment in Luton because no arrangement had been made for an interdenominational 'drumhead' Thanksgiving Service. The National Federation of Discharged Soldiers and Sailors had wanted this to be at a place called Wardown Park, but the Town Clerk rather crassly had turned it down. Birdie had offered Luton Hoo grounds instead, but in the ensuing row this had had to be turned down also, much to local people's fury.

July 19th arrived; the procession did assemble in Luton Hoo park and then made its way to the Town Hall. The Mayor attempted to speak but was quickly drowned by jeering and shouting. The crowd surged forward. The Mayor hurriedly retreated, and escaped in disguise. The Town Hall's front door was broken down, furniture and windows were smashed, decorations and illuminations were torn down. Police were called in and roughly handled. Later in the evening, after fireworks, a crowd of about eight thousand returned to the Town Hall and set it on fire. Shops were looted, and a piano was dragged out into the street. There were 'wild dances' to songs such as 'Keep the Home Fires Burning'. When the fire engines arrived, their hoses were cut. More police and troops had to be called in.

Birdie was very distressed at such a shameful incident, and wrote to the Federation: 'I shall consider it a privilege as well as a pleasure if the sailors and soldiers of Luton will accept my invitation to sports and tea on Saturday, August 16th. Sports 2 p.m. Tea 4 p.m. to members. Their ladies at 6 p.m. for dancing.' She also arranged for a drumhead service to be held at the Hoo on the Sunday following the riot. This service went off peacefully and successfully. The Comrades, another association, sent a band, and there was an estimated congregation of 20,000, with ten clergy (four Anglican and six Nonconformist). Harold was also present.

The 16 August 'monster fête' was deemed by all a memorable occasion, with 'ex-servicemen mingling with a distinguished house-party', including the eighteen-year-old Lord Louis Mountbatten, a midshipman, who won one of the races. Sir Charles Russell, the eminent solicitor, was awarded a booby prize, and Lady Wernher herself made a speech begging the town to 'wipe out the stigma'. In September she gave a party for 6,300 local children.

The cry now was for a new Mayor. Who better to take his place than Lady Wernher? Lady Wernher for Mayor!

But Lady Wernher, unusually for her, never answered letters about such a proposal, and it had to be assumed that silence meant refusal. The reason, however, soon became clear. Harold wrote this letter on 25 September from Bath House to Zia, about to have another child (Georgina, or Gina, born on 17 October):

> Imagine my surprise on arriving here to find that the 'secret' was that Mother was marrying Lord Ludlow today at 12 o'clock. She seems very happy and I feel sure he is devoted to her. I think she was wise to keep it all quiet. Meanwhile I am staying here tonight with Margie as naturally she feels it all rather . . . I feel rather gaga & don't know what to think as there are so many questions to this marriage. Apparently he is going to live here. Margie says he is 'terribly in love'. I am apparently the cause of it as she was so lonely & the fact that we do not want to live at Luton Hoo decided her.

Society papers were of course very excited about this news. It had been known that some 'mystery lady' had been ordering quantities of expensive mauve and purple silk lingerie and boudoir wraps embroidered with coronets from a shop called Eno's, and there had been another large order for sable and chinchilla furs, paid for in cash. A vast quantity of purple orchids had been sent to Christ Church, Mayfair. Now it was revealed that the new

Lady Ludlow's favourite colours were mauve and purple, and that she had also ordered a purple Rolls-Royce with a coronet on it, and purple uniforms for her chauffeurs. At her wedding, attended only by Lord Bledisloe as best man, her son Harold who gave her away, and Margie Pryce, she had looked 'radiant', wearing a mauve dress and an ample purple velvet hat 'sprouting osprey feathers at every pore'. It was also noted that Lord Ludlow made a habit of marrying rich widows. His first wife had been Blanche, Lady Howard de Walden, famed for her emeralds. She had died in 1911 whilst putting on her hat at Monte Carlo.

Henry Ludlow was aged fifty-three, and his bride fifty-seven, though she admitted to fifty-four. Descended from Manasseh Lopes of Jamaica, he was a lawyer and regarded as one of the best-dressed members of the House of Lords. His grandfather had been the 'friend and support of Lord Beaconsfield', and his father, a Lord Justice of Appeal, had been raised to the peerage. He was President of the Cancer Hospital and Treasurer of St Bartholomew's Hospital: his recreations were given as shooting, hunting, stalking and coaching. Unfortunately he had a reputation for being 'difficile at times'.

One unpleasant cloud hung over the wedding. Derrick again. Once an acting captain, though claiming to be a major, he was back in London, having been found guilty by a court martial of selling Army goods at Salonika. 'Penniless', he had been threatening to become a taxi-driver; but nevertheless he had been going to the races every day. There had been an Appeal to the King, and it so happened that on the very day of the wedding news had come that His Majesty 'had been pleased to quash the conviction'. Much seems to have depended on whether Derrick could have been considered a liar. The King had decided that he was not a liar.

Harold had told Zia of a 'most frightful attack on us' in *John Bull*. 'Please don't tell your father, and if you buy the papers do it yourself and don't send the servants as it is on the front and middle pages.'

The article dragged in all the succulent details. This baronet, disinherited son of a multi-millionaire, brother-in-law of Lady Zia Wernher, was of German blood. Then Lady Wernher/Ludlow was attacked on such unlikely grounds as having ill-treated girls who were land workers at Luton Hoo – they had to sleep on straw in rooms full of mice, and were only paid two shillings a week. 'It is just the sort of thing one expects to find in a household founded by someone descended from a Privy Councillor of Darmstadt.' As for Lady Zia, she had been recently fined £5 for driving a car without a licence to a shooting party, at a time when using precious petrol for pleasure was strictly forbidden. The writer then brought up the case of a young soldier during the war having been shot 'for a sudden failure of nerve'. Why should titled people have any different treatment?

There was an unsuccessful attempt to have the matter raised in Parliament. Derrick, looking bloated and untidy, according to Harold, disappeared to New York. The Ludlows went on their honeymoon to Paris, Biarritz and Granada. They returned to find that Margie had resigned her position as Birdie's secretary.

Lady Ludlow and the Great Robbery

Harold being still in the Army, Zia was busy furnishing Thorpe Lubenham and Someries House. She found herself having to bear the brunt of her parents' unhappiness. Judging from the Grand Duke's letters, he seemed to be getting on well with 'Christo', Prince Christopher of Greece, but was full of grumbles about the Imperial family. Possibly he was going a little mad. Gina, when older, was terrified of him. He would try to trip her with a walking-stick, or suddenly snatch her up on to his knees. With the crook of that same stick he caught a housemaid by the neck. Gina was shocked when she saw him chasing Nada with a cigarette lighter. As usual, he was inclined to be rude about servants, making comments, for instance, about the nose of a footman in his hearing. Countess Torby had become a diabetic. She 'smoked like a chimney', and kept up her jokes, which were not always appreciated by the King. Once at Buckingham Palace he told the Prince of Wales to tell her to get off a seat because it was reserved for royalty, and she refused. In November she and the Grand Duke returned after six years' absence to Cannes, not to Villa Kazbeck, which was let, but to the smaller Villa Luna Nuova nearby.

Boy was considered by all to be very good-looking and for a while had a job at Vickers. He drank too much, a bottle of port a day, and – complained his mother – was no joy to her, only thinking of himself. After losing his job, he went to his parents at Villa Luna Nuova, but would hardly talk to them and when they questioned him continued to answer back in a very unpleasant way. In any case he was out most of the time, sometimes doing his painting. Every evening around midnight he would go out to dancing clubs, coming home at 4 a.m. He would be up again at 8 a.m. His father thought such a life would give him a complete breakdown. Only Nada seemed to have any influence over him, and when she left, Boy announced that he was going to Paris, but would give no address. As for Nada, Countess Torby wrote to Zia: 'Papa is furious with her. She met that Countess Valombrosa and from that day on they became intimate friends. She even went to live with her.' Rumours were already beginning to circulate about Nada's peculiar women friends.

By 1920 Zia's letters to her parents give the impression that she and Harold were at some grand house party or other virtually every weekend: Polesden Lacey, Grimsthorpe Castle, Mymms Park, Cortachy Castle, Holkham, Warren House, Drummond Castle, and even Luton Hoo. In October they were at a ball given by Cornelius Vanderbilt, and it was there that Dickie Mountbatten first met Edwina Ashley, granddaughter of Sir Ernest Cassel. She and Dickie became engaged in 1921.

Boy met Edwina in Paris. He was obviously delighted to be on his own there, and wrote several letters to Zia, mostly in pencil. One was dated 11 November:

I had great fun at Edwina's. Her cousin Marjorie Brecknock was also there – most amusing. I have found out (which will please Harold!) that Edwina is a real dirt & anything but as innocent as Dickie thought her to be!! They were awfully funny, as they both had a go at me to find out what sort of chap I was and were delighted when they found out I had a dirty mind like their own!!

The plan that Georgie Greece should marry Elizabeth of Romania had been revived. On 23 February 1920 he wrote to Zia from his exile at St Moritz: 'Thanks for your kind wishes re engagement. But I am not really engaged yet, only sort of preliminary state of affairs.' Then on 21 November he wrote again: 'Just back from Romania. I really am engaged this time! Besides me, Sitta has also got engaged to Carol of Romania! . . .

You can well imagine what a great excitement I found here on my arrival, and the most wonderful results of the elections in Greece.' His brother King Alexander, who had been virtually a prisoner in his palace, had died that autumn after being bitten by a monkey. An election had followed, Venizelos had been defeated and thus forced to resign and leave the country. After a plebiscite George's father King Constantine returned, to a tremendous welcome, though the Allies refused to recognize him. 'You see I was right,' Grand Duke Michael told Zia, 'not to allow you to marry a Balkan.' Perhaps this particular Balkan had regrets though, for he wrote to her on 13 December from Bucharest: 'I do wonder, Zia dear, when we shall meet again. I would simply love to see you again. It seems so funny to be engaged, rather nice in a way, but horribly shyifying at times!! y.e.d.f. Georgie.'

Both the Greek-Romanian marriages were disasters. Georgie and Elizabeth were to divorce after fourteen years, with no children. King Carol in any case was a great womanizer and his first marriage, to Zizi Lambrini, had been dissolved. Sitta gave birth to a son, Michael, and soon afterwards King Carol started his notorious affair with Madame Lupescu.

The gossip columns in society papers had pursued the Ludlows on their return from honeymoon. As always, Birdie's clothes were the great fascination.

> She was just little Miss Alice Mankiewicz, living quietly in Bayswater, playing her piano. Now she has arrived from Paris hardly visible behind a huge cape of ostrich feathers tinted mauve, with only a few ropes of her pearls visible. She had remarried it seems when we were thinking of something else.

The bridegroom, Lord Ludlow, owned Heywood House near Westbury and had rented Lamport Hall, Northamptonshire, from the Ishams, hoping that his wife would want to live in the former – though he said he intended to 'use' Bath House. A dandy, always to be seen with violets or a carnation or two in his buttonhole, his looks were considered typically Sephardic Spanish. He had hunted with the Pytchley, 'a fine concourse of fashionable sporting folk', according to Siegfried Sassoon, and was rumoured to have spent £40,000 of his first wife's money on improving his stables. His hasty temper had brought him into frequent hostilities with 'peers, parsons and peasants', and he had sometimes even come to blows. He might dismiss employees on the spot, but reinstate them the next day. A journalist from the *Northamptonshire Independent* arrived for an interview at Bath House, expecting to be told to go to hell, but to his surprise found Ludlow in a good mood. It was revealed by this journalist that Ludlow had been unfit for active service during the war, so had done his duty as an ordinary constable, rising to sergeant. He had often been on the beat outside Buckingham Palace, although well known to the royal family. If summoned to Scotland Yard, he would arrive in his own limousine. Once during a zeppelin raid, he had been bundled into a vehicle with other police and kept up all night. 'I wonder,' remarked the journalist, 'how his temper stood the test.'

Nobody, therefore, could have been more different from Lady Ludlow's first husband, Sir Julius Wernher. Ludlow's pretentious behaviour irritated many people. Sir Gyles Isham quoted a remark by Mrs Claude Beddington: 'He was educated at Eton and Balliol, but nobody who met him would ever have guessed it!'

So it is not surprising to learn that Birdie soon discovered that she had made a terrible mistake. She refused to live at Heywood. When he decided he would after all move into Luton Hoo, he made her change the servants' liveries from mauve to blue. He was now in command, and from the hard line of her mouth in photographs it is evident that she did not like it. She took refuge in her piano playing. Harold was worried about what his step-father intended to do with the Luton Hoo stables after he became Master of the Hertfordshire Hunt.

At any rate Birdie was delighted about one thing: she was godmother to Nada's son David. She was offered the OBE for her war work but declined it. In January the Ludlows went to the Chelsea Arts Ball with Zia, Harold and Dickie Mountbatten. Birdie wore a Spanish gypsy costume from Granada. At Luton Hoo she set about improving the parterres in the garden that had been laid out by Romaine Walker for a huge garden party, 'graced by royalty'. There were also musical soirées and a dance at Bath House; she was quoted as saying that it was criminal to own Bath House and not give parties. In June she was spotted with Zia and Nada at Ascot, 'resplendent in cream lace with a large black hat out of which emerged a tremendous emerald feather'. She kept up Julius's tradition of presiding at Leet dinners and organized a second thanksgiving service in the Hoo grounds for 'Those Who Returned'. Her Southdown sheep continued to win all the prizes at agricultural shows. She was also steadily building up her fine collection of English porcelain. No one could compete with her bidding at Christie's if she was determined to get rare pieces.

It was obvious that Lord Ludlow was settling in well at Luton Hoo, even if his wife was patently unhappy. Servants noted that her expression had hardened and that she always arranged for an enormous vase of flowers to be put in the middle of the dining-room table, presumably so that she could not see him at meals. His phaeton was the winner at the Richmond Horse Show. He opened such events as the Costers' Donkey Show, presided over Motor Speed Trials and Retriever Trials. For her part Birdie organized charity fêtes – one of these was for Luton's unemployed fallen girls. She was invited to the Princess Royal's wedding and the Mountbatten wedding. Dickie had been to India with 'David' (the Prince of Wales), so on their return Birdie invited Edwina to watch their State carriage from Bath House on their way to the Palace.

The Grand Ducal finances were a continual worry, both for her and Harold. Rather pathetically, when asked by Birdie what he would like for his birthday, he said he would like a new suit. This at a time when she herself had just returned from Paris, dressed, according to the *Sketch*, 'no longer in mauve but in a "gorgeous pink and gold turban with marvellously becoming osprey feathers . . . The endless succession of elaborate and ornate gowns worn by Lady Ludlow leave but a confused maze in my memory.'*

---

* Not everyone was quite so complimentary about Birdie's clothes. When she set off for one of her cures at Baden-Baden, it was noted that she was 'wearing a peculiar sort of bellrope with gold tassels hanging from neck to knees' and that her dress was 'embroidered with countless geegaws'.

40. Wedding photograph of Nada and Prince George of Battenberg,
15 November, 1916.
Bridesmaids: Princess Louise of Battenberg, Zia, Princesses Xenia and Nina
of Russia.
Taken at Kenwood.

41. Zia and Harold leave the Chapel Royal, 20 July, 1917.

42. Lady Wernher at the opening of the Bazaar for the National Children's Home and Orphanage, Harpenden, 5 July, 1911; accompanied by the Rector of Harpenden and the Mayor of St Albans.

43. Lord and Lady Ludlow at the Richmond Horse Show, June 1921, when Lord Ludlow's mail phaeton won first prize in the Marathon Class.

44. Nada at Cannes.

45. After polo: Harold, Zia and Grand Duke Michael, late 1920s.

46. Alex and Gina
with Tiny at Thorpe
Lubenham.

47. Alex and Gina
out hunting with the
Fernie, 1927.

48. At the Fernie Hunt Horse Show, Thorpe Lubenham: Myra, Zia, the Maharajah of Jaipur, Harold.

49. Garden party at Someries House in aid of University College Hospital, London, July 1939: Zia and Myra.

50. Party at Luton Hoo, 1937, from Lady Jean Ogilvy's album.

51. Harold and Zia with Brown Jack and Steve Donoghue, Thorpe
Lubenham, 1934.

52. Sir Alfred Munnings painting Brown Jack's portrait, September 1934;
with the Wernhers' groom, Dawes, impeccably dressed.

53. Mulberry 'B', Arromanches. Concrete caissons or Phoenixes in the foreground, with four Liberty ships at anchor in front. Far left: some blockships or Gooseberries visible. Further inland the Whales: interconnected floating Spud pierheads from which flexible floating roadways run ashore for the berthing of coasters and unloading of vehicles and stores.

54. Hospital ship berthed at pierhead, Mulberry 'B'. Vehicles waiting to be discharged on right.

55. Lady Zia Wernher in the uniform of St John Ambulance Brigade County President, Leicestershire, and Major-General Sir Harold Wernher, November 1944.

56. Wedding of Colonel Harold (Bunnie) Phillips to Gina, 10 October, 1944. Princess Alexandra and Myra as bridesmaids.

57. At the wedding of Major David Butter to Myra, 5 November, 1946: Princess Elizabeth, Princess Marina, Queen Mary, Harold.

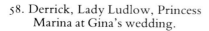

58. Derrick, Lady Ludlow, Princess Marina at Gina's wedding.

59. Harold.

60. Alex.

61. Zia, holding the
newly born Sacha,
Harold and Myra; at
Tucson, Arizona,
February 1947.

62. 'Alex dry shod',
before leaving for
Tunisia.

63. Prince Philip and
Princess Anne, Hallo-
we'en, Thorpe
Lubenham.

64. The Queen and Gina
holding cigarettes in self-
defence against midges.

65. Balmoral 1954. The
Queen leads the Earl of
Westmorland with Prince
Charles and Princess
Anne. Bunnie with Sacha,
Nicky and Fiona.

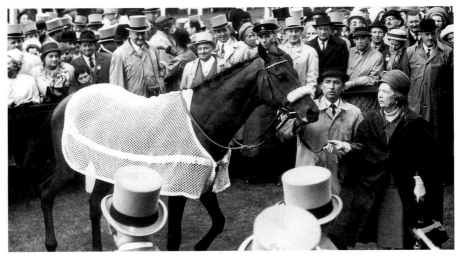

66. Charlottown wins the Derby, 1966: Zia in the winner's enclosure.

67. Zia with the Derby Cup.

68. Zia leads in Meld,
winner of the St Leger, 1955.

69. M. René puts the finishing touches before Sacha's coming-out ball,
Luton Hoo, 10 July, 1964; watched by Nicky, Myra, Harold,
Sandra and Gina.

70. The marble hall and staircase at Luton Hoo, designed by Mewès and Davis. In the centre *Cupid and Psyche* by Borgonzoli; in the alcove a group by Ferdinand Faivre.

71. From Zia's Fabergé collection: spray of gypsophila with flowers in translucent green enamel with rose diamond centres, engraved stalk, yellow and red gold moss, in a green nephrite jar.

72. From Lady Ludlow's English porcelain collection: Bow figure of Flora, based on the statue in the Farnese Palace, Rome, *c.* 1756–9.

73. Harold and Zia's golden wedding anniversary at Luton Hoo, July 20, 1967. *Left to right*: Rohays, Marilyn, Sandra, Myra, David, Bunnie, Gina, James Hamilton, Sacha, Fiona, Nicky. *In front*: Georgina, Charles, Natalia, Marita.

74. The wedding of James Burnett of Leys to Fiona Phillips, July 1971. *Back row*: Sir Cecil Boyd-Rochfort, Lady Boyd-Rochfort, Strongbow Cecil, James, Fiona, Bunnie, Gina, HRH the Duke of Edinburgh, KG KT. *Centre*: Edwina Hicks, HRH Prince Edward, Harold, the Queen, Queen Elizabeth the Queen Mother, Zia, Natalia. *Front row*: Lady Emma Guinness, Mary Clare Younger, Rupert Cecil.

75. The wedding of Lord Ramsay to Marilyn Butter, 3 October, 1973. *Back row*: Fiona Harvey, HRH Prince Charles, Lord Ramsay (James), Marilyn, James Hambro, HRH Princess Anne, Georgina Butter. *Centre*: David, Myra, the Queen, James Strabane, Queen Elizabeth the Queen Mother, the Countess of Dalhousie, the Earl of Dalhousie. *Front row*: Leonie Bailey, Toby Keswick, David Keswick, Marina Ogilvy.

76. Nicky, Edward, Charlotte and Lucy, Luton Hoo, 1990.

Harold had wanted the Grand Duke to sell Villa Kazbeck, but Countess Torby was suggesting that he might take out a mortgage on it. Harold was not too keen on this, as he told his mother: 'The only thing is, if they refuse to sell I can't let them starve, in which case the Kazbeck as security is better than nothing, and I personally don't think it is worth more than a million francs.' He found the Grand Duke 'very livery', chiefly no doubt because he kept himself shut up in an airtight room, smoking all day long. 'I don't believe he takes any exercise.' And the news about Boy was very bad. 'He becomes more gaga than ever', and had been seen on the Embankment in Paris looking like a tramp. Nada had been very distressed and was having him watched. The final disaster had been when he absentmindedly jumped into a car owned by a strange woman, who started screaming for the police. So now he was in a mental home near Uxbridge, which 'needless to say I am paying for'. Harold had actually visited Boy, and found him normal 'except when his parents are mentioned'. 'He has all the peculiarities of his parents only a thousand times accentuated. That is to say that he has the G.D.'s nervousness and his mother's mania for thinking they are being persecuted by the Government. He also has a horror of men, and barricades his door, and thinks all men are what they should not be!! Anyway so long as he is locked up tant mieux.'

The treatment lasted for a few months. Birdie was sorry for Boy and suggested that Harold should find rooms for him near Bath House, which was duly done (in Clarges Street). Harold also arranged for him to do fashion drawings for illustrated papers. Alas, it was discovered that much of the allowance that Boy received from Harold and Birdie was spent in Soho nightclubs.

Early in November 1922 Birdie was waiting at Luton Hoo for Lord Ludlow to come back from hunting. In the dusk his horse tripped on some rabbit wire around the cricket pitch in the park, threw him and rolled on him. He was concussed and had two ribs broken. This developed into pneumonia and on 8 November he died. Sir Gyles Isham wickedly suggested that the servants at Luton Hoo hated him so much that they had deliberately put the wire there, but no doubt, as so often, Ludlow had been drunk. It was a shock to discover that in his will he had asked to be buried with his first wife Blanche. In order to avoid any more scandal about the unsuccessful marriage, it was decided to ignore his wishes and bury him in the Lopes family vault at Heywood.

There was a different kind of shock some weeks later, when Harold broke the news that Derrick in New York had married a Miss Theodora Romanoff. Newspapers had been pestering Harold for photographs of the girl. He told his mother: 'Finally I got so sick of it all that I refused to see the *Daily Sketch*, so of course they published an account which included a half page on the Court Martial.' He went to see their old nanny, who had had a letter from Derrick sending photographs of the girl, one with straight hair, one curly, quite pretty with an Odol toothpaste smile. 'Of course the name Romanoff or Romanov is as common as Smith, so the Russians tell me. None of the colony here have ever heard of her. What a coincidence. Two Romanoffs for daughters-in-law!'

The mystery continued when Derrick wrote to his mother asking her not to make any inquiries. As there had been some dubious liaisons in the past, Sir Charles Russell was asked to make investigations. Harold also knew the Chief of Police in New York, who said he would check the immigration files. 'One does not like the element of mystery, although the girl looks innocent enough. I suppose she couldn't be the Czar's daughter!' (By that time the Anastasia legend had already begun to circulate.)*

Such correspondence with Russell as still survives on this matter mentions some tantalizingly exotic names in his investigations: Madame Viroubova, Desirée Duval and Laura Mollie McCall. A private detective was instructed to join an organization in Genoa called the 'Conti Rosa' and to travel to New York. Photographs of past 'ill-fated girls' were obtained, but none resembled Derrick's wife, who it was proved had indeed been born in Petrograd and had been in New York for the past two years.

---

* Zia's bridesmaid Princess Xenia was one of the main supporters of Anna Anderson's claim to be the Tsar's daughter Anastasia.

The suspicion, no doubt unfounded, always remained that 'Romanoff' had been invented to spite Harold and Zia, but the name was accepted and appeared in Burke's *Peerage*, where she was shown as the younger daughter of Nikita Romanov. Her mother, according to Harold, was said to have been born in Germany. The fuss was probably more to do with Julius Wernher's trust fund, but one wonders why so many of the papers had to be destroyed. In 1924 a daughter was born, Alexandra, who grew up an attractive girl and trained to be a ballet dancer. But the mother remained in New York and always seems to have been kept apart from the family.

Under the circumstances, therefore, the fact that Zia was worrying about Georgie Greece must have seemed of less importance. One of the few remaining letters that Zia had kept from him was written on 23 December 1922. His father had been forced to abdicate a second time, after a disastrous defeat by the Turks and the even more appalling massacre of Greeks at Smyrna, and had died of a broken heart in exile. Now Georgie was allowed to become King, but like his late brother was as good as a prisoner in his palace. He had been forced to sign the death warrants for the execution of Cabinet ministers and the former Commander-in-Chief. His uncle Prince Andrew would have been shot but for British intervention; instead he was banished for life. Georgie's endearingly naïve little letter to Zia ran:

No doubt you have heard all about the terribly difficult times we have been living through in these parts. I have been passing through such awful ordeals that I really wonder I have not gone quite crazy. Because the ruling people of the moment give one the impression of being escaped lunatics . . . Events have been too disgraceful and beastly for words, simply ghastly. But then on the other hand it does seem rather ridiculous that I should be King, of all things!! I can't get used to the idea! When I get addressed as Majesty I am the whole time wondering what people mean and whom they are talking about. According to my idea it is one of the most obnoxious professions I have ever come across!

Within a year there was to be another revolution in Greece, and he was exiled, having refused to abdicate. A republic was declared; all royal property was confiscated. Georgie eventually settled down to live at Claridge's in London, where it was said that 'those who managed to penetrate his reserve appreciated his dry sense of humour'. It was not until 1935 that he was recalled to Athens.

In April 1923 there were already rumours that Lady Ludlow was likely to be married again. This time an unnamed Earl, 'short of cash', was said to be the candidate. Perhaps something would have transpired had she not become very ill whilst in Egypt, which necessitated another long cure at Baden-Baden. Meanwhile Margie Pryce had returned – nicknamed 'Priceless' by Countess Torby, and 'the Pearl of Great Pryce' by the inhabitants of Luton – and took over not only the running of Bath House and Luton Hoo, but most of Birdie's correspondence. Even Christmas presents from Birdie had notes signed in Margie's hand. The daughters of her brother-in-law Alex Marc looked forward to boxes of cast-off coroneted underclothes, hardly used and generally mauve, perhaps with a cheque for five pounds also enclosed. 'Lady Birdie', as she liked to be called, was remembered by them as 'dripping with lipstick', and it was noticed that she and Margie used the same scent – women in her position who used scent at that time were considered fast. She also liked scented chocolates with crystallized violets or rose petals on top; in the Marc family they would say: 'Look, I've got a Lady Birdie.'

Birdie also had a slight accent, which some people unkindly said was East End. She developed a disconcerting habit of nudging you in the ribs when making a joke, and this too was thought excessive. A tic in her eye was often mistaken for a wink. She had a box at Covent Garden, but talked during performances and had to be shushed.

Harold kept his mother informed with royal news. The Prince of Wales had asked him to 'arrange things' for hunting with the Pytchley, and had been to tea. 'I must say he has a wonderful nerve out hunting and takes terrific obstacles. I only hope he doesn't have a bad fall as he does ask for trouble.' The Spanish

Infantas had been to stay. Prince Nicholas of Greece and his wife Helen, a Russian princess, were in London with their three daughters, Olga, Elizabeth and Marina, and Zia had taken them to watch Harold playing polo at Hurlingham and Ranelagh, and to Wimbledon for the tennis. Zia had given a ball for four hundred people whilst Birdie was at Baden-Baden, and everyone had decided, Harold said, that on that night Prince Paul of Serbia, later of Yugoslavia, had fallen for Olga (they were married in October that year).

It had now become more than plain that Birdie was thoroughly enjoying her power, and her status as a great property owner of unimaginable wealth, a lavish hostess, benefactress, owner of fabulous jewels, leader of fashion and friend of royalty. If she had been seriously tempted by the chance of becoming a countess, she must have decided that independence was more important. Her portrait had been painted by de Laszlo and was duly exhibited. She gave after-dinner 'musicales', at which sundry Greek royalties, the Vanderbilts and leaders of society such as Lady Cunard would be present. On 13 November 1923 there was a huge reception at Bath House for Dominion Prime Ministers and representatives from the Empire in London for the Imperial and Economic Conference; the Princess Royal was Birdie's guest of honour.

It was noted by columnists that the white streak in her hair had become much larger. Unfortunately her relationship with Zia was not as warm as it used to be. Derrick, on the other hand, had been making overtures, though without much success. He had been working in an advertising agency in New York, but in May turned up in London – ominously – for discussions with his trustees. His mother went abroad, presumably to avoid the pain of seeing him.

On 12 June 1924 news broke in the papers about a burglary at Bath House – 'the biggest jewel robbery of all time'. The jewels in question had been Sir Julius Wernher's Renaissance collection, 'unique and irreplaceable', valued possibly at £250,000, though some said worth a million. It transpired that Lady Ludlow, just returned from Switzerland, had been asleep in the house at the time, having gone to bed at 11 p.m., locking her bedroom door as usual. The burglary had been discovered at 6.30 a.m. by a maid, who found the Red Room overlooking Piccadilly, where the jewels had been kept in locked cases, resembling the 'aftermath of a snowstorm'. Silk cushions had been ripped open to carry the loot, and the floor in some places was ankle-deep in white flock and feathers. The thief or thieves had obviously been expert lock-pickers and had known how to discriminate between the best and the least important – though few objects had been left. And yet the police felt that they had not really been professionals. Judging from the trail of flock, it was obvious that they had escaped via a skylight, through which they must also have entered.

The jewels were insured only against fire. A £5,000 reward was offered, and a complete list of the 109 stolen items was published in *The Times* and elsewhere: 'Gold enamel pendant jewel of a crocodile, the back and head set with opals and a ruby collar; Portion of a gold enamel chain in six square pieces decorated with leaves, fruit and flowers, open work back, each piece set in centre with a pearl, Lask diamond, or ruby, etc. etc.' Some of Birdie's own Fabergé had also been taken.

Five days later, on 17 June, Derrick was arrested. Unable to find securities, he spent the night in Brixton prison. The next day his trustees put up £1,000 bail. In spite of the inevitable 'buzz of excitement' the charge had nothing to do with the burglary but was in connection with Derrick's allegedly having committed perjury in the bankruptcy proceedings of 1912. A French money-lender was claiming £400. The magistrate at Bow Street, remarking that 'there have been some very absurd rumours', dismissed the case, since one of the deponents had died in 1918.

Nevertheless the rumours persisted, and in a certain degree have lingered on to this day. Nor is it possible to find the real truth, because Lady Ludlow once more ordered her solicitor Sir Charles Russell to destroy papers. Such few documents as do still exist only make the matter more tantalizing.

A letter of 13 July from Russell reported on a visit to Scotland Yard. No further warrants against Derrick were outstanding, he said, but Derrick had visited Russell and 'to my horror' his main debts were revealed at over £100,000. Russell had told Scotland Yard that Lady Ludlow was anxious the thief should be caught and convicted, since the proceedings at Bow Street had cast a dreadful and unjustified slur on Sir Derrick's name in connection with the robbery. The police had said that they were pretty sure that the thief was a man called McCraig, known as 'The Cat', who worked with one Higham Harris and had operated from an empty house nearby. It would seem that the jewels were likely to be in the hands of another member of the gang, called 'Cocky Cohen'. Scotland Yard had asked for patience. Lady Ludlow was also asked to maintain absolute secrecy, and not even to confide in Margie Pryce or Harold Wernher.

From the public's point of view the whole matter of the burglary went very quiet, apart from an occasional rumour that they had gone to Chicago to a collector who had died whilst the crook was still at sea, or had been sent to a Paris fence who had become nervous and had offered only a few hundred pounds. Then, in December, it suddenly leaked out that not only had the jewels been returned intact to Lady Ludlow but that this had happened in July!

So now Sir Charles Russell was forced to make a statement to the press. It was an involved and not altogether satisfactory story. An anonymous letter in red ink had been sent to Lady Ludlow and passed on to Scotland Yard. As a result, the man called 'Cocky Cohen' had been taken by Superintendent Fred Wensley to Russell's office, on condition that his real name would not be revealed. £15,000 had been asked for the return of the jewels, but after some bargaining £6,500 had been paid.

But why such secrecy hitherto? The scandalmongers could not be silenced. Harold was also mystified as to why he had not been allowed to 'share the burden'. Another letter from Russell that survives is dated 6 November, and shows that Scotland Yard had wanted to drop the case but that Lady Ludlow was still 'extremely dissatisfied'. The only remaining documents are some extremely large solicitors' bills from London, New York and Paris, not only for the burglary but in connection with Derrick's bankruptcy and marriage. Perhaps Harold never knew the whole truth, though he did keep a cutting from the *Express* of 6 July 1928, which reported on the sentencing to four years' penal servitude at Newcastle, for a jewel robbery, of James McCraig, alias George Enright. This man had boasted that he had taken part in the raid on Bath House on 11 June 1924.

McCraig, who was known in America as the 'Human Fly', because of the ease and agility with which he climbed up the front of the houses which he raided, came to London in 1922, after being liberated from Sing Sing Prison. Within a few weeks he had, with catlike activity, climbed up the porticoes of so many London mansions and secured such a quantity of valuable jewellery that he was able to establish himself, with other criminals, in a luxuriously-furnished flat in Jermyn Street.

McCraig said that he had hidden in the basement of Bath House, and confirmed the other details about putting the jewels in cushion covers and escaping through the skylight and down the fire escape. The police, according to the *Express*, had continued their inquiries, and whilst satisfying themselves that McCraig was the thief had decided that there was not enough evidence to justify his arrest. 'The facts about the final episode, the return of the treasures, have yet to be disclosed.' And Harold in his own writing added: 'It is a curious fact that the men who carried out this theft – McCraig and another and also Cocky Cohen – have all been convicted in connection with other thefts and all three are in penal servitude.'

Curious indeed. Birdie never lost her love for Derrick, and later had him staying with her at Bath House. She probably settled all his debts. In the 1930s she took him on trips to Florida and the West Indies. 'He could charm the birds off the trees.'

20

The Game of Business

Harold had left the Lancers and was now commanding the 5th Beds and Herts, a Territorial battalion, while at the same time looking for some more substantial occupation.

He was known as a munificent and jovial host at Lubenham (if sparing on the drinks), and never more so than when entertaining friends up for the hunting or shooting. But men had to be on his wavelength, which often meant finance or horses, and although he had many close male friends such as Ronnie Tree and Jack Lowther (both Masters of the Pytchley), Joe Airlie, and Alick Poklewski-Koziell (son-in-law of Baroness Stoeckl), he probably got on best in those days with women, especially pretty ones – a fact of which Zia was only too conscious. His voice was soft and he still had his limp. His sense of humour did at times tend to be schoolboyish; some found his language 'unbelievably frank'. He loved his children and they adored him, and he was a 'good employer' – an ex-housemaid, Dorothy Jelley, recalled him as 'one of the nicest gentlemen I have ever met'. On the other hand, out hunting he could give you the 'most frightful rocket' if your car passed over the scent, and in that way he was 'certainly not the most tactful man in the world'.

He was generous towards charities, but they had to be of his own choosing and without prompting. He also helped individuals, but hated being asked for money, and that applied to his wife's Russian and German relations. Soon after the war he was appointed a trustee, and afterwards Honorary Secretary, of the King Edward VII Hospital; later he became Chairman. When the

Rockefeller Foundation gave an enormous donation of over £1,200,000 to University College Hospital, followed by £65,000 from Geoffrey Duveen, he was asked to take over the chairmanship of the Hospital's House and Finance Committee. He himself launched an appeal fund for a new obstetric wing and nurses' home by giving £10,000, and shrewdly organized dinner parties where guests were faced with blank cheques on their plates to be filled in before the meal. The Hospital minutes show that he made inspections with military thoroughness, finding dust on lampshades and objecting to urine samples being kept in view of patients when eating food.

As Honorary Secretary of the King's Fund he was the main organizer during 1922–3 in raising £500,000 for postwar hospital rehabilitation, the sum required to qualify for a similar sum from the government. He persuaded Otto Beit to launch the Radium Fund with an initial donation of £50,000.

In contrast to his parents he liked English furniture, especially Queen Anne, and he bought a Claude, two Guardis, a number of Dutch seventeenth-century paintings, including a possible Rembrandt, and some Nasmyths. During the 1926 General Strike he bought the Duke of Leinster's Kildare silver toilet set at Christie's (exhibited at the Treasure Houses of Britain Exhibition at Washington in 1987). The best furniture and pictures tended to be kept at the more formal Someries House. At Lubenham he built a covered tennis court, and a recreation hall for servants, and he also created a private golf-course for the estate.

There was a staff of about twenty-six at Lubenham, including grooms. All was superbly managed by Zia. 'She was a tremendous executive,' a neighbour has said. 'She could run anything. She said exactly what she thought. Scratch the surface, and my God was she an aristocrat.' Her standards were of the very highest; the food had to be of the very best. The servants also ate well. Although still Russian Orthodox, she attended the local church. She had a prejudice against Roman Catholics, but employed Roman Catholic servants. Her sense of humour was rather more limited, at any rate different from Harold's, who liked to tease her. 'If she told you something, you knew it was exact.

She never embroidered a story.' Harold did like to embroider stories, to make them funnier.

Reggie Winn and his wife Alice, a niece of Nancy Astor, whilst on their honeymoon in 1924, met Zia and Harold at Granada, and it was the beginning of a lifelong friendship. 'Zia was so pretty,' Alice Winn has said, 'like a Greuze, with a retroussé nose. She had blue eyes and a wonderful complexion. She seemed very foreign, and had a foreign accent, and rolled her Rs. Nada had a much harder voice. We shared carriages, sniffing the orange blossom together. Harold was a very astute man, with a Peter Pan quality, like Reggie. He was amused by simple things. I never saw him in anything but a good humour. Zia was quite a flirt, the old-fashioned sort, nothing serious. She couldn't resist flirting, and quite a lot of people fell in love with her. She got her charm from her mother. She knew all about royalty, and who was related to whom. Harold never talked about his parents' families.'

In fact others have said that Zia was 'basically shy'. Some of her county friends got bored when she spoke about her Pushkin descent, especially those who had never heard of the 'damned fellow', though in effect she was much more interested in her Imperial ancestry. Everyone of course was impressed by the succession of royal personages who came to stay at Lubenham. She was also still recognized as an all-round sportswoman: a very good shot, golfer and tennis player. She had been a founder member of Wimbledon; even Suzanne Lenglen was prepared to play against her. Zia also loved fishing, and had done so ever since fishing in the lake at Keele Hall, a place for which she had a special affection.

After the birth of her third child, Myra Alice, on 8 March 1925, a new wing was added to Lubenham. The family always spent June and July at Someries House for the Season, taking with them some of the Lubenham staff. In August and September they would be in Scotland, where first they rented Cortachy Castle and then Downie Park, belonging to their great friends the Airlies. Lady Airlie had been one of Zia's childhood friends, so close there seemed to be a kind of telepathy between them. Again the Wernhers would bring their staff, also a quantity of china, silver, and even cushions. Later they rented Invermark, belonging to the Dalhousies.

Zia spoke German, French and Russian, but none of them well. She and Harold supported 'endless causes' and she virtually ran the village, but an attempt by her to help Harold raise money for University College Hospital had distressing consequences. She had arranged a Christmas dinner dance, with a cabaret, on Boxing Day 1926, which was a Sunday, at the Kit Cat Club, and on 22 December received a severe letter from Lady Bertha Dawkins at Buckingham Palace. Queen Mary had been sent details of this entertainment by a 'lady of position' and was very surprised by it. 'Have you really given your name in this manner?' wrote Lady Bertha. 'Her Majesty and the King feel very strongly with regard to due observance of Sunday. Her Majesty doubts whether in the end hospitals will benefit from such entertainments.' The lady of position had said that she would not continue to contribute to hospitals if these means were adopted for raising funds.

Such a letter was a great blow, and Zia at once cancelled the dinner dance. It was not the end of the story, however. On Christmas Day another letter arrived from Lady Bertha. The Queen had now learnt that the Duchess of York had never been consulted about putting her name as a patron on the invitation card. 'The Duchess is a good deal annoyed, and is going to say that in future her permission must be asked before her name is used.' Perhaps this affair marked the beginning of the slight chilliness towards Zia and Harold by the Yorks, which continued when they were King and Queen.

At the end of 1924 Harold had become Joint Master of the Fernie with Lord Stalbridge. He was reluctant to take it on, but subscriptions were down and there was a deficit of £2,000 which he was expected to make good. Because of foot-and-mouth disease hunting was in any case restricted for the next year or so.

He remained Joint Master until 1935, and when Lord Stalbridge retired, with Charlie Edmonstone and Commander F. J. Alexander. The 1920s and '30s have always been regarded as a glorious period in the Shires for hunting, and the Fernie and the Pytchley were the leaders in traditional social life. But hard, or dedicated, riders to hounds might choose to hunt with the Quorn on

Mondays and Fridays, the Cottesmore on Tuesdays, the Belvoir on Wednesdays, the Fernie on Thursdays, the Belvoir or Cottesmore again on Saturdays. At that period the Fernie hunted twice a week, Mondays and Thursdays, but Thursday was the fashionable day. The Prince of Wales came to hunt with the Fernie and the Pytchley, sometimes joined by his brothers Princes Henry and Albert (Bertie), sometimes with Fruity Metcalfe, and kept a stud at Craven Lodge.

The Fernie country was entirely within Leicestershire, only about ten miles by eighteen. One reads how the going was 'perfect in any weather': the nearer to Market Harborough the better the land. The fields were large, mostly 'good sound grassland' with little plough, and in those days there was not much wire. There were no big woods, only small blackthorn coverts, some specially planted, such as Charlie's Gorse and Botany Bay, so named because it was the furthest from the rival Quorn. Lord Stalbridge has written that the very word *Fernie* 'sent a thrill down the spine, not only of every fox-hunter but of every sportsman the length and breadth of the land'. The pack of hounds had been methodically bred. In the old days such characters as the renowned late Victorian courtesan Skittles and the Empress Elizabeth of Austria rode across these very fields. Harold's huntsman was Bert Peaker, the successor to another renowned personality, Arthur Thatcher, who in turn had served with Charles Fernie, after whom the Hunt was named.★

The expenses faced by Harold Wernher were mainly connected with the kennels, poultry claims, problems of wire fencing and coverts maintenance, and sometimes the organization of hunt balls. He had started his career as Master with surprising bad luck. Almost on his first day his horse broke its back while jumping a brook. He then mounted another which dropped dead on returning to the stables. His Irish hunters, however, were much admired, 'a brilliant stud', and he scooped most of the

★ C. W. B. Fernie had been Master from 1888 until his death in 1919, hunting a country claimed by the Quorn. He left his pack of hounds to the Hunt Committee on condition that the Quorn gave up its claim – which was successfully negotiated.

prizes at point-to-points. Every summer he would mount some young officers, usually from the Lancers, for his own Someries House polo team in London, mainly on Argentinian ponies.

Zia of course was always immaculately turned out at meets, riding her grey horse side-saddle, as most women then did, and wearing a top hat. Although energetic in other sports, and regarded as a first-rate rider, she was not a thruster and never followed the hounds, sticking by her rough riders Tom Hobbs, a horseman of Olympic standards, or Frank Jones.

Zia may have been a flirt and even encouraged some admirers, but she did not like Harold flirting. She was suspicious of his relations with Nada, who she thought was promoting infidelities (and she was probably right). When she was in Paris buying clothes, she knew he went to parties and nightclubs with Nada and George, now Marquess of Milford Haven after his father's death. When Nada came to Lubenham she would stay on in the dining-room with the men after the ladies had retired, making risqué jokes and smoking cigars, until Zia hammered on the door and told her to come out. It is clear that Harold was discreetly helping with the Milford Haven finances.

It was noticeable to many delighted observers in Leicestershire that Zia was finding her millionaire American neighbour, Marshall Field III, attractive. He was indeed good-looking, an Anglophile old Etonian, and a keen follower of the Fernie; he was also president of the *Chicago Sun-Times* (and later director of the New York publishers Simon and Schuster and Pocket Books, Inc.). His racing interests in England and Ireland were looked after by Zia's old friend and contemporary, Cecil Boyd-Rochfort, once Sir Ernest Cassel's manager at Newmarket; it was Marshall Field who lent Boyd-Rochfort the money to buy the famous Freemason Lodge training stables. Zia and Marshall bought a horse in partnership, and CBR placed this 'very moderate hurdler' to win two races in the flat. Thus began Zia's great enthusiasm for racing, which was to make her a household name in the world of sport.

Zia's relations with her mother-in-law were becoming increasingly uneasy. Ostensibly this was because she disapproved of 'Lady Bird's' being weak over Derrick, and felt that she had always treated Harold badly, and that she resented his being so successful. On the other hand observers considered that she was probably ashamed of having this mother-in-law of obscure Polish descent. The two of them were, as someone said, total opposites, and Zia found Lady Ludlow only too eager to invite her grand relations to the parties and musicales at Bath House.

These gatherings were indeed on the most lavish scale. The stairs and drawing-rooms were banked with magnificent flowers brought up from Luton Hoo. Once a room was entirely decorated with Magnolia Grandiflora blooms. On another occasion a room was filled with singing birds in cages. Sometimes up to four hundred invitations were sent out for entertainments that started at 10.30 p.m., after a dinner party for fifty or so, including royals. The assumption seems to have been that only about half would accept. Journalists were never invited, so these musicales were rarely reported in papers. However, Birdie's faithful admirer in the *Sketch* was able to report that the 'divine' Madame Suggia played the cello at a party in July 1924, when Chaliapin also sang 'snatches' from *Boris Godunov*.

It was reckoned that Birdie was prepared to pay about a thousand guineas a night in fees to her performers. Madame Suggia played again in December to 140 guests. She was there again in June, with Chaliapin and the Don Cossack choir, playing to 180 guests, in the presence of the Princess Royal. Her Spanish dances were a success, but Birdie upset her by saying that a Max Bruch piece was 'too long and classic' for a drawing-room. So she refused to play again ten days later, and her place was taken by Gaspare Cassado; the Don Cossack choir sang once more, and Baronessa Mendelssohn-Gordigiani was at the piano. But not all the parties were highbrow. Harrods supplied a Charlie Chaplin film for Christmas Day, and there was also a 'negro spirituals evening'. In June 1927 110 guests listened to Os-Ke-Non-Ton, the Mohawk chieftain, singing songs such as 'The Scalp Dance' and 'Navajo Love Song', and in July the entertainers for 170 guests were Jack Hulbert and Cicely Courtneidge, the de Groot orchestra playing Viennese waltzes, and the Revellers.

Alice Winn found Lady Ludlow slightly frightening, frank and direct, indeed 'downright bossy'. Servants have said that Birdie was 'too conscious of what she had', and they disapproved of Margie Pryce, who 'tried too hard to be a lady'. Birdie was closest to Florence Marc, to whom she poured out her heart about Derrick, Harold and Zia, and she was enormously generous to Florence's family. She loved giving children's parties, with surprises such as gas balloons shaped like animals. 'She was the sort of person who would jump round a corner at you and say *Boo*.' At Luton Hoo she organized children's cricket matches and built a sports club with a bowling green, cricket pitch, tennis court and a specially sprung dance floor in a coach house. A thousand guests were invited to the jubilee of the Luton Chamber of Commerce, and were entertained by Madame Italia Conti's troupe.

1924 had been the great year for the success of the Luton Hoo flock of Southdown sheep, which had carried away most of the important prizes. There had always been interest in the flock abroad, notably from New Zealand, but also Canada, China, Japan and Peru, resulting in exports of rams and ewes. The original strain descended from Madame de Falbe's day, but had been carefully improved and nurtured. The champion sheep were attributed to the efforts of Lady Ludlow, but in fact it was Harold who deserved the credit.

Lady (Otto) Beit was one of Birdie's best friends; and the Beits and the Wernhers were easily the grandest of the *nouveaux riches*. Birdie was also a friend of Sybil Colefax and Lady Desborough, and the ill-assorted alliance of these three was considered comic: Sybil Colefax, *nouveau* but not *riche*, with a flair for decoration; Lady Desborough aristocratic and beautiful; Lady Ludlow, as we should now refer to her, an 'overflowing' character, of immense wealth, at the mention of whose name everyone would smile. In reality Lady Ludlow's great entertainments, her expensive furs, her extraordinary and fashionable clothes covered in jewels and coronets, her Rolls-Royces, were a compensation for her loneliness. But she was now much respected as a leading connoisseur of English porcelain.

Harold could not resist telling tales against Zia to his mother. In August 1925 he and Zia were staying with Marshall Field at Saratoga Springs, New York. The trip was not an unqualified success, he said, as Zia had got it into her head that he was in love with Marshall's sister-in-law, who was a 'wonderful dancer but not attractive in any way'.

During the weekend we went out together a good deal chiefly to tease Zia, and more as a reprisal than anything else. Zia was very angry and rude to her, then apologised. But at a nightclub Zia took up an attitude of mad jealousy, following me about, dancing next to me and abusing me like a pickpocket. At first I laughed then it became so childish I had to do something. I have never seen anyone act with such lack of dignity and stupidity. Really she might have been the Grand Duke. Personally I can imagine no worse thing for any man than to show your adoration for him by open jealousy. When I think of her own behaviour [presumably with Marshall Field] last winter it makes me laugh but then she says 'That was different'. It always is for any member of that family.

In March 1926 Harold told his mother that Zia was suffering from another attack of 'Saratoga fever'. This time it was about 'the charming Nancy Tree' (another niece of Nancy Astor, and Ronnie Tree's wife – the Trees were neighbours). 'If she goes on like this we shan't have a friend in the world. I notice Zia gets attacks just before Marshall Field arrives or on parting from him. I remain quite calm, but oh so bored by all the childishness and pettiness of the whole thing. I expect jealousy the moment Nada appears on the scene.'

In 1923 Louise Mountbatten, Nada's sister-in-law, married Gustav Adolf, Crown Prince of Sweden. Zia and Harold went to the wedding. 'Give a kiss to the King of Sweden,' Countess Torby wrote to Zia. 'I love him dearly.' This connection was to be important for Harold, who was to become a Chairman of the Swedish-owned firm of Electrolux, maker of vacuum cleaners and, eventually, refrigerators.

Electrolux had been founded by Axel Wenner-Gren in Sweden in 1913, and had been an instant success. Wenner-Gren set about raising money there from the Wallenberg family and others. By 1920 it was a worldwide organization, the British agency having been acquired by James Scrivener, who operated at first from a London basement on a working capital of £5,000. Then in 1922 Wenner-Gren acquired the patent in a new system of refrigeration invented by two young Swedes, Munters and Platen. He decided that the time had come to build a factory and asked Birger Dahlerus, also Swedish, the managing director of Skefco, the ball-bearing firm at Luton, to find a wealthy Englishman to put up the money.

In view of Harold's connections with Luton, his relationship with the Swedish royal family and his friendship with the Wallenbergs, he was an obvious choice. He went to Sweden again and immediately he and Wenner-Gren 'sparked it off'. The deal was done, but it seems that Harold may have put his capital mostly if not all into the parent firm. At any rate Electrolux Ltd was formed on 1 February 1926 with Harold as Chairman and Dahlerus and Scrivener as joint managing directors, and with a capital of £1 million. In that same month Harold presided at a luncheon at the Savoy Hotel and demonstrated the new refrigerator, which as he explained was operated by a system whereby heat actually generated cold.

In April he went to stay at the Royal Palace in Stockholm, evidently feeling a little uneasy about protocol. 'I do wish you were here,' he wrote to Zia, 'as you would know exactly what to do!' 'I have a suite to myself with dining room and sitting room. The palace is very like Madrid and is huge, it has lovely tapestries and a wonderful silk carpet, also an English Mortlake tapestry.' He went to the opera with the King's brother Charles, although 'quite deaf!' After visiting factories with Wenner-Gren, he stayed with Gustav Adolf and Louise at Gothenburg. 'Gustav spoke of nothing else except archaeology.' Later he wrote from Stockholm: 'I thought of you yesterday when Louise turned out all her jewels, and some very fine. Most are such huge things you want to be Queen Mary to wear them.'

An old wartime aircraft factory building at Luton with several acres around it was bought as the site of the new factory, which was opened on 18 May 1927 by the President of the Board of Trade. In that time of slump it was a great boost to employment at Luton. Harold, a Colonel now, retired from the Beds and

Herts. His experience as a soldier made him determined to build a spirit of loyalty in the company: what he called Electrolitis. Although not Chairman in an executive capacity, he would often tour the factory in an informal way. With his keen eye for detail he was quick at spotting weaknesses in machinery, on which he would remark as if casually at the end of his tour. The workmen liked and respected him, and he would ask after their families as though they were his friends; again this was a sympathy that went back to his days in the trenches with the Machine-Gun Corps.

The more successful Electrolux salesmen with consistently good quotas were invited to a three-day convention at Luton, which included sales training and sports. This privileged band slept in bell tents loaned by the 5th Beds and Herts. 'The object of the Convention,' Harold wrote, 'is to give the salesmen a good dose of Electrolitis. When Electrolitis attacks a salesman he radiates loyalty and enthusiasm and just as horses love racing and dogs love hunting so he loves his work. That man is already marked for promotion.' Electrolitis was also injected into the lower echelons. Jack Rosser, then a tooling engineer, has said: 'The company was one big happy family. We all believed in the future.' Promotion was from the shop-floor.

Harold joked that he wanted to make refrigerators because he was tired of lukewarm Martinis. In due course he brought George Milford Haven on to the board. He did not get on well with Scrivener, whom he found pompous and who bored him with long lectures about details in the balance-sheet. Scrivener did not always appreciate Harold's type of humour. He habitually wore a long white coat in the factory. One day Harold entered his office and said: 'Hullo, I've come to have my hair cut.' There were worrying times in those early days, due to competition from compressor-operated refrigerators which could be plugged into electric points; Electrolux refrigerators required the extra expense of plumbing. Harold's manner in business was very different from his father's. As an old colleague has said: 'He might have appeared overbearing to people who didn't know him. He had a very gruff manner and could be rather brusque. He spoke as he thought and said what he thought. You shouldn't be offended by that. His criticisms were generally very good, and accepted.'

Another has said: 'He was merciless with pig-headed fools.' But with Wenner-Gren, a brilliant entrepreneur, he was 'like a blood-brother', though this was probably an exaggeration. 'Harold Wernher enjoyed the game of business, and was not out to make money for himself.' Details of many of his City interests have been lost, destroyed during the Blitz in the Second World War, when No. 1 London Wall was fire-bombed. He was known as a powerful and brilliant businessman, extremely hard-working. All the same, it was evident that he was determined not to be like his father, all work and no play.

As Chairman of the Anglo-Swedish Society, of which he was later President, Harold was made Knight Commander of the Swedish Order of Vasa and much later received the Grand Cross of the Northern Star. He also became Chairman of the Swedish-owned L. M. Ericsson Telephone Company. In 1933 he gave a reception at Someries House for Nobel Prizewinners, and the guests included George Bernard Shaw, Rudyard Kipling and Guglielmo Marchese Marconi.

The Grand Duke continued to be troublesome. Indeed Harold in 1925 found him 'perfectly crazy' at Cannes, abusing everybody. Alice Winn played bridge with him sometimes in London and was terrified. 'I never knew what he was going to say next.' Once Gina told him, 'You're cheating', which he was, and he immediately sent her to her room. As Felix Yusupov said, the man was not responsible for his actions. At Luton Hoo he got in a rage with one of Lady Ludlow's footmen trying to take off his boot, and kicked him across the room. Harold saw this, and his 'blood boiled'. The Grand Duke couldn't bear noises such as crackling paper and crunching sugar, and noses had to be blown outside the room. The only people he seemed to like were taxi drivers, because he enjoyed saying: 'Take me to Buckingham Palace.' His humour was excruciating. He had a butler called Abel, who therefore was 'able to pass the soup'; and this was repeated at every meal.

Sophie Torby on the other hand was loved by her grand-children, and she would hide presents for them under the satin cushions. The Grand Duke was furious, as was George V, when it was reported in the papers that Nada and Prince George (later

Duke of Kent) had won a Charleston competition at Cannes. He grumbled constantly that Zia was not seeing enough of them and was irritated by Boy, who talked about nothing except ladies' clothes.

Nada and Zia gave a Russian ball to help émigrés, thereby causing the wrath of Zinoviev, supposed author of the notorious letter inciting British workers to rebellion and chairman of the executive committee of the Communist International. The Wernhers were in the South of France early in 1927 when Diaghilev gave a performance of his Ballet Russe with Serge Lifar dancing at Monte Carlo. Countess Torby was already a great admirer of Diaghilev, having been to the production of *Boris Godunov* at the Paris Opera before the war and to *Swan Lake* with Kscheshinka and Nijinsky at Covent Garden. In March she arranged a charity gala, again for Russian émigrés at Nice. Diaghilev was enchanted to discover that she was the granddaughter of Pushkin, and she was enchanted by Diaghilev. As a result, she promised to leave him in her will one of Pushkin's letters that she owned. It seems that she knew she had not long to live.

Sophie Torby owned twelve of Pushkin's letters, eleven to his beautiful fiancée Natalia Goncharova in 1830 and an angry one to her mother after the marriage. The letters were in French and were written from Moscow and Boldino, where Pushkin had been marooned during a cholera epidemic. The Boldino letters were punctured with pinholes, reported to be effective in releasing infected air. It was Pushkin's most productive time as a poet. All the letters had been published in an edited form by Turgenev, and in the days of the Tsar Sophie had been incensed by a peremptory letter from Grand Duke Constantin Constantinovich, President of the Imperial Academy of Arts and Sciences, demanding that she should return Russia's heritage to Russia – this when she herself had been refused permission to return to Russia on account of the morganatic marriage. According to Lifar, she had sworn on oath that her grandfather's letters should never see Russia again.

She died that same year in September. She had not altered her will, but the family gave Diaghilev a letter. Again to quote Lifar, Grand Duke Michael needed money, as he was continually ill and 'cared little for what went on around him'. 'His daughters fell wholly under Sergei Pavlovich's [Diaghilev's] charm. Thus, for a ridiculously small sum (if I am right, only some 30,000 francs), Diaghilev acquired [the rest of] this priceless treasure.'

Diaghilev died in August 1929, and Lifar felt it his duty to buy all his library and archives, including Pushkin's twelve letters. Apparently it was his hope that they eventually would be returned to Russia. Lifar died in 1986, and with the coming of the Gorbachev era the letters were sold to the Soviet Ministry of Culture and are now housed with the State Pushkin archives.★

George V may have been irritated at times by Sophie Torby, but he wrote a warm and affectionate letter of condolence to the Grand Duke about 'the terrible shock to May and me when I opened your telegram this morning', ending:

> God bless you.
> I remain Yours very affectionately George.

Much of her will was concerned with the disposal of her jewellery. Among the many bequests Queen Mary was left 'in grateful and devoted remembrance my ruby brooch with ruby pendant given to me by my brothers-in-law and originally chosen for the Empress Alexandra'. The pearl necklace which she had worn every day was to be sold for death duties. Birdie was left her best bracelet of rubies and sapphires. Her great collection of Fabergé was to be divided among her children; in Zia's share was one object that is nearly always illustrated in books as a master-piece of Fabergé's art, a spray of gypsophila in rose diamonds and green enamel on gold in a jade jar, so delicate that the stalks and flowers quiver at the slightest movement of air (it had once belonged to Queen Olga of Greece). Zia also inherited her mother's umbrellas and parasols, which had Fabergé handles.

In December Harold told his mother that the Grand Duke had been to dinner and had 'behaved quite well for him', the reason being that he no longer had his wife to argue with. He added:

★ The proceeds of the sale are to be used for an annual Prix Lifar, to be awarded to talented dancers.

'The Queen wishes Zia to have tea with her Tuesday and I am quite sure it is in connection with some stupidities the G.D. has told her. I told Zia to put all the blame on me if H.M. reviles her for not having the G.D. to live with us. He is such an ungrateful old devil that one never knows what "potions" he is stirring up.'

Negotiations began to sell Kazbeck to pay the French death duties. While Harold and Zia were in Cannes to discuss this, 'We came face to face with Cynthia Mosley and her disgusting husband [disgusting because Sir Oswald Mosley was then a Labour MP]. We cut them dead.'

Otto Beit and Margie Pryce, 'after great suffering', both died in 1928. Margie left nearly £90,000 and was buried at East Hyde near Julius Wernher's mausoleum. In April 1929 Harold reported that the Grand Duke was dying, and he was not sorry. 'He has never shown any gratitude or one single endearing quality since I have known him.' Evidently the Grand Duke had been moved from Cambridge Gate, for he died in lesser premises on the 27th at 41 York Terrace. He was buried with his wife in an appropriately Imperial tomb, now almost concealed by rambler roses, in West Hampstead cemetery.

Then in 1930 Friedie Eckstein died: the last of the great trio of Empire pioneers, so an obituarist wrote, referring of course to Julius Wernher and Alfred Beit.

The year 1928 was memorable for Harold and Zia in a quite different way. For it was the beginning of Harold's successes with Brown Jack, one of the most brilliant racehorses in English racing history, and Zia's acquisition of Double Life, also to be a spectacular winner – but more importantly the foundation mare of their Someries stud that produced the famous horses Precipitation, Persian Gulf, Meld and Charlottown.

Harold had bought Brown Jack, a gelding, for a mere £750, with a contingency of £50 to the trainer Aubrey Hastings at the Wroughton stables in Wiltshire if the horse won a race. Having once been a 'gentleman jockey' he was then more interested in National Hunt racing than the flat. His ambition was to win the Cheltenham Challenge Cup, so he had asked the Rogers brothers, leading Irish trainers and dealers whom he had known before the war, from whom he had bought some of his hunters, to look out for a top-class hurdler. Brown Jack had been foaled in 1924, by Jackdaw (a horse with a certain reputation) and Querquidella, and when entered at the Dublin sales this placid little yearling had failed even to attract a bid. Later he was bought for £110, then sold to Charlie Rogers for £275. After a year Charlie Rogers had telephoned to say that he thought he had two possibilities, though the horse was as yet untried.

Harold was in Sweden with Wenner-Gren at the time, on his way to Berlin to make a deal with Siemens. A paragraph from his letter of 2 June 1928 to Zia reads: 'Aubrey wired me advising me to buy the 2 horses from Rogers, he wants £800 for the one by Jackdaw & I think it worth it as the other was so cheap.'

In his first race, at Bournemouth, Brown Jack finished third, but he ended the season by winning five out of eight races. He next proceeded to realize Harold's ambition by winning the Cheltenham Challenge Cup with extraordinary assurance, and it was then that he was spotted by Steve Donoghue, the champion jockey, who suggested to Hastings that the horse ought to be trained for the flat. The result was a famous partnership between Donoghue and Brown Jack, who also proved to be a horse with a quite exceptional character, adding to his enormous popularity. It established the fame of Wroughton stables, and made racing history.

Zia had bought, through Cecil Boyd-Rochfort, a yearling called Lilyon, which won three races in the summer of 1927. She also had interests in other horses. Encouraged by the success of Lilyon, she asked CBR to find her another yearling; and this was to be Double Life, a small chestnut filly, bought at the Newmarket sales for six hundred guineas. Apparently Norman Field, a cousin of Marshall Field and an owner at Freemason Lodge, said: 'Why have you bought this little rabbit?' CBR replied that he was sure that she would make a good brood mare even if she proved no good at racing. It was true that her dam Saint Joan was little known, but her sire, Bachelor's Double, had descendants that were impressive.

Double Life's breeders had been R. J. Russell Ryan in Ireland and the lightweight jockey Johnny Dines. As a two-year-old, she won twice, and in her second and final season in 1929, ridden by Johnny Dines, she won four more, including the Chesterfield Cup and the Cambridgeshire, under Zia's colours of green and yellow. This last was a thrilling race, with Double Life starting tenth and then moving up past one horse after another, Dines riding 'like a man inspired'. Zia was the first woman to have won the Cambridgeshire. Gina, then aged ten, remembers flowers and telegrams of congratulation pouring in, the telephone constantly ringing and her mother 'being rather coy about it'.

Harold wrote to his mother: 'The little filly looked like a polo pony next to the other horses. She stayed on well to the last. So we got a good cup after all, and accomplished what we had set out to do, namely to win a race at Ascot and Goodwood in the same year.' But, he said, the Irish market was being spoilt, because Jim Joel, Barney Barnato's nephew, was busy buying up 'everything he can get hold of', paying ridiculous prices. 'So typical of that family. Father would have been amused.' Sister Agnes had been to stay at Lubenham, ostensibly 'to talk about horses'. Instead 'we had an ample ration of her usual obsession, His Majesty, and heard all about what he says, does, eats etc! . . . The canny old thing is still very much all there and at bridge remembers every card.'

Harold at that time was also backing plays in the West End of London, though without much success. His other great enthusiasm was polo, and he made a dashing figure on the field. The Someries House team in effect started in 1927, playing at Roehampton, Ranelagh and Hurlingham, and was 'very well mounted', in part thanks to the remarkable trainer F. H. Thomason. Harold himself could only find time to play occasionally, and the main components of the team were young officers from the 17/21st Lancers, usually Desmond Miller, R. D. B. Cooke ('Cookie') and H. C. Walford ('Chicken'), and sometimes R. G. Hamilton-Russell and Colonel V. N. Lockett. During that first season King Alfonso of Spain was staying with the Wernhers at Someries House and was a frequent and enthusiastic spectator – Lady Ludlow also had him staying at Luton Hoo.

It was said that Zia never missed her daily inspection of polo ponies before they played. Followed by Thomason, she would examine each one meticulously, checking the grooming and such things as maladjustments in the saddling.

A great deal of gossip circulated about Desmond Miller and Zia. There was no doubt that she developed an obsession about this good-looking and well-dressed young man, some twelve years younger than herself, and he kept clothes at Lubenham. In fact the relationship was 'innocent', as it became clear later that he preferred men to women. Harold may not have realized this at first, but tolerated him not only because he was a good polo player and generally well liked, but because it meant that Zia could not complain too much if she had suspicions about his own indiscretions. As Cookie's widow Joan said years later, Desmond was a kind of ADC to the Wernhers. 'Zia hated being alone, and loved to dominate people.' Desmond was insecure socially, with little sense of humour and dazzled by the Grand Ducal glamour and all the royal 'rigmarole'. The rest of the family thought him boring. Zia was very good to his elderly mother, who lived with a companion at Rugby.

In June Harold was knighted, a KCVO. The citation mentioned his services to agriculture and the fact that he was Honorary Secretary at the King Edward VII Hospital.

21

Brown Jack

'Lady Bird' Ludlow continued to give her spectacular musicales at Bath House and enormous summer garden parties at Luton Hoo. She dressed rather more sedately now, though she had gained a reputation for being an expert on furs and lace. She employed a butler, three footmen, a French chef, a hallboy and two 'odd men' for cleaning. There were also five chauffeurs, dressed in purple livery with velvet collars and crested buttons, as well as four housemaids, a housekeeper, and five kitchen and scullery maids. Mr Edwards the butler was her great support. A sometime kitchen maid who later worked for Zia has said: 'With Lady Ludlow you were a servant. With Lady Zia you were a friend. Lady Ludlow talked gruff like a man. She was very conscious of what she had.'

Although there were complaints about small tips, Lady Ludlow is remembered for tremendous generosity and of course lavish entertaining. 'A lot was always going on in her life.' She was indeed one of the great hostesses of the time. She was also popular in the town of Luton and loved presiding over Court Leet dinners. At that period she did not spend as much time at Luton Hoo as she did when her eyesight began to fail. Mr Edwards would be sent in advance with other servants from Bath House. The first footman would sit by the chauffeur in the purple Rolls, with Lady Ludlow behind, possibly accompanied by her granddaughter Gina, who was so embarrassed by Grandma Alice's regal progress that she felt like hiding on the floor. The second footman would be in charge of taking the staff in a special purple bus. At Luton

Hoo there was a small resident staff, not counting the fifteen or so gardeners, the firemen, the gamekeepers, the blacksmith, the carpenter, the laundry maids, the night watchmen and the man who came in to clean the copper pans and pluck fowls. It was the job of the fifth chauffeur to take orders each morning from the chef for buying things from shops. When there were house parties, especially for the pheasant shoots, perhaps a dozen people worked in the kitchen. It was considered nothing less than a disaster if a thousand birds were not killed on the first day.

On Sundays when Lady Ludlow was in residence at Luton Hoo there were services in the chapel built by Street for the Gerard Leighs in 1874. This superb late Victorian building had a Romanesque arcading of alabaster, stained glass by Clayton and Bell, Minton floor tiles and a moulded ceiling decorated by David Bell. But the high standard of music, under the direction of the organist Frederick Gostelow, had a certain fame. Only guests and estate and mansion staff were generally admitted to these services; others on application might be allowed in with special passes. The full choir consisted of ten boys and six men, dressed in purple cassocks, Eton collars, bow-ties and surplices edged with lace. Rehearsals were exacting, for Lady Ludlow was quite liable to call out after the anthem: 'That wasn't good enough. Sing it again.' George of Greece when in exile used to come to stay and had a special seat in the chapel. He would always ask for one particular anthem, having been 'overwhelmed' on his first visit by the top boy's tenor solo.

It was in 1929 that Chaliapin, after a recording session at Queen's Hall, asked the celebrated accompanist Ivor Newton to play for him at the next Ludlow soirée. Three hundred and thirty-five invitations had been sent out for that evening. Thereafter Ivor Newton was often engaged for the musicales. In his autobiography he lists Flagstad, Grace Moore, Gladys Swarthout, Conchita Supervia, Yvonne Printemps, Sacha Guitry, Alexander Kipnis, Gigli and Tauber as having sung at Bath House, with Kreisler and Piatigorsky among the instrumentalists. The front row of seats, sometimes the first two rows, were reserved for royalty, and applause after each piece of music would be somewhat muted, on account of the ladies wearing long white gloves. Lady Ludlow would always ask for an encore, and, according to Newton, the only time Chaliapin was nonplussed was when she called out: 'Do sing me some Brahms' (which does not seem quite in character).

After the concert Lady Ludlow would escort the royals to the supper room, followed by Harold with the rest of the guests. The artists would then retreat to the red drawing-room, where Sir Julius's collection of Renaissance jewels, Limoges enamels, bronzes and ivories was kept. They had to wait until Lady Ludlow sent a message inviting them to supper. 'She once came into the artists' room for this purpose and was astonished to find the short, portly Gigli and the tall, slim Piatigorsky dancing a minuet with proper stateliness.'

When Queen Mary visited Bath House for tea, certain prize objects would be hidden away in advance. If the Queen did suggest that she might be given something that attracted her, the usual reply would be: 'Oh no, that's an heirloom.' In 1932 a huge and sumptuous volume, limited to a hundred copies, was published, entitled *Old English Porcelain: The Lady Ludlow Collection*. The excellence of the production and the high quality of the colour printing caused quite a sensation in the art world. It was now recognized that this collection of English procelain was one of the best in the country. Queen Mary, on receiving a copy of the book, wondered why she had never been shown the Worcester vase illustrated as the frontispiece and some rare Derby figures of 1764–9.

Lady Ludlow spent three weeks every year at Baden-Baden. The budding novelist Barbara Cartland sometimes coincided with her. It was the fashion, but you also went there to get thin. The first week was spent unwinding, after an enormous dose of salts. The next week was for relaxing, and the third week for building up. Walks up the mountain and running were part of the curriculum. 'It was very hard work.'

After the Prince of Wales arrived at Luton Hoo in July 1930 in his blue monoplane, to watch a police athletics meeting, Lady Ludlow took to flying to race meetings in a private aeroplane. The successes of her son's and daughter-in-law's horses had turned her into a racing enthusiast. Indeed in 1930 a newspaper report described her as a 'race-horse owner and art expert'. So she bought a large house at Newmarket, Warren Towers. Her best horse was a brown gelding called Greenore, foaled in 1929, recognized as a high-class sprint handicapper. Between 1931 and 1935 Greenore ran forty-two times and won on thirteen occasions, ridden usually by Michael Beary or Harry Wragg.

Harold and Zia were now determined to begin breeding racehorses. Double Life was therefore boarded at Cecil Boyd-Rochfort's family estate, Middleton Park, County Westmeath, and in 1931 after one barren year she was mated to Hurry On, sire of three Derby winners. The result was a filly, Nymph Errant, of no great consequence, and, as in any case CBR was convinced that Hurry On's colts were superior to his fillies, he persuaded Zia to send Double Life to Hurry On once more in 1932. This time there was a chestnut colt called Precipitation, with a magnificent career ahead, which included winning the Ascot Gold Cup.

Double Life's success as a foundation mare for the Wernhers' eventual stud at Newmarket was to prove truly amazing. For she also bred Persian Gulf, the Coronation Cup winner, and the filly Doubleton, from whom descended the great Meld, winner of three Classic races in 1955. And Meld's son was Charlottown, winner of the 1966 Derby. As CBR's biographer wrote: 'It is fair to say that this little "rabbit" of a filly was one of the greatest bargains in the history of racing.'

The combination of Brown Jack and Steve Donoghue came to be known as the 'old firm'. 1928 was their first season together, and on 19 June that year they won – with surprising ease – the Queen Alexandra Stakes at Ascot, over two miles, the longest race under Jockey Club rules. This was the beginning of a great series of triumphs. In that same season Brown Jack earned £5,334 in prize money. Altogether he was to run in 65 races, winning 25 and being placed 14 times, notching up £23,150 altogether.

In 1929 Brown Jack, by then aged five, won the Salisbury Cup. He lost the Ascot Stakes by a short head but once more won the Queen Alexandra Stakes, beating one of his main rivals by four lengths. His failures – so magnificent, they were almost like duels – all added to his popularity. Brown Jack reacted to crowds and was obviously excited by applause. It came to be realized that here was a horse of unusual intelligence, not to say eccentricity, and the public loved him. But Aubrey Hastings died before seeing Brown Jack's second victory at Ascot, so henceforward Ivor Anthony was to be trainer.

Generally Brown Jack spent his winters turned out to grass at Lubenham. In February 1930 Harold, as Joint Master of the Fernie, gave a party for 650 farmers and landowners in the covered tennis court. The endless flow of champagne and its effect on some of the guests are still remembered in parts of Leicestershire and Northamptonshire. 'Even the chandeliers began to swing.'

'Sir Harold kept the good will of the farming community and knew every inch of the Fernie country, and exactly where the hounds would go,' so an old neighbour of those days has said. 'He was such an enthusiast . . . In some ways between the wars was the most glorious time in the Shires. One appreciated the value of long masterships. And, what's more, with Sir Harold you knew that there was always that imp of mischief lurking behind whatever he said, even when ticking you off.' It was true that he seized every chance to get away from London to be in time for the Thursday meets. If possible he hunted three days a week, often changing into hunting kit in the car. His horses were in the care of stud grooms 'of the old school, wizards at stable craft'. He worried because Alex seemed rather afraid of horses. But Gina was mad about hunting. 'She thinks of little else and is absolutely fearless,' he told his mother. 'Charlie Edmonstone rides like a flat race jockey, but is nothing to her.'

The stream of visitors at Lubenham seemed to observers 'positively endless'. Princess Elizabeth, being about the same age as Myra, first came to tea when she was two and a half – 'two little things running about'; later they had swimming lessons together. The King of Sweden, 'Uncle Gustav', apparently preferred golf to hunting. In November 1930 he invited Harold and Zia for three days' elk-shooting near Gothenburg. 'Lady Zia grassed one massive beast herself,' so a local Leicestershire paper recorded.

Later that month Harold was writing one of his newsy letters to Lady Ludlow: 'Zia is still heavily occupied with her young man [i.e. Desmond Miller] which is a good thing as I am allowed out with Nada. Last night Gloria [Vanderbilt] gave a party which was great fun. The Queen of Spain has been very irritable of late, but last night at the Berkeley she was dancing wildly until 1.15 a.m.'

Zia disapproved of Gloria, which was hardly surprising in view of insinuations in the press four years later about her relationship with Nada. It was becoming well known in the Wernhers' set that Nada was frequenting lesbian bars at Cannes, all of which fuelled the gossip, especially and absurdly when Nada and Edwina Mountbatten went travelling in Persia and elsewhere – absurdly, since they would be accompanied by Edwina's lover Bunnie Phillips. Zia was also becoming jealous and suspicious of the Milford Havens, after seeing pictures of them at Ciro's in the *Daily Mail* with Harold and an exceedingly beautiful girl named Joan Clarkson, who had been in C. B. Cochran's revues. Worse, it turned out that this girl was advertising Amami shampoo. Zia may not have known at that time that the liaison with Joan Clarkson was common knowledge among their friends, who also called the girl 'The Pearl in the Oyster'.

Then to everybody's surprise Prince Friedel Hohenlohe-Langenburg proposed to Gloria. She turned him down. Within three weeks, as Harold gleefully told his mother, Friedel had proposed again, this time to Princess Margarita of Greece, Georgie Greece's cousin and Prince Andrew's daughter, and had been accepted. 'I suppose it is his idea of revenge.'

It was Gloria's twin sister, Thelma Furness, who claimed later to have introduced Mrs Simpson to the Prince of Wales, though Dickie Mountbatten insisted that the first meeting had taken place at the Milford Havens' house near Maidenhead, Lynden Manor.

Harold spoke at a Mansion House dinner in aid of the University College fund. He was also invited to join the board of Imperial College as Crown Nominee. His business interests were spreading fast, and he was a powerful figure in the City. He put up money for building the new Cambridge Theatre at Seven Dials, completed in 1931. Backing plays was proving a disastrous venture; owning theatres looked a safer investment – you got your rents and income from the bars. In that same year, 1931, he formed a group to acquire the ATP, Associated Theatre Properties

Ltd, from W. C. Gaunt, the Yorkshire woollens tycoon, and the Shubert brothers, New York theatre proprietors. ATP owned the freehold of the Apollo Theatre and leases and subleases of the Gaiety, the Adelphi, His Majesty's and the Shaftesbury. The purchase price was said to be £400,000, though ATP had been registered in 1925 with an authorized and issued capital of £500,000. Harold Wernher was recorded as owning 99,503 out of 100,003 ordinary shares. He also owned an undisclosed amount of the preference shares. His group now acquired the freehold of the Cambridge.

Harold's manager was Tom Bostock. A plan to take over the Piccadilly was thwarted, but subleases on the St James's and the Lyric were easily acquired. An arrangement had quickly to be made with Gilbert Miller, one of the foremost presenters of plays in both London and New York, whereby Miller could continue to make use of the St James's and the Lyric, and, if need be, of other theatres controlled by the company. In December an important deal was struck with C. B. Cochran whereby all his future productions would be staged in ATP theatres.

Harold was now the 'big white chief' behind the scenes in London theatreland, though Noël Coward was a little sarcastic about this. Dickie Mountbatten wrote to Georgy Milford Haven on 25 October 1932 that Coward had been spending a week with him and Edwina in Malta. 'He told me that he had met Harold and liked him and that what he particularly liked was that he didn't pretend to be particularly interested in the play [*Words and Music*] but only in the business side.' A refreshing change, he said, from the people who gush about a play when they are not interested.

Actually 1933 was a memorable year for Cochran productions, including Margaret Kennedy's *Escape Me Never* with Elizabeth Bergner at the Apollo, following *Fifteen Wild Decembers* (about the Brontës) at the same theatre, starring Emlyn Williams, Ralph Richardson, Beatrix Lehmann and Diana Wynyard, and *Nymph Errant* with Gertrude Lawrence and a Cole Porter score at the Adelphi. Noël Coward's *Conversation Piece* was performed at His Majesty's in 1934, but that play marked a break between him and Cochran.

Financially, the thirties was not a happy time for the theatre. As Basil Dean said, it was still awaiting its messiah, with Hollywood drawing away some of the best London talent. Dean had an idea. Why not 'combine the current influence of the film studios with the wealth of past achievement of the theatre?' He knew Tom Bostock, who was also 'desperately worried' and wanted to sustain the interest of his 'magnifico' as well as balance the accounts. So Dean was summoned to a meeting at Someries House. Harold, however, would only give him – as he put it – a loose understanding and it was agreed that his headquarters could be at the Cambridge Theatre.

The Cambridge was not proving very popular, and Harold was worried. Dean therefore had the auditorium redesigned: the lighting was improved and warmer colours used for the decorations. This made all the difference. Harold having become interested in going into films, on 7 February 1934 a lunch was arranged at the Savoy, with R. D. Blumenfield in the chair, and Harold and Stephen Courtauld on each side of him. John Galsworthy, Dodie Smith and Clemence Dane were among the authors present. There was big press coverage and several star actors and actresses were lured to Ealing Studios. But war disrupted all these grandiose schemes, and in 1943 Harold had to sell ATP at a loss to Prince Littler, but without His Majesty's, whose lease had already come to an end. The Adelphi had also by then been sold to Jack Hylton. In later life Harold used to say: 'I have lost two fortunes.' One was to do with the theatres; the other possibly with an Anglo-Spanish construction company, ruined by the Civil War.

Nada had met Douglas Fairbanks, Junior, through the Mountbattens, who had spent part of their honeymoon with his father. She visited him in Hollywood, and her stories inspired Harold and Zia to go there too. Fairbanks was amused that the Wernhers were disappointed to find the place so sedate. 'They thought Hollywood would be terribly gay. Then they went to San Francisco, which was so wild they were rather shocked!'

Douglas Fairbanks thought Harold 'very attractive to look at, charming to meet, the decisive one in the family'. Zia hadn't so much humour as Harold and sometimes didn't seem to catch on to his jokes. 'Harold was jolly, with a great twinkle about life in general. He liked informal social life, she liked formal. I was told she could be quite temperamental . . . No, I didn't play polo. Couldn't afford it frankly.'

During 1931 and 1932 Harold played in most of the leading polo tournaments, winning a few cups. He was the owner of a champion polo pony, Nube de Plata. In the mid-thirties the Maharajah of Jaipur was often in the Someries team, as were Captain Mike Ansell, the famous showjumper, and the usual young officers from the 17/21st Lancers, mounted as always by Harold. Harold and Zia went to India with the Reggie Winns to stay at Jaipur and with the Viceroy, Lord Willingdon. It was probably then that Harold hit on the idea that the wonderful new Electrolux refrigerator was just the thing for India. He would laugh about it later. 'My first big mistake. I launched out with an ambitious sales campaign only to find that these fridges wouldn't stand 120 in the shade. They went into reverse, and became hot enough to cook a joint.' Soon afterwards air-cooled refrigerators were introduced, but by 1936 Electrolux refrigerator production had moved into 'All Gas', with the slogan 'The Flame that Freezes'.

In the year before, Harold had given a Victory Dinner to celebrate record sales both in refrigerators and vacuum cleaners. He would turn up at board meetings at Electrolux in his most casual clothes with leather patches on the elbows, but was always elegant at formal evening occasions, wearing all his decorations. He presented a silver rosebowl for the best golfer in the company, and then proceeded to win it himself, so that his name would be inscribed on it first. He would have been surprised to know that nobody had dared beat him. He was remembered for the dictum: 'Never invest in a company that has a large and well-furnished head office,' though his counterparts in Ericsson Telephones in Sweden had extremely luxurious offices.

He smoked a lot. The smell of Balkan Sobranie cigarettes wafting upstairs at Someries House meant that he had returned home. One of Myra's memories of those days is of him coming home from the City and sitting with his battered old briefcase on his knees and taking out papers, while ash from his cigarette-holder dropped on the carpet (to Zia's annoyance). In the mornings Myra would watch him shaving with a cutthroat razor.

But to return to Brown Jack, Harold's greatest pride. In 1930 he had won the Alexandra Stakes yet again, also the Goodwood and Doncaster cups. This 'gallant old gentleman', as he was called in the press, was as lively as ever. That year was also memorable for the arrival of Zia's Mail Fist, another gelding, for training at Wroughton stables. He had once shown great promise but was now behaving disappointingly. To quote R. C. Lyle, Brown Jack's faithful chronicler: 'She [Lady Zia] little knew that her five-year-old would never win again a race of any kind but that he would gain fame and popularity as the familiar and willing attendant [as pacemaker] on her husband's Brown Jack in nearly all his future successes.' Racegoers became fascinated not only by the friendship between the two horses but by the way Mail Fist would speed ahead at the beginning of a race and then drop back to allow Brown Jack to win. Steve Donoghue, Brown Jack and Mail Fist became an almost invincible triumvirate.

It was recalled that in the early days in Ireland Brown Jack had had another inseparable friend, a donkey. Stories began to circulate about his intelligence and fads and fancies. One admirer went so far as to say that 'a kindlier brain no horse or man or woman ever possessed'. He liked to sleep sitting on his manger; when the rails were padded to make him more comfortable he tore away the padding with his teeth. He could never bear wearing a blanket and would only have a linen sheet. He hated his siestas being disturbed by the noise of tennis balls. He loved humbugs and éclairs, and would snatch his stable lad Alfie Garratt's bread and cheese sandwiches. He was easily bored and had to be introduced to any newcomer at Wroughton. Before a race he would begin sweating in anticipation, and just before reaching the winning post would make a curious little 'shuffle dance' as if to show his delight at yet another triumph. It was plain that he thoroughly disliked racing at Newmarket.

1931 was considered Brown Jack's peak year, when he won the Chester Cup, the Queen Alexandra Stakes and the Ebor Handicap, and came second in the Goodwood and Doncaster Cups, carrying 10 stone, a big handicap. Harold told Lady Ludlow how he had had a hunch about the Ebor Handicap. 'I took the night train to York arriving at 3 a.m. so as to see the race. It was run at great speed, B.J. just drew out 3 furlongs from home, and was in at a canter at 10 to 1. Luckily I played on my inspiration and had a really good bet. I have never seen a Derby winner have such a reception. The crowd jumped over the barriers and simply mobbed the horse and jockey.' Just before the winning post Donoghue had leant forward and patted him on the neck. Brown Jack's ears pricked at once, knowing that he had won once more.

Unbelievably Brown Jack won the Queen Alexandra Stakes in 1932 and 1933. By that time his fan mail was as large as any film star's. In 1934 he was ten years old. The great question was, could the old fellow do it yet again? Could he win the Queen Alexandra Stakes for the sixth year in succession?

Ivor Anthony could not bear to watch that race and sat apart under a tree. The great rival was Solatium, six years younger. Mail Fist at first as usual went well into the lead, Brown Jack several lengths behind. Then gradually Brown Jack began to move up. The suspense was intolerable, so *The Times* correspondent wrote. Donoghue lost his whip, and had to talk Brown Jack home. 'I am certain the old rogue was laughing at me for having dropped it, and I know he enjoyed giving me that fight. Just as he had done every time, he pricked his ears as he approached the post and did his comic little dance.'

Ivor Anthony knew Brown Jack had won because of the terrific cheering, and R. C. Lyle wrote afterwards:

'I have never seen such a sight anywhere . . . Eminently respectable old ladies in the Royal Enclosure gathered up their skirts . . . Hats were raised in the air . . . There were cheers from all parts of the course. Such a scene could be witnessed only in this country. Crowds round the unsaddling enclosure were many times deep. Brown Jack at last came in, looking to the right and left, his ears pricked again, as he was patted from all sides.

As Harold told Lyle afterwards: 'Half his tail was pulled out.'
The King sent for Harold to congratulate him. Now it was

decided that Brown Jack and his friend Mail Fist had earned their retirement. They were transported from Wroughton to Luben-ham, where they enjoyed a new life carrying their owners out hunting with the Fernie. In racing history Brown Jack ranks as one of the greatest racehorses of the twentieth century, along with Arkle, Shergar and Desert Orchid, not to mention Meld.

It was a time when Oswald Mosley's Blackshirts were causing alarm in the East End of London. Rather unwisely and out of curiosity, Harold and Zia decided to go to one of those meetings. Suddenly there was a shout of 'Oi, 'ere comes Brown Jack!' They had been recognized, and had quickly to retreat.

Harold had a disappointment with his horse Ballasport in the Grand National. The second time round, another horse fell, his rein catching Ballasport's jockey's leg and pulling the stirrup; the jockey managed to carry on for eight fences but eventually fell exhausted at the last fence. Red Bee was another of Harold's horses that ran in the National. His ambition was to ride at Aintree himself, but Zia, on hearing this, took good care that they would always be in the South of France at the time of the race. Gina later used to ride Ballasport out hunting. One day when out with the Quorn she jumped a fence and Ballasport fell on the spikes, piercing his stomach and killing him.

Both Cecil Boyd-Rochfort and Zia had great hopes for Double Life's son Precipitation, now a fine chestnut and very like his sire Hurry On. In the meantime Zia had had some success with Casanova, which had won the Dewhurst Stakes and had just failed to win the Two Thousand Guineas. It was also realized that Precipitation ought eventually to be great at stud, and with this in view, at CBR's suggestion, the Wernhers decided to buy part of Sir Alec Black's Compton Park stud at Newmarket. They named it the Someries Stud, and eventually it was expanded to 182 acres.

Precipitation won seven races, worth £18,419, and these included a memorable triumph in the Ascot Gold Cup. The Someries Stud was ready to receive him for the covering season in 1938. He too knew he was a star and had many idiosyncrasies, for instance, refusing to be touched by a brush and thus having to be groomed with a stable rubber. He liked his liberty in the paddock, wet or fine, at a time when most stallions were usually kept in solitary confinement apart from exercise periods. Indeed if he had not been allowed to roam free he would have been unmanageable. His fee at first was 300 guineas. In due course he sired three St Leger winners and a Derby winner, Airborne, and his grandson Sassafras won the Prix de l'Arc de Triomphe. The stud was managed by CBR with the assistance of Peter McCall.

Harold's curious nickname for Zia was 'Prut'. As a hostess, she was supreme, 'minding desperately' about making guests comfortable; and Lubenham with its chintzes and brocades had a cheerful atmosphere, very English. The garden, although on a grand scale, was with its great herbaceous borders also much more English and informal than Luton Hoo's. Zia was not at all intellectual, but loved the theatre – also her gardening and animals. In so many ways she seemed the opposite both to Nada and Harold, and it was considered that her relationship with Desmond Miller, who most people thought was a charmer, could have begun as a kind of defence. Many thought she had another admirer, Eric Stocks (whom the family despised as a wet), but she treated him simply as a useful spare man. Nevertheless one notices that both men featured in the Luton Hoo visitors' book when Harold and Zia came to stay there – again as spares no doubt. Or perhaps it was a little game hatched by Harold and Lady Ludlow.

Desmond also sometimes went to Scotland with the Wernhers. The children loved those six weeks at Downie Park and Invermark. 'We worshipped Scotland. The house was packed with friends. It was absolutely marvellous, the highlight of our lives. We were out all day fishing or up in the hills. Papa came and went.' The girls were being very strictly brought up, but Gina was inclined to be rebellious. Myra, small and bright, much younger, a great mimic, seemed set to be a brilliant musician. The choirboys at Luton Hoo admired Gina from afar, especially for her athletic skills and the fact that her spaniels were trained to be gun dogs. Alex looked very much like his mother, fair with slightly Slav eyes, but unlike her was interested in the arts and music. He soon got over his nervousness with horses, and when he went to Sandhurst in 1938 won the much coveted 'Saddle' for the best rider. Like both his parents, he shot and played golf very well.

Some letters from Harold to Lady Ludlow in the early 1930s seem to indicate that Zia was not altogether happy at the time, obviously because of jealousy. As friends have since said, she was essentially vulnerable, even immature.

December 5 1930. Zia determined to be very gay and insists on going to a night club every time we go to London.

May 20 1932. Nada in Paris, staying as you may guess with Gloria. The Desmond business is still going strong, but there is friction because Nancy Tree asks him out fairly frequently. I suppose to tease! Anyhow for the peace of the house I hope no marked cooling off takes place.

Oct 18 1932. Back from Sandringham. All very homely and pleasant and not frightening at all. Place ugly. Comfortable, but decoration is not our style. Venetia James was there and of course immediately wrote forty letters on Sandringham paper to all her friends. Zia suddenly gone south. You can put these in order: (1) to say goodbye to Nada (2) to have her hair done (3) to see Desmond.

February 13 1933. The gap between the sisters is broadening, chiefly on account of Gloria and every effort is being made to compromise me, so as to put me against Georgy and Nada and vice versa.

March 16 1933. Zia going to Baden-Baden. Sisters more friendly because Nada refuses to be drawn into academic arguments.

August 5 1933. Dickie Mountbatten most intelligent, with remarkable memory. Zia had one of her anti-Georgy outbursts which upset him very much. As you know he worships Georgy and looks up to him like a god. Maharajah of Jaipur staying, and Sister Agnes before returning to her royal summer quarters.

August 16 1934. Going to Gleneagles. Cynthia Pole Carew coming which will balance up Desmond! Zia's energy is amazing. After a full day on the hills she drags the tired and rather reluctant Desmond to fish or shoot rabbits.

August 26 1934. Downie Park. Awkward incident. Zia is always asking me to take Cynthia out or for her to go to my butt in order to salve her conscience for the previous week when Desmond was here! At the same time she was spitefully jealous. One evening we came in having been to Kirriemuir and Glamis and Zia says to me 'Oh have you had a nice day lying in the heather?', and to Cynthia 'Your cheeks are red'. I said nothing at the time but later tackled Zia alone and asked her why she made such horrid remarks which could only create a strained atmosphere and embarrass everyone. To which she had no answer. I must say it gets pretty boring and I can hardly feel it contributes to the calm and peace one expects on holiday.

Soon after this Desmond was sent with his regiment to India, and there he remained until just before war broke out.

In 1935 Harold had to resign from being Joint Master of the Fernie, partly because of business pressures, partly because he had dislocated his shoulder playing polo. His place was therefore taken by Zia, in conjunction with Commander F. J. Alexander and Captain Derrick Hignett.

The Villa Kazbeck at Cannes had to be sold. It was bought for 600,000 francs by a Russian named Davidowski and some others. Subsequently it was turned into flats.

Harold as usual was touchy when Zia received begging letters from impoverished Russian relatives, though without prompting he put up the money for a Wernher cousin to start a garage in North London. Zia's Uncle Sandro, Grand Duke Alexander, had published with some success a book of memoirs, *Once a Grand Duke*. He was in Paris, separated from his wife, Grand Duchess Xenia, the sister of the late Tsar, who had a Grace and Favour house at Hampton Court. In February 1932 he wrote to Zia saying that he was ill in bed, and asked for a loan of £500. He would pay her back when his second book was published. He was also writing a series of articles for the *Red Book Magazine*. Zia was instructed to reply that she could lend him £250, which had to be repaid within a year. She gave high taxation as an excuse, and the fact that Boy was ill. Harold also turned down the suggestion that he should help Alexander's daughter, Irina Yusupov, in her lawsuit against Metro-Goldwyn-Mayer over their Rasputin film. Probably Zia's offer to Alexander was refused, for when *Always a Grand Duke* was published in 1933, 'Sandro' was not complimentary about Zia and Nada, scorning their 'well-groomed and highly admired beauty', and describing them as 'playmates and friends of the Prince of Wales' and 'leading the carefree existence of typical rich Londoners', with whom he could have nothing in common.

Zia was of course far from being a playmate of the Prince of Wales, any more than she was a playmate of Gloria Vanderbilt and Thelma Furness. Nor did she approve of Mrs Simpson, who was indeed a friend of Nada. However, she did attend a dinner at which Mrs Simpson and the Prince were present, and this was in the year of the Silver Jubilee, 1935. It had been given by the German ambassador, Leopold von Hoesch, in honour of Zia's cousin, Crown Princess Cécile of Germany (wife of 'Little Willie'), and the Otto von Bismarcks, who were all staying with the Wernhers at Someries House. It has been claimed that it was at this dinner that Princess Cécile urged the Prince to make his notorious appeal at the Queen's Hall for friendship with Nazi Germany.

According to Harold, it was Nada who had encouraged Princess Marina to marry Prince George, later Duke of Kent, in 1934. True or not, it hardly matters, but Princess Marina (who was of course her cousin) was to become one of Zia's closest friends. The Duchess of York invited Zia and Harold to a supper party after the wedding. Zia was asked to bring her guests and anyone else she liked. There would be a little dancing 'if people are not too exhausted', and dress would be informal; no decorations.

1934 was also the year in which Prince Philip, aged thirteen, came to school at Gordonstoun. Previously he had been at Kurt Hahn's school in Germany, but Hahn had been driven out by the Nazis and had founded Gordonstoun on the same principles. Earlier, when he was eight, Prince Philip had been at school at Cheam, and had then stayed on occasions at Lubenham. Since his parents had been left impoverished he moved about in an extended family system. His uncles George Milford Haven and to some extent Louis (Dickie) Mountbatten were acting *in loco parentis*. His grandmother was living at Kensington Palace. Harold kept a 'watching brief', and he and Zia were regarded as honorary uncle and aunt. The Milford Havens' son David and Alex Wernher became Prince Philip's great friends. Philip generally came to Lubenham for Christmas, and has been remembered locally as having been 'fair-haired, boisterous and very polite and handsome'. He gave Myra his old bus tickets.

Prince Philip has considered Harold as being one of the early influences on his life. He enjoyed their long discussions, and would arrive with a list of questions for advice.

During Jubilee year Zia was one of those organizing a Russian Exhibition in London, which of course included some of their mother's wonderful collection of Fabergé. The Princess Royal agreed to lend the sapphire and diamond necklace that had once belonged to Countess Torby, but wanted it back for evenings and the Ascot Weekend; this necklace was believed to have been owned by the Empress Elizabeth of Russia. Various relations were approached for loans. Queen Marie of Romania ('Aunty Missy') sent a diadem and a writing table. Whether it was the same as the 'beautiful sapphire Hesse diadem my husband bought me and now kept in a bank in Switzerland' is not clear. She explained that her pearls had been sent to Moscow for safety, but 'taken by the Bolsheviks at the Revolution'. She added: 'Now I am at the other end of the world. I have become a sort of recluse who lives as best she can, not as she would!' 'Cousin Juliana' of the Netherlands didn't want to send anything. Queen Mary lent some Russian silver, but wrote that the King had a rule about not lending pictures owned by the Crown, except for exhibition at Buckingham Palace.

In February 1934 something happened that would have surprised but ultimately delighted Sir Julius Wernher. Harold was offered the chairmanship of Central Mining in place of Sir Evelyn Walters. He told his mother that it was the unanimous wish of the directors, and had the blessing of General Smuts and Montague Norman, the Governor of the Bank of England. He told Lady Ludlow that although a very high salary had been offered he had turned the job down.

1. I do not believe in being a part time Chairman for such an important Company. *2.* I should have no spare time for myself at all, unless I gave up all the things I have helped to create and which are my real interests. *3.* I would have to go out to South Africa at times when I am most wanted for other jobs. *4.* It would be an entirely new field, i.e. mining. *5.* I am not dependent on a salary and can afford the sacrifice.

I often think of father and the Sundays spent at Luton Hoo when he was immersed in papers and correspondence. He really got very little enjoyment out of his country place and all that he had spent on it, and doubtless you would have seen much more of him than you would have done had his interests been less exacting.

Still, the offer had been a very great honour, especially after the slights Harold had felt during his childhood, realizing that his parents had a poor opinion of his intelligence compared to his brothers'. Further distinctions came when George V nominated Harold to the Council of the Duchy of Lancaster. Harold also succeeded Lord Somerleyton as Senior Honorary Secretary, in effect chief executive, of the King's Hospital Fund.

A biography of Brown Jack was commissioned, with illustrations by Lionel Edwards. Brown Jack and his 'lad' Alfie Garratt were painted by Munnings, who also at George V's suggestion made a bronze statuette of Brown Jack, a duplicate being sent to Ascot. Harold gave a farewell dinner at the Piccadilly Hotel for Steve Donoghue; a telephone was specially rigged so that Donoghue could speak to Brown Jack in his stable.

1935 as Jubilee Year was particularly busy for entertaining. Georgie Greece spent his last weekend in England at Lubenham, having been recalled after a plebiscite to his throne. Zia gave a purdah party at Someries House including Queen Mary and the Maharanis of Cooch Bihar and Jaipur, who arrived in limousines with darkened windows. No manservants were allowed on the premises during the party.

The cook at Lubenham was Mary Mawby, and years afterwards she described the meticulous attention paid by Zia to the daily menus, and the extraordinary standard of perfection for all the dishes, some of which might have taken two days to prepare. 'Lady Zia would always come to thank and compliment us afterwards.' Mary Mawby was married to the head gardener. 'On our days off we had to be in by 10 p.m. You had to be reliable and of good character, and mind your ps and qs, otherwise you would be sacked immediately. My husband had to provide flowers for the exquisite flower arrangements in every room. Lady Zia had a great sense of colour. Everything had to be just right.'

The servants all loved Count Michael Torby – Boy – who was forever coming down to chat to them in the pantry. But fellow guests at Lubenham found Boy 'decidedly odd, mooching about'; his long white pointed face, high forehead and large eyes were typical of the old Grand Dukes. He was always very polite, 'courtly', and painted well, often on rice paper or silk. In 1938 he was naturalized British.

'We loved Miss Gina, and Miss Myra too. They were never allowed to get sunburnt, and when out with their mother always had to wear gloves and hats in summer.' The girls were usually immaculately dressed, and at children's parties jealous mothers noted that they arrived just after the royal princesses and generally dressed in the same way. Myra, like her father, knew how to 'mob up' Zia, especially when her mother made surprising remarks such as 'Just remember this. You're not in this world to enjoy yourself.'

Once Myra made the mistake of saying she was bored, to which Zia retorted sharply: 'There must be something wrong with you. There is always something to do.' It was a lesson well learnt.

As in the past, when there had been great royal processions, Lady Ludlow arranged for friends, and especially children, to watch the funeral of George V from the terrace at Bath House. Prince Philip was there. Harold and Zia were abroad at the time, and Myra – thrilled to be wearing black – wrote to them:

I went to watch the funeral from Grandma Alice's. Aunty Nada I saw in a carriage, the Queen and lots of people I knew. The King looked as if he was going to fall down. He

341

trudged along like anything. Everyone was pitying him. Alex wore his khaki suit and was the second boy in the line outside St George's Hospital. He had his head up and when Uncle Georgy went past he winked, but he quickly put his head down when he saw the Queen coming.

Lady Ludlow would give summer tennis parties for her grand-children at Luton Hoo, needless to say on an extravagant scale. 'Teas' would consist of mountains of lobster sandwiches, straw-berries and ice-cream, éclairs, 'wonderful salads' with white wine dressing, and jugs of orangeade and cider well laced with brandy for grown-ups. Nevertheless many young people found her alarming. 'It was her blunt way of speaking.' Otto Beit's grandson Theo Bull was riveted by the pearl buttons bobbing up and down on her blouse. She was getting a little lame, and Freddie Shaugh-nessy has written how at one of these parties she came hobbling along on her stick, eye twitching. 'Come along, boys and gels,' she said in her curious grating voice. 'Help yerselves, it's all free, yer know.' That evening there were champagne cocktails, served on silver salvers with small embroidered napkins for each guest. Up she came to Freddie and a girl, and said with a wink, out of the corner of her mouth: 'Don't you pinch these things; most of my guests do, use 'em as pocket hankies.' Then she hobbled off to another group.

Nine royal personages and six ambassadors were counted at a gala musicale in the spring of 1935, to be entertained by Grace Moore singing 'One Night of Love' and excerpts from *La Bohème*, in which she had been performing at Covent Garden. Dino Bagiolo, Grace Moore's operatic partner, also sang. Gregor Piatigorsky played the cello, and there were Viennese waltzes. This was in aid of Harold's University College Hospital appeal. In May, 233 people came to hear Maria Müller from the New York Met, and such was the crowd of vehicles in Piccadilly outside that police had to be summoned from Vine Street. Lady Ludlow received her guests from the top of the great sweep of stairs, lined as usual with Luton Hoo hothouse flowers. Hephzi-bah and Yehudi Menuhin played at another of her concerts. In that year she began to have serious trouble with her eyes, and her sight began to deteriorate badly. Nevertheless she was able to give a series of sherry parties to view the new arrangement of her china collection in its rosewood cases. She also gave an enormous party to hear Kreisler and Gladys Swarthout (her first appearance in England), at which she was obviously determined to appear at her best, wearing 'rows and rows of pearls over sea-green silk'. Zia was there, dressed 'most becomingly in pink satin with panels of purple tulle'.

'Lady Bird' now wore double lorgnettes, and began to spend much more time at Luton Hoo. 'When there were no white shutters up you knew Her Ladyship was at home.' Derrick would visit her sometimes, and Mr Edwards would say to the staff: 'He's down for the cheque book.' Derrick was huge, twice his mother's size, with a monocle. Generally he had some impractical business scheme to put across to the trustees. Perhaps it is not surprising to learn that he was an expert bridge player and chairman of the American Bridge League of New York.

Georgie Greece gave Zia news of the visit of Edward VIII and Wallis Simpson to Corfu. 'David's visit was great fun . . . He was very restless and fidgety, but charming and doing his best to be nice. I must say a certain lady was being quite a help and I think she will stay put quite a while.' He thought the King appreciated being left in peace for a change. Georgie then wrote of the forthcoming reburial of his parents and grandparents at Athens, since they had all died in exile. 'Sitta and sisters are arriving with Christo and wife. I feel rather nervous, as I'm on my own and it's so long since I have entertained, *and* the house is still very far from what it ought to be.'

By the time of the burial Edward VIII had abdicated. 'I am sorry for David,' Georgie wrote. 'Poor Bertie. I'm sure he will do his best, and she has *all* the charm.'

The change in Sovereigns was a relief for Zia, who could not visualize having to invite Mrs Simpson to Gina's coming-out ball in 1937, which was planned to be on a scale such as had not been seen since pre-war times. The ball would be at Someries House on 30 June, some six weeks after the Coronation of George VI, at which Queen Mary invited Zia and Harold to sit in her box.

Unfortunately some foreign relations felt they could not make another journey so soon to London for Gina's party. Still it was a tremendous and sparkling occasion, the first time the new King and Queen had attended a large private party since their accession. There were about a thousand guests, and a large double queue of waiting cars stretched into Portland Place. Ambrose the band leader flew over specially from Paris, where he had been playing at the Exhibition, in order to conduct at the dance, which began at 11 p.m. The flowers were a sensation, but the masses of orange-coloured antirrhinums seemed to have struck people most. The ballroom was built on the lawn with awnings of pale pink muslin. There was a clairvoyant and Larry Adler played the mouth-organ. The jewellery worn by 'Jai', the Maharajah of Jaipur, was described as breathtaking.

The party ended at six, and the King and Queen stayed till five – the papers reported that prostitutes in Bond Street waved to them as they drove home.

'There is no doubt,' commented one columnist afterwards, 'that the beautiful Miss Georgina Wernher is a catch.' Michael Astor must have thought so, for when he bought a Rolls-Royce he annoyed his mother by asking: 'Do you think this will do for Gina?' The car was promptly put in a garage and had to be sold. Lady Astor did not know that Michael then gave Gina a brooch. All the same, Miss Georgina Wernher had strong ideas of her own about how to conduct her future life.

Prince Philip again came to Lubenham for Christmas, but it was a time of great sadness. On 16 November his pregnant sister Cecilia and her husband Grand Duke George Donatus of Hesse, with their two sons and the Grand Duke's mother, had been killed in an air crash on their way to England for his brother Ludwig's wedding to Margaret Geddes.

MULBERRY

22

Appointment to Combined Operations

Everyone who knew Alex Wernher speaks of him today as a delightful, unspoilt boy. 'He had all the charm in the world.' His great friend both at Eton and in the Army was Bobby Peacock, with whom he shared digs, tents and girlfriends. Alex never boasted about his grand connections and was always telling funny stories about his mother, who would have been horrified by the sort of girls with whom he consorted, and even more horrified had she known that Cecil Boyd-Rochfort (his godfather) had arranged a dinner for Alex and Bobby with some girls from the Windmill Theatre.

Alex loved the freedom. He felt very Russian, and when wearing his black boots with his blues would sometimes do a Cossack dance. 'Once he was in the Army,' Joan Cooke has said, 'he took life with both hands.' 'My God, life is good,' he would exclaim. Zia objected to the way he let his hair grow longer, and complained that he never brought his friends home. Once he and Bobby were stationed at Dunstable, not so far from Lubenham. Zia telephoned their digs when Alex was in London with a girlfriend, and Bobby foolishly told her that Alex could not speak to her because he was ill in bed with a cold. The next morning Alex returned with a tremendous hangover, only just before Zia arrived in her Rolls. Bobby had to rush to the Colonel to explain the situation.

When Harold gave Alex a large car for his twenty-first birthday, he said he didn't want it; he only wanted a small one. Remembering the disastrous effect of a large allowance on Derrick, Harold let him have only £500 a year, but when Alex went to Meerut in India this was enough for him to keep three polo ponies. He had joined the 17th/21st Lancers partly because of the possibility of polo, but when war approached the regiment was converted to tanks.

Gina, needless to say, was being groomed by her mother to marry a duke at least, to give her 'stability'. But she told Zia that she had no intention of marrying anyone with a title, and spending her life 'opening flower shows'. That did not stop eligible young men proposing to her – she had eighteen proposals of marriage in all. In any case she preferred older men to those 'spotty' youths – 'They would all decide they were in love with the same girl, and then move to another.' Her mother finally decided that the future Marquess of Linlithgow was the one for Gina. But he already had a girlfriend, whom he eventually married, and it was his twin brother who was the more keen on her.

When Desmond Miller and Dick Hamilton-Russell suggested taking Gina to a theatre, Zia put her foot down. Again, on one occasion at Lubenham, Gina and Prince Philip wanted to go to a party, and Zia forbade it. But Gina said that she was going to go, and locked herself into her room. Later she and Philip did go out. Next morning at breakfast there was no reprimand from Zia, who simply asked if the party had been a good one.

In March 1938 Gina was at Kitzbühl and wrote furiously to her mother, who had apparently leapt to conclusions when Gina had said that she had found the brother of Hugo Windischgrätz 'too attractive for words'. She had seen him staring at her for days and after being introduced he had invited her to dinner and then to a party.

> I have never been so surprised or annoyed in my life at the things you have imagined . . . I really don't think you trust me a yard and I have never done anything that I shouldn't although when I receive a letter like that I feel I would like to . . . Lots of men come up and click their heels and ask me to dance but you will be pleased to hear that I decline their charming offers.

Only a few months after the death of George Milford Haven, in November 1938, his son David took Gina to the 400 Nightclub. Zia was scandalized on both counts, and wrote a stern letter to David when she heard from Gina about this. Part of his reply is also worth quoting, including the misspellings:

Dearest Aunty Zia,
. . . I wish sometimes you would immagine you were Gina's age, as you were once, and then you would go out occassionally at night, and then you would realize how much Gina wants to enjoy herself, as indeed all young people of our age do.
    I know that you can trust Gina, so what is the objection of her going where she wants, whatever the place is. As long as her conscience isn't pricking, she knows she is not dissgracing anyone, either you or her, and Gina is the one girl that disslikes any dirty night clubs.
    I immagine that you are afraid of what people will think.
    Well what does it matter what people think, it is no concern of theirs, and it is only nasty people with dirty, evil minds that start gossiping and inventing stories . . .
    I can assure you that we need never have told you that we went out on Thursday night, and you will find that this summer, with a war threatening and so on, that if you don't let her go to nightclubs occasionally, she will go out without telling you. Remember she will soon be twenty-one, and then you can't stop her . . . All love, from your respectful nephew David.

Gina's hopeful suitors might be asked to stay at Someries House and in the afternoon would be driven in the Rolls to watch Harold's team playing polo at Ranelagh or Hurlingham. The 'formidable Someries House team', with its yellow and green colours, was now well known in the sporting columns, even though its name was not so dashing as most of its opponents' – Les Diables, the Panthers and the Gauchos. In July 1938 Someries House beat the Cowdray team in the Ashton Cup, and also won the Coronation Cup at Ranelagh, but this last was Harold's final game, as he fell and dislocated his shoulder.

That winter Lady Ludlow contracted facial shingles, affecting an eye. A royal aeroplane flew her to Switzerland for treatment. She had to be back by 14 February, when Queen Mary came to visit the Luton and Dunstable Hospital and lunched at Luton Hoo. For the occasion Lady Ludlow ordered that banks of red, white and blue flowers should be obtained, regardless of cost, to decorate Luton Hoo's entrance. A French chef was specially employed and his creation of two baskets, looking like stripped willow, one topped with roses; the other with chrysanthemums, all made out of sugar, was a sensation. People in Luton were shocked to see Lady Ludlow sitting next to the Queen in the car with her face so painted, but this was to disguise the disfigurement from shingles. To commemorate the Queen's visit, she gave £6,000 to the Hospital, and Harold gave £1,000. She then flew to Aix-les-Bains.

Life at Luton Hoo was very quiet on her return, though she did give one big lunch party in her traditional style at Bath House. It was a place that badly needed children, so the servants thought. The Sunday services in the chapel continued. Mr Edwards the butler would wait for her to come down in the lift, and then would escort her on his arm into the chapel, one hand under the tails of his coat.

The approach of war also brought back to Lady Ludlow memories of the elder Alex, her son. She had a miniature of him made into a ring. Not long afterwards she developed neuritis. In August she flew to Lausanne for a cataract operation, and was still there when war broke out.

Harold earlier in 1939 had been invited to serve on a government committee under the chairmanship of Sir Charles Wilson (later Lord Moran, Churchill's doctor), to plan for dealing with civilian casualties in the event of war. As he wrote in a small volume of reminiscences, the Air Ministry's estimate of casualties was 'terrifying'. In that same book there is also a tantalizingly brief mention of an 'event of unusual interest' that took place just before the war. He wrote:

I had been approached by a Swedish friend, Mr B. Dahlerus, with a view to making a proposal to Lord Halifax, the Foreign Secretary. Dahlerus had been a business associate of mine for a number of years and lived for a long time in England. He had married a second time, in 1934, a German lady, and during that time had made the acquaintance of Field–Marshal Goering.

This was of course Birger Dahlerus, who had been managing director of Electrolux. Harold went on to say that Dahlerus believed that Goering was anxious to avoid war, and that 'some steps should be taken for members of the business community in England to have informal talks with him.' Consequently it was arranged that a delegation should meet Goering secretly on an island in North Friesland early in August 1939. Harold was not part of this delegation.

Another name associated with Electrolux, that of its founder, Wenner-Gren, is absent from Harold's book. Perhaps by now he was becoming wary of Wenner-Gren, even though he and Zia had been his guests in the Caribbean on his yacht *Southern Cross*. Wenner-Gren had also been seeing Goering, who had told him that he did not want war. A much more enigmatic character than Dahlerus, and ultimately held to be suspect by the British and American governments, Wenner-Gren seems originally to have met Goering independently of Dahlerus. In his diary he records having had lunch with Sir Harold Wernher on 22 May 1939: 'We discussed mainly politics – rather pessimistic.' Did Harold encourage or discourage him from plunging into the treacherous world of international politics? There is no clue. At any rate after that meeting Wenner-Gren did go to see Neville Chamberlain, and on 10 June reported back to Goering, who actually suggested that the *Southern Cross* might be the venue for the meeting with the English businessmen.

From then onwards Dahlerus seems to have been the intermediary between Goering and the Foreign Office, and shuttled between them several times in the last week before the invasion of Poland, as Harold records. He even managed to see Hitler, who by then was 'in such a state of hysteria that it was impossible to get a word in edgeways.' One assumes that Harold continued to see Dahlerus on some of those visits. He might have given opinions, but his role now presumably was that of a spectator.

When Harold and Zia heard the BBC announcement at 8 a.m. on 3 September that the Prime Minister would be broadcasting at 11, they knew it meant war would be declared. They were in London, and decided to drive immediately to see Alex, then stationed at Colchester. Petrol rationing was inevitable, and they feared that bombing might start immediately. They stopped in the East End to hear the broadcast, and at 11.15 there was an air raid warning, but a false alarm.

Luckily they managed to see Alex. Harold was haunted by the memory of his time in the trenches. It was almost as if he had a presentiment of what was going to happen to this boy whom they both idolized.

Lady Ludlow at once decided that she would offer Luton Hoo to Sister Agnes for her hospital. Sister Agnes was in her mid-eighties, and the administration was in the hands of Sir George Ogilvie, retired from a distinguished career in the Indian Civil Service. It therefore fell to Sir George to supervise the packing at 17 Grosvenor Crescent, Sister Agnes's home, to which the hospital had returned from Grosvenor Gardens. Lady Ludlow also decided that she must move into the Gables, a modern half-timbered house occupied by her agent for the past three years. The agent, Robin Coventry Barrett, known as Covie, was told that he had three days in which to transfer his family and his belongings to the Hermitage, a smaller house on the estate (and where Sydney and Beatrice Webb had stayed). Worse, she told Covie that she now could not afford to pay him full time and he must find another job to supplement his income.

'Sister Agnes was a real case,' Frank Field, the then second footman remembers. 'Lovely corn-coloured wig, red enamel cross, buttoned boots, a stick.' She would tip the gardeners a shilling each. But as Covie's son has also said, the two strong-minded old ladies did not get on. In any case during the Phoney War there were few patients. So in April 1940 the King Edward VII Hospital moved back to 17 Grosvenor Crescent. Even after

Dunkirk Sister Agnes found that there was little scope for a voluntary hospital.

Meanwhile Lady Ludlow had also decided to dismantle and close down the Luton Hoo chapel. The last service was held there on 11 February. She sold the organ, built by Henry Jones of Fulham in 1875, with its magnificent case by G. E. Street, to Luton Parish Church for a hundred guineas. She would not be responsible for its removal. 'That's the last word with the organ,' she said, and because she had her double lorgnettes across her nose her staff knew her mind had been made up. To many it was the end of an era, and a great loss to lovers of music. But the church was slow in paying up, and before long she sent a note through a messenger: 'Where's my money?' At Lubenham the horses had to be disposed of, and the farm put on a war basis. As Harold wrote: 'The good old days of foxhunting were over.' Evacuees from Zia's Children's Home in Hampstead were billeted in the laundry and stable flats.

Harold was among those summoned to act as liaison between the War Office and the LDV, Local Defence Volunteers, later known as the Home Guard. It was thanks ultimately to him that some million rifles and 50,000 automatic weapons were obtained for the Home Guard from the USA. After Dunkirk, General Sir Henry Pownall became Inspector-General of the Home Guard and he appointed Harold liaison officer with Eastern Command, which eventually had its headquarters at Luton Hoo. Harold reckoned that within nine months he covered over 30,000 miles in his car visiting units. When in the spring of 1941 Eastern Command was split into two, he was appointed GSO 1 Home Guard for South-Eastern Command under General Bernard Paget, who was eventually succeeded by 'Monty', Lieutenant-General Bernard Montgomery.

But Harold was desperate for what he considered a proper war appointment.

Zia was President of the St John Ambulance Brigade for Leicestershire, and later its Assistant Lady County Superintendent. As such, various convalescent hospitals came under her special care: at East Langton Grange, for instance, and West Langton Hall where she became Commandant; then there was a training centre for nurses at Dingley Hall, and a residential nursery at Stoke Golding. Her capacity for organization came into full play. She was notoriously outspoken, saying exactly what she thought, yet she could be tactful when inspecting private houses that might be used as annexes for hospitals. One lady was embarrassed because her floors were not carpeted. 'Much better,' Zia said kindly. 'It's healthier to have rugs.' Princess Marina and Edwina Mountbatten were St John Superintendents and therefore were on occasion invited to Lubenham for tours of the local hospitals, in which Gina and after a while Myra worked as nurses. Patients would sometimes be taken to see the great Brown Jack in his stable at Lubenham.*

On 18 September 1940 a land-mine dropped near Someries House, virtually destroying it. Zia's new Swiss lady's maid, Odile Barbier – to become a devoted friend of all the family – was in the house at the time. In compensation for her ordeal Zia gave Odile a ruby bracelet. The Wernhers now took an apartment at the Dorchester Hotel, like a number of other wealthy people during the war. Since the hotel was built of steel and concrete it was thought that it would be safe against bombs.

About this time Zia was in the Dorchester with Myra, who had been invited to a party for the Princesses at Windsor. She met Lady Allendale, whose daughter Ela had also been invited. Ela was terrified of Zia, whom she thought more royal than the royals. The Queen, Lady Allendale told Zia, had said no lady's maids. To which Zia replied: 'Queen or no Queen, Myra must have a lady's maid.' And a lady's maid duly accompanied the embarrassed Myra to Windsor. The Queen was furious.

Nobody could give parties like those at Windsor Castle during the war. Officers on duty from the brigade of Guards would be invited to dances. One party at Christmas is especially remembered, with the King jumping on the radiogram and the Queen sliding on the parquet floor. 'You couldn't imagine Zia doing that!' Princess Elizabeth was in the Kingfisher Patrol of the 1st

---

* Fans of Brown Jack would save up their sugar ration for him. Letters were also received begging for hairs from his tail for sending as talismans to husbands and sons overseas.

Buckingham Palace Girl Guides, Patricia Mountbatten being patrol leader. Myra was in the Robin Patrol. They went for treks in Windsor Park and were taught useful things like how to throw ropes from a rock to save someone from drowning in a river. Fires with damp sticks were always a failure, but they enjoyed the singsongs in the bus.

Zia was not told that Gina, on receiving a letter from an able seaman who had seen her photograph in the *Tatler* and made her his pin-up, had agreed to go to the cinema with him. At any rate Gina by then was twenty-one. He wanted to see her home, but home was now the Dorchester Hotel, which he did not know. So Gina had to make the excuse that she had a very difficult father, and it was imperative that she should go back alone.

When a land-mine exploded ten yards from No. 1 London Wall, Harold's office inside it was destroyed except for the contents of the safe, containing the most vital papers; however, the massive structure of the building stood up well. Newmarket was bombed, so those two valuable stallions, Precipitation and Casanova, were removed to Lubenham. When Newmarket was bombed again, their famous mother Double Life was wounded, so she too was taken to Lubenham. The treasures at Bath House, after some delay, had already been crated up after the start of the Blitz; some were stored at Lubenham, some in the Luton Hoo chapel. Nissen huts were built in the woods at Luton Hoo, and Capability Brown's lake was drained in case they might be used as landmarks by German bombers. Churchill tanks, made by Vauxhall Motors, were tested out in Luton Hoo park and the drives were concreted over for the purpose. At last, early in 1941, Lady Ludlow decided to leave altogether, and bought a house near Godalming. It was a hard decision and she hated it.

Before she left, Harold went to see her in order to discuss the future of the estate,* as she was now in her late seventies. He reported to Zia – by now on extremely cool terms with her

---

* The total area of the estate in 1941 was 4,362 acres, as compared to 5,218 when bought by Sir Julius Wernher. The average value per acre was reckoned at £116.

mother-in-law – that the meeting had been stormy at times, but they parted good friends.

I shall summarize the conversation. Send this to Alex before he meets his Grandma.

Father's [Julius's] *intentions*: She produced a list of all my capital and legacies, i.e. Alex [his brother], my uncle [Franz Mankiewicz] and the marriage settlement she forfeited on marrying Ludlow. She more or less said I ought not to have been the heir, to which I replied that it was not my fault and that the blame should be laid on my Father. I said I knew she had always held it against me.

Alex. She asked why he who had seen so little of Luton Hoo should feel sentimental and proud of it. Pointed out he could hardly have seen much as never invited & asked her to look at the visitors' book to see how often our names appeared! Moreover I said that the film 'Gone with the Wind' had impressed Alex as to the perpetual nature of land & anyone could change their views.

Her money. She resented my suggestion that this should be left to the family, & said it was her business & her money & she could do as she liked.

Books. Would not have sold them [after Julius's death] if I could have stored them. I said this was absurd as they took up little room & to denude the bookshelves was as unnecessary as to tear the silks off the walls. Alex [his brother] teased her about selling them & asked if she was short of cash! She is genuinely ashamed & looking for an excuse to blame me.

Art collection. She was furious about my attitude. I said I was sorry if I offended her, but felt that her dillydallying attitude whilst London was burning had been unnecessary & my minute checking of all articles had been a reflection of my integrity.

In due course it was decided to offer Luton Hoo and the art collection, with a thousand acres of land, to the National Trust, provided that the family could live in part of the house after the war. James Lees-Milne was met there by Harold and Zia. Evidently they set out to charm him, and he was impressed; Harold was 'simple and forthcoming', Zia 'pretty and sweet'. He did not at all like Luton Hoo, either inside or out, and hated the Mewès and Davis top storey and mansard roof. But then much of the interior was boarded up to eye-level as protection against the military occupants.

A sharp letter from Harold to Zia, headed HQ South-Eastern Command, Home Forces, and written in June 1941, shows that she still had reason to be jealous – a reason well founded:

> If you are going to write me such letters I would rather you did not communicate with me as it is too unpleasant and boring. I refuse, at my age, to submit all my movements to you for your approval. I shall lunch or dine where I like and with whom I like, so what? It is really too boring & you see Alex, from his letters, feels the same. I cannot see what Bush or Pratt [staff at Lubenham] have to do with my movements. I do not discuss you with employees.

Evidently there was some sort of surrender in her reply, as his next letter was as cheerful and intimate as ever. In her middle age Zia had come to terms with situations such as these, and it made no difference to her affection for him, or for that matter to his for her.

Desmond Miller was dead, and the details of his death were so shocking that they were kept from Zia. She was of course upset, but perhaps she was not quite so affected as she would have been a few years before. Desmond had been on the abortive expedition to Norway and had come back badly shell-shocked. It seems that by then he had already realized that he had lost ground in Zia's affections, and this may have added to his depression. He visited her at a time when she was very preoccupied with her war work, and he felt then that he was not being sufficiently welcomed. In any case it appeared that whilst in hospital he had formed a relationship with a young officer, and the Wernhers felt that he was trying to come to terms with this. After being in hospital he went to Sandhurst. One morning he seemed exceptionally happy, and went for a walk. When he did not return an officer was sent to look for him. The officer returned green and shaken. He had found Desmond hanging – horribly – from a high tree.

Another inhabitant of the Dorchester Hotel was Dr Chaim Weizmann, the great Zionist. Harold now found himself involved in a curious episode. Mountbatten, who had recently been appointed Chief of Combined Operations, asked Harold to look into the feasibility of synthesizing rubber, which Weizmann considered could be made from fermented wheat.

Weizmann, a distinguished scientist, was attached to the Ministry of Supply, and was already known as the inventor of a synthetic acetone and a synthetic quinine. His contention was that the large store of wheat in Canada could be used for this synthetic rubber, now that most of the world's rubber supply had been cut off by the Japanese conquests in East Asia. So Weizmann and Harold had a meeting with Lord Beaverbrook, who was then Minister of Supply. Unfortunately, Weizmann was a poor advocate, and seemed perturbed by a kettle steaming constantly in the room on account of Beaverbrook's asthma. Beaverbrook was not impressed. There were other meetings and a correspondence with Harold Macmillan, but to no avail. Weizmann therefore went to try his luck in America. He failed once more, as the American oil chiefs were determined that their product was the one to make synthetic rubber. This was a blow to the Canadian economy, and ultimately detrimental to the United Kingdom, as it meant that the Americans would have the monopoly for making such things as tyres after the war, until normal production resumed.

Mountbatten was expecting the imminent arrival of General George Marshall from the United States, to open discussions for the invasion of the Continent, and decided that it was imperative to have a 'Transport Dictator' under him, with wide terms of reference, and who in effect would be co-ordinator in matters of supply and labour between the three Services. It would, naturally, have to be someone of outstanding organizing and managing ability, with both military and business experience. Mountbatten had already come across petty interdepartmental jealousies and resentments, not to mention power conflicts between the Services, so the chosen individual would have to be exceptionally tough. He thought immediately of Harold Wernher.

'Dear old Dickie,' a former colleague has remembered. 'Philip Ziegler was right in his book – he never felt at ease unless supported by those he liked and trusted. In Harold's case his personal wealth meant absolute self-confidence. He was not interested in power as such. After all, he was already well known as an important and very successful industrialist.'

'Surely this fellow is some sort of relation of yours?' Churchill asked Mountbatten. He was then reminded that Duncan Sandys, Financial Secretary to the War Office, was even more closely related to the Prime Minister, being his son-in-law. Mountbatten thought that he had convinced Churchill, but a few days later had to tell Harold he had been turned down. 'I need hardly tell you,' he wrote, 'it is no use arguing with the Prime Minister, although I do not believe we can find anybody who could do the job as well as you, apart from the fun of having you in the party.'

That was on 24 March 1942. Suddenly Churchill changed his mind. Why he did so, Mountbatten never knew. Harold had a theory that in the first instance Churchill had decided that it was he who had 'muffed matters' with Weizmann, when it had really been due to Beaverbrook's 'disgraceful behaviour'. This, however, does seem unlikely, since Churchill had deliberately avoided getting involved, being afraid that Weizmann would start bringing up the Zionist question. Or it could have been to do with Harold's association with Electrolux and Wenner-Gren, recently placed on the government's blacklist.

Harold was given the rank of Brigadier; his title of Co-Ordinator of Port Facilities was later changed to Co-Ordinator of Ministry and Service Facilities (for Combined Operations), CMSF for short. The 'Most Secret' Directive sent to him on 20 April and signed Louis Mountbatten included these paragraphs:

Your responsibility will embrace the whole problem of preparing facilities for the launching of the Assault and of maintaining supplies and reinforcements during the earlier phase of a major Combined Operation against Northern France. The phase of the operation with which you are

chiefly to be concerned is that between the time that the
assault force is about to embark in England and the time that
sufficient French Ports have been captured and put into
operation, for the supply problem to proceed on normal
lines.

The aspects of the problem to which you should devote
particular attention include the following: – (a) Road and rail
systems in Southern England in relation to the embarkation
problem. (b) Loading and other harbour facilities for
shipping taking part in the operation. (c) Direct embarkation
of all forms of military vehicles into landing crafts, etc., on
the South Coast. (d) Assembly and modification of shipping
for the cross-Channel journey. (e) Ships' discharging
facilities for stores and motor transport on the French Coast.
(f) The raising and training of skilled labour to fulfil the
foregoing tasks under active service conditions. (g)
Questions relating to priority requirements.

The Directive also gave him right of access to all Cabinet
Ministers, and any major plans prepared by the Joint Planning
Staff, by the Commander-in-Chief Home Forces, or by Combined Operations Headquarters, 'and should you entertain doubts
on their possibility from the supply point of view, it will be your
duty to bring this doubt both to the notice of the originator of the
plan and to me.'

As Mountbatten also wrote in his letter of introduction to
various Ministers, Harold's terms of reference would embrace
'special shipping, railways, roads, communications, wharves,
dock labour, smoke screens, etc. etc., and, indeed, the co-
ordination of all the many activities which have to be brought to
life again in the South, before it can be used as the base for any
considerable operation.' In effect the South of England was being
turned from a defensive area to an offensive one; from a bastion to
a springboard. Railways, for instance, that had been torn up had
to be relaid, minefields had to be cleared, barbed wire had to be
removed. During 1941 virtually all the South and East Coast
ports, including the Port of London, had been out of commission.
Not surprisingly, people like Sir Findlater Stewart, in charge of

Security at Home Forces Headquarters, viewed Harold at first with great suspicion. 'But later,' as Harold said, 'it was through his co-operation that I was able to effect many of my official "stunts".' In fact Harold typically took great care to make friends with secretaries and juniors, which helped when he needed to make appointments with their chiefs at short notice. He insisted on having his own secretary, Miss Lainson; as she was a civilian, she had to take the oath of secrecy, and he had to pay her out of his own pocket.

The first task entrusted to Harold by the Chiefs of Staff was to make arrangements for the construction of 'hards' from which landing-craft carrying tanks and personnel could land on beaches for the projected invasion. This necessitated a complete survey of the coast from Plymouth to Dover and in the Glasgow area by Lieutenant-Colonel Ian Mackillop, whom Harold managed to secure as his deputy after a fierce battle with General Sir Noel Holmes, Director of Movements. A way had to be devised to make it possible for tanks and vehicles to cross the beaches between high tide and low water. To lay permanent concrete, except at high-water mark, was impracticable. A solution was devised by Lieutenant-Colonel Vassal Steer-Webster: pre-cast concrete mattresses, reinforced with steel wire to make them flexible, each element capable of being carried by four men, and weighing 360 lbs, measuring 3 ft 4 in. by 2 ft 4 in. A mattress looked like a great slab of flexible chocolate. It took 4,000 to make one hard. Harold wrote in his *Personal Experiences*: 'I arranged a demonstration for the Admiralty, who were to undertake the construction of the "hards" and, after a considerable amount of opposition, also from the War Office, the principle was adopted. Hundreds of miles of this mattress were constructed and eventually used in all theatres of the European war.'

There was a major clash with Admiral Sir Frederick Dalrymple-Hamilton at the Admiralty over creating assembly points for the hards at Dartmouth College, which involved making concrete standings for tanks and widening roads in the beautiful grounds. Harold argued that 'everyone had to make sacrifices' and that equivalent damage was being done in the parks of many private estates (including Luton Hoo, though he may have avoided mentioning it). The Admiral finally succumbed. 'It is interesting to note,' wrote Harold, 'that shortly afterwards the College was badly bombed and was finally taken over by Combined Operations Headquarters for training of Landing Craft crew. The rubble collected from the bomb damage was used in the construction of roads.'

There were soon to be other clashes with less co-operative personalities. Being merciless with those whom he considered 'pig-headed fools' was to cost Harold dear personally, even if it benefited the country, as will be shown later and as Michael Harrison has commented on in his book on 'Mulberry', the project to which Harold was to become vitally linked: 'In the single-minded pursuit of what he considered to be his duty, he was completely careless of the "feelings" of incompetent jacks-in-office . . . The result was that he offended several people who, unimportant in themselves, wielded considerable power.' Indeed, as anyone knows who has fought in war among the lower echelons, and has studied the background of the higher commands, it is impossible not to be appalled when reading of the way some of the individuals in power allowed their jealousies and vanities to control their judgement. Admiral Sir Ronald Brockman, who was Personal Secretary to Mountbatten when he was Viceroy of India, looked upon Harold as a person used to command: 'There was no question of it. He was a tremendous man.' Prince Philip has summarized the qualities that made Harold into such a good businessman: clarity of mind, very down-to-earth, practical, when faced with a problem would at once pick on essentials; always with an original view, never formed opinions as a result of books or what people said – his opinion might be completely different; when he asked you to do something it was difficult to say no. In some ways he was a man ahead of his time.

He himself said that 'opposition came not so much from persons as the system, though there were quite a few persons who objected to me or my methods,' and this applied more to the War Office than the Admiralty.

In addition to the construction of 171 embarkation points, Harold had to supervise the erection of maintenance depots and accommodation for the crews, and also to provide storage tanks so that the landing-craft could be refuelled immediately they returned from the Continent.

Meanwhile Harold and Zia were active in sending parcels to friends in German prison camps through the Red Cross. One friend in particular was Mike Ansell, who had been virtually blinded at St Valéry in 1940 and had been operated on without success by a German surgeon. 'Chicken' Walford, another member of the Someries House polo team, had been in command of the 17/21st Lancers, but was killed in an air crash near Newmarket where he had gone up to watch a squadron training. A month before the regiment, including Alex, went abroad, Dick Hamilton-Russell took command. 'Cookie' Cooke, another former team member, was on the Corps staff.

Zia had been driven 'nearly frantic' when Alex had wanted to volunteer to fight on the Russian front, after the German invasion of Russia in June 1941. Harold, through his War Office connection, of course knew that the 17/21st was to be in the spearhead of the 1st Army in Algeria and Tunisia, but kept this from her.

23

Co-ordination and Tragedy

One of Harold's allies at the War Office was Brigadier C. S. Napier, Deputy Director of Movements, a man – in Harold's words – of outstanding vision and ability. Napier was worried by the mood of pessimism at the War Office, and the view of so many that an assault on the heavily defended French coast would be suicidal. He was also concerned about insufficient preparation for the arrival of American troops.

Napier went to see Harold with a long agenda. 'As you have been given a post and an obscure title which nobody can understand,' he said, 'why don't you set up a committee? I can suggest names.' Thus it was that the CMSF Committee was created under Harold's chairmanship, with some permanent members and usually numbering about twenty people, mostly from the Admiralty, War Office and Ministry of War Transport. Not surprisingly, there were grumbles about time wasted, but after a while the importance of those weekly meetings was conceded, especially when Mountbatten made Harold his deputy on all administrative committees.

'Mountbatten had immense drive and go and life,' a survivor from those days has said. 'It was a bit of a joke in Whitehall that Lord Louis had in all his friends and relations. But he had a way of picking 'em. My God he had. Many things had to be insisted on that were highly unpalatable.'

Mountbatten was overworked and of course inexperienced. Commando raids also came within his scope. Churchill said: 'You must carry on with the raids on the coast of France, because not

362

only are they good for keeping the Germans on their toes and killing some of them too, but it keeps up morale in the country. But your main object is to prepare for the invasion of France.' Harold was not concerned with raids, but it was vital that he should be conversant with the strategic picture so that priorities could be realized within departments if the strategic plan were changed. Security was strict, and departments tended to be 'water-tight'. Thus Harold also had the job of passing on selected information to those in responsible positions.

Mountbatten relied on Harold to keep him briefed on administration concisely and in broad lines, but not to trouble him with details that could be solved elsewhere. Many years later he was asked why there should have been jealousy between the forces in time of war, when everyone was expected to pull together. One simple reason, he replied, was that it was human nature to prefer your own show, be it club or school or Service, and feel it superior to the others. Each Service knew that funds for defence were limited: the more one Service got, the less for the other two. This led to a power conflict, a competition for expansion and prestige. Serving officers also knew only too well that in peace-time rates of pay would be reduced. 'You'd try to improve your bargaining position almost subconsciously in war-time by acquiring the main jobs, the main responsibilities, the main share of resources and manpower.'

But, as Harold was to discover, those were not the only sources of hostility.

An immediate problem was that of coasters. Because of the bombing and the submarine menace all shipping had been diverted to the West Coast. Now, in the absence of landing-craft, shallow-draught vessels had to be found, and converted, by installing lifting gear, to be capable of carrying five to ten tons of stores across the Channel. Harold now made an inventory of the entire port capacity from the Wash to the Bristol Channel, and produced a list of every single ship's berth in the whole of that area. The early minutes of the CMSF committees were divided into heads such as Hards, Camouflage, Provision of Cranes, Loading of Barges, Anti-Aircraft Protection, Anti-Gas. Preparations had also to be made for assembling an invasion force.

Thus 'Concentration Areas' were located twenty-five to thirty miles from the coast; 'Assembly Areas' five to ten miles; and 'Transit Areas' on the coast itself. For all those camps, roads and standings for vehicles had to be constructed or ordered.

One of the great secrets of the war, which proved of vital importance after the Normandy landings, was the invention known as PLUTO, the initials of Pipe Line Under The Ocean, which was eventually capable of pumping a million gallons of oil a day across the English Channel to Normandy. Harold was involved in the early discussions. The actual idea is said to have evolved in April 1942 when Mountbatten was invited by Geoffrey Lloyd, Minister in charge of the Petroleum Warfare Department, to watch a demonstration of flame-throwers. At the end of the demonstration Lloyd asked Mountbatten whether anything further could be done on the petroleum side to assist the projected Continental operations. Mountbatten replied: 'Yes. Can you lay a pipeline across the Channel?' Much of the development of PLUTO (if not the original inspiration) was due to the initiative of Captain Tom Hussey, another man whom Harold found to be blessedly above small pettinesses and lust for empire-building. The first reaction of the experts to Mountbatten's question was that it would be impossible, but that engineering feat was eventually made possible by the firms of Siemens and Anglo-Iranian Oil. Harold was invited by the Admiralty to the launching of the first trial on the Thames of a giant drum carrying many miles of flexible pipe. By Christmas another trial oil pipeline had been successfully laid across the Bristol Channel from Swansea to Ilfracombe.

Meanwhile, lurking irritatingly for Harold in the background during the spring and summer of 1942 were anxieties about the multi-millionaire Wenner-Gren, who had been blacklisted by the Americans and British as a possible German spy or at any rate a Nazi sympathizer. Wenner-Gren was also a friend of the Windsors in the Bahamas, and was always ready to put his *Southern Cross* at their disposal. The Duke was trying to build up the economy of the colony, and Wenner-Gren had brought in substantial and welcome foreign capital.

All this had temporarily brought Electrolux under the scrutiny of the Trading with the Enemy Department, with inquiries about

Wenner-Gren's shareholdings. It did not take long to show that the British firm was a self-contained entity and separate from its Swedish parent – from whose board Harold Wernher and its English general manager, Harry Faulkner, had in fact resigned in 1940. There was some relief when it was learnt that Wenner-Gren was also on the German blacklist. 'From which it appears nobody trusts the man', so the Departmental report ran.

Harold therefore felt constrained to call a meeting at the department with members of the British firm, and said that he was convinced that Wenner-Gren no longer had active control in Sweden and that another member of the board, certainly not a Nazi, had power of attorney. He expressed worries about shareholders' dividends being affected (in other words mostly his own and Faulkner's), and the stigma of Electrolux UK after the war if its name appeared on a blacklist. The affair eventually did blow over, and the Duke of Windsor felt angry and humiliated. In the view of the British Embassy at Stockholm Wenner-Gren was nothing more than a 'pompous ass', a social climber and tax-dodger.

Harold's first major clash with the established Civil Service was in July 1942. Mountbatten was worried about the inefficiency of the petrol supply system, as the four-gallon cans used by the British Army were made of such flimsy material that they were easily squashed. It had also been shown that in North Africa the cans became damaged by the vibration of trucks, and it was reckoned that in this way 40 per cent of the petrol was wasted. The Germans were using cans of a much stronger material, and of a design invented by the Americans. They were known as jerricans, and it was this design that the Petroleum Committee was trying without success to get adopted by the War Office.

Mountbatten therefore asked Harold to tackle the Secretary of State for War, Sir James Grigg, a bureaucrat of the bureaucrats, variously described as a 'graceless fellow' and 'an able chap but slippery', and who already despised Mountbatten as a playboy and an amateur who was being pushed along because of his royal connections. The thing started badly for Harold because he had to make an appointment through Grigg's secretary, Sidney

Redman, with whom for some undisclosed reason he had already clashed in his Home Guard days.

Harold is recorded as having given the following account. 'When I was shown in, Grigg looked at me in the rudest possible way. "And what do *you* want? I am a very busy man." ' Harold was the last person to lie down under such behaviour. 'You know perfectly well what I want,' he replied. 'I explained to your secretary why I wished to see you. If your secretary didn't tell you, then you haven't got a very competent secretary, nor a very well conducted office.'

Grigg looked at Harold 'as though he was going to shoot me'. Then he muttered something like: 'Well, yes, he did tell me. I've many more important things to attend to. What exactly is it that you want?'

Harold then produced photographs of thousands of crushed cans in the hold of a ship, and patiently explained the advantages of the jerrican. But Grigg had made up his mind from the start, to do nothing. 'I expect you're right,' he said. 'You may be. I can't say. It's no concern of my Department.' At which Harold jumped at him, reminding him that he held the ultimate responsibility and if things went wrong there would be questions in the House.

'I thought he would have a stroke,' Harold said. 'He glared at me for a minute or two, as though he'd lost all power of speech. Then he half-shouted: "Are you *threatening* me, Sir Harold? No one threatens me! I won't be threatened! How *dare* you speak to me like that? I assure you, you'll regret having spoken to me like that!" '

From then onwards Grigg became the personal antagonist and opponent both of Harold Wernher and Mountbatten. Although he had agreed to look into the matter, nothing of course was done. Only after Operation TORCH, the invasion of North Africa, when more cans were crushed with terrific wastage, was Harold able to galvanize interest through what he called a dramatic stunt. At a Combined Operations meeting his suggestion that jerricans should be adopted was again rejected by the Quartermaster General and the Air Ministry representative. He then asked Sir Ralph Metcalfe, the Director of Sea Transport, to come in, and photographs of the holds of ships were shown with piles of ruined cans. At this the Fourth Sea Lord, Sir John Cunningham, thumped on the table and said that something must be done immediately. The Americans concurred. A special committee was therefore set up under Sir Findlater Stewart, and production was put in hand for 20 million jerricans, half of them to be manufactured in Great Britain.

But an awkward matter had now to be glossed over, though it was not missed by Sir James Grigg. As Harold put it in his book of wartime reminiscences: 'The Ministry of Supply selected factories for the manufacture which possessed welding facilities; and for that reason one of the Companies of which I was Chairman was asked to go into production.' That company was Electrolux. The pressing was carried out by Vauxhall Motors, also in Luton, and then – in spite of union struggles – finished off at a factory hitherto making paper bags.

In fact Electrolux during the war was also engaged in producing depth-charge cases (over a million), ammunition boxes, shell cases, refrigerators for smaller Admiralty vessels, bridge-building material for the Army, electric motors and alternators, and such items as target markers, bomb tails and parachute containers for the RAF. Officers from the Admiralty, War Department and RAF were also housed in the factory. Harold was also involved in arranging for secret missions by Mosquito aircraft to Sweden to pick up ball-bearings for the firm of Skefco at Luton.

The requisitioning of private property in the Glasgow area and the commandeering of civilian labour were other unpopular battles. But a less exacting job for Harold was as Chairman of the club for Combined Operations officers at Montagu House, overlooking the Thames. This club was useful for more informal discussions – and making friends. Here elegant ladies, mostly wives and daughters of the officers, served the drinks and food, and glamorous figures might be encountered such as Douglas Fairbanks, Junior, 'Wild Bill' Donovan of the American Office of Strategic Services, Robert Henriques the author, Solly Zuckerman the 'monkey man', Ian Collins the publisher and with luck Generals Eisenhower and Mark Clark.

Eisenhower dined at the Dorchester with Harold, who seems

afterwards to have taught him bridge. As Harold had been involved in Operation BOLERO, the code-name for the Committee set up to prepare for the arrival of American troops – camps, airfields, hospitals, stores – he became friendly with General J. C. H. Lee, in charge of all American supplies, and accompanied him on many occasions in his sumptuously equipped train to exercises in Scotland and the South-West.

Operation ROUNDUP was the name given in 1943 for the planning of the full-scale invasion of northern France; this later turned into OVERLORD. From the beginning in 1942 Harold was called to several of the operational meetings, attended by General Sir Bernard Paget, Air Chief Marshal Sir Sholto Douglas and Mountbatten. Paget and Douglas at that stage could not visualize any site for a limited operation except in the Calais-Boulogne area, partly because of the limited range of fighter aircraft; this plan was known as SLEDGEHAMMER. But Mountbatten was always strongly against SLEDGEHAMMER and believed that the only suitable stretch of coastline which was lightly defended was in the neighbourhood of Cherbourg and along the Normandy coast. Harold wrote:

> Mountbatten stated that it would be possible to increase the range of fighter aircraft by some means, such as subsidiary petrol tanks. General Paget pointed out that there were no harbours capable of supporting an offensive in that area and that those which existed would certainly be destroyed. Mountbatten replied that even that problem could be solved and he would put up a further plan. It was in fact made possible by the construction of Mulberry harbours.

The idea of what became 'Mulberry' was still embryonic. Eisenhower wrote how at a conference of service chiefs Mountbatten had remarked: 'If ports are not available, we may have to construct them in pieces and tow them across,' and that this had been greeted by 'hoots and jeers'. Mountbatten always attributed the original conception of Mulberry to Commodore John Hughes-Hallett, but even in 1941 there had been suggestions about artificial breakwaters and sheltered anchorages. Ideas were in circulation about a 'Bubble Breakwater', a 'Lilo' and a 'Swiss Roll', a floating affair of timber and canvas supported on wire cables. Arguments against the Pas de Calais also included the shallowness of the beaches, and the ease of mining.

The possibility of floating piers was also being investigated, and this inspired the famous and often quoted Minute written by Churchill from Downing Street on 30 May and addressed to CCO (Mountbatten) 'or Deputy'.

Piers for Use on Beaches

They must float up and down with the tide. The anchor problem must be answered. Let me have the best solution worked out. Don't argue the matter. The difficulties will argue for themselves.

Harold first knew of TORCH when Mountbatten asked him to go to the Ministry of War Transport to obtain a list of the ships which were being used in the operation. He was surprised to learn that they consisted almost entirely of ocean liners. He then guessed correctly that the destination must be North Africa. The attention of the German Luftwaffe was now temporarily diverted from Britain, so Harold had the task of arranging with the Ministry of War Transport for the delivery of over 2 million tons of reserve coal to various South Coast ports.

There was no diminution of the U-boat menace, however. And this led to another proposal: the construction of a gigantic floating aircraft carrier made of solid ice, known as 'Habbakuk', named after the prophet (who was really spelt *Habakkuk*). It was the brainchild of an eccentric, unkempt genius of fertile imagination named Geoffrey Pyke, friend of the scientist J. D. Bernal, who with Solly Zuckerman formed part of Mountbatten's so-called Department of Wild Talents. Habbakuk was designed to be unsinkable and would be mixed with a compound of paper-pulp know as Pykcrete. It was expected to float off the north-west tip of France and thus be a base for fighter aircraft. Not surprisingly, this suggestion generated more hoots and jeers, though Mountbatten was to claim that Mulberry at first was considered an even more outrageous concept.

369

Mountbatten, Harold Wernher, Bernal (who was Professor of Physics at London University), Zuckerman and Tom Hussey (given the job of Co-Ordinator of Experiments and Development, known as CXD) all assembled in Pyke's bedroom in Albany off Piccadilly where he was recovering from an illness. Zuckerman has described this meeting:

> Pyke was sitting up, looking, with his strange beard, like some jaundiced Christ. Mountbatten tried to assure him that work was proceeding as fast as it possibly could. Pyke was not satisfied. 'Without faith,' he kept protesting, 'nothing will come of the project.' 'But I have faith,' replied Mountbatten. 'Yes,' said Pyke, 'but have the others got faith?', and turning to Harold Wernher he asked solemnly: 'Have you got faith, Brigadier?' Poor Wernher did not know what to say, but before he could offer a word, the CCO had chipped in with the remark: 'Wernher's on my staff, to see that I am not over-lavish with my own faith.'

Harold, as it happened, had no faith in Habbakuk, but loyally continued to give Mountbatten 'practical construction advice', and Churchill was excited by it. The Americans certainly had no faith in Pyke, who had already annoyed them over another of his inventions, Weasel, a light tracked vehicle useful for partisan warfare. In the end Habbakuk was abandoned, because the Allies were able to occupy the Azores, and also because long-range fighters had been developed. One negative side of Habbakuk was that it made the Admiralty look with suspicion on any further ambitious project put up by Combined Operations Headquarters.

At the end of his account of Habbakuk Harold wrote these stark words:

'Mr Pyke committed suicide after the war ended.'

On 25 August 1942 a great tragedy hit the royal family. The Duke of Kent was killed in an air crash when flying over Invergordon in Scotland to Iceland.

The funeral was held at St George's Chapel, Windsor four days later. Nada was there and wrote to Zia:

What a ghastly horrible tragedy – that poor darling George. You know how fond I was of him and I always considered him my best friend in the world. Marina asked me to call her next day after the accident & she was so wonderful & spoke so calmly & sensibly, but since then she has quite broken down. The last thing he said to Marina and Zoia [Baroness de Stoeckl's daughter] before he left was 'Remind me to call Nada up as soon as I return, as I want to see her.' The funeral was the most awful tragic thing I have ever been to. After the ceremony they all broke down. The King sobbing like a child. Queen Mary too – in fact the whole room.

Zia too had broken down when she heard of his death.

By that autumn Alex was with the 17/21 Lancers in Tunisia. On 2 December he wrote to his mother after ten days' fighting. It was to be his last letter. He told her that he was writing from the top of a mountain. The enemy was not far off, so there was very little time for writing. There had been a rapid advance of four hundred miles before an encounter. He had been in two battles. It was awful seeing shells coming straight at you, but one's sensations were strange, he said. One became quite detached, almost without hatred, and without much fear. There was just a desire to finish it all as soon as possible. He had been dive-bombed twice and machine-gunned a good deal. His knowledge of German had come in useful when prisoners were brought in. He had been four days without washing, but 'it keeps you warm'.

Well, Ma, so far all is well, and I hope my luck goes on. I feel it will somehow, as I seem to come out of all our engagements better than most.

I think of you all a great deal. Give my best love to Pa, Gina and Myra. I will write again soon. Much love Alex.

That night the tanks of his squadron were going back to harbour. Alex's tank had trouble, and he was waiting on foot to guide the squadron across a gully. One tank stuck, and on its being towed out, Alex's leg and hip were crushed between the towing tank and another. He was evacuated before midnight but was amazingly cheerful.

There had been no time to build up proper medical facilities, and this was in the days before penicillin came into general use. Gangrene set in. The doctor gave him a pint of his own blood. Sometimes Alex was conscious. His last words were to send his family all his love. He died at 11.15 a.m. on 4 December.

Zia was writing letters in the drawing-room at Lubenham and Myra was playing the piano on the morning that the butler brought in the telegram about Alex's death. He was ashen. It seemed that the postman had known about its contents and had been unable to ride his bicycle to the house; he had sat down in the kitchen, speechless.

Gina was sent for from the hospital where she was working, and Zia drove to London to tell Harold. That night the two of them went to the theatre. Some people were amazed at this; others saw it as an act of courage. As Myra has said: 'You just couldn't sit and brood. If you had done so, you'd have been finished.'

Both Harold and Zia were devastated, and never wanted to speak of Alex's death in public. 'I'm all right if you don't mention it,' Zia said. Harold postponed his CMSF meeting for a week. He looked as if he had aged ten years, people thought.

Of all the letters they received, Princess Marina's was the most moving. She had gone to stay at Lubenham after her husband's death. Derrick wrote from New York. Lady Ludlow offered to come and see Harold in London, but he said it would only hurt more. She wrote him a long and affectionate letter, and a separate one to Zia, and it was clear from these that in the last years a special bond had grown up between her and the boy.

I understood him and he knew it, and he honoured me with his confidence tho' I never sought or asked for it. Seeing the great disparity of our ages, our relationship was extraordinary and the most precious thing in my life. We had much in common, not only in our tastes but in our outlook in life and he liked to discuss those with me and never felt I was too old to understand.

It took a long time for Gina to recover. So many of her contemporaries were being killed or wounded, and this was to continue during the subsequent campaign in Italy. Platoon commanders or squadron leaders, always in their early twenties, were expected to be the leaders in an attack, and were often thus among the first casualties.

Bobby Peacock arrived in Tunisia two days after Alex's death. There followed three weeks of hectic fighting and other officers were killed. Afterwards he went to see Alex's grave, marked with a wooden cross and stones, and put flowers on it. He sent a photograph to Zia. Her comment was: 'Is this the best you can do?'

She seemed completely out of touch with the realities of war, as if she could not understand the way the world was changing. Her grief obscured all. She was hurt when Dick Hamilton-Russell, as Alex's commanding officer, was only able to write briefly in pencil at the height of battle, and she took his wife out to lunch to complain that no one had come home to break the news to her.

Then at Christmas a card arrived from Prince Philip, simply with the words 'Love Philip'. He was now second-in-command of the destroyer HMS *Wallace*, which was doing patrol work in the particularly dangerous waters of the Channel and North Sea. He had not heard of Alex's death, but Zia could not appreciate this and complained angrily to Mountbatten (who was also executor of Alex's will).

Philip eventually wrote to her on 10 January, and it was a letter that swept aside any possible resentment. 'Ever since I got the telegram from Uncle Dickie,' he wrote, 'I have been in a daze.'

Alex filled a place in my life that was very important to me, he filled a place of a brother and for that alone I am eternally grateful to him. As the older boy he was the guide and the pillow and in a great many ways I tried to model myself on him. As I grew older I was able to find many of my shortcomings by just comparing myself to him and in some cases I managed to put them right . . .

It is not easy for me to try and say what I thought of him because there are no words which can describe a friendship between two boys, those things just are and one does not stop to think why.

Dear Zia, I know you will never think very much of me, I am rude and unmannerly and I say many things out of turn which I realize afterwards must have hurt someone. Then I am filled with remorse and I try to get matters right . . .'

In May 1943 Harold attended a debate in the House of Commons when it was known that the Prime Minister would be making an important announcement. During the debate Churchill was handed a cable, which he proceeded to read aloud. It was from Field Marshal Alexander, saying that in accordance with instructions given him by the Prime Minister the previous year, the German Army had been driven back from El Alamein to Tunis and had now surrendered. He awaited the Prime Minister's further instructions.

At the Casablanca Conference of January 1943 between Churchill, Roosevelt and the Combined Chiefs of Staff it was agreed that a D-Day for the invasion of Northern France should be planned for, even if this had to be in 1944. There would also be a Supreme Allied Commander, as yet not chosen. Meanwhile General Sir Frederick Morgan was named as Chief of Staff to this future Commander, and given the initials of COSSAC. This placed Mountbatten in an advisory capacity, and, as Ziegler has said in his biography, it said much for Morgan's common sense and tact that there was no misunderstanding or ill-feeling. Mountbatten thus put at COSSAC's disposal the planning and intelligence of his own headquarters.

Still the argument continued over the choice of the Pas de Calais or Normandy for the invasion, and on this depended both the availability of harbours, and especially bombing strategy. COSSAC's own plan was based on the preference of Combined Operations, which was for Normandy. A decision was becoming urgent in view of the Chiefs of Staff conference at Quebec in August. 'From this appalling quandary,' as Morgan wrote, they were rescued by Mountbatten, 'always a leader of progressive thought and somewhat of an enfant terrible to his more elderly confrères'. Mountbatten decided to organize a conference at Largs in Scotland, to which all those on the highest level concerned with the organization of the invasion were invited, such as the COSSAC staff, General Paget as commander of the British Home Forces, Air Chief Marshal Sir Trafford Leigh-Mallory, and Admiral Sir Charles Little from Portsmouth. It was a brilliant diplomatic success. Mountbatten chaired the conference, which included among others twenty generals, eleven air marshals and eight admirals.

The COSSAC plan was accepted, provided that the three main principles were observed, namely complete air protection, complete sea protection and artificial harbours. A minute was sent to the Chiefs of Staff recommending that there should be a single authority appointed to deal with all aspects concerned with this last. As a result, it was agreed that Harold Wernher, while remaining CMSF, should be appointed to the staff of COSSAC to undertake the 'co-ordination of ports, sheltered anchorages, port and landing facilities' between the various Service Departments and the US authorities, and the supervision of the 'progress of supply material and stores.'

'I at once realized,' Mountbatten was to write afterwards to Eisenhower, who eventually became Supreme Commander, 'that without the personal drive of a really great man, such a project [artificial harbours] could not possibly succeed. I therefore put Harold Wernher on to this task and arranged to transfer him to Freddie Morgan's American staff pending your appointment.' To be truthful, on 5 July at the Largs Conference it was Admiral Little who had suggested to Harold that he might make himself responsible for this huge job, and it was Little who then reported back to Mountbatten.

Harold flew back to London with Mountbatten from Largs in Mountbatten's private plane. On the way Mountbatten asked him how he thought the Conference had gone.

I told him I thought it was the culminating achievement for himself and therefore for his headquarters, but that the virtual end of his activities was in sight because the Commanders in the field, such as Montgomery, would say that his veterans would be able to undertake operations without advice from other quarters. I therefore advised Mountbatten to look for another job, and this was to come to him sooner than anyone could have expected.

Ziegler has commented that this advice was superfluous, since Mountbatten had already worked it out for himself.

On 24 August Harold was promoted to Acting Major-General, to give him the requisite rank to carry out his new duties. He was summoned by telegram to proceed to Quebec with eighteen Service and civilian experts.

24

The Victory Harbour

It has generally been agreed that the spark behind the acceptance of COSSAC's plan for 'sheltered water' was Hughes-Hallett's remark at Largs: 'Why don't we get some old ships and sink them as breakwaters?' Two sites for artificial harbours had been selected, one in the American sector at Saint Laurent known as Mulberry A, and the other in the British sector at Arromanches known as Mulberry B. Harold had spoken energetically in favour, and was said to have been 'in his element'.

Each of the harbours was to be approximately the size of Dover's, and between them they were to supply 12,000 tons of stores a day whatever the weather. The block-ships, old merchant ships about sixty in number, were given the name of Gooseberries and were to be scuttled in about twelve feet of water, on an even keel and – another important point – overlapping. They were expected to last ninety days from D-Day. 'No mean horticultural feat,' was the well-worn joke. In the end some redundant warships had also to be used to make up the number.

Out to sea from the Gooseberries would be about a mile of floating steel structures called Bombardons, moored in the open sea in two rows and designed to break the waves. Both these breakwaters, the Gooseberries and Bombardons, were the responsibility of the Navy. The concrete caissons known as Phoenixes and the Whale piers (of which more later) were to be an Army commitment. Before setting out for Quebec, Harold was able to arrange with the Ministry of Supply that his old friend Jack Gibson of Pauling & Co. should be in charge of the constructional side of the Phoenixes, although according to his diary the appointment was not confirmed until 24 September, over a month later. He wrote of Gibson: 'A Yorkshire man, he had started life contracting for Pearson & Co., and later, when the first Lord Cowdray retired from business, he had made Gibson a present of over £100,000 worth of plant in gratitude for his services. With this plant Gibson had carried out some big contracts in Lower Egypt and Sudan.' Somehow those old polo contacts at Cowdray Park must have played their part. All the same, Gibson was a splendid choice, and the success of Mulberry owed a great deal to him.

R. A. Davis, once of Vauxhall Motors, was to handle the remaining work such as pierheads, flexible floating roadways and pontoons. Captain Harold Hickling, a New Zealander, was to liaise with the Admiralty. Like Gibson and Davis, he became a 'firm friend' of Harold Wernher, though, being also unafraid of speaking his mind, he admitted that there had been 'initial bickering' (which was a polite understatement) at Whitehall. Other members of Harold's inner team included Colonel Basil Bunting, his assistant, and the Americans Brigadier-General H. B. Vaughan and Colonel C. M. Spainhour, all hard workers and likewise with 'no feeling other than getting on with the job'.

With Colonel Bruce White, who was responsible for port engineering at the War Office, there was a more difficult relationship. To get things done quickly, according to Hickling, you generally had to deal with Colonel Vassal Steer-Webster. It was with Bruce White that Harold travelled to Quebec for the 'Quadrant' Conference of August 1943, on a very tedious eighteen-hour journey, sleeping on the floor of a Liberator bomber with boots in each other's faces.

It is hard not to look on Harold's existence during the next six months or so as a catalogue of confrontations, in spite of his outstanding achievements. He fought back, not caring what he said, and as a result left a reputation with some for being 'overbearing', which was to work against him when Mulberry had been successfully launched, and even when the war was over.

Harold had once been a Regular officer, having passed through the Royal Military College, and had served with great distinction as a cavalry officer and with the Machine-Gun Corps in the First War. This was not enough for many of those at the War Office who had made the Army their career; they insisted on looking upon him as a 'temporary gent', and regarded his new rank of Major-General as 'administrative fiction'.

At Quebec he at once found himself in conflict with American officers who had taken it upon themselves to prepare a report on artificial harbours for General Marshall without having consulted the British. Only when Harold threatened to return to England was the report withdrawn. Then there was difficulty with Admiral Ernest J. King of the US Navy over the provision of American tugs – hardly surprising since he was known as Limey Hater Extraordinaire. Harold was depressed by his grudging attitude. Soon afterwards Mountbatten summoned him to his room at the Hôtel Frontenac, where they were all staying, to tell him of his appointment as Supreme Commander in South-East Asia. He was understandably exultant, and it was a very great compliment for someone of his age (forty-three). All the same, after his recent experience with Admiral King, Harold could not help warning him that he was likely to be very low on the Americans' priority list for supplying men and materials. But Mountbatten was not deterred; as Ziegler has said, his naïvety over this was sublime.

It was decided that Harold and his delegation should proceed to Washington to thrash out the details of the Mulberry plan with the Combined Chiefs of Staff. Before leaving Quebec, he had been promised a gala lunch by the Italian chef at the Frontenac. Alas, ten minutes before this lunch he was called away by Mountbatten to see the Prime Minister, who now had a new scheme for constructing steel pontoons for towing to the Pacific, to be used instead of aircraft-carriers. Churchill wanted him to oversee the job. Harold put up a number of valid objections to the idea and added that he felt he had enough on his plate with Mulberry, and could not divert his energies to anything else:

Whereupon the Prime Minister was extremely annoyed and obviously regarded me as an obstructionist. However, when the conference broke up half an hour later, the Prime

Minister asked me to remain. I felt rather like a schoolboy in the presence of the Headmaster as I imagined what was coming to me. However with a beaming smile on his face he said: 'Those good old days, when we used to play polo together, do seem a long way off now, don't they?' After this I knew I had been forgiven.

Harold had missed that lunch.

At Washington the more minute details of Mulberry were discussed, and a signal was sent to London on 26 August authorizing the construction of the caissons. It took over a week to decide that these should be an Army responsibility. Almost with a sinking heart, one reads that Harold became aware that Vice-Admiral O. C. Badger, the American chairman of the committee for supplies in all theatres of war, had some sort of grievance against him. However, Badger did not allow this to interfere with his attitude towards the British delegation at large, which Harold felt at least showed an impressive generosity of mind. Later this rather niggling little grievance was settled amicably after Harold had made Steer-Webster ply the Admiral with a lot of strong drinks. Churchill, however, was in an irritable mood when he met Harold again; it seemed because he was not wearing his hearing aid, and this probably did not help Harold in the long run either.

The final plan for the Mulberry Harbours was approved by the Chiefs of Staff on 3 September, nine months before the invasion of the Continent was planned to start.

Bruce White headed the Harbour Committee, and all seemed to be going harmoniously until the return to London. With the departure of Mountbatten, Harold now realized that White was attempting to assume overall direction of the Mulberry project. It is not worth while to delve into the preliminaries of these dramas, mainly technical, which have been said since to have been based on the 'deepest psychological differences'. Bruce White was a man who had rows with a number of people, his strong point being the support of Churchill, who seemed to enjoy having men at odds with the majority. The trouble with Harold centred mainly at first upon the construction of the Phoenix caissons, Bruce White having been responsible for the original designs.

The Phoenixes, concrete caissons, were the inner main breakwaters for the harbours, some against the Gooseberries for further protection and stretching out on each side of them to the east and west. They would be in different sizes according to the depth of water into which they would be 'planted'. The largest, ultimately, was 200 feet long and 60 feet high. As only eight dry docks were found to be available, some slipways and wet docks were used. Nearly half the caissons had to be constructed in pits excavated along the banks of the Thames. Rectangular in form, flat-bottomed with square bows and stern, they had to be towable over some 100 miles, and of course proof against capsizing. These enormous concrete hulks of perhaps 6,000 tons were nicknamed 'blocks of flats' and had to be sunk in exactly the right places, within a deadline of fifteen minutes: a question of inches, not feet. All this would require a considerable feat of seamanship. Bruce White, as Harold said, could not appreciate that once they were manufactured and floating they would come under Admiralty jurisdiction, being classified at that stage as ships.

Twenty-five contractors were employed at various sites and 10,000 men were required for prefabricating about a million tons of concrete. Later, as work proceeded, a further 12,000 men were drafted in. Ernest Bevin, as Minister for Labour, was very helpful to Harold on this, especially when skilled operatives – scaffolders and steel fixers – had to be released from military service. Harold had to convince the Services that, Americans being unable to contribute to the work, it would be undesirable to mix civilian and military labour owing to the disparity of pay. Thus the men were drafted as civilians.

The Whale piers were to be inside the breakwaters. They were described as the most ingenious pieces of engineering in modern times, and the Prime Minister's dictum, 'They must float up and down with the tide', was often quoted. The essence of Whale consisted of pierheads – rectangular steel ships, like the Phoenixes 200 feet long, and with a 60-foot beam and 11 feet deep. They were known as Spud pierheads, because of the four legs, or spuds, 90 feet high, fitted with winding machinery to enable them to be moved up and down. When ready to be towed across to France, the legs would be up above the hull; on arrival a button would be pressed and the legs would be lowered until they were buried in the seabed. From these pierheads ran the flexible floating roadways for the unloading of cargoes. Ten miles of these were ordered. Each was divided into sections or spans of 480 feet for towing purposes. Each of the piers used at Arromanches could take a 40-ton load such as a tank. A LST (Landing Ship Tanks) could unload about seventy tanks and trucks in eighteen minutes. There were about 240 firms concerned with the building of Whale.

If Whale required 50,000 tons of steel, on top of that the Bombardon breakwaters needed a further 30,000 tons, a great problem in a time of wartime shortage. Each Bombardon was about 200 feet long. Harold admitted that he never had much faith in them, and his suspicions were to prove well founded in the storms following D-Day.

The construction of the hards was also continuing. Security and air raids were other problems. Attempting to keep the peace and reconciling conflicting interests and priorities was, needless to say, almost as difficult a task.

The actual siting of the Mulberries on the other side of the Channel now became of paramount importance, and Admiral Sir William Tennant was brought into COSSAC to plan the movement and erection of the harbours. Captain Hickling was transferred to Tennant's staff, which was helpful to Harold as they were able to keep in daily touch. The first difficulty that Tennant found was that the designs for Phoenix, produced by Bruce White's department at the War Office at the end of October 1943, were too complicated and would cause delays in construction. Harold, as usual the troubleshooter, consulted the Controller of the Navy, who brought in a concrete expert to submit modifications. It was now becoming doubtful whether the job could be finished by 1 May 1944, the date set for the invasion. 'You can imagine,' Harold said later, 'that all this made for no good will. But it was in the winter that the real crisis arose between the War Office and the Admiralty. It really boiled down to a matter of prestige against tradition.'

It was also a race against time. 'Second Front Now!' was being splashed on London's walls. Given the gigantic nature and size of the project, everyone was overstretched. Allowances therefore have to be made for this 'war within war', or what Harold was tactfully to describe in his book as 'misunderstandings and disappointments', but the outline needs to be recorded here to show the pressures under which he had to work. Although a Major-General, he was still regarded as an interloper by the War Office. His CMSF reports now had to be prepared for COSSAC, General Morgan, who relayed them on to the Chiefs of Staff Committee under his own signature. Typical headings in these reports indicate some of the scope involved: Design of Mulberry, Types of Breakwater, Labour, Sites (Dry Docks etc.), Tugs.

Bruce White and his colleagues still would not accept that the Phoenixes for which they had been responsible would move into the domain of the Admiralty as soon as they were afloat. The situation became so bad that the Controller refused to deal any more with Bruce White. Harold had no alternative but to take up the matter with COSSAC, as the whole future timetable was being jeopardized by the quarrel.

Morgan was ill, so it was decided to refer it to the Chiefs of Staff. But the Chiefs of Staff were with Churchill, Roosevelt and Stalin at the Teheran Conference (28 November – 1 December 1943). Their deputies were under the orders of General Nye, who proved unsympathetic and simply snapped at Harold: 'You're supposed to co-ordinate. Why don't you co-ordinate?' It was difficult for Harold to restrain himself. 'How can I co-ordinate,' he replied, 'if people refuse to be co-ordinated?' Now Admiral Sir Bertram Ramsay, Allied Naval Commander-in-Chief for OVER-LORD, who had already had trouble with Bruce White, came to the defence of Harold Wernher. We read that a 'most acrimonious argument followed'. Back it all went to General Morgan, and 'the matter as we all thought was settled'.

Harold next had to go to the Admiralty, and arranged for a directive to be drawn up with the staff of the First Sea Lord, Admiral Sir Andrew Cunningham. At a subsequent meeting of the Chiefs of Staff Cunningham altered that directive. Thus Harold was put in an absurd position, and he decided to confront

Cunningham himself. He found him in a bad temper, because of a misunderstanding with the US Navy and because the windows of his office had been blown in by a bomb. Harold had to be patient, listening to his 'tales of woe' for a good half-hour. At last Cunningham agreed to restore the directive to its original form.

In spite of this, Bruce White determined to continue the fight. He wrote and signed a letter to Harold dated 9 November on behalf of General McMullen, Director of Transportation, to the effect that the work would never be finished in time and that the blame lay with Harold because of his *lack* of co-ordination, giving preference to one Service over another and misusing building facilities, in particular pushing forward the construction of Bombardons to the detriment of Phoenixes. 'My goodness,' Steer-Webster said later, 'this did cause a flap! Wernher, justly I think, decided that this was an issue of such importance that it must be taken to the highest level, which would probably have meant the end of Bruce White. However, Wernher relented, rang up General McMullen and told him to withdraw the letter – which he did.'

According to Harold, he had quoted to McMullen a similar type of incident concerning Prince Louis of Battenberg, Mountbatten's father, when he was First Sea Lord, who had received an insubordinate letter from an admiral whom he admired. Prince Louis had merely acknowledged this letter and had sent it back, saying that he had not read it.

The name of Sir James Grigg was never mentioned in any of the accounts of this clash of bureaucrats, but undoubtedly he would have been well aware of it.

It was the redoubtable Jack Gibson, the great authority in engineering, who now emerged as a hero. He had once said about Phoenixes: 'It isn't a question of whether it can be done, but how it can be done.' At this late stage he had to point out that there were still fatal flaws in the design of the Phoenixes. His advice was taken, and once taken he worked 'night and day' on this gigantic task, producing, so it was said, 147 Phoenixes in 147 days – the final drawings only having been approved on 27 November. No less than 142 alterations or additions had been made. The short hours of daylight and the nightly air attacks added to the difficulties. It was then that the question of finding the dry docks became one of the most urgent priorities, although, as Gibson was to say afterwards, 'our main headache was labour'.

When the appointment of Eisenhower as Supreme Allied Commander of SHAEF (Supreme Headquarters, Allied Expeditionary Force) was announced, it was Harold who had to write him a warning that the completion of Mulberry might not be until the end of April; dangerously near D-Day:

The project is one of almost unprecedented magnitude.
Apart from the production it entails the movement of this
vast quantity of equipment (approximately one million tons)
from its point of manufacture to the assembly point, and its
subsequent movement across one hundred miles of open
seas, and its erection under considerable difficulty to a time
schedule.

He regarded the shortage of tugs as a potential disaster, unless the United States was able to provide more.

Eisenhower's arrival in January 1944 also helped to settle some of the qualms of the Americans, who had become irritated by the internecine British squabbles and were thus suspicious of the progress reports. Harold wrote of Eisenhower's tact and charm, and how on his first day as Supreme Commander, after an address to his staff at the headquarters and an appeal for co-operation between British and Americans, he 'took the senior officers into another room and asked each of us in turn what we were doing and again addressed us'.

As the constructional stage of Phoenixes, Whales, Bombardons etc. gave way to the operational stage, including the assembling of parts, so the burden of co-operation gradually passed to Admiral Tennant and Commodore Hickling, and they also became directly responsible for PLUTO. A new decision to equip the Phoenixes with anti-aircraft guns caused further anxieties about delays. Indeed, it is clear that if Montgomery, in command of Land Forces, had not insisted on a month's delay for the invasion, so as to make possible a landing on a wider front, Mulberry would probably not have been ready in time.

One construction site for Phoenixes was at Stokes Bay near

Portsmouth. The local contractor came to see Harold with a grievance, for his most important engineer had been forbidden by the Admiralty to work in the area. Harold was amused to find that this man was the son of Alexander Kerensky, the Russian Prime Minister in 1917 and thus a *bête noire* of Zia and all other White Russians. Nevertheless he managed to have the ban withdrawn and young Kerensky continued to work throughout the construction period. But it was a different problem when General Morgan ordered his staff to give every facility to a Soviet delegation which had arrived to study the OVERLORD plan. Harold had to insist that they should not be told about Mulberry.

There were some madcap schemes which Harold was asked to investigate. One was proposed by an unnamed but prominent United States engineer in the Corps of Engineers, who suggested that old aeroplane engines could be mounted on barges and anchored some way from the shores. The general thought that in the case of a gale these engines could be started up and so deflect the wind from the Mulberry harbours. As Harold said: 'It was sometimes difficult to give a polite answer to this kind of proposal.'

The various units had finally to be assembled on the South Coast of England and parked at strategic points, often difficult to find because of the gathering of assault forces. Although this was outside Harold's responsibility, he had to arrange for dredgers to be brought in advance from the Clyde. More tugs had at last arrived from the United States, bringing the total to about 200, for towing the various 'monstrosities' from all over the British Isles – 'Undoubtedly the biggest towing operation ever mounted.' All had to be protected from gales and enemy attacks. Harold was also involved in the task of requisitioning or otherwise obtaining old ships for block-ships. Many of the skippers of these 'crocks' were not told, for security reasons, what was to be their destination until the last minute, and partings were often 'emotional'.

In the view of Harold and 'unprejudiced' observers the assembly was only completed in time because the stranglehold of the War Office on Production and Movement had been eased in the last vital weeks. As Harold said: 'I felt that Director of Transportation [McMullen] had taken on more than he could hope to achieve with the military labour at his disposal.' Gibson agreed with him that matters were not proceeding in a 'businesslike manner'.

Harold's account of the inevitable row was bland enough but gave a revealing picture of the side of his character that brought him unpopularity:

> Furthermore, there were insufficient electricians to complete the work on the pierheads. I accordingly went to the Admiralty and the Ministry of Supply to see whether we could mobilise any extra labour from those sources.
>
> Meanwhile I asked General Sir Humfrey Gale, who was the Chief Supply Officer at SHAEF, to summon a meeting. Before this I had been in touch with General McMullen. He stated that everything possible had been done, but that there were insufficient light cranes for the job. I asked him what steps he had taken to procure cranes and received an unsatisfactory reply. Before going into the meeting, I rang up the Ministry of Works and discovered that there were numerous cranes in the country which were being held in order to shift the coal which we had deposited in various dumps along the South Coast. They stated that these could be moved at short notice if necessary.
>
> At the meeting, General McMullen stated his case, whereupon General Gale asked me for a solution. I denied General McMullen's remark that cranes were not available and stated that, if I were given authority, I would guarantee to deliver the cranes in a short time. Furthermore, I stated that I had seen the Americans and, if necessary, they would place at our disposal a large number of Sea Bees (Marine Engineers). I also advised that if teams of Sea Bees and British Engineers were placed side by side healthy competition would ensue. It was by this means that the equipment was all completed and assembled in time.

D–Day was fixed for 6 June. By superhuman efforts the main assembly was indeed completed, and just in time. Some units only arrived on D minus 1. The Mulberry advance forces sailed on the evening of D-Day. 'This magnificent port,' Churchill was eventually to signal, 'has made possible the liberation of Europe.'

Some weeks beforehand Harold decided, to the surprise of some, that his duties as CMSF had been accomplished, now that the work had moved into the operational stage. He went to see General Ismay at the War Cabinet to recommend that his appointment should be terminated. He followed up this visit with a letter:

> . . . The position is that the task which was allotted to me is in sight of completion, and all the arrangements have been made, and all the Ministries are now so closely in touch with each other that even additions to the equipment can be undertaken without any action on my part. Large staffs have been set up to deal with the operational aspects of 'Mulberry', and the responsibility therefore falls on them.

The Prime Minister gave his approval for the termination on 11 April. Harold's rank was changed from Acting to Honorary Major-General. He went to say goodbye to Admiral Ramsay, reminding him that they were the only two who had been involved with the plans from the beginning, starting with SLEDGEHAMMER. He could not help telling him privately that the more he thought of what lay ahead, the more appalling the prospect appeared, being so dependent on weather conditions during the time of operation. Ramsay replied in somewhat blimpish fashion:

> Have you ever been in Scotland on August 12 in a really good grouse year? You go to your butt with two guns and a loader, hundreds of grouse pass over the butt, you shoot quite well, and perhaps pick up thirty birds; thousands go on untouched. Well, that is just what this operation is. We have 5,000 craft, we have supremacy of the air and sea. Many ships may be hit but many will arrive and it is impetus that will win the day.

He was right though. In the long run numbers count when ground forces are engaged.

There was indeed trouble with the weather after the landings, but in the case of Mulberry A not quite as terrible as Harold had gloomily feared. The losses of Bombardons and Phoenixes were negligible, but 50 per cent of the pierheads were lost, as were two tugs. This great storm on D plus 13, which lasted for two days, almost totally destroyed Mulberry A at Saint Laurent, and was reckoned to have been the worst in eighty years, comparable to the one that dispersed the Spanish Armada. All the Bombardons broke loose and came adrift. Further work had to be discontinued and the harbour abandoned.

Harold understandably left the job with a mixture of regret and relief. At last he would be able to spend more time with his family. For the last two years he had been up all hours, liable to be called to emergency meetings in the middle of the night, perhaps by the Prime Minister. He sometimes snatched a night or two at Lubenham, and Zia tried to spend a couple of nights each week at the Dorchester. To the family he always seemed very controlled, outwardly at least. They would know he was worried by the way he would sit in an armchair, gazing at nothing and biting or picking at his thumbnail. 'All things are possible until proved impossible,' he would tell them.

He wrote to Mountbatten in India to tell him of his departure. It was a somewhat flat letter, praising the co-operation of the Controller of the Navy and the 'help and understanding' of some other Admiralty officers, though admittedly the War Office had been difficult and in most cases 'narrow-minded in their outlook'. 'But in the end I managed to reconcile the various parties and got on with it.' He was sad to be 'out of the hunt just at this exciting moment'. He also wrote to Sir Andrew Duncan, Minister of Supply, thanking him for their 'pleasant relationship'.

Mountbatten replied by return, now with his headquarters in Ceylon: 'I shall always bless the day when I had the good sense to realize: (a) that a CMSF was wanted, and (b) that you were the chap to do it.' He also suggested that when the war in Europe was over Harold might consider an appointment as a 'go-getter for the war in South East Asia', making sure in London that Mountbatten's requirements were being met. He added: 'I am so glad to think that your unique talents have been properly used in this war and know how much the success of OVERLORD will owe to you.'

Meanwhile Harold had put up a scheme for using civilian builders who had been employed for Mulberry to work on the rehabilitation of captured French ports, under the leadership of Jack Gibson. This in due course was turned down by General Gale, Chief Supply Officer for SHAEF, and one cannot but suspect that personalities lay behind the rejection of this apparently reasonable plan. Another scheme was suggested by both Harold and Jack Gibson. This again was connected with Mulberry contractors, and was for a national campaign for housing after the war, which they felt would help Churchill when the time came for an election. But it was again rejected, somewhat rudely, by Duncan Sandys at the Ministry of Works.

From the letters that Harold kept after his departure it is clear that his admirers and supporters were those with 'no feeling other than getting on with the job.' In Whitehall there were too many who felt they deserved the credit for any major projects, and who thus resented outsiders 'butting in'.

In fact the government was already concerned with the housing shortage, and plans were being made for the production of prefabricated houses. Because insulation was likely to be poor and kitchen space limited, refrigerator manufacturers were approached to quote for built-in models. Electrolux won an initial contract for 50,000 refrigerators. Harold expected Electrolux to go into production with new refrigerators in October, which was one reason why his reply to Mountbatten – written the day after D-Day – was ambivalent. 'Naturally,' he wrote, 'I would go to any lengths to carry out your wishes.' After a clear hint about possible opposition from the War Office, he said that he was looking forward to getting back to some of his civilian obligations. He was certainly not interested in 'taking on a job which many other people could do'.

By early September Mulberry B was well established, and Harold was invited by SHAEF to Arromanches, there to be received by his old friend Hickling, who was in charge of the port. He learnt that up to the end of August a million tons of stores were landed in the British sector, half of them via Mulberry. Even at the height of the storm 800 tons of ammunition had been landed. Harold's conclusion about the disaster to Mulberry A was that it was due to inadequate soundings having been made, and that the Americans had hurried too much with its erection on site, 'trying to beat us to it'. Mulberry A had not been repaired, since the port of Cherbourg was about to be captured.

He flew home in a Dakota and had a lucky escape. The young American pilot lost his way in the clouds, and Harold was just able to stop him in time from heading towards the North Sea and Germany. That night, telephoning the family from the Dorchester, he watched a flying bomb drop on the roof of Lansdowne House a few hundred yards away.

General Brownjohn, who had been with COSSAC, was one of those who received an honour – a CB – following the Normandy landings. When Mountbatten wrote to congratulate him, he replied modestly, realizing that Mountbatten would be disappointed and upset that Harold had been overlooked, but saying:

> I expect you will have seen Harold Wernher when you were in London [in August], and that he will have told you of his trials and tribulations over the Mulberry. The fact that the Phoenix were ready on D-Day was due, in my opinion, very largely to his efforts, but I do not think this will ever be recognised, except by the few who know – he made too many enemies in official circles by his forceful methods!

Mountbatten forwarded this letter to Harold.

Because of his connections in peacetime with hospital work Harold was being consulted over the new Health Act, the forerunner of the National Health Service brought in by the Labour government. This to some extent compensated for earlier rebuffs.

There was also the question of reviving the Edward VII Hospital. During the Blitz in January 1941, 17 Grosvenor Crescent and its neighbour, 16, the lease of which Sister Agnes had acquired, were badly damaged by bombs. It broke the heart of

Sister Agnes, then aged eighty-eight, and she died on 11 May that year.* In the following July Harold had been elected Chairman.

At Lubenham Harold had enjoyed supervising the harvest, and Myra often drove the tractor. She regretted the departure of boyfriends who left with the American 82nd and 101st Airborne, which had been stationed near Market Harborough. Thanks to Harold's friendship with General Ridgway, the family had been allowed to watch the mass parachute drop held as a top-secret practice exercise before the Normandy landings.

There was also light relief when the Wernhers had a racing success at Newmarket: Persian Gulf, a four-year-old son of Double Life by Bahram, won the Coronation Cup. He was also the favourite for the Gold Cup, but disappointingly was lamed in a trial gallop beforehand, due to some rough ground. (Harold had contemplated suing the Jockey Club agent about this).†

Lady Ludlow had decided they must get rid of Bath House. Harold had wanted to use it for his office. When she was approached about his taking over the Gables instead, she relented and he was able to move the office into Bath House, which, however, was subsequently damaged in an air raid.

In his letter of 7 June to Mountbatten, Harold had written about Edwina Mountbatten's having been to Lubenham for a 'mammoth St John affair organized by Zia'. Edwina was now Superintendent-in-Chief of the St John Ambulance Brigade Nursing Division. She had delivered a brilliant speech, he said, to two thousand Brigade members, and this had been followed by a parade and all-star concert at Leicester which had raised £1,700.

---

* On 29 April Sister Agnes had sent this message to a committee meeting at Grosvenor Crescent: 'My friends, I have been very ill, so I could not come to meet you today. As long as our houses were standing up I could be happy making plans for the future; but when the bomb came and destroyed both houses I felt there was nothing left. I am making arrangements for the future; try to help me to have a little happiness after all these years.'

† Persian Gulf's sons included Zarathustra, the 50–1 outsider who won the Irish Derby in 1954, and also the Irish St Leger and Ascot Gold Cup, and Parthia the 10–1 winner of the Derby in 1959; his daughters included Zabara (One Thousand Guineas) and Queen of Sheba (Irish One Thousand Guineas).

I cannot speak too highly of the way Edwina carried out her duties, first of all the speech, then the wonderful knack of saying the right thing to so many people. She has all the grace and charm which one wishes the Royalties had, and of course as she has double the brains she is able to ingratiate herself to all. She really is a clever girl.

There is a reason for quoting this letter, since on 10 October 1944 Gina Wernher married Colonel Bunnie (Harold) Phillips, with whom for years Edwina had been in love. Bunnie had accompanied Edwina on many of her often arduous travels in wild places before the war, sometimes with Nada, sometimes with Marjorie Brecknock or Jean Norton. The liaison was well known to the Wernhers, including Gina, as well as Mountbatten, who, as Philip Ziegler has said in his biography, had on several occasions thought of divorce but nevertheless had been very fond of 'the Rabbit', as he called him.

Bunnie Phillips, quiet and very tall, and in some ways not unlike Mountbatten in appearance, was in the Coldstream Guards and attached to the Allied Mission in Washington. He came from a well-known family of brewers. Early in the war he had been with an organization in New York known as British Security Co-ordination, under the 'Quiet Canadian', Sir William Stephenson, with an assortment of colleagues such as A. J. Ayer, General Telfer-Smollett, F. W. D. Deakin, David Ogilvie, Giles Playfair and Montgomery Hyde. Descended from Carlos Gonzalez Candamo, a President of Peru, he had worked for the Secret Service in Chile, and more recently in SOE (Special Operations Executive) with Mountbatten in India. Neither he nor Gina was mentioned by name by Ziegler, who did, however, quote the extraordinary and tender letter from Mountbatten commiserating with his wife for the breaking of the relationship. Janet Morgan in her biography of Edwina has written of how Bunnie went to Broadlands to give the news to her.

When Zia was told of the engagement she had sat down to write to Queen Mary with tears of disappointment streaming down her face. She also wrote to the Queen.

Nearly a year before the wedding Edwina had been at Lubenham for St John Ambulance. She had returned to London by train with Gina. They were sitting alone, Gina reading and Edwina staring out of the window. Suddenly Edwina asked Gina whom she would like to marry. Then she said: 'I think you ought to marry Bunnie.' Gina had first admired Bunnie on the polo field, and so, since she knew he was ill with jaundice in India, she felt encouraged to send him a Christmas card. He was surprised, and kept the card by his bed.

Early in August 1944 Gina came out of the Dorchester and ran into Bunnie in Park Lane. Edwina asked them both to dinner and put them next to one another. It was Nada who pushed the affair along. She had invited Bunnie and Gina to her house Lynden Manor, and on the way there by train Bunnie had asked Gina several times to marry him, but Gina could not make up her mind. Gina's cousin Paul Chavchavadze was also staying at Lynden Manor, and played the guitar while Bunnie continued to press Gina. At last Nada said to Gina: 'I'm fed up. This is wearing me out. Are you going to accept him or are you not?' She went out of the room, and Gina accepted. Then Nada rang up Zia with the news.

The tension was by no means over, for at 5 a.m. the next morning Bunnie was off on a secret mission to France. Gina of course was afraid that he might never return.

Zia's letter to Queen Mary was in fact formal and controlled. She said that they had known Bunnie and his family for many years and were very pleased. It would be hard parting from Gina, they were such a united family, 'but we are happy to think he is so charming and that he will make a good husband'.

The wedding was at St Margaret's, Westminster, with Myra and Princess Alexandra as bridesmaids. Edwina did not come. It took her about two years to recover, but later both families settled down and 'we all went about together.' After the honeymoon at Lynden Manor, Bunnie had to return to Washington, later to be joined by Gina.

In October 1944 the government released details of Mulberry, and there were articles in newspapers under headings such as '*The Victory Harbour*', '*Invasion Port Epic*', '*Trumpcard of the Invasion*'.

The Times wrote of Mulberry as 'one of the most memorable achievements of the war', a 'vast undertaking, in which daring imagination was combined with the highest engineering skill and ingenuity'. In the list of names of those connected with the success of Mulberry Harold's name was not included.

Not surprisingly, Harold was upset. He wrote to General Morgan and told him that several people who had been associated with him, including some from the Admiralty and the Ministry of Supply, had written to ask why this had been so. He admitted that in an 'enterprise of such magnitude' he could not have avoided treading on toes and being ruthless, but felt that in the end all difficulties had been settled. He also wrote to Mountbatten.

Morgan replied somewhat evasively, saying that at the press conference he had assumed that it was common knowledge that Harold had been one of the prime movers. Harold wrote back that it could never have been common knowledge because of the security measures at the time, and in any case in a recent communiqué all the names of people working under Harold, but not Harold himself, had been mentioned. Morgan promised to look into the matter, but Harold never heard anything more from him.

Meanwhile Mountbatten promised to 'enter the lists'. He had thought of writing to Eisenhower, he said, but felt that 'Ike' had come into the show too late to know all the details and would only refer the matter back to General Gale, 'who apparently is one of those in the woodpile'. So Mountbatten had decided to write to 'Pug' Ismay, Chief of Staff to the War Cabinet, and enclosed a copy of his long letter to him. He was gratified, he said, that Combined Operations had been mentioned as having first put forward the idea of artificial harbours, but 'I was painfully surprised that there was no mention of the one man in the whole Kingdom who made the Mulberry possible.' He added:

I refer, of course, to Harold Wernher, who from the beginning was the man I put in charge of this project, and whom I transferred to COSSAC's staff when I left. I had enough talks while I was in London, and also have had sufficient letters to convince me that, but for Harold

395

Wernher's indomitable energy and fearless moral courage,
Mulberry could never have been got ready in time if at all.

He also said that he noted that Bruce White had been knighted
for the part he had played in Mulberry. 'By the same standard
Harold Wernher should be made a peer.' As he had dealt with
both men he knew what to think of their respective contributions.
He quoted Ernest Bevin, who had said to him in August: 'You
certainly put the right man in charge of getting Mulberry finished,
because Wernher was not afraid to come and see me when all
other means of getting labour had failed, and I was glad to be able
to help him.' Mountbatten considered the whole thing a real
miscarriage of justice, and felt that the Prime Minister should be
made aware of the situation.

Ismay advised him to draw up a full citation, *and* to write to
Eisenhower. He said that it was unthinkable to draw the Prime
Minister into arguments about the relative merits of various
officers. It was only in about March or April 1944 that Churchill
had taken a keen personal interest in Mulberry and started holding
conferences on the subject. By that time Harold Wernher was
leaving the job, so the Prime Minister would not in any way
connect him with the project.

25

Return to Luton Hoo

Mountbatten's struggle to obtain recognition for Harold took a long time to bear fruit. That he was genuinely very fond of Harold is absolutely without argument. His own vanity has been much written about, and later he often asked Harold to provide biographers and journalists with material, in effect as complimentary as possible, about the Combined Operations days. On the other hand he realized well enough that his achievements then had also depended on Harold's efforts. This is proved by his diary entry of 17 August 1944 when he flew over the Normandy coast and looked down on Muberry B:

> My greatest thrill was to see the artificial harbour at Arromanches, which I and my staff at COHQ had been responsible for originating and Harold Wernher for putting over. This vast port . . . is like a great commercial harbour, with breakwaters, piers, quays etc., at which ships were busily unloading.

Harold offended people but could charm them if he wished. In a certain way he was also modest about himself. He might have seemed thick-skinned to some, but he was sensitive enough to be hurt (and Zia more so) by the cold-shouldering he had received, and it is hardly surprising that he felt bitterness towards Bruce White. Even so he was often at pains to acknowledge White's successes.

Mountbatten recommended Harold for the CB in the Birthday

Honours. The reply from Eisenhower was kind, but his promise to take up the matter with Generals Morgan and Gale did not augur well.

Steer-Webster told Harold that he had run into the Prime Minister and had been congratulated as the inventor of the flexible mattress for the hards. He had said that several people who had contributed most to Mulberry had never been mentioned, and the Prime Minister had asked, 'Who?' Steer-Webster replied 'Werner'. The Prime Minister gave a slightly sibylline reply: 'Men's bad deeds are always remembered and so are the good, and this is no exception.'

When VE Day arrived, Harold took Cookie's wife Joan to cheer with the crowds outside Buckingham Palace. 'He held one arm, and a drunk sailor held my other as we swayed about.' The Birthday Honours came and went, and still there was nothing for Harold. He went to Sweden on Electrolux business and stayed with Gustav Adolf and Louise. There he met again Count Folke Bernadotte, who was to be assassinated by Jewish terrorists as United Nations mediator in the first Arab-Israeli conflict, and who told him about a secret meeting with Himmler, surprisingly naïve about his ambition to be Hitler's successor.

Lady Ludlow was unwell for most of the year, and came to a nursing home in London. She saw a great deal of Derrick, as full of charm as ever and with all sorts of impossible business ideas. None of Harold's family had ever seen Derrick's wife, who was believed to be in a mental home in America.

On 30 November 1945 Lady Ludlow died. Newspapers described her as 'Madam Midas'. Obituaries mentioned that she had been a Dame of Grace of the Order of St John of Jerusalem, but concentrated more on the achievements of Sir Julius. Her enormous will had been signed on 17 December 1943, evidently hastened by her grandson Alex's recent death in action. A few weeks before her death she added a long codicil.

Queen Mary was left a number of Chelsea, Worcester and Bow items from the porcelain collection, 'particularly admired by Her Majesty on the occasion of a visit to Bath House'. Harold, as an executor, wrote to Queen Mary, saying that he was happy to feel that 'some of this collection is passing to a connoisseur who will appreciate them'. Not quite so tactfully he also said that the will was 'a remarkable document, as everyone has been remembered, even the florist at Harrogate who attended my mother when she stayed there'. In thanking him, Queen Mary generously replied that she did not wish to spoil the collection, so that if there were any pieces he wished to keep, 'I beg that you will not hesitate to do so'. Some months later when she had received her legacy she wrote again, saying that she was superstitious about peacocks and therefore wished to return the Bow peacock and peahen. She also did not want what she described as the Dr Wall Worcester Silhouette Portrait Mug, 'as it does not fit in with my room'. She trusted that Harold would not be offended.

Actually the English porcelain collection was not Harold's property. Lady Ludlow was determined that it should not pass to Zia. In her will she said that she understood that there was an intention to give the Luton Hoo estate to the National Trust, in which case the collection was to be bequeathed to the Trust, to be displayed in the house as a memorial to her grandson. If the conveyance to the National Trust did not take place within five years of her death, then the collection would have to be sold and the proceeds added to the residuary estate.

There were legacies to forty-five charities in the main will, totalling £82,700. She also left £50,000 to form a trust towards the prevention and cure of blindness and deafness in the United Kingdom and British Empire, in memory of her son Alex,' who sacrificed his life in the Great War when he might on account of his partial blindness have avoided military service altogether'.

There was to be a trust for Derrick of £200,000 from which he would receive the income. He also received a legacy of £100,000, to be paid out of the residuary estate. Besides other legacies, Lady Ludlow left a number of specified objects such as pictures and jewellery to Derrick, Harold, Gina, Myra and Derrick's daughter Alexandra, and directed that the proceeds of the residuary estate (which included the freehold of Bath House) should be added to the trust in memory of her son.

Oddly, the clause about household linen, plate, silver, china, books, etc. at Luton Hoo was left vague. She merely said that she had excluded them from other wills because Harold had once 'expressed the determination that neither he nor his son would ever reside there'.

Zia was remembered only in the codicil, with two bits of jewellery and a sable cape. A great deal of the codicil concerned the disposal of the many other jewels and furs, but she revoked the legacy of £100,000 to Derrick out of the residuary estate, as she did not think this was 'now necessary'. Either she had meanwhile been giving Derrick money or she did not think there would be enough left in the residuary estate for his trust. By the time the remainder of her jewellery and other things had been sold at Christie's and Bath House had been sold (in 1948 for about £400,000), the residuary estate amounted to over £1 million. The trust to help the blind and deaf is in operation to this day.

The codicil went into some extraordinary details, even mentioning pillowcases and eiderdowns. Derrick was allowed silver, glass and china for eight guests; Alexandra for six guests. The disposal of the rest of the household linen was at last specified: half to Harold, a quarter to Derrick, a quarter to her secretary, a woman disliked by the family, who did rather well in other ways too (inheriting, for instance, a mink coat and several jewels).

The sale of the remainder of Lady Ludlow's jewellery – evidently those bits she had forgotten about, some 200 pieces – at Christie's in October 1946 fetched £120,317, the most valuable piece being Boucheron diamond ear pendants, 17 carats each, fetching £25,000.

In the New Year's Honours for 1946 Zia was awarded the OBE. (She was to receive the CBE in 1956 'for political and public services in Bedfordshire.)

Bunnie had a touch of TB, so he and Gina were advised to spend some time in the dry air of Tucson, Arizona, and it was there that their first child, Alexandra Anastasia, known as Sacha, was born on 27 February 1946. Harold, Zia and Myra came over for the birth, bringing with them a bag of Lubenham earth, so that the baby would be born on English soil.

They came back on the *Queen Mary*, to discover that General Gale – he of the 'woodpile' – was another passenger. The general was not pleased to find himself thus trapped, and Zia was not going to allow him to escape. As Harold reported to Mountbatten, she 'submitted him to a pretty severe cross-examination'. Evidently she won him over, or overpowered him, since from then onwards General Gale was a supporter of Harold's 'case'.

Bunnie was pronounced cured in March. In the hope of regaining possession of Luton Hoo, Harold and Zia had decided to make over Lubenham to Bunnie and Gina. Luton Hoo was still occupied by the military, and the Ministry of Supply had dumps on the estate. On their return to England they began momentarily to wonder if they had been too hasty about Lubenham. Zia was terrified of the Labour government's plans for nationalization, almost as if they were a preliminary to a new Russian Revolution. On the other hand there was the encouraging news that Harold had been awarded the American Legion of Merit, which was a considerable boost to Mountbatten's efforts on his behalf at home.

Mountbatten came back for the Victory Parade. He went to see the Military Secretary about recognition for Harold, and at Zia's suggestion met Gale. He also spoke to the King, who he thought was sympathetic.

Soon, though, the truth was revealed about Harold's exclusion from any Honours List. On 24 July Mountbatten told him this:

I have ascertained from Wemyss [Military Secretary] that you were put in for a C.B. but that P.J. [Sir James Grigg] personally scratched it out after it had passed through every committee stage, saying that so long as he was in office he would never pass your name. This is extremely confidential and secret, and must on no account be used, but it explains everything.

In the meanwhile I have got both Lawson [the new Secretary of State for War] and Attlee to agree to reconsider your case . . .

Harold and Zia spent the August Bank Holiday with Mountbatten at Broadlands and told him of another plan: in place of a decoration Harold would prefer to have Luton Hoo back, so that he could use part of it and leave the rest for perhaps an agricultural college or even as some sort of military establishment. For the

National Trust plan had by then foundered. Mountbatten duly relayed this suggestion to Lawson, explaining that 'at the end of this year he [Harold] will have nowhere else to live, which would make it particularly difficult for him since he farms extensively and is Chairman of the Electrolux Company, whose factory is in Luton'.

There the matter rested for a while. Whilst at Broadlands, Harold agreed to be trustee for Edwina Mountbatten's money inherited from her grandfather, Sir Ernest Cassel. He was also now Chairman of University College Hospital (until 1951), and was negotiating to buy two war-damaged houses in Beaumont Street, Marylebone, as a new site for the Edward VII Hospital, which it was hoped could remain independent. A tender of £45,450 for the Beaumont Street buildings was eventually accepted on 22 October 1947 (quite a bargain), about three-quarters of the sum being supplied by the War Damages Commission and some from a trust formed by Harold. He was also a keen liveryman of the Fishmongers' Company in the City, whose ornate and beautiful building had been burnt during the war, and was playing a strenuous part in having it restored to its original glory.

After Broadlands he and Zia were invited by Princess Marina to Birkhall on the Balmoral estate. 'Bring all your fishing gear!' she had written. Zia was pleased to find a picture of her father on one of the walls. They met the King, who told Harold that he felt that the essence of Combined Operations HQ should be reconstituted, and that the only man able to do this with the right amount of vision, prestige and capacity was Mountbatten. All this welcome praise was relayed at once to Mountbatten, who was of course delighted and often was to ask Harold to repeat it for the benefit of biographers. In fact such a post did in a sense come to pass thirteen years later when Mountbatten was appointed Chief of the Defence Staff.

It must have been an awkward meeting both for the Wernhers and the King, and obviously Harold's own particular grievance would not have been mentioned. For in July the Lord Chamberlain, Lord Clarendon, had written to tell them that their right of entrée to Buckingham Palace for the royal garden party had been withdrawn. This meant that they were forbidden to park their car in the palace courtyard.

Zia treated the thing as a most terrible humiliation. In October she wrote to Mountbatten to ask him to take the matter up with the King, and pointed out that since 1939 there had been a series of indications that she and Harold had 'caused some dissatisfaction at Court'. To mention one, Zia's name had been omitted from every official function at Buckingham Palace, although she was the County President of St John Ambulance Brigade for Leicestershire. Then there was this question of the right of entrée. And finally that of Harold's being overlooked after his distinguished war service.

Once again Mountbatten gladly obliged, this time mentioning that Harold had served as senior Honorary Secretary of the King's Fund for twenty years, and was a member of the Duchy of Lancaster, being on a special committee for forestry policy. In 1938 he had also collaborated with Lord Davidson over the redecoration of the Royal Chapel, personally raising all the large donations.

The King was believed to have replied to Mountbatten: 'The decision is mine. Too many people have the right of entrée.' The Queen also may have taken part in the decision, since it was said that 'she couldn't do with lesser foreign royalties'. Whatever she really felt about Zia, it should be noted that she continued to sign letters to her in an affectionate manner. Nevertheless Zia in her old age used to enjoy dipping into her box of royal letters and reading out one from George V to her father, in which he had apparently said that he didn't mind Bertie's marrying Elizabeth Bowes-Lyon since he would never be king.

Possibly relevant was a letter from the Queen of Spain after staying at Buckingham Palace, in which she said she had 'been unable to do anything' there.★

On 5 November 1946 Myra married Major David Butter of the Scots Guards. The wedding was again at St Margaret's Westmins-

---

★ Zia had lent Queen Ena her fox fur for the visit. About that time a gossipy friend had spotted a note from Zia in somebody's hall. 'Looking forward to tomorrow,' it ran. 'Don't change. Only Queen of Spain coming.'

ter, and Princess Alexandra was bridesmaid once more, with Diana Herbert, and with Prince Michael of Kent as page. Queen Mary and Princesses Elizabeth, Margaret and Marina were among the guests. David Butter's mother was American and his father a Scottish landowner; he had been awarded the Military Cross in North Africa. In later years he became Lord Lieutenant of Perthshire and Kinross. Zia was especially pleased about the connection with Scotland, which she loved so much and felt was like her father's descriptions of Georgia.

The Butters' first child, Sandra Elizabeth Zia, was born on 26 July 1948. Princess Elizabeth was a godmother. Gina meanwhile had had a son, Nicholas Harold, or Nicky, born on 23 August 1947, with Prince Philip as godfather. Gina was to have three more daughters: Fiona Mercedes, Marita Georgina and Natalia Ayesha, known in the family as Tally, born respectively on 30 March 1951, 28 May 1954 and 8 May 1959. The name Ayesha was after the Rajmata of Jaipur, one of Tally's godmothers. Myra also had three more daughters, and one son: Marilyn Davina, Rohays Georgina, Georgina Marguerite and Charles Harold Alexander, born respectively on 22 March 1950, 9 April 1952, 9 July 1956 and 10 April 1960. Rohays was named after Cecil Boyd-Rochfort's wife.

At last the War Office capitulated and agreed to release Luton Hoo, and without restrictions. Harold and Zia therefore decided to turn part of the house into a museum. A decision had to be made about Lady Ludlow's china, which they felt ought not to be dispersed and which they were determined to display.

A tremendous amount of adaptation and redecoration was necessary. Whilst plans were in progress they moved into the Gables and had to live there for three years. But Mountbatten was not going to relent over obtaining some form of personal recognition for Harold, so he sent a recommendation to the Duke of Gloucester, as President of the King's Fund, for his promotion from KCVO to GCVO. At last, in this he was successful, and it came to pass in 1948.

The engagement of Prince Philip to Princess Elizabeth, officially announced on 10 July 1947, had been no secret to the Wernhers, who were at the Princess's farewell party before she went to South Africa with her father in February. Harold was worried about Mountbatten's tendency to 'over excitement' and to 'boss everybody about'. Indeed, according to Ziegler, Prince Philip had gently to put his foot down. After the official announcement Prince Philip wired back to the Wernhers, thanking them for their congratulations and adding: 'Have no fear I shall certainly pop in and see you as of old whenever I get a chance.' He saw to it that they had the best seats in the Abbey and arranged for Boy to watch the 'proceedings' on 20 November from Buckingham Palace. David Milford Haven was best man, and the first part of the honeymoon was at Broadlands. Prince Philip wrote from there, describing his relief when they got away at last from the wedding breakfast.

The attention of the popular press began to turn on the unfortunate David's love life, which was becoming complicated, to say the least. His aunt Louise in Sweden kept writing to Zia for further news. 'How my heart aches for poor Nada. Really the tragedy to see one's son caught up in a fast, pleasure-loving set . . . His father died just when he most needed him.' Nada, however, could hardly herself complain about this sowing of wild oats.

For journalists David's most exciting romance was to be with the actress Eva Bartok. Zia felt that under the circumstances Douglas Fairbanks was the right person to make him 'see sense', but that was a forlorn hope. 'David is a fool,' she wrote to Mountbatten. 'In my Cannes days any man could go about with a woman without the newspapers hounding him and taking photographs of all their trips abroad!! I am *not* taking his part but I think it is bad luck in a way.' Nada was delighted when at last he married an American, Mrs Romaine 'Toodie' Dahlgren, in 1950. 'Lots of money! You know I'm mad about good manners, well hers are the best.' But she was annoyed when they started sporting a huge coronet and initials on their notepaper. 'Too vulgar for words. Georgie, myself and Aunt V. [her mother-in-law] did away with all that.' In the end she was glad when the marriage broke up.

Nada still spent half the year at Cannes. A typical letter from her to Zia ran as follows:

I've crossed the Channel eighteen times in the last year. Have any of you made a move to come and see me except Myra. You have money here and no excuse for not coming except your damned social dates. I have them too and have chucked the lot. If royalties did not exist in the world you would be the most miserable creatures in the world, and would not know what to do with yourselves . . . Glorious weather here and casino going fine. Adini [Queen of Denmark] has just left. 'Uncle Gustav' I've not seen! What a relief!!

This letter was in fact written on 17 April 1948, and was thus a little unfair to Zia. For one thing she and Harold had only just returned from South Africa, where, incidentally, they had stayed a weekend with Smuts at Groote Schuur – Harold had written to Mountbatten that he had found Smuts to be 'a man of calibre, because he is a soldier, politician and philosopher, and the only really great man I have ever met who has real simplicity'. But Smuts was soon to be defeated by the National Party, the beginning of the age of apartheid.

Then on the way home by ship there had been a message over the radio that Derrick had died. He had fallen from his seventh-floor flat in Prince's Gate, Knightsbridge, and suicide was suspected. His daughter Alexandra had been in the flat at the time, and had admitted that he had been depressed and quiet for some weeks. The coroner's verdict of suicide remained open, however, since there had been evidence of giddiness and dizziness which might have caused him to fall over the parapet.

Derrick's death meant that Harold was now the third baronet.

Probably the most valid excuse of all for Zia's not visiting Nada was the immense effort of getting a house that was really a palace into working order. 'It was a terrific affair', a friend has said. 'She felt Luton Hoo was exactly the right size for her, and of course she had natural taste and a wonderful sense of colour. Then there was the garden which had got into a mess. She was trying to put the clock back fifty years when everyone else was cutting down and struggling with rationing.' It was reckoned that there were 1,900 objects to be exhibited in the Collection.

Zia kept sending over to Lubenham for items of furniture. Gina could not use the main bedroom in case her mother still wanted it. After Zia turned up herself one day with a bucket for the goldfish, Gina could stand it no more and said to her father: 'From now onwards I have got to be free to do what I like here, burn the house down if I want to.'

Many people thought that the tension of setting up Luton Hoo on the grand scale, on top of Alex's death, brought on Zia's aneurysm, a ringing in one ear, caused by a broken blood-vessel, which gradually became so severe that grandchildren have said that if you put your head against hers it was like listening to a train coming into a railway station.

Zia had refused to get rid of the attic floor of Luton Hoo, which Lees-Milne had so disliked. 'Where else could I put my footmen?' she said. She had of course played a considerable part in helping to choose the important English furniture that Harold had bought, though he had a 'very good eye' for it. At the Kenwood sale, for instance, before that house was bought and furnished by Lord Iveagh to be presented to the nation, Harold had acquired a few pieces of furniture that she had known as a girl. He was certainly the more responsible for the acquisition of the pictures that were added to the Collection. There were various Dutch landscapes, including a van der Heyden, a de Hooch, a Cuyp and a Hobbema, and paintings by Turner, Constable and Marlow. He sold his father's Zuccarelli but bought another by the same artist. Experts from the Victoria and Albert Museum and the British Museum gave advice about the arrangement of Sir Julius's collection and such matters as attributions and authenticity. Objects that seemed like fakes were quickly disposed of. As Harold 'couldn't abide' Victorian furniture, most of that description had to go too.

The chapel was kept boarded up, its stained-glass windows and magnificent carved ceiling out of view, and was used instead as an art gallery for most of the main masterpieces such as the Altdorfer, the Bermejo, the Filippino Lippi and the Titian, and for a display of the Renaissance jewellery. The original main entrance hall contained the Gobelin tapestries, the Sèvres porcelain, the Kildare silver-gilt dressing set and Zia's large collection of Fabergé inherited from her parents and including her own set of miniature Fabergé eggs. Special rooms were dedicated to ivories, bronzes and ceramics, which included of course Sir Julius's famous Aldobrandini tazza and the two Castel Durante plates. The arrangement of the great dining-room would have pleased its creator Mewès, with its Beauvais tapestries around which the room had been originally designed. The dining-room table was laid to seat eighteen people, the silver-gilt cutlery and the cut glass, again inherited by Zia, having been kept in store at Cannes after the Grand Duke's death. Other silver, including dishes and ewers once belonging to the Duke of Cumberland, later King of Hanover, had been bought by Harold.

Zia's Pushkin relics and Russian Imperial portraits and memorabilia, including Court dresses, had also been brought out of store and put on display. The most interesting portrait of all was of Christian-Augustus, Duke of Anhalt-Zeibst, father of Catherine the Great. A happy solution had also been devised for Lady Ludlow's collection of English porcelain, which occupied three rooms on the upper floor. This had been sold to the National Arts Collection Fund, with a large donation by Harold on condition that it could be kept on permanent display at Luton Hoo.

There was also a Brown Jack room, which included racing mementoes from the Wernhers' innumerable successes, to which were added many other trophies and paintings of Double Life, Precipitation and Meld. The old Wonder Horse had died on 22 September 1948, aged twenty-five. His brain was preserved, and his skeleton acquired by the Natural History Museum in London.

Later Harold acquired a great prize: a silver racing trophy, 'The Emperor's Plate', a copy of Falconet's famous statue of Peter the Great on horseback overlooking the River Neva. Zia's great-grandfather Nicholas I had visited Ascot in 1844 and had promised to present a silver trophy, to the value of £500, in every succeeding year in place of the Gold Cup. The race, known as 'The Emperor's Plate', continued to be run until the outbreak of the Crimean War in 1854, when the Gold Cup was restored. Harold's acquisition was believed to be the first of the trophies, which were of different design every year, and probably the only one surviving. It was placed in the Russian Rooms.

Harold played a large part in local politics. On 26 June 1948 a

Conservative fête was held at Luton Hoo. Winston Churchill addressed a crowd of 114,000 people from a platform in front of the house. Part of the speech was a castigation of Labour Party politics, part about European Union and the need for its 'fraternal association' with the United States and British Commonwealth. It was in fact prepared for him by Reginald Maudling. He had lunch with the Wernhers at the Gables.

Harold was Prime Warden of the Fishmongers' Company in 1948–9, in honour of which he presented a silver-gilt cup by Paul de Lamerie and a chandelier from Bath House. It was largely thanks to him that Prince Philip became Prime Warden in 1961–2. He was instrumental in commissioning for the Fishmongers the world-renowned and much-reproduced paintings by Annigoni of Queen Elizabeth II and Prince Philip as Duke of Edinburgh. On 15 October he opened the new premises of the King Edward VII Hospital in Beaumont Street, in the presence of Queen Mary. As a hospital by Royal Charter, it was therefore allowed not to be part of the National Health Service. In his speech Harold said that in the history of the hospital 12,000 patients had been treated. At present there were beds for thirty-one patients.

By 1972 the hospital would be treating 2,000 patients in a year. Sir George Ogilvie was still Governor-Administrator, but in 1950 his place was taken by his daughter Vere, Lady Birdwood, who remained in that post for twenty-two years. 'Sir Harold was a marvellous Chairman,' she has said, 'leaving you alone to get on with it. Sometimes he would realize you needed backing up. He was a hard man, but fair, and always had an eye for the coming man. He never missed the monthly meetings. Obviously the hospital was very high in his interests.'

Similarly it has been remembered at University College Hospital, which was taken over by the National Health Service in 1947, that Harold's easy manner smoothed the transition, and new members nominated by the government quickly fitted into the board – so much so that when a controversial matter cropped up and Harold presented the case, saying afterwards 'All agreed?', no members liked to disagree even if they had not understood.

'An eye for the coming man' has been echoed by others who were connected in business with Harold, in phrases such as 'great flair to be able to pick right people'. This was an important aspect of his character, and certainly applied to his time with Combined Operations and COSSAC, and to the team which worked loyally under him. 'He was a taskmaster, but fair,' a colleague has said. 'If he wanted something done, he expected it to be done. He was not interested in excuses. He always gave you a feeling of being very well organized, the days and months ahead were well planned. He was a stickler for punctuality.' The success of his new venture, hotels in Bermuda, was to a great extent due to good teamwork, though success did take some time to materialize.

Harold already had a large shareholding in the Bermuda Property Development Company, which owned the Bermudiana Hotel, badly run down after the war. The banker Sir Harry Butterfield had suggested to Harold that he might buy the hotel outright, since at that time real estate held abroad did not affect British death duties. Harold decided to make it an apartment hotel, but there were delays owing to the shortage of materials, which annoyed him. Finally, in March 1951, the Bermudiana reopened. In spite of his capable manager Robert Sanson, it ran at a loss. Harold summoned out one of his financial advisers, Robert Spooner, and it was decided to turn it into an ordinary hotel. In due course the situation changed, and Harold found himself enjoying being an hotelier. He therefore bought a small country hotel, the Harmony Hall. He also bought a piece of beach, to be known as the Bermudiana Beach, which had a restaurant. Nearly every winter he and Zia went to the West Indies or Florida, and would therefore stop at Bermuda on the way there or back, staying at the Mid-Ocean Club, of which Harold was a life member, since Zia disliked the air-conditioning at the Bermudiana. Later still he acquired the lease of the Belmont Manor House Hotel and Country Club, which had an eighteen-hole golf course; so Zia decided to switch her allegiance from the Mid-Ocean to the Belmont.

Harold also acquired a flat at 15 Grosvenor Square, after they had given up the rooms at the Dorchester. In October 1949 he held speed trials along the drive at Luton Hoo which had been laid out for tanks during the war. The trials ended in disaster when a driver was killed, so they were not repeated.

Earlier that year, in April, Princess Elizabeth had been taken to see Luton Hoo. She and Prince Philip stayed at the Gables.

When Queen Mary heard that Princesses Olga and Marina had been invited to see the final arrangement of the collection on 23 April 1950, she asked if she might join them and have a wheelchair provided. In her inimitable manner she was full of praise and enthusiasm.

The house was opened to the public on 4 May.

26

Grandparents

In March 1951 Harold Wernher bought Blackhall Stud in County Kildare, in partnership with Lord Astor and his brother J. J. (Jakie) Astor. The price was around £50,000. Two years later Lord Astor died, and Harold bought J.J. Astor's share on his death in 1966. Foals would be sent from Someries Stud after weaning, and then Harold and his manager would decide where they would be trained – the Wernhers had become somewhat uneasy about having their horses trained at Newmarket after the trouble with Persian Gulf.

Cecil Boyd-Rochfort, now also the royal trainer, continued to help with increasing Someries Stud. For a while Zia sent horses to be trained at Epsom by Johnny Dines, who had ridden Double Life so successfully. She and Harold shared the same colours, green and yellow, but Harold's jockey wore a quartered cap. As Curling has said in his biography of CBR, the key to the 'whole successful Wernher story' in racing lay in the acquisition of Double Life, many of whose winning descendants CBR had trained, including her grandson Double Eclipse, which finished third in the Derby in 1951, and her great-granddaughter Meld, which was responsible for making Zia the leading racehorse owner on the flat for 1955 and from then onwards a well-known sporting character. Friends said that when Princess Elizabeth became Queen her jargon about horses with Zia was incomprehensible to the layman. Indeed ever since the acquisition of Double Life hardly a year passed without Zia having a winner, and this continued over the decades ahead.

Zia after the war was becoming increasingly worried about Nada, who was drinking too much. Consequently she found herself taking over responsibilities for Nada's retarded daughter Tatiana. Boy also spent much time at Luton Hoo. Zia's grandchildren were to become very fond of him, and he showed them how to paint. There are some sad letters written to Zia from his hospital about 'all these terrible pills fighting inside me'. When staying at Luton Hoo, he sometimes felt his depression returning and would say, 'I am afraid I must go back', and have to be rushed to Roehampton. He died on 25 April 1959.

The grandchildren seem to have had mixed feelings about Nada. They found her 'fun', but some of her habits were occasionally too boisterous, like squirting you with the garden hose or pouring a night pot full of water on people out of the window.

When Zia failed to see Nada's name listed in *The Times* as having been in the funeral cortège of George VI, she became suspicious, as if it were all Nada's fault. Her accusing letter elicited a typical response on 21 February 1952:

Don't you worry about my name not being mentioned. I could not care less! If you want to know I was in the *first* carriage behind the *Queen's*! I was up at 5.45 on the morning of the funeral . . . A Royal car was sent for me from Buckingham Palace and guarded by a constable until I got into it!! We drove for 3 hours from Buckingham Palace to Paddington, frozen to the bone. You could not hear literally a sound except feet marching. I saw darling Queen Mary at her window watching and bowing when the Queen passed by. David and I lunched with Philip and the Queen after I arrived at Clarence House. She was looking *too lovely* and very composed. A charming lunch – Louise, Gustav and Juliana were also there etc. Philip looked very well but very thin. After the funeral we all went down to Broadlands for the weekend. Eighteen of us in all! . . . On the Sunday Philip came over to lunch and told me his one idea was to get to Coustalado [her villa at Cannes] as soon as possible . . . Sunday I am lunching with Marina at Coppins. More

Kings etc.! I'd collected Mama's sapphires from the Bank for
the occasion.

Nada was to develop acute arthritis and had to spend much
time in a clinic. She died at Cannes on 22 January 1963, David
Milford Haven having by then married a second time. David had
married Janet Bryce, a cousin of Bunnie – the Bryces had been a
Scottish shipping family, and it was a clerk called Grace in their
office who started the renowned Grace Line in America.

In the summer of 1952 a musical pageant was held at Luton Hoo,
a much greater success than the previous year's Bedfordshire
Agricultural Show, which had lost money. Nearly 100,000 people
came to it. Guests that year included Sitta and her son Michael of
Romania, Cécile and Fritzi from Germany, and the Douglas
Fairbankses (who were later lent the Gables for two years when
he was filming at Elstree). The Queen and Prince Philip also came
for the weekend in November, the first of many weekends more
or less coinciding with their wedding anniversary, as well as with
the first pheasant shoot of the year. Their rooms had furniture
from the Great Exhibition of 1851. Fellow guests were the
Brabournes, Gina and Bunnie, Myra and David, David Milford
Haven and Boy. The Queen wrote afterwards, saying she hadn't
laughed so much for a long time. It was such a relief, she said, to
get away from dispatch boxes and telegrams.

One of the butlers employed in the 1950s at Luton Hoo was
Peter Whiteley, who has written of the galaxy of royal visitors:
'You name them we had them all.' The visits of the Queen and
Prince Philip caused the most flutterings. They were supposed to
be 'quite informal', but, as he said, 'Heaven knows what we
would have had to do if they had been formal.' Yet when the
Queen did arrive the atmosphere would relax at once.

The only person who did not relax on these visits was the cook
Laura Allen, creator of marvels such as a meringue swan on
mango ice-cream, strawberry trees, glacé quails, boned and
walnut-stuffed poussin, and chocolate almond cake – a secret
recipe. Harold had to get the watchman to send Laura Allen to

bed; otherwise she would be working all night. Even so she would be up again at 4 a.m.

Zia always arranged an entertainment, perhaps a film, for the Queen. It would be held in the ballroom, and all the staff and estate workers would be invited. On the first occasion they had the Balalaika Players. At other times entertainers included Winifred Atwell and her honky-tonk piano (the Queen asked for 'Roll out the Barrel'), Val Doonican and Victor Borge. There were also excursions to places such as Woburn or to see Jim Joel's horses.

Peter Whiteley has described how butlers and footmen at Luton Hoo had to wear livery, unusual at the time: green with gold piping, stiff white shirts and white ties. Servants hated the way Zia kept a silver-edged pad by her plate on which she noted down (among other things) their faults and mistakes. 'You've got it coming to you tomorrow,' a temporary cook was told after Laura Allen's retirement. Luton Hoo time meant putting clocks five minutes forward. If guests were late, Zia would start a meal regardless. Also disconcertingly for guests, she would gobble up her food, making you feel you had either to keep up or leave something before the plates were swept away. Small children had to eat at a round table at the end of the dining table.

On one occasion Princess Alexandra, who was staying, came into the dining-room after the soup. Everyone stood up except Zia. 'You're late, Alexandra!' Zia said sternly . . . And here it can be mentioned in passing that it was at Luton Hoo that Princess Alexandra met Angus Ogilvy.

Zia was known once to have knocked on the Queen's door when she looked like being late, calling out: 'Are you ready?' Prince Charles on hearing about this said: 'If that happens again I shan't dare to come to Luton Hoo.'

In the early 1960s Gina's eldest daughter Sacha was aghast when told by Zia to go upstairs and hurry the Queen along for dinner. Sacha was relieved when she saw the Queen running towards her down the corridor, holding up her skirts. On another occasion some servants hid behind a screen to watch the Queen go by. The screen fell over, obviously giving her a shock.

The problem of finding and keeping staff was a kind of

nightmare for Zia, but it was partially solved when she hit on the idea of importing relays of servants from the island of St Helena.

'Extraordinary sense of grandeur.' 'A snob but with every right to be one.' 'Not so pompous as she looked or behaved. Really a very warm person.' 'Always looked a million dollars. Perfectly dressed.' 'Strong dynastic feelings.' These are some comments by people who knew her best. Harold would tickle her if he felt she was becoming unbearably pompous, and she would then 'cry blue murder'. Alice Winn used to love listening to her telling Princess Marina about their Russian relations, all with peculiar nicknames: 'You see, my dear, Bobo was a cousin of Aunt Pupu, and Uncle Cici's brother was . . .' Princess Marina, with her slightly foreign accent, would try to look interested: 'Oh no, Zia, is that so? Really? Really?' It was also understood that there was an element of competition between Zia and Lord Mountbatten over princely and royal connections. The great relief to her was that the right of entrée at Buckingham Palace had been restored.

Barbara Cartland was a neighbour, and had worked with Zia for St John Ambulance. She felt it a great privilege to have known her. 'Lady Zia had that marvellous aristocratic air, something you can't invent. She was not putting it on. She was never condescending. You always felt you ought to curtsy. She had beautiful manners. She worked frightfully hard during the war and afterwards. She was adored by everyone on the estate.'

Evidently for many years there had been a rift of some sort between Zia and Grand Duchess Xenia, her aunt by marriage and a sister of the late Tsar. Perhaps the Grand Duchess had complained that she was not receiving enough financial help from Harold, and had then been cut off. It was Olga of Yugoslavia who begged Zia to visit Xenia – apparently very lonely – 'now that the ice is broken'. After this Zia would call regularly on Xenia at Hampton Court, staying for not more than twenty minutes, perhaps bringing a gift of a brace of pheasants or asparagus.

There was a temporary disaster on the Luton Hoo estate in August 1954 when a vat of cyanide at Vauxhall Motors overflowed into the River Lea, killing most of the animal and plant life in Capability Brown's lakes. Harold sued for damages. This was a sensational case in the history of Luton, but of more far-reaching importance was one brought by the Inland Revenue against Zia, and which she lost, involving a sum of around £10,000. This latter case was reported either as Sharkey (the name of the Inspector of Taxes) v. Wernher, or as Trading with Yourself. Since Zia was hopeless over business matters, Harold had to fight on her behalf, and eventually of course had to pay out.

It all began when five of Zia's colts and fillies were transferred from her stud farms to her racing stables. Naturally when the horses were being bred, the expenses were debited in the accounts of the stud farm. It followed that when the horses were transferred to the stables, the accounts were credited with the cost of the breeding. Inland Revenue's contention was that the proper figure to be brought into account was the market price, not the cost, since racing and training was regarded in law as recreational activity and not taxable, but a stud farm was a trading activity and therefore taxable. Comparisons were made with farmers producing eggs: if an egg was worth sixpence in the market, but cost a shilling to produce and the farmer consumed that egg, then the figure which he should credit to his account should be a shilling, not sixpence. It was a complex, much debated case affecting, as the QC Sir Reginald Manningham-Buller predicted, all racehorse owners who bred their own horses. Harold took it to the House of Lords but was overruled.

The case had additional notoriety since it happened in the year of Zia's triumphs with Meld, recognized then and since as one of the greatest fillies of the century, 'if not of all time'. A handsome bay, by Alycidon out of Daily Double, Meld had shown promise in 1954 as a two-year-old. The name, as Zia would explain, came from a term in canasta. Ridden by Harry Carr, she easily won the One Thousand Guineas in April 1955. After the race Zia delighted onlookers by pushing aside photographers and rushing to kiss not only CBR but Meld. The excitement exhausted her, so she did not go afterwards to Freemason Lodge to celebrate. But the Queen went there, and wrote to congratulate Zia on the wonderful sight, having seen Meld beforehand 'striding away up the hill to the winning post'. She described how she had managed to peep into Meld's stable and had seen her quite unconcerned by all the fuss. Her own horse Belladonna had come last, but, as she said: 'We must renew our rivalry at the Oaks.'

As it happened, the Queen had no luck at the Oaks either. Meld won easily, her second Classic, and she also won the Coronation Stakes at Ascot. Before racing in the third Classic, the St Leger, it looked as if she was about to succumb to the alarming coughing epidemic then rife at Newmarket. She coughed just before the race. But a 'combination of class and courage' gave her a three-quarters of a length victory over Nucleus, ridden by Lester Piggott, who afterwards furiously lodged an unsuccessful complaint. As a result of this victory, Cecil Boyd-Rochfort had altogether earned over £1 million for his patrons. Meld's five wins had also netted £43,051 for Zia, who was, incidentally, the first woman owner to win the St Leger.

Meld, unfortunately, was to turn out a disappointing brood mare, though with one outstanding exception: Charlottown, which won the Derby in 1966.

Zia was superstitious. She also liked to put sick, injured or unsuccessful horses 'on the Box', a system known as radionic therapy, based on 'energy patterns', whereby hairs from tails would be sent to a practitioner in Oxfordshire. These hairs would be analysed, and treatment 'projected' through special instruments, without direct contact with the animal. She found the Box so successful that she used it for her dogs, and later for herself.

Zia also had dreams about winners, which came to pass. The Queen, on hearing about this, wrote that she wished that she could have such dreams about her Belladonna.

In August Harold was at last elected to the Jockey Club, having been proposed by Sir Humphrey de Trafford and seconded by Lord Rosebery. To many of his friends the honour seemed long overdue, considering that he had been one of the leading figures on the British Turf for at least twenty years. But he still had enemies, dating back to Mulberry days, and this had previously resulted in his being blackballed. It was said that some other members had been afraid that he would 'take over'. To his supporters, however, he was the ideal 'live wire to light up all the dead wood'. And he did prove to be a live wire in the Jockey Club, becoming President of the Thoroughbred Rules.

The prejudices against him also reared up when Bernard Fergusson was commissioned to write the history of Combined Operations, *The Watery Maze*. On reading Fergusson's draft, Mountbatten complained that the references to Harold's appointment as CMSF were too cursory. Fergusson replied that in his interviews he had come across various ill-wishers, none of whom, as it happened, had much liking either for Bruce White or Grigg. 'I can't tell you how many similar jealousies I have turned up under stones in the many avenues I have explored.' Mountbatten wrote back, admitting that Harold Wernher had not been 'everybody's cup of tea', but insisted as usual that Combined Ops would never have been such a success without his drive and energy. In the final version Fergusson summed up Harold's predicament fairly neatly, but all too briefly:

> Wernher was to have a roughish time in his job. Whereas he himself was made privy to all the secrets relating to invasion he was unable to pass them on. Many of the things he had to insist on were highly unpalatable to those he was dealing with, and he could not disclose his reasons. It was not surprising that a good many corns were trodden on.

Probably when Harold came to read the book he had almost given up caring about that old struggle for proper recognition. After all, anyone who achieves anything creates enemies and jealousies. He rarely used his honorary rank of Major-General – usually on official occasions. With such a strong character, he was a man about whom there were varied opinions. As a public figure, he was grand in stature, grand in appearance. 'Ever the businessman, first and foremost.' 'Fatal to get across him or there'd be hell.' 'Not interested in excuses. If he wanted something done, he expected it to be done.' 'A taskmaster, but not a hard taskmaster in the nasty sense of the word.' 'Went out of his way to help people.' 'Common touch to a very high degree.' 'Ready to give the red carpet treatment to the most obvious cowboys if good for business.' 'A gentleman in every sense of the word.' 'He knew he

was important but never oppressed you by appearing overgrand.'
'Enormous range of knowledge.' 'Made every woman feel she
was beautiful.' 'Extraordinary sense of humour. At home it was a
laugh a minute.'

He kept a list of funny stories and jokes, some excruciating, for
speeches, some quoted from Winston Churchill, others from
newspapers.* There were those who were shocked by his language when making jokes. Others were offended by his brand of
humour. When, for instance, he and Zia were in Paris, they
stayed either at the Ritz or with Lady Granard, an American, at
her magnificent house in the Rue de Varennes. There was a love-
hate relationship with Lady Granard, who was not at all pleased
when Harold told her in his bread-and-butter letter that it was so
much cheaper staying with her than being at the Ritz. Nor was
she pleased when instead of flowers from a florist Zia simply sent
lilac cut from a friend's garden.†

'As with all the very rich he had a mean streak.' Lady Granard
thought that this also applied to Zia, who was 'mean about things
like paper-clips', and expected her laundry to be washed at Rue
de Varennes. At Luton Hoo people complained that both Harold
and Zia were 'very tight on the booze.' A tray was kept behind a
screen. A husband might be offered a tiny glass of sherry and
would have to ask for a Martini instead. 'That's not good enough,'
one of their old friends would have to say. 'I want twice that.'
Then, referring to his wife: 'Can Rachel have one too?' It seemed
that Zia, who did not drink herself, thought that women should
not drink before meals. Harold knew that Sir John Carew Pole
liked whisky, but always had to 'send down' for it. Wines,
however, were always 'the best, superb'.

A guest was also taken aback, when invited to tea and asked if
she would like to see the Collection, to find that she had to pay
the entrance fee. This even also happened to some directors of

---

* 'There is no fool like an oiled fool.' 'Familiarity breeds attempt.' An
advertisement: 'Working single lady wants digs – must have bath – urgently.'
Daily Mirror: 'Magistrates may act on indecent shows.'
† Lady Granard was very thin and had wonderful jewels. Harold nicknamed
her Stones and Bones.

Electrolux from Sweden and their wives. They had not understood that to Harold this had been a joke.

A favourite story in the family concerns one of the shoots at Luton Hoo, where 'barking' deer were and still are a pest. A Colonel Barker, an old buffer, was in the party. He had missed a pheasant, as usual, and at that moment a deer jumped out of the woods. Harold shouted: 'Shoot that bloody barker.' Colonel Barker took it personally and would not speak for the rest of the day.

Everyone agreed that Harold was 'divine to his family'. 'It was a very close-knit family group. The grandchildren worshipped him. He never spoke down to them. He cut out funny pictures and remarks in newspapers and sent these to them at school.' There was no question either of his love for Zia, in spite of his well-known 'eye for the ladies'. People were amused to watch Zia keeping a 'beady eye' on him when they had a box at Goodwood. She knew he was still seeing Joan Clarkson, and would stab angrily with her finger at this woman's picture in the *Tatler*. On the other hand, on her biennial visits to Paris, to buy dresses from Patou, she would ring up in advance if she had to come back early.

Harold's next most famous racehorse after Brown Jack was Aggressor, bred in 1955 at Someries Stud. He had been bought 'in utero', his dam Phaetonia having been acquired for 15,500 guineas on Boyd-Rochfort's recommendation. As usual, Aggressor was sent to Blackhall after weaning. Harold decided there that he was below standard and decided to put him up for sale with a reserve of 1,000 guineas. Luckily for him, as it turned out, the bidding stopped at 750 guineas. Aggressor, trained by Towser Gosden, was to win eleven races, worth £36,203. His last victory, as a five-year-old and before being retired to Someries Stud for the covering season of 1961, was against the brilliant Petite Étoile in the King George VI and Queen Elizabeth Stakes. Meanwhile Zia continued with her successes. In Meld's Classic year she had also won the Cambridgeshire with Retrial. Sonsa, another descendant of Double Life, and 'on the Box', won the Ebbisham in 1956. Every year Zia visited Electrolux to make trophy presentations to the Luton Football League, and would give tips for local punters. This became an eagerly awaited event, reported in the press, especially after Zia successfully tipped Parthia, son of Precipitation but owned by Sir Humphrey de Trafford, as the Derby winner. She also tipped her own horse Dickens, which won various races including the Dante Stakes at York at 100–8.

On 23 September 1958 the Bermudiana Hotel had been burnt to the ground. Nothing but the girders was left. Zia telephoned their accountant Robert Spooner at 7.30 a.m.: 'Have you heard the news? It was on the wireless. Harry Butterfield says it's still burning.' Mr Spooner tracked down Harold on the factory floor at Electrolux, but he had already been told. 'It was typical of Sir Harold,' he has said, 'that he just got on with what he was doing. "All right, Spooner, get on a plane as quickly as you can and see what's going on. Get on to Insurance. I'll follow when I am able."' Within a week the two of them, with the Bermudiana's manager Carroll Dooley and an architect, Fitzroy Robinson, worked out guidelines for a new hotel; for Harold had instantly taken the decision that he would rebuild. It had been the worst fire in Bermuda's history. The new hotel was built on a palatial scale with rooms for 460 guests, costing at least $4 million. The approved contractors were E.G.M. Cape, a Canadian firm; local people were at first annoyed about this, but reconciled when the hotel was ready for opening with such amazing speed, in April 1960, only fourteen months after the fire.

Harold had insisted that the new Bermudiana should be multi-racial, with black people admitted. The success of the hotel was in large part due to his knack of choosing the right individuals for the right job. For instance, the eventual general manager at the Bermudiana was Pierre Rollinger, who had originally impressed Harold and Zia as a waiter when they stayed at the Mid-Ocean Club. Most of the guest staff would be picked by Harold or Spooner. Harold came out to Bermuda twice a year, and had Dooley as his deputy for the Company, which was known as the Harmony Hall Co. Ltd, and included the Belmont and South Shore Beach Club.

Harold looked on the Company very much as a family concern, and thoroughly enjoyed himself. He used to say that in running it he had benefited from past experience. Zia was always afraid that if he stayed at the Bermudiana he would get 'too involved' in business, so they continued to stay either at the Belmont or the Parkland, which also had the essential golf-course. But as the years went by, and he reached his seventies, he decided that he had 'too many eggs in that one basket', and he had to think about his grandchildren's futures. So in 1968 the Company was sold to Charles Forte.

Harold also had an interest in the Plaza Hotel in New York, in connection with which there are two irresistible Zia stories, which could be apocryphal. She and Harold would stay at the Plaza. One morning Zia became impatient because her breakfast had not arrived. She therefore rang up the President of the Corporation at his home on Long Island, where it happened that he was still asleep after a late-night party. 'This is Lady Zia Wernher,' she said. 'I've been waiting for my breakfast for thirty-five minutes, and I want it sent to me at once.' That is one version of the story. The other is that she rang up her cousin Serge Obolensky, who was in charge of public relations at the Plaza.

She would also refuse to make reservations for dinner (which again would be gobbled up at speed). Entering the dining-room one evening, she found that no tables were available. 'I am Lady Zia Wernher,' she said in a voice so loud that all the guests stopped talking – as someone present has said, forks in mid-air. 'I want you to send me the manager.' He duly arrived, and she then lectured him on how she considered dining-rooms should properly be managed.

She was quite capable, as friends have recalled, before setting out in the *Queen Mary* or *Queen Elizabeth*, of ringing up the Chairman of Cunard and arranging with him where her deckchair would be placed. She always went to the top, even if a telephone had to be installed, and when thwarted would begin to flirt. Similarly, she always expected to be in the Royal Box at Wimbledon. She would telephone Lord Glendevon, who was in charge of such things, not to ask if she could have seats but to tell him on which days she wanted them.

Zia kept her extraordinary complexion to the end of her life. If she was always impeccably turned out, changing her dresses several times a day, Harold liked to hold on to his old clothes. Once, on the *Queen Elizabeth*, Zia arranged with her lady's maid Odile Barbier for an ancient pair of his trousers to be thrown out of the porthole, 'buried at sea'. 'Some of Sir Harold's clothes were so old,' Odile has said, 'but it made no difference. He would stand out in a crowd.' Zia's reliance on Odile Barbier (and she acknowledged this) was so great that she was quite shocked when she learnt that not only had Odile secretly been taking driving lessons but she had bought herself a car.

In August 1961 Harold and Zia, accompanied by Odile, went to Moscow and Leningrad. It was Zia's first visit to Russia, and she was hoping to have a 'confrontation' with Khrushchev. Unfortunately, in a sense, they arrived during the celebrations after the descent of the astronaut Gheman Titov, the second man in space, and found themselves marooned in their hotel while processions took place. Zia was almost surprised to find that Russians were more interested in her descent from Pushkin than from Nicholas I. Nevertheless she was determined to speak her mind, and fearlessly upbraided the Communists for the murders of her uncles and the Tsar's family. She refused to visit Lenin's tomb.

Lady Granard attacked Zia for 'betraying' her father's family by daring to go to Russia. 'There you are. Wrong again.'

It was suspected that in any case Zia had not really enjoyed Russia. After her visit people she had met would send her May Day cards. She sent them back, with a note: 'We do not go in for such things.' Instead she sent Christmas cards.

A delegation of Russian engineers wanted to look round the Electrolux factory to see how refrigerators were made in Britain. When Zia heard about this she said to Stanley Broughton, the Managing Director: 'I'll come. I'll pretend to be the Welfare Officer and go round with them. I'll listen to what they say and I'll tell you.' Broughton said: 'You'll do nothing of the sort, because you're well known to the factory workers. Our shop steward is a Communist [as she well knew] and the gaffe will be blown immediately. You're welcome to come but you'll come as the Chairman's wife.' She was annoyed, argued back, but eventually gave in. The Russians turned out to have known all about her and were thrilled about her descent from Pushkin. At tea afterwards in the canteen they all gathered round her and sat at her table. 'They got on famously,' Broughton has said. 'I was left with the Embassy Secretary and the Commissar chap who looked very black about it all.' The shop steward was called Ted Baker. He had a picture of Stalin above his desk. Zia therefore sent him a book on Stalin (with not much effect). When Harold promoted him, he demanded to see the books, but Harold was absolutely firm. 'You stick to the machines and the boys. I'll look after the books.'

It was in 1961 that the firm Automatic Telephone and Electric Ltd, and Ericsson Telephones, of which Harold had been Chairman now for thirty years, merged with Plessey, thus doubling Plessey's size and producing an important diversity in a company that was already regarded as a national institution and a leader in the production of radio, television, telephone and electronic components. Ericsson had an association with the Bendix Corporation of America and manufactured a number of industrial and scientific instruments. The merger thus became a huge telecommunications group, employing 47,000 people. Harold's association with Electrolux was a valuable link, as was the fact that he was Chairman of the National Institute of Agricultural Engineering. He joined the board of Plessey as a part-time director.*

It took about a year to assess this great new potential, and in May 1962 the Chairman of Plessey, Sir Allen Clark, announced a major reorganization. But in June Sir Allen died suddenly, and this left a power vacuum, for he had ruled like an autocrat, drawing an immense salary of over £260,000, apparently with little thought of his sons becoming top men in the business. As a result, there was a boardroom crisis, a group of directors led by the Chairman of Automatic Telephones, A. F. (Sandy) Roger, claiming that the sons were not sufficiently experienced to run a firm of such vast size and importance, and that one of the existing directors should be promoted instead.

Just before his death Sir Allen had 'persuaded' Harold Wernher to be Deputy Chairman. The succession crisis broke within

---

* Plessey designed and produced the first portable wireless in Britain and the first commercially produced telephone set in the world.

hours of the funeral. These stormy battles took place at Harold's flat in Grosvenor Square. Harold was quoted in the press as saying that there was a 'clash of personalities and not of politics', though salaries for directors, especially for future Chairmen, came into it and there was alarm about Sir Allen's diktat over reorganization. Rumours therefore had to be staunched quickly and Plessey's credibility (its shares had dropped sharply) restored in the City, and this was done thanks to the iron hand of Harold. He became Chairman – on condition that he was *unpaid* – and forced Sandy Roger and two other directors to resign. It was an extremely painful affair, as all three were well known and liked in the City.

Then came the sensation. The Prime Minister Harold Macmillan had in that same month, in his 'night of the long knives', purged some of his Cabinet Ministers. Harold Wernher announced that two of the vacancies on the board were to be filled respectively by the ex-Minister of Defence Harold (later Lord) Watkinson and the ex-Lord Chancellor, Lord Kilmuir (originally Sir David Maxwell-Fyffe). The third vacancy was taken by Field Marshal Lord Harding of Petherton, the distinguished soldier and recently Governor and Commander-in-Chief in Cyprus. The eldest Clark son, John, was to be managing director, with the younger, Michael, his deputy. It was clear, however, that control would be in the hands of Harold and his powerful new team.

There was an immediate row in the Commons, led by the Labour backbencher Roy Mason; for Plessey was deeply involved with government work. But Harold Macmillan refused to bring in legislation to prevent ex-Ministers going into industry.

It was widely acknowledged that Harold had saved Plessey, and he would say it was one of the biggest challenges in his life. He retired at the end of the year, and Kilmuir became Chairman. One notes that just before the row in the Commons Harold Macmillan was chief guest at the Midsummer Fête at Luton Hoo. This was in aid of the Lady Zia Wernher Spastics Centre.

Harold's resignation from Plessey also meant the end of his Chairmanship of Ericsson. He was now nearly seventy. Then he announced that he was also going to retire as Chairman of Electrolux. The sudden decision took the other directors by surprise. He was succeeded by Lord Luke, and was given the title of President.

The visits by various European crowned heads or deposed monarchs continued at Luton Hoo. Gustav Adolf of Sweden was a favourite, and he and Zia afterwards would exchange letters on such things as asparagus crowns, trout flies, roses and special ways to smoke fish.

Queen Elizabeth's letters to Zia show that she invariably enjoyed herself and are full of warmth. She would bring her own gun dogs and dog-handler, and would help to pick up the pheasants. In 1959 the bag was over 1,000. She was at Luton Hoo when news came about the assassination of President Kennedy.

In 1964 Sacha would be eighteen, so Zia decided to launch her with the 'most perfect ball ever given', even better than Gina's at Someries House before the War. There would be over 800 guests, and it would be the first at Luton Hoo since Harold's coming of age exactly fifty years before. Joe Loss with his fourteen-piece band was hired to play.

Sacha's ball was the sort of evening for which the Mewès and Davis ballroom had been designed, and Lady Ludlow would have been proud. Many foreign relations were there, including 'all the Badens'. The great dining-room, hung with the famous Beauvais tapestries of the Roi de Chine, and with the long table laid with crested Imperial crystal and gilded plates, was used to entertain the Queen and the Duke of Edinburgh, and forty-four other guests. The terrace and rose garden were illuminated, and – in spite of rain at 2 a.m. – the event was indeed remembered as an outstanding success. 'It was a perfect evening,' one of the royal guests wrote afterwards, 'the dance floor always full of smiling people and everyone at their BEST. Sacha was a dream with flowers in her hair and, I noticed, surrounded suitably by the smashingest of young men.' Princess Margaret and Lord Snowdon were among the last to leave, 'clambering happily into bed at 6 o'clock'.

One young man who was not present, however, was James Hamilton, eldest son of the Duke of Abercorn. He hardly knew the Wernhers and thought that going to a ball with white ties and tiaras would be a bore. He met Sacha the following year at a weekend party, and soon afterwards they became engaged. Zia had told Sacha that the whole point of the ball was to get her married. Harold joked that he had therefore wasted £14,000.

The year 1966 seemed to many like Zia's apotheosis. Her favourite grandchild was married in Westminster Abbey, with a reception afterwards at St James's Palace for over 1,000 guests. And she won the Derby.

In the early sixties the Wernhers had had various racing successes, notably with Zia's Duplation and Harold's Tahiri. Meld's fifth foal by the stallion Charlottesville was the famous Charlottown, winner of the French Derby and the Grand Prix de Paris. As a two-year-old, Charlottown won three races, trained by J. M. Gosden, but for the rest of his career he was trained by Gordon Smyth. In the Derby he was ridden by the Australian jockey Scobie Breasley; the race had to be delayed when he tore off a plate and a blacksmith had to be called. It was a thrilling race, Charlottown suddenly shooting into the lead, and winning by a neck at 5–1. Zia's stock in Luton, where she had tipped her horse for a win, was thus never higher. Bookies had to pay out £74,489. She admitted that she nearly fainted from excitement.

The solid gold Derby cup joined the eleven others on display at Luton Hoo, to be followed by another for the Coronation Stakes, again won by Charlottown. But he was just beaten by a length by his arch-rival Sodium in the Irish Sweeps Derby. Altogether he won seven races, worth £116,863, and was voted Horse of the Year for 1966. Harold was reported as saying: 'He is a grand horse, but probably not the best we've had. Meld had that something extra.' And he was right.

Charlottown was to prove a disappointing sire over nine covering seasons. He was exported to Australia, where he broke a leg and had to be put down.

Harold's Harmony Hall, named after his Bermuda property, son of Tahiri and grandson of Miss Pecksniff, also won three races in 1966. The successes continued, if not quite on the same scale. Between 1925 and the end of the 1976 season, Zia won

196 races, with prize money totalling £305,299. She had bought 20 horses, and had bred 75 at Someries Stud. Harold won 88 races, worth £117,829. He bought 5 horses and bred 22. Gina, Myra and Nicky became part-owners of the Stud. By 1976 Double Life's descendants had won 114 races in Zia and Harold's colours, 3 in Gina, Myra and Nicky's colours, and 36 in other colours.

Gina and Bunnie had sold Thorpe Lubenham and had moved to Checkendon Court (where John Buchan got his idea for the thirty-nine steps), near Henley, in order to be closer to their children's schools. Gina had decided that she would not want to undertake the running of Luton Hoo after her parents' death, and, as David and Myra had their Scottish estates, it was decided that Nicky should be the heir. Harold therefore began the gradual process of putting the estate into his grandson's name. The decision about Nicky was made about the time of two compulsory purchases of Luton Hoo land. Twenty-seven and a half acres were acquired by Luton Town Council for two secondary schools; and after a long struggle Harold agreed to sell 137 acres, for £127,000, for the extension of Luton Airport. One important objection to this last, not only by Harold and Zia but by neighbours, was the annoyance from low-flying aircraft which they considered would be made worse when runways were extended. The question of noise from aircraft was to become an obsession with both Harold and Zia for years ahead. Harold also feared that vibrations might affect the Ludlow collection of porcelain. Later he had to give up more land for the M1 motorway.

A family party, including the ten grandchildren, was arranged for Harold and Zia's golden wedding. Most of the grandchildren, especially when young, were in awe of Zia, but it was the opposite with Harold, who was endlessly joking and spoiling them. When they grew up they became more at ease with Zia. Sacha was always the one who got on with her best. All the grandchildren had striking good looks, but hers were among the most outstanding, inherited from Countess Torby and Julius Wernher. Unlike her mother, she was more receptive to Zia's ideas of conventions and dress (James, for instance, could not understand why she was always wearing gloves).★ Zia also approved of the two boys, Nicky Phillips and Charles Butter. Nicky was temperamentally different to the others, introverted and less communicative. Charles was the youngest, and, aged seven, was made to propose the toast at the golden wedding. He was relieved when it was all over, but Zia called out: 'Come here, child. I couldn't hear a word you said. Say it all over again.'

She tended to be intolerant with the children. They were expected to watch their manners. She criticized especially Fiona Phillips, whom she called the 'little Communist', and Sandra Butter, because she thought they both were untidy and dressed badly. This would infuriate Harold. Actually Sandra became a dress designer and studied in Paris. Her ideas were unconventional and very much of the period. '*Sandra*,' Zia would say. 'What *have* you got on? You look like a common Bond Street tart.' She tried to make Lady Granard take an interest in the girl, but this proved yet another irritation, for Lady Granard, ever the rival (the implication being that Zia married for money, and Lady Granard was rich – very rich – in her *own* right), knew that Zia only wanted her to produce suitable, well-connected boyfriends who would take Sandra to Longchamps; and after all she had her own grandchildren to look after.

Zia loved the intrigue of matchmaking. Marita Phillips was furious when, aged sixteen, she was told: 'You have to use your head in marriage. It's absolutely out of the question just using your heart.' She thought Marita's taking ballet lessons and learning mime was a waste of time. In fact, in 1978 Marita was the co-founder of the successful Mime School (with Adam Darius), of which she was the administrator, and in succeeding years performed in the West End, on the Continent, and in Brazil and Africa. She also acted in films, and wrote lyrics that were sung by Demis Roussos, Peter Skellern and Art Garfunkel.

Natalia Phillips was another granddaughter who annoyed Zia.

★ Sacha was Mountbatten's god-daughter. Philip Ziegler has described how in Mountbatten's lonely old age she became 'as dear to him as a member of his closest family', the most notable of a 'galaxy of young, attractive and devoted women' who rallied to 'ride with him, listen to his stories, imbibe his wisdom'.

She was known as the Screecher. 'Take that screeching child away,' Zia would say. Natalia liked going down to the basement at Luton Hoo to see Albert the odd-job man tap-dancing like Fred Astaire. 'You are not to go down there again, Natalia,' she said. 'You might catch a disease.' What she really meant was that Albert 'drank', and she felt that he would therefore be a bad influence. Once at a Christmas Eve tea Natalia was made to sit at a nest of tables behind a pillar, because Zia did not like the way she ate. Perhaps Zia saw too much of herself in Natalia, who even as a child would not give ground. As Charles has said: 'You could never win an argument with Grandma.' The main excitement for the children at Luton Hoo was the staff dance. After Boxing Day at 10 a.m. sharp they all had to leave.

Like Grand Duke Michael, Zia could not abide rustling paper. Thus Christmas presents were not allowed to be wrapped up, which took half the fun away. Myra, many years before, had been reduced to tears because she had been attacked for daring to give her mother a specially wrapped present. At Luton Hoo all was a matter of routine. The children would be taken up to see Zia in bed in the mornings, and little presents would be hidden for them in the bedclothes. Odile would lay out the jewels on the dressing-table for Zia to choose from. It was like a levee. Actually Zia never wore many jewels, usually just a brooch, her pearl choker and a cabochon ruby ring. Marita was with her when Zia was surveying a selection of dresses put out for some special occasion. '*Really*,' Zia said, 'what can Odile be thinking? None of these will do.' At which Marita burst into tears. 'You're not to say that, Grandma. Odile works very hard for you and she is my best friend.'

The grandchildren tended to find Zia's succession of adored golden retrievers pretty terrible: Bracken, Fern, Cedar and Twig. The dogs were taught tricks, which Zia found almost hysterically funny, like 'dying for England', leaping on some unsuspecting male guest and snatching his handkerchief, and playing the piano ('thump, thump, thump'). When Twig trampled all over a friend's flowers, Zia said: 'Very stupid of you to put a flowerbed there.' Visitors, however, were impressed to be greeted by her in the pillared hall, 'like the goddess Diana with faithful hounds on each side'.

Yet Zia was perpetually being teased by Harold; she was in charge at Luton Hoo, but if he put his foot down she 'gave in like a shot'. If he did not like one of her guests, he would hide in the bushes and make animal or bird noises. The children loved all this, just as they loved his imitations of Harold Macmillan and General de Gaulle. 'Go on, Grumpy, do it, do it,' they would shout. He was forever making up rhymes and limericks for them, and seemed to understand what would most amuse a particular child. Out of the blue he would send a letter including a photograph from a newspaper with something absurd ballooning out of a person's mouth. 'Grandma was good with people but bad with the family,' Marita has said. 'Grandpa was good with the family but not always good with people. He was gruff on the outside but sensitive inside. To us he was always very relaxed.' He still smoked strong Turkish cigarettes and surreptitiously dropped the ash on the carpets: 'Good against moths.' His favourite grandchildren were Marita and Rohays, and when they were nine he took them to Bermuda for two weeks. 'Grandma told us to stick by him. He would swish off and we had to run along behind him. We thought we were there free, but Mr Spooner said our parents were paying for us all the time. It was all part of his hotel business. That sort of thing gave Grandpa a kick. Like a game.'

The staff in hotels at Bermuda were terrified of Zia and once a manager had to fly to New York to get some special biscuits that she wanted.

It was agreed that as a hostess at Luton Hoo she was still the perfectionist. But Luton Hoo time had still to be observed, and clocks continued to be put forward five minutes. Once the Phillips girls hid behind the dining-room curtains. Zia entered and was enraged at not seeing them. She told the butler to lock the door, and then they all sprang out at her. She was not much amused, though of course Harold was.

Harold and Zia both continued to enjoy their autumns in Scotland, including one week with the Butters at Pitlochry and one with the Phillipses at their house in Aberdeenshire. Zia would send her huge maroon and black Rolls ahead with all the luggage, and be met at the airport. Usually she would take over the wheel herself, with a golden retriever beside her, and hooting at every corner. Passers-by were amazed by the sight, as though Queen Mary had been reincarnated. The children teased her about her luggage, all marked with her racing colours, green and yellow. One year the Butters counted twenty-seven pieces. Marita also counted twenty identical beige cashmere twinsets.

'You all look like beatniks,' Zia told the Butter girls. 'You'll never get married.' She still had her passion for fishing, spending hours in the river, and would wear beautifully cut, waterproof clothing and carry the most expensive rods. She attacked some-body's head keeper for not wearing a hat: 'Hats are put on so that they can be taken off.'

In her old age, after being so abstemious and disapproving of drink generally, she unexpectedly developed a taste for sloe gin and Dubonnet, having been introduced to them by Geoffrey Hull, manager at Someries Stud, and his wife. 'She was lovely,' Joan Hull has said. 'I put myself out to enjoy her. If you were aware she wanted things, you gave them to her. One telephoned Sir Harold with the bad news, Lady Zia only with the good news. He was always full of fun. Time didn't seem to matter. He was the easiest person in the world. Once the site of a garage annoyed him. He said to Geoff "Go and see if they'll sell the place." He bought it and just got rid of it.'

When the aged Kerensky came to visit Luton Hoo in July 1966 Zia was ready for the attack. But as with the Russians at Electrolux they both delighted in one another. He told her he had been very friendly with her eldest uncle Grand Duke Nicholas, and said that if Nicholas had been Tsar the revolution would never have taken place. He also claimed that he had done everything possible for the Imperial family to leave, provided the British sent a cruiser to Murmansk.

If Russians from the USSR came to visit Luton Hoo, Zia would make a point of meeting them in the Romanov room. Out would come that stabbing finger, pointing at a picture of a cousin or uncle: 'Murdered by Bolsheviks! Murdered! Murdered!'

The Phillipses and the Butters each had a floor in 15 Grosvenor Square. They called it Coronation Street, after the television series. Zia was in the Grosvenor Square flat at the time of the big anti-

Vietnam demonstration in 1968. The story goes that she went down into the square and tapped a woman, said to have been Vanessa Redgrave, on the shoulder. 'What have you done for the world?' she asked her. 'What have *you* done?' this putative Vanessa Redgrave replied. 'I've done a lot,' retorted Zia. 'Go and do something useful in life. Get off your bottom and do something.'

The late Sir Charles Johnston, then High Commissioner in Australia and a translator of Pushkin's *Eugene Onegin*, was an amused observer of the Wernhers, being married himself to a White Russian. In his diary he recorded how at a party given by the Douglas Fairbankses he was put between a lady endlessly talking about servants in Canberra and Zia, who kept fixing Princess Marina 'with a basilisk eye'. Zia explained to him: 'I'm trying to get her to go.' Finally, as he said, by sheer force of will she achieved her object, although Princess Marina was enjoying herself and didn't want to leave at all.

Zia always hated late nights (unlike Harold) and when at home would go to bed at 10, even if guests were present.

Sir Charles was also at the ball at Checkendon in July 1969 given by Gina and Myra for Fiona and Marilyn. There were about four hundred guests, including various members of the royal family, who could have, he said, been expected to 'cast a damper'. 'But they were all relaxed and in a cosy mood. Thanks to the Russian link, there was a sort of Tolstoyan feeling of family togetherness – it could have been a ball at the Rostovs' . . . We were surrounded by chums . . . the warm feeling of being welcomed and liked and wanted.'

At least Harold could not say that the ball had been wasted. Two years later Fiona married one of the guests, Cecil Boyd-Rochfort's stepson, Jamie Burnett of Leys, who had inherited his mother's old home Crathes Castle on Deeside. By then CBR had retired, and had been succeeded at Freemason Lodge by Jamie's brother Henry Cecil.★ If the newly-weds were not quite so obsessed by the world of horses as their parents, it was certainly – as reported in the press – a 'spectacular union between two great racing families'.

★ Jamie had changed his name from Cecil to Burnett of Leys, his mother's maiden name. Crathes Castle is now a National Trust property.

27

Last Years, and an Epilogue

The great Luton Airport row continued all through the 1960s and beyond. Committees were formed, protests were made to Cabinet Ministers. Zia kept a notebook, listing every time an aeroplane flew over or near the Hoo. It was true that some planes after take-off, only a mile away, did fly very close, sometimes at night. Often when this happened Zia in a fury would ring Flight Control, the Airport Director and the Town Clerk of Luton. Finally she decided to get everyone concerned to lunch. She charmed them all, and was in consequence taken up in a plane (a Jumbo) herself, which she thoroughly enjoyed. Maybe her efforts (and Harold's) were not quite responsible for improving the situation, but improved it was in due course. At least Someries Castle and the farm where Joseph Conrad had lived were not demolished to make way for a new runway.

Harold resigned as Chairman of the King Edward VII Hospital in 1969, and was elected a Vice-President. 'Old age is creeping on,' he said, but it was a hard decision, almost as hard as giving up Bermuda, for the hospital had always been his special interest. The death of David Milford Haven in April 1970 was a blow to the family. He had collapsed when catching a train at Liverpool Street Station. To Zia he had been almost like a son; to Gina like a brother; and Harold had often been involved in disentangling David's wilder adventures before his first marriage. He agreed with Mountbatten that David's early love, Robin Dalton, an Australian, should be made welcome if she came to the memorial service – as indeed she did (Mountbatten himself escorted her to the second row).

A different kind of blow was the public revelation of Harold's long association with Joan Clarkson. It was probably more painful than shocking for the family to see *Evening Standard* posters displayed in Grosvenor Square, to the effect that a 'millionaire friend of the Queen' was being sued as co-respondent in a divorce case. Harold, aged seventy-eight, was being sued by the husband of Joan Clarkson, now Mrs Dennis. It was disclosed that she even had a flat in Grosvenor Square, not far from No. 15. The grandchildren knew about 'Grandpa's girlfriend', simply as a joke. One Butter daughter remembers being in Claridge's with her mother, and Myra saying: 'Quick, look behind you, there she is.'

Evidently 'Joanie' had wanted a divorce, but her husband, who was well known in the racing world, had named Harold in a cross-petition. Harold was determined to fight the charge, and it was noticed that when he and Zia went to the Two Thousand Guineas they walked arm-in-arm, something which had not been seen before.

Within months Harold was diagnosed as having cancer. His family and friends, including Joan Dennis, were convinced that the strain had somehow ignited it. The citation was dropped, and the divorce case delayed. He went into the Edward VII where he had three massive operations. He became very weak and was often in severe pain, but kept up his spirits in an extraordinary, and typical, way. All the family took turns sitting with him, and helped to feed him. He died at Luton Hoo on 30 June 1973, aged eighty.

A memorial service was held at St Margaret's, Westminster. Mountbatten gave the address, and spoke of his courage and modesty, describing him as a 'fierce patriot' and recalling his contribution to Combined Operations, so important to the success of the invasion of Northern France. A letter from Gavin Astor in *The Times* was especially valued by Zia. He spoke of Harold as having been 'always ready to give time, help and advice to anyone who approached him, no matter how young or humble'; of his 'well-informed mind' and his sense of humour, which 'cast a comfortable and relaxed atmosphere over any gathering – a business meeting, an annual staff dinner, a social occasion, a chat on the factory floor, a stroll with friends.'

Zia was to remain at Luton Hoo for her lifetime. Being totally unbusinesslike, she was always convinced that she would run out of money. Nicky, who had been at Lausanne University and was now working with Lazards in Paris, had to make constant visits, to prevent her from selling family treasures. She would be 'livid' if he wanted to cut down diseased trees in the park. She was harassed by a prospective MP who wanted to turn the Hoo estate into a garden suburb of Luton with houses for 3,000 people and children's playgrounds. Zia was reported as saying: 'If he were a Communist, I could understand it, but it sounds very strange for an Englishman.' When she heard that in London a councillor wanted to sell the contents of Kenwood for financing a similar purpose, it seemed to her that a repetition of 1917 in St Petersburg was fast approaching. She decided to run a garden centre, was delighted when it showed a small profit, but had no idea about turnover.

In fact there were genuine worries about there being sufficient ready cash to pay off death duties and maintain the expenses of the estate. This was due to Harold's efforts to make sure all his descendants would be properly provided for during his lifetime. As a result, some important ivories from the Wernher collection, thought to have been worth £700,000 on the open market, had to be made over to the nation in lieu of tax. Chief among these was the superb tenth-century Byzantine triptych of the Virgin and Child that had previously passed through the hands of many famous nineteenth-century collectors such as Soltykoff, Seillère and Spitzer.

Not long after Harold's death Marilyn Butter married James Ramsay, eldest son of Lord Dalhousie. This was especially happy because of memories of family holidays at Invermark, the Dalhousies' house in Scotland. Marilyn had worked at Asprey's, and was one of Zia's favourites, like her sister Georgina.

James Ramsay asked Zia what he should call her. After some hesitation she said 'Zia'. When he told his father this, Lord

Dalhousie said: 'Good Lord, it took me forty years to reach that stage.'

The Joan Dennis affair flared up again in the press in 1975, and in a way that was extremely hurtful to Zia. The Dennises had been divorced in 1974, but now Joanie was suing her former husband in the High Court for nearly £40,000 that she said was due to her. It was revealed in court that until 1970 Harold had been giving her a regular allowance of £5,000 a year as well as presents of jewellery and sometimes cheques of up to £50,000. He had also given her a house in Sussex and two houses in Bermuda, and money to decorate a mews house in Mayfair.

Aged sixty-eight, she admitted that she had become his mistress when she was twenty (as anyone in the Wernhers' circle would have confirmed), but said that after her marriage he had simply been a close friend. The Dennises had married in 1941, and she had written to Harold after the death of his son Alex, and after that she had begun seeing him again. Newspaper accounts of the case described her as still being a very beautiful woman, even stunning. The marriage had, according to Joan, become 'turbulent', and had broken up in 1969. Captain Dennis claimed that rows had mainly occurred because of the presents and money that Harold gave her.

Friends have said that she was good fun, 'dripping with jewels', and 'liked her tipple'. Her circle included Tallulah Bankhead, Noël Coward and Beatrice Lillie. She loved having houses redecorated, and in court you could see she was 'ever the actress'.

The curator at Luton Hoo remembered seeing Zia on the terrace at Luton Hoo, 'looking awful'. 'Do you know what has happened?' she said to him. 'The editor of a newspaper has just rung up from London. "Lady Zia," he said, "I am so sorry about this terrible trouble you are having. Shall I send down a reporter, and we can put this matter straight?" "No," I said, and slammed down the receiver.'

It is perfectly clear that Harold did 'adore' Joan, as she claimed in court. He also adored Zia. They were totally different characters, and Joanie fulfilled a part of life that he needed. Zia accepted this. She even managed a kind of joke: 'After all, everyone needs friends.' The family never felt threatened by Joanie. A friend of

Joanie's has admitted: 'She was simply a good-time girl, from a quite different milieu.'

The case was reported during Wimbledon. Zia had her seat in the Royal Box. She dressed immaculately as usual, and sat there as though unperturbed, knowing that people were staring at her and that she was being photographed. Only when she got back into the car did her face begin to show the tension.

Joan Dennis won her case and was awarded £43,380 damages. She regretted that Harold's name had ever been mentioned, and there is no doubt that she was sincere in this. In fairness to Harold it should be recorded that during all that time he had been quietly giving money to many people who were genuinely in need. Nor had he been her only lover, 'Bert' Duke of Marlborough having been another.

Friends wrote to Zia to show their support, but for her it was like receiving condolences all over again. All the letters had to be answered. She never let herself go. Her eyes might fill with tears, but she would quickly turn away. The trouble in her ear became worse, and she would have to spend much time lying down.

She still loved meeting attractive people, and even had drinks on view. 'You see I've become quite modern,' she said. The Queen and Prince Philip continued to come to Luton Hoo every November, and in August Zia had her annual visit to Balmoral. The traumas of the past years were relieved when Nicky married Countess Lucy Czernin, from a family famous in the days of the Austro-Hungarian Empire, especially in Prague. Natalia was at last in favour when Zia heard that she was being taken out by Gerald Grosvenor. 'Don't let him go. Don't let him go,' she said. 'You must come down and bring him to lunch.' Neither Natalia nor Gerald needed her encouragement, for they became engaged – though by then Zia had died.

She appreciated Nicky's tremendous sense of duty, which she felt was like Nicholas I's. They became very close in those last years. She still could not understand the importance of jobs and office hours for young people. She expected grandchildren not only to keep ringing up but to be able to drop everything and come to lunch. Sandra was back working in London, and would be telephoned rather angrily, almost barked at: 'Sandra, I'm alive!'

'Grandma, I've never doubted it. It's been very difficult these past weeks.' That was not a good enough excuse. She would be annoyed when she thought she was not being given enough information about the family's lives.

The stud at Newmarket remained her great interest. It was said that she never sat down to a meal without discussing horses. In the mornings at Luton Hoo she would watch the gardeners through field-glasses from the bathroom. Then down she would come to show them how to hoe properly. She once found an American woman on a seat in the private part of the garden, and ordered her to get off. The American refused. 'Madam,' she said, 'I have paid my shilling to see your garden, and here I mean to stay.' She was thereupon invited into the house for tea.

'In Russia we wouldn't have allowed it' was a favourite remark. The younger Butter girls would 'cringe with embarrassment' when she started talking about her Imperial connections. She would insist on their being taken to school in the Rolls, but they would ask the chauffeur to let them out at a corner so as not to be seen arriving in such grandeur.

In the autumn of 1977 she realized she would not have the strength to entertain the Queen and Prince Philip that year. It was therefore left to Nicky and Lucy to be hosts. Gina, Bunnie, Myra, David, Mountbatten, Sacha and James were going to be there. Before leaving, she kissed the servants. They knew that she never expected to return. She had made all the arrangements about menus and flowers. For this was to celebrate the Queen's thirtieth wedding anniversary.

The Queen wrote to Zia on 22 November, thanking her for all the thought and kindness that had gone into the organization of the weekend, and for the fire in her bedroom, 'now such a rare thing'. She wrote about the clouds of pheasants, and about running out of cartridges and dry stockings, and how she and Prince Philip could hardly believe that they had been married so long. 'But now that I have a lovely grandson of my own it is perhaps more believable that time has passed like that.'

As always, it was an affectionate letter, but inevitably with a sad undertone. The weekend had not been the same 'without *you* being actually there.' Zia died on 7 December. There was no specific illness; 'she just curled up and died'. At her funeral it was noticed that Nicky seemed the most deeply upset. There was a memorial service in the Grosvenor Chapel, taken by Robert Runcie, Bishop of St Albans and soon to be Archbishop of Canterbury.

Nearly thirteen years before, she had written a letter for Odile Barbier, 'to be opened after my death – if neither of us is alive to be burnt'. It was a testimony to a side of her character of which people not close to her might perhaps have been unaware. She wrote to say how grateful she was for Odile's devotion to her for so many years. 'For you have given up your life to me, a thing I was always deeply touched by, and you must know how devoted I was to you.' And she ended:

> Who knows we may meet again in another world? Thanks for all you have done for me.
> A kiss
> from your devoted
> Zia Wernher.

★ ★ ★

The family tree on page 449 gives details of the marriages and births of descendants of Harold and Zia Wernher since 1977. The twenty-second great-grandchild, Hugh Grosvenor, was born on 29 January 1991.

Bunnie died in 1980. Checkendon Court was sold, but Gina kept the family home in Aberdeenshire. She succeeded Lady Brecknock as Chief President of St John Ambulance Brigade but resigned in 1990. 'Both our parents,' Myra has said, 'were a terrific example of self-discipline and service. They made us aware of our good fortune in life. Pa was completely unmaterialistic but admired good things and would have been happy anywhere. Ma was very demanding but would always have made herself comfortable if in different circumstances. They were people of great strength and courage.'

This tradition of public service was transmitted also to the grandchildren. Sacha trained and qualified in the work of C. J. Jung, and later conducted workshops and training programmes on psychotherapy and counselling in Northern Ireland. She also became a Governor of Harrow School. Fiona raised a million pounds within eighteen months for a hospital wing for premature babies in North-East Scotland. The vitality of the family was also shown in Marita's and Georgina's writings, and in Rohays's murals.

There was a great family tragedy in 1988 when Marita's husband, Randall Crawley, was killed with his brother Andrew in an air crash in Italy. Marita's second son, Galen, was born two months afterwards.

The death of Nicky was an appalling shock. He was found in the garage at Luton Hoo, with the engine running, on 1 March 1991. He was aged forty-three, and to most people it had seemed that he had everything that life could offer. The verdict was that his death was an accident.

Like all his family, he had an extraordinary sense of public duty, but temperamentally he was apart. In an obituary in the *Daily Telegraph* a friend wrote: 'He was reserved, but somehow his reserve was not of an ordinary nature. Nicky was a most attractive man in every sense. That he was strikingly handsome there is no question. But he carried a palpable air of mystery.' To which could be added a grace of manner and a grace of mind, a quiet authority and wit, and an essentially kind nature, never patronizing. He was an exemplary father, and loved flowers and trees. Perhaps he owed less to his Russian ancestry than did his sisters. He was an enigma in life as he was in death.

He had been suffering from overwork and a bad attack of influenza. He was also depressed, particularly by the sale of Someries Stud in January; for racing had been his great passion. He had driven himself hard, in what seemed to many people an alarming way, and was obviously conscious of carrying the weight of family tradition and responsibility. All this was matched by some undoubtedly brilliant achievements.

One such achievement was his management of Luton Hoo itself. He and Lucy had moved into the Gables after Zia's death. The part of the mansion that had been occupied by his grandparents was now used for banquets, conferences, films, television and fashion photography. Nicky was ready to organize firework displays, musical accompaniments, floodlighting, marquees. It was a splendid solution to the upkeep of this vast building, which in the first instance, after Zia's death, had had to be subsidized by his own successful investments, particularly in North Sea Oil, and by the sale of the Altdorfer painting to the National Gallery.★

Capability Brown's park is still an amazingly peaceful oasis, with geese and swans on the lake, and – of course – pheasants, so numerous that one fears to run over them on the drive. The cedars sometimes lose limbs in gales, but are still a glorious feature. Nicky had taken a particular pride in replanting the great rock garden created by Julius Wernher as a surprise for his wife. One part of the estate, however, comprising seventy acres, had been cut off by new roads and visually spoilt by overlooking an industrial area, which included Vauxhall Motors. So it was converted by Nicky into a business park, landscaped with avenues, fountains and pavilions, and connected to Luton Airport and the M1 Motorway. It was given the name Capability Green, and opened by the Duke of Edinburgh in 1987. A million feet of office and business space was envisaged, and a Japanese company was the first to acquire a site. The whole project was an immense contribution to the prosperity of the town of Luton.

During the winter of 1990–1 Nicky and, especially, Lucy set about – with tremendous enthusiasm – making changes to the arrangement of the entire Wernher Collection, including the Russian and Fabergé rooms. G. E. Street's chapel was also restored to its dazzling Late Victorian glory.

Nicky's interest in commercial design, reflected in Capability Green, has been shared by his sister Natalia, who in 1985 founded the Eaton Hall Design Workshop, now given charitable status. In February 1987, with Nicky as host, a series of events was held at Luton Hoo to pay tribute to the 150th anniversary of the death of Pushkin. About 170 Pushkin scholars and admirers, as well as

---

★ Luton Hoo and the Julius Wernher Collection had been left to Zia for her lifetime. After her death Nicky inherited the mansion and estate. He was joint owner of the Collection with the five Butter grandchildren. Proceeds from the Altdorfer sale went to fund and perpetuate the newly formed Luton Hoo Foundation for urgent repairs and future conservation.

descendants, attended two days of readings from his works, with music and lectures. It was a unique and special experience.

In February 1987 the words *glasnost* and *perestroika* were unknown in the West. To the palatial grandeur of Luton Hoo there came Professor Yuri Mann from the Institute of World Literature in Moscow, the Russian poets Alexander Mezherov and Yuna Moritz, and the Russian cultural attaché in London. Other guests included a Galitzine and an Obolensky, the Pushkin scholar Tatiana Wolff, Professors Paul Debreceny from North Carolina, Louis Allain from Lille, A. D. P. Briggs from Bristol, and John Bayley, with his wife Iris Murdoch, from Oxford. Beneath a cloudburst of chandeliers in the ballroom there was music by Glinka, Tchaikovsky, Shostakovich and Britten; and readings by the actors Alan Howard and Jeffry Wickham, and by Nathalie Brooke, granddaughter of Count Benckendorff the last Tsarist ambassador in London. In this neutral ground, as a guest wrote afterwards, it was possible to believe that these people, from such diverse backgrounds, all participating in Pushkin's honour, were accomplishing something that politicians had hitherto failed to achieve.

Pushkin for the Russians has been compared to Shakespeare for the English and Goethe for the Germans. He freed the language from artificiality and archaism. His influence on contemporaries and all the great Russian novelists was immense. At Luton Hoo in those almost dreamlike mornings and evenings we who participated knew once more that his voice was the enduring voice of Russia, that he expressed a whole national consciousness regardless of politics, uniting Russians wherever they might be throughout the world.

The Wernher Fabergé collection was also on display. New additions had also been placed with the Imperial relics inherited by Zia: furniture associated with the Tsarevich in the House of Special Purpose in 1917, that had been given to Nicky by the son of the Tsarevich's tutor, Charles Gibbes. None of this seemed incongruous.

One participant at that weekend might have come for an additional reason. He was Anthony Sampson, author of *Black on Gold*, subtitled *Tycoons, Revolutionaries and Apartheid*, and editor in the 1950s of the black South African magazine *Drum*. Perhaps Sir Julius Wernher, whose huge portrait watched benignly above the staircase in the Marble Hall, would not have thought this incongruous either.

That experience gave a new inspiration to the whole family. Marita began to write her play about Pushkin. Sacha launched her scheme for the Pushkin Prizes in Ireland, inaugurated in June 1988.

These prizes, given at Barons Court in County Tyrone, were for imaginative works by children of eleven to twelve; six primary schools in Northern Ireland and two in the Republic took part. They were interdenominational and the first judges were Roald Dahl, Jennifer Johnston and Martin Waddell. Sacha felt that Pushkin's poetry and ideals had a particular relevance to Ireland. 'Men like Pushkin,' she has written, 'have sought to articulate the truths of the heart that lie deeper than politics. This applies as well to Ireland's heritage. In Ireland it has been the great literary figures who have given shape and form to the undying identity of this country and who help us to see or understand the emergence of a new sense of this land's cultural and spiritual identity.'

The scheme was a great success. Seamus Heaney was at the prizegiving in 1989. The next judges were Brian Friel, Ted Hughes and Sam McAughtry. Sacha was encouraged to plan for extending the prizes to published works by adult Irish writers. In 1990 a group of schoolchildren, sponsored by herself and the Education Boards of north and south Ireland, and accompanied by a team from Ulster Television, visited Pushkin sites in Russia.

Sacha's example gave Myra (a Trustee of the Duke of Edinburgh Award Scheme) the idea of starting Pushkin Prizes in Scotland – but for secondary schools, children of twelve to fourteen. Her pilot scheme was in Tayside, and by then *glasnost* had become familiar. She hoped that her venture would help young people to forge friendships with others in Ireland 'who share our Celtic heritage' and in the Soviet Union. Both she and Sacha were planning exchange visits for prizewinners. Myra's first judges were Edwin Morgan, Mollie Hunter, Magnus Linklater and Norman MacCaig.

Accompanied by Prince George Galitzine, members of the

Phillips and Butter families went to Russia to visit places associated with their ancestor. They met Pushkin relatives, and were interviewed by *Pravda* and Soviet television. In Leningrad Gina and Myra were shown Pushkin's letters that had once belonged to their grandmother Countess Torby and had been acquired by Diaghilev. Gina commissioned a bust of Pushkin by the sculptor Anikushin for the new Pushkin room at Luton Hoo.

In 1988 Rohays Butter married Alexander 'Konky' Galitzine, eldest son of Prince George Galitzine.

In 1990 Gina and Sacha went again to the USSR, this time to Georgia, where they saw the old palace of Grand Duke Michael Nikolaievich, Gina's great-grandfather, and the mountain of Kazbeck after which the villa at Cannes had been named. They were welcomed enthusiastically as the first descendants to come there since the Revolution. However, in this case, it must be admitted, the descent from Pushkin was of rather less account, since he had been a Russian and the Georgians were then looking forward to early independence from the Russians.

Nicky died just before the completion of the chapel, and his funeral was the first service to be held there. Lucy continued with her spectacular work in the reorganization of the Collection and the redecoration of the rooms. On 18 May 1991, as the anniversary of the birth of Tsar Nicholas II, there was an event at Luton Hoo, at least as remarkable as that in February 1987: an event for which Nicky and Lucy had worked so hard. The chapel was rededicated to St Nicholas in the Russian Orthodox faith by the Metropolitan, Anthony of Sourozh. The chief guest was the Grand Duke Vladimir Kyrilovich, pretender to the Imperial throne and accompanied by his Grand Duchess. Also present were the Cultural Attaché and the Second Secretary from the Soviet Embassy, and Dr Sergei Mikhailovich Nekrasov, Director of the Pushkin Museum in Leningrad. Such a gathering would have been inconceivable only a few years before.

It was a long service in Russian, and under the circumstances particularly moving, with music by the choir of the Russian Orthodox cathedral at Ennismore Gardens in London. Huge ornate wrought-iron gates, with the monogram A W – for Alice Wernher – divided the chapel from an antechamber. These gates, not unlike those seen outside palaces in Leningrad, had once stood at the entrance to Birdie's gardens but had been taken down for safety in 1940. In the main chapel were ikons given to Charles Gibbes by the Tsarina. In the antechamber were all Zia's family portraits and busts of her ancestors Nicholas I and Peter the Great. The procession passed the Tsarevich's chair and desk, and a chandelier from the house in which the Imperial family had been massacred.

After the service the family and others from the old and present regimes gathered in the new, and deliberately simple, Pushkin room where Anikushkin's bust had been placed. Then Dr Nekrasov produced his surprise, presenting Lucy with a copy of Pushkin's death-mask.

In the pillared hall vodka later flowed. Once again it was an evening of animation and splendour, of the sort for which Luton Hoo had been created.

Pushkin by himself

WERNHER

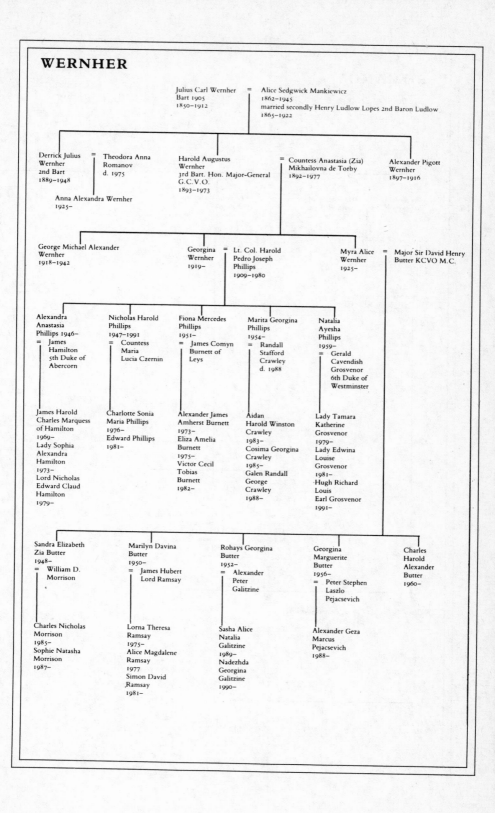

Julius Carl Wernher = Alice Sedgwick Mankiewicz
Bart 1905   1862–1945
1850–1912   married secondly Henry Ludlow Lopes 2nd Baron Ludlow
            1865–1922

Derrick Julius = Theodora Anna   Harold Augustus = Countess Anastasia (Zia)   Alexander Pigott
Wernher   Romanov   Wernher   Mikhailovna de Torby   Wernher
2nd Bart   d. 1975   3rd Bart. Hon. Major-General   1892–1977   1897–1916
1889–1948   G.C.V.O.
        1893–1973

Anna Alexandra Wernher
1925–

George Michael Alexander   Georgina = Lt. Col. Harold   Myra Alice = Major Sir David Henry
Wernher   Wernher   Pedro Joseph   Wernher   Butter KCVO M.C.
1918–1942   1919–   Phillips   1925–
        1909–1980

Alexandra   Nicholas Harold   Fiona Mercedes   Marita Georgina   Natalia
Anastasia   Phillips   Phillips   Phillips   Ayesha
Phillips 1946–   1947–1991   1951–   1954–   Phillips
= James   = Countess   = James Comyn   = Randall   1959–
Hamilton   Maria   Burnett of   Stafford   = Gerald
5th Duke of   Lucia Czernin   Leys   Crawley   Cavendish
Abercorn   d. 1988   Grosvenor
            6th Duke of
            Westminster

James Harold   Charlotte Sonia   Alexander James   Aidan   Lady Tamara
Charles Marquess   Maria Phillips   Amherst Burnett   Harold Winston   Katherine
of Hamilton   1976–   1973–   Crawley   Grosvenor
1969–   Edward Phillips   Eliza Amelia   1983–   1979–
Lady Sophia   1981–   Burnett   Cosima Georgina   Lady Edwina
Alexandra   1975–   Crawley   Louise
Hamilton   Victor Cecil   1985–   Grosvenor
1973–   Tobias   Galen Randall   1981–
Lord Nicholas   Burnett   George   Hugh Richard
Edward Claud   1982–   Crawley   Louis
Hamilton   1988–   Earl Grosvenor
1979–   1991–

Sandra Elizabeth   Marilyn Davina   Rohays Georgina   Georgina   Charles
Zia Butter   Butter   Butter   Marguerite   Harold
1948–   1950–   1952–   Butter   Alexander
= William D.   = James Hubert   = Alexander   1956–   Butter
Morrison   Lord Ramsay   Peter   = Peter Stephen   1960–
        Galitzine   Laszlo
            Pejacsevich

Charles Nicholas   Lorna Theresa   Sasha Alice   Alexander Geza
Morrison   Ramsay   Natalia   Marcus
1985–   1975–   Galitzine   Pejacsevich
Sophie Natasha   Alice Magdalene   1989–   1988–
Morrison   Ramsay   Nadezhda
1987–   1977   Georgina
    Simon David   Galitzine
    Ramsay   1990–
    1981–

ROMANOV

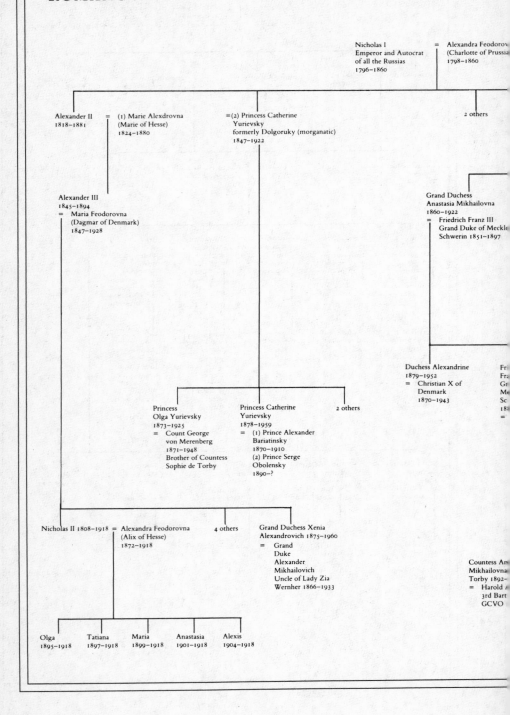

Nicholas I
Emperor and Autocrat
of all the Russias
1796–1860
= Alexandra Feodorov
(Charlotte of Prussia
1798–1860

Alexander II
1818–1881
= (1) Marie Alexdrovna
(Marie of Hesse)
1824–1880
= (2) Princess Catherine
Yurievsky
formerly Dolgoruky (morganatic)
1847–1922

2 others

Alexander III
1845–1894
= Maria Feodorovna
(Dagmar of Denmark)
1847–1928

Grand Duchess
Anastasia Mikhailovna
1860–1922
= Friedrich Franz III
Grand Duke of Meckle
Schwerin 1851–1897

Duchess Alexandrine
1879–1952
= Christian X of
Denmark
1870–1943

Fri
Fra
Gr
Me
Sc
18
=

Princess
Olga Yurievsky
1873–1925
= Count George
von Merenberg
1871–1948
Brother of Countess
Sophie de Torby

Princess Catherine
Yurievsky
1878–1959
= (1) Prince Alexander
Bariatinsky
1870–1910
(2) Prince Serge
Obolensky
1890–?

2 others

Nicholas II 1808–1918 = Alexandra Feodorovna
(Alix of Hesse)
1872–1918

4 others

Grand Duchess Xenia
Alexandrovich 1875–1960
= Grand
Duke
Alexander
Mikhailovich
Uncle of Lady Zia
Wernher 1866–1933

Countess An
Mikhailovna
Torby 1892–
= Harold
3rd Bart
GCVO

Olga
1895–1918

Tatiana
1897–1918

Maria
1899–1918

Anastasia
1901–1918

Alexis
1904–1918

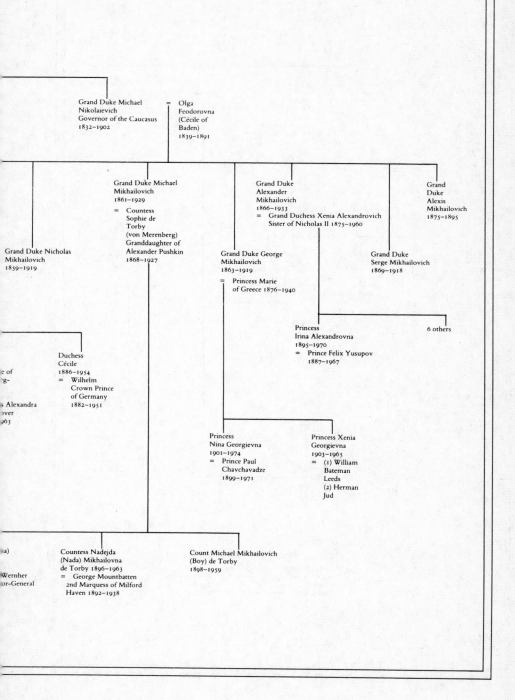

Grand Duke Michael
Nikolaievich
Governor of the Caucasus
1832–1902
= Olga
Feodorovna
(Cécile of
Baden)
1839–1891

Grand Duke Michael
Mikhailovich
1861–1929
= Countess
Sophie de
Torby
(von Merenberg)
Granddaughter of
Alexander Pushkin
1868–1927

Grand Duke
Alexander
Mikhailovich
1866–1933
= Grand Duchess Xenia Alexandrovich
Sister of Nicholas II 1875–1960

Grand
Duke
Alexis
Mikhailovich
1875–1895

Grand Duke Nicholas
Mikhailovich
1859–1919

Grand Duke George
Mikhailovich
1863–1919
= Princess Marie
of Greece 1876–1940

Grand Duke
Serge Mikhailovich
1869–1918

Princess
Irina Alexandrovna
1895–1970
= Prince Felix Yusupov
1887–1967

6 others

Duchess
Cécile
1886–1954
= Wilhelm
Crown Prince
of Germany
1882–1951

e of
rg-

s Alexandra
over
963

Princess
Nina Georgievna
1901–1974
= Prince Paul
Chavchavadze
1899–1971

Princess Xenia
Georgievna
1903–1965
= (1) William
Bateman
Leeds
(2) Herman
Jud

a)

Wernher
or-General

Countess Nadejda
(Nada) Mikhailovna
de Torby 1896–1963
= George Mountbatten
2nd Marquess of Milford
Haven 1892–1938

Count Michael Mikhailovich
(Boy) de Torby
1898–1959

NASSAU

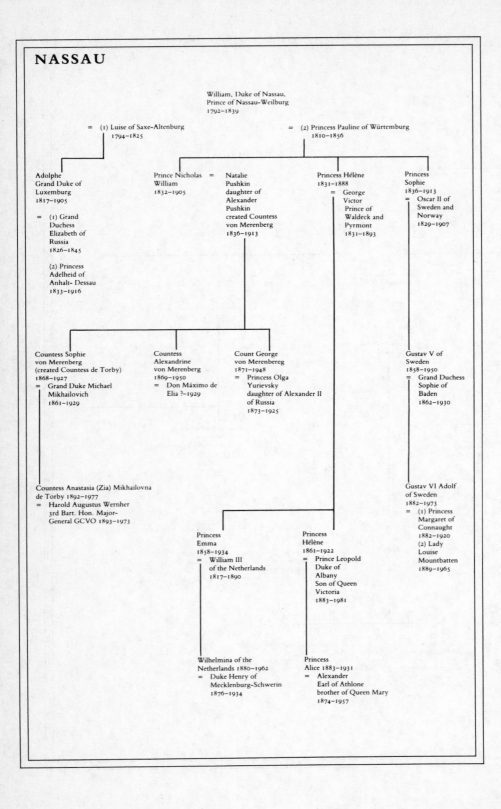

William, Duke of Nassau,
Prince of Nassau-Weilburg
1792–1839

= (1) Luise of Saxe-Altenburg
1794–1825

= (2) Princess Pauline of Würtemburg
1810–1856

Adolphe
Grand Duke of
Luxemburg
1817–1905

= (1) Grand
Duchess
Elizabeth of
Russia
1826–1845

(2) Princess
Adelheid of
Anhalt- Dessau
1833–1916

Prince Nicholas =
William
1832–1905

Natalie
Pushkin
daughter of
Alexander
Pushkin
created Countess
von Merenberg
1836–1913

Princess Hélène
1831–1888

= George
Victor
Prince of
Waldeck and
Pyrmont
1831–1893

Princess
Sophie
1836–1913
= Oscar II of
Sweden and
Norway
1829–1907

Countess Sophie
von Merenberg
(created Countess de Torby)
1868–1927
= Grand Duke Michael
Mikhailovich
1861–1929

Countess
Alexandrine
von Merenberg
1869–1950
= Don Máximo de
Elia ?–1929

Count George
von Merenberg
1871–1948
= Princess Olga
Yurievsky
daughter of Alexander II
of Russia
1873–1925

Gustav V of
Sweden
1858–1950
= Grand Duchess
Sophie of
Baden
1862–1930

Countess Anastasia (Zia) Mikhailovna
de Torby 1892–1977
= Harold Augustus Wernher
3rd Bart. Hon. Major-
General GCVO 1893–1973

Gustav VI Adolf
of Sweden
1882–1973
= (1) Princess
Margaret of
Connaught
1882–1920
(2) Lady
Louise
Mountbatten
1889–1965

Princess
Emma
1858–1934
= William III
of the Netherlands
1817–1890

Princess
Hélène
1861–1922
= Prince Leopold
Duke of
Albany
Son of Queen
Victoria
1883–1981

Wilhelmina of the
Netherlands 1880–1962
= Duke Henry of
Mecklenburg-Schwerin
1876–1934

Princess
Alice 1883–1931
= Alexander
Earl of Athlone
brother of Queen Mary
1874–1957

Published and Manuscript Sources

I have listed the names of authors of my main books of reference, which are given in the Bibliography, and these are shown chapter by chapter.

Part One

The Luton Hoo archives are not catalogued and broadly include the letters from Julius Wernher to his parents and his wife, the latter particularly interesting in connection with the Lemoine scandal and Derrick's misdemeanours. There are also papers in German concerning his family and a few letters from his wife, as well as certain printed documents relating to business activities, various wills, some notebooks with prices of *objets d'art* and correspondence concerning them, the Mewès and Davis blueprints, his manuscript 'Notes on the Diamond Fields', draft speeches, and assessments of his character etc. written in the 1920s by surviving ex-colleagues.

In 1975 Mrs Maryna Fraser compiled her *Inventory of the Archives of H. Eckstein & Co. 1887–1910*, which greatly facilitates research at Barlow Rand. I consulted vols 3–6 in connection with the Markham Affair; vol. 98, *Private Letters to London Mar. 1907–June 1908*; vols 100–101, *Newspaper Cuttings on the Death of Alfred Beit*; vols 130, 144 and 167, *Private London Letters from Wernher Nov. 1902–July 1908, Nov. 1895–1910, Nov. 1895–1902* respectively; also certain letters in vols 116, 130 and 175 for the months of Aug.–Sept. 1899. Mrs Fraser's *All that Glittered: Selected*

Correspondence of Lionel Phillips 1890–1924 and Duminy and Guest's
FitzPatrick, South African Politician: Selected Papers 1888–1906 also
includes important papers from the Eckstein archives; these were
supplemented by Mr and Mrs Hunt's Phillips papers; a collection
of Phillips papers copied by Thelma Gutsche in the Africana
Museum, Johannesburg, and the FitzPatrick papers at the English
Language Library, Grahamstown. Other manuscript sources consulted include 'Half a Century in South Africa' by J. B. Currey at
the South African Library, Cape Town, the Rolleston family
papers, Sigismund Neumann's diary owned by Lady Newman,
correspondence at Rhodes House (MSS Afr S228: C24, C26, C28
and De Beers C7a, C7b, 9, 10/1, 26 and 28) and the Rothschild
Archive (RFam FD6, XI 111 18, XI 130A Z, X 112 7, and B17
RH XC).

Chapter 1, *The Young Julius*; Chapter 2, *Life in the Diamond Fields*:
Carl Wernher. Also private communications Coffey, Carl Udo
Wernher, Woodger. Rolleston MSS.

Chapter 3, *Turn of the Tide*: Beet. Boyle, Emden. David Harris.
Murray. Reunert. Roberts. Rosenthal. Taylor.

Chapter 4, *Centre of Important Interest*: Beit (*The Will and the Way*).
Cohen. Emden. Fort. Trollope. Turrell. Wheatcroft – an invaluable general source throughout the diamond- and gold-mining
chapters.

Chapter 5, *Farewell to Kimberley*: Chilvers. Roberts.

Chapter 6. '*Duties and Cares of the Sterner Sex*': Chilvers. Emden.
FitzPatrick. Newbury. Phillips. Roberts. Rotberg – for all
chapters concerning Rhodes. Turrell and Worger for all succeeding chapters concerning the diamond industry.

Chapter 7, *The Politics of Gold*: Allen. Bode. Cartwright – an
essential reference throughout the rest of Part One. Chilvers.
Graumann. Gutsche. Fraser – another main reference in chapters hereafter, including her editing of Phillips's *Some Reminiscences*. Jackson. Kiewiet. Kubrick. Lockhart. Longford.
Newbury. Reunert. Roberts. Taylor. Wagner. Gardner Williams. Also Hunt archives.

Chapter 8, *Gold into Art*: Bode. Emden. Fort. Longford. Magnus.
Pakenham.

Chapter 9, War Clouds: Beit. Belloc. Blainey. Blunt. Chilvers. Duminy. Edwards. FitzPatrick. Gutsche. Jackson. Judd. Kiewiet. Kubrick. Long. Longford. Pakenham. Rumbold. Walter. Also FitzPatrick papers.

Chapter 10, Forward to La Belle Epoque: Belloc. Duminy. Emden. FitzPatrick. Gutsche. Frank Harris. Judd. Long. McCarthy. Pakenham. Rhodes James. Richardson. Sampson. Taylor.

Chapter 11, South Africa Again: Brinnen. FitzPatrick. Gray. Gregory. Montgomery-Massingberd. Newbury. Pevsner. Phillips. Richardson. Van Onselen. Also re Mewès and Davis, Bouvet papers and Fenwick dissertation.

Chapter 12, Pinnacle of Achievement: Beit. Fort. Frankel. Haldane. Kubrick. Ted Morgan. Phillips. Richardson. Russell. Searle. Simpson. Webb.

Chapter 13, Alone without Beit: Beit (*The Will and the Way*). Chilvers. Cornwallis-West. Epstein. Gutsche. Richardson. Rosenthal. Stoeckl.

Chapter 14, Imperial Interlude: Bainbridge. Chavchavadze. Graves. Nariskin-Kurakin. Grand Duke Michael. Pless. Pope-Hennessy. Stoeckl.

Chapter 15, A Couple of Scrapes: Gutsche. Epstein. Milly. Painter. Rosenthal. Webb. Rothschild archives.

Chapter 16, An Era Ended: Brümmer. Epstein. Frankel. Kubrick. Phillips. Ritchie. Rosenthal. Stoeckl. Walker. Lady Wernher's letter to Phillips in Africana Museum, Johannesburg.

Part Two

The Luton Hoo archives contain letters to Lady Ludlow from Sir Harold and his children, a few documents concerning the Witwatersrand versus Cape Town University controversy and the Bath House burglary, and Lady Ludlow's scrapbooks both for Luton Hoo and Bath House. In the Royal Archives there is correspondence with Lord Stamfordham about Harold's commission in 1912 (RA GV F388), lengthy correspondence over the worrying question of Lady Zia's being granted the style and precedence of an Earl's daughter in 1917 (RA GV 1153/IV, XIII, XVIII), Lady Zia's letter to Queen Mary about Gina's engagement

in 1944 (RA GV CC47 2169) and correspondence between Queen
Mary and Sir Harold over Lady Ludlow's bequest in 1946 (RA
GV CC47 2256). The letters from George V and Queen Mary to
Grand Duke Michael and Countess Torby in 1917 are with Lady
Zia's correspondence, the property of Mrs Harold Phillips and
Lady Butter; this collection also includes the letters between
Countess Torby and the Queen of Greece. At Luton Hoo there is
also a number of papers concerning Combined Operations and
Mulberry, some 'Top Secret', which to some extent complement
the Record Office files WO32, DEF2 and ADM199, essential for
a full-scale history of Mulberry; also many letters from Mountbatten. Mountbatten's official papers concerning Combined
Operations are in the Library of Southampton University, and I
consulted B50, B76, I197, J168. At Broadlands I consulted family
letters in S339–44. Again at Luton Hoo there are papers, letters
and scrapbooks about racehorses, Someries Stud, Bermuda hotels
and the Luton Airport row; also Sir Harold's First World War
diary.

Chapter 17, *Legacies, Love, War*: Brümmer. Cartwright. *Lettres
des Grand-Ducs*. Rawlinson. Ritchie. Walker. Letter to Sister
Agnes in Royal Archives, RA GV F388/5, by gracious permission of Her Majesty the Queen. Rube letter in Luton Hoo
archives.

Chapter 18, *Murders and Marriages*: Benois. Brümmer. Chavchavadze. Cooper. Grand Duchess George.

Grigg. Gutsche. *Lettres des Grand-Ducs*. Marlow. Masson. Grand-
Duc Nicolas. Paléologue. Ritchie. Rose (for more on George V
and rescue of Tsar). Summers. Ziegler.

Chapter 19, *Lady Ludlow and the Great Robbery*: Alexander Mikhailovich. Curling. Dean. Goldsmith. Hayden. Lyle. Newton.
Shaughnessy. Vanderbilt. Isham papers 1/807, Northamptonshire Record Office, courtesy Trustees of Lamport Hall Estate.

Chapter 20, *The Game of Business*: Blackwood. Blow. Buckle.
Carr. Curling. Lifar. Lyle. Snowman. Thompson. Private –
Broughton.

Chapter 21, *Brown Jack*: Curling. Dean. Lyle. Newton.
Shaughnessy.

Chapter 22, Appointment to Combined Operations: Harrison. Irving. Lees-Milne. Harold Wernher. Ziegler.

Chapter 23, Co-ordination and Tragedy: Fergusson. Gilbert. Goldsmith. Harrison. Hartcup. Irving. Harold Wernher. Ziegler. Zuckerman.

Chapter 24, The Victory Harbour: Harrison, Hartcup. Janet Morgan. Harold Wernher. Ziegler.

Chapter 25, Return to Luton Hoo: Harold Wernher. Ziegler. Private – Spooner.

Chapter 26, Grandparents; *Chapter 27, Last Years*: Curling. Fergusson. Rosina Harrison. Trace.

Bibliography

Airlie, Mabell Countess of *Thatched with Gold*, London 1962
Alexander Mikhailovich, Grand Duke *Once a Grand Duke*, London 1932
   Always a Grand Duke, London 1933
Allen, Vida *Early Kimberley: A Photographic Souvenir*, Kimberley 1986
Les Arts, 'Collection de M. Rodolphe Kann', Paris Jan.–March 1903, nos 13, 14,
   15; Feb. 1908, no. 14

Bainbridge, Henry Charles *Peter Carl Fabergé*, London 1966
Beet, George *Grand Old Days in the Diamond Fields*, Cape Town 1931
Beit, Sir Alfred, and Lockhart, J. G. *The Will and the Way*, London 1957
Beit, Otto *Catalogue of Collection of Pictures, etc.*, intr. and described by Wilhelm
   von Bode, London 1913
Belloc, Hilaire *The Jews*, London 1922
   Sonnets and Verse, London 1923
Benois, Alexandre *Memoirs*, London 1962
Blackwood, Caroline *In the Pink*, London 1987
Blainey, A. G. 'Lost Causes of the Jameson Raid', *Economic History Review*
   XLVIII, 1969
Blow, Simon *Fields Elysian*, London 1983
Blunt, Wilfrid Scawen *My Diaries, 1888–1910*, London 1921
Boyle, Frederick *To the Cape for Diamonds*, London 1873
Brinnen, John Malcolm, and Gaulin, Kenneth *Grand Luxe: The Transatlantic
   Style*, London 1988
Brümmer, N. J., and others, *Gedenkboek van het Victoria-Kollege*, Cape Town
   1918
Buckle, Richard *Diaghilev*, London 1979

Camplin, Jamie *The Rise of the Plutocrats*, London 1978
Carr, Raymond *English Foxhunting: A History*, London 1976
Cartwright, A. P. *The Corner House*, London 1965
   Gold Paved the Way, London 1967
   Golden Age, Cape Town 1968
   The First South African, London 1971
Chavchavadze, David *The Grand Dukes*, New York 1990

Bibliography

Chilvers, Hedley A. *The Story of De Beers*, London 1939
Cohen, Louis *Reminiscences of Kimberley*, London 1911
 Reminiscences of Johannesburg, London 1924
Cooper, Ken *Luton Scene Again*, Chichester 1990
Cornwallis-West, G. *Edwardian Hey-days*, London 1930
Curling, Bill *The Captain: A Biography of Captain Sir Cecil Boyd-Rochfort*,
 London 1970

Dean, Basil *Mind's Eye*, London 1973
Denoon, D. J. N. 'Capital and Capitalists in the Transvaal', *Historical Journal*
 23, 1, 1980
Dictionary of National Biography London 1885–
Dictionary of South African Biography, Pretoria 1968–
Duminy, A. H., and Guest, W. R. *FitzPatrick: South African Politician, Selected
 Papers*, Johannesburg 1976
 Interfering in Politics, Johannesburg 1987

Edwards, Anne *The Matriarch*, London 1984
Emden, Paul H. *Randlords*, London 1935
 Jews of Britain, London 1944
Epstein, E. J. *The Diamond Invention*, London 1982

Fenwick, Justin *Architecture of the Entente Cordiale*, unpublished dissertation 1971
Fergusson, Bernard *The Watery Maze*, London 1961
FitzPatrick, J. P. *The Transvaal from Within*, London 1899
 South African Memories, ed. G. H. Wilson, London 1932
Fort, G. Seymour *Alfred Beit*, London 1932
Frankel, S. Herbert *Capital Investment in South Africa*, Oxford 1938
Fraser, Maryna, and Jeeves, Alan *All that Glittered: Selected Correspondence of
 Lionel Phillips 1890–1924*, Cape Town 1977

George, Grand Duchess *A Romanov Diary*, New York 1988
Gilbert, Martin *Road to Victory: Winston S. Churchill 1941–1945*, London 1986
Goldsmith, Barbara *Little Gloria – Happy at Last*, London 1980
Goldsmith, Maurice *Sage: Life of S. D. Bernal*, London 1980
Graumann, Sir Harry *Rand, Riches and South Africa*, London 1936
Graves, Charles *Royal Riviera*, London 1957
Gray, A. Stuart *Edwardian Architecture*, London 1985
Gregory, Theodore *Ernest Oppenheimer and the Economic Development of Southern
 Africa*, Cape Town 1962
Grigg, John *Lloyd George: The People's Champion*, London 1985
Gutsche, Thelma *No Ordinary Woman: The Life and Times of Florence Phillips*,
 Cape Town 1966

Haldane, Richard Burdon *An Autobiography*, London 1929
Harris, David *Pioneer, Soldier and Politician*, London 1931
Harris, Frank *My Life and Loves*, London 1925, 1964
Harrison, Michael *Mulberry*, London 1963
Harrison, Rosina *Gentlemen's Gentlemen*, London 1976
Hartcup, G. *Code Name Mulberry*, Newton Abbot 1977

Bibliography

Haydon, Arthur, and Perkins, W. Leslie *Old English Porcelain: The Lady Ludlow Collection*, London 1932

Heald, Tim *The Duke: A Portrait of Prince Philip*, London 1991

Hickling, Rear-Admiral H. *The Prefabricated Harbour*, United Services Institution, London, August 1945

Irving, David *Göring*, London 1989

Jackson, Stanley *The Great Barnato*, London 1970

Judd, Denis *Radical Joe*, London 1977

Kiewiet, C. W. de *The Imperial Factor in South Africa*, Cambridge 1937
  A History of South Africa: Social and Economic, Oxford 1941

Kubicek, Robert V. 'The Randlords in 1895', *Journal of British Studies* XI, 1972
  Economic Imperialism in Theory and Practice, Durham, NC 1979

Lampe, David *Pyke: The Unknown Genius*, London 1959

Lang, John *Bullion Johannesburg*, Johannesburg 1986

Lees-Milne, James *Ancestral Voices*, London 1975

Leslie, Anita *Jennie*, London 1969

Lettres des Grand-Ducs à Nicholas II, trans. M. Lichnevsky, Paris 1926

Lifar, Serge *Ma Vie*, London 1970

Lockhart, J. G., and Woodhouse, C. M. *Rhodes*, London 1963

Longford, Elizabeth *Jameson's Raid*, London 1982

Lyle, R. C. *Brown Jack*, London 1934

McCarthy, John P. *Hilaire Belloc*, Indianapolis 1979

Magnus, Philip *King Edward the Seventh*, London 1964

Marlow, John *Milner, Apostle of Empire*, London 1976

Maurois, André *Cecil Rhodes*, London 1953

Mawby, A. A. 'Capital, Government and Politics in the Transvaal 1900–7', *Historical Journal* 17: 2, 1974

Merriman, J. X. *Selections from Correspondence*, ed. P. Lewsen, 4 vols, Cape Town 1960–9

Michael Mikhailovitch, Grand Duke *Never Say Die*, London 1908

Milly, Jean *Les Pastiches de Proust*, Paris 1970

Montgomery-Massingberd, Hugh, and Watkin, David *The London Ritz*, London 1950

Morgan, Janet *Edwina Mountbatten: A Life of her Own*, London 1991

Morgan, Ted *Churchill 1874–1915*, London 1983

Murray, Richard William *The Diamond Fields Keepsake for 1873*, facsimile edition, introd. Brian Roberts, Kimberley 1979

Nares, Owen 'Luton Hoo and the Wernher Collection', *Country Life*, 5 May 1950

Narishkin-Kurakin, Elizabeth *Under Three Tsars*, New York 1931

Newbury, Colin 'Out of the Pit', *The Journal of Imperial and Commonwealth History* 10:1, 1981
  'The Origins and Functions of the London Diamond Syndicate 1889–1914', *Business History* XXIX: 1, Jan. 1987
  The Diamond Ring, Oxford 1989

Bibliography

Newton, Ivor *At the Piano*, London 1966

Nicolas Mikhailovich, Grand Duc *La Fin du Tsarisme: Lettres inédites à Frédéric Masson 1914–18*, Paris 1968

Obolensky, Serge *One Man in His Time*, New York 1958

Onselen, Charles van *Studies in the Social and Economic History of the Witwatersrand 1886–1914*: vol. 1, *New Babylon*, vol. 2, *New Nineveh*, Johannesburg 1982

Painter, George D. *Marcel Proust* vol. 2, London 1968

Pakenham, Thomas *The Boer War*, London 1979

Paléologue, Maurice *La Russie des Tsars pendant la Grande Guerre*, 3 vols, Paris 1922

Pallister, David, Stewart, Sarah, and Lepper, Ian *South Africa Inc.: The Oppenheimer Empire*, London 1987

Parliamentary Blue Books, *Reports from Committees (2) British South Africa*, vol. IX, Session 19 Jan.–6 Aug. 1897

Parliamentary Report Select Committee on Jameson Raid, presented to House of Commons 17 July 1896

Phillips, Lionel *Some Reminiscences* (originally pub. 1924), ed. Maryna Fraser, Craighall S. A. 1986

Pevsner, Nikolaus *Bedfordshire* (Buildings of England Series), London 1968

Pless, Daisy Princess of *From My Private Diary*, London 1931

Plomer, William *Cecil Rhodes*, London 1933

Pope-Hennessy, James *Queen Mary*, London 1959

Rawlinson, Commander A. *The Defence of London 1915–1918*, London 1931

La Renaissance de l'Art Français 21, 24 (re Kann and Porgès), Paris 1920

Reunert, Theodore *Gold and Diamonds in South Africa*, Cape Town 1983

Rhodes-James, Robert *The British Revolution*, 2 vols, London 1976

Richardson, Peter *Chinese Labour in the Transvaal*, London 1982

Ritchie, W. *The History of the South African College*, Cape Town 1918

Roberts, Brian *The Diamond Magnates*, London 1972
    Kimberley, Turbulent City, Cape Town 1976
    Cecil Rhodes, Flawed Genius, London 1987

Rose, Kenneth *King George V*, London 1983

Rosenthal, Eric *Here Are Diamonds*, London 1950
    Gold! Gold! Gold!, London 1970

Rotberg, Robert I. *Cecil Rhodes and the Pursuit of Power*, Oxford 1988

Rothschild, Miriam *Dear Lord Rothschild*, London 1983

Rumbold, Sir Horace *Final Recollections of a Diplomat*, London 1908

Russell, Bertrand *The Autobiography of Bertrand Russell*, vol. 1, London 1967

Sampson, Anthony *Black and Gold: Tycoons, Revolutionaries and Apartheid*, London 1987

Sanderson, George *Theatre Ownership in Britain*, London 1953

Schreiner, Olive *The Story of an African Farm*, London 1883

Searle, C. R. *Corruption in British Politics*, Oxford 1987

Shaughnessy, Alfred *Both Ends of the Candle*, London 1978

Shorten, John R. *The Johannesburg Saga*, Cape Town 1963

Simpson, Colin *The Partnership*, London 1987

Bibliography

Snowman, Kenneth A. *The Art of Carl Fabergé*, London 1962
Solododkoff, Alexander von *Fabergé*, London 1988
Standard Encyclopaedia of Southern Africa, Cape Town 1970–
Stoeckl, Baroness de *Not All Vanity*, London 1950
   My Dear Marquis, London 1952
Stokes, Eric 'Milnerism', *The Historical Journal* VI, 1962
Summers, Anthony, and Mangold, Tom *File on the Czar*, London 1976

Taylor, J. B. *A Pioneer Looks Back*, London 1939
Thompson, George *History of the Fernie Hunt*, Leicester 1987
Trace, Dr Keith *A History of the Plessey Company Ltd.*, privately printed, n.d.
Trollope, Anthony *South Africa*, 2 vols, London 1978
Troyat, Henri *Pushkin*, London 1951
Turrell, Robert Vicat *Capital and Labour on the Kimberley Diamond Fields
   1871–1890*, Cambridge 1987

Vanderbilt, Gloria, and Furness, Thelma Lady *Double Exposure*, London 1959

Walker, Eric A. *The South African College and the University of Cape Town*, Cape
   Town 1929
Wagner, P. A. *The Diamond Fields of South Africa*, Johannesburg 1914
Walter, J. P. R. *Fitz*, London 1955
Warwick, Christopher *George and Marina*, London 1988
Webb, Beatrice *My Apprenticeship* (new edn 1979), London 1926
   Our Partnership, ed. Barbara Drake and Margaret Cole, London 1948
   The Diary of Beatrice Webb, vols 2 and 3, Norman and Jeanne MacKenzie,
      London 1983 and 1984
Webb, Sidney and Beatrice *The Letters*, ed. Norman MacKenzie, London 1978
Wernher, Carl *Chronicle of the Wernher Family*, Cambridge 1931
Wernher, Sir Harold A. *Personal Experiences*, privately printed 1950
Wheatcroft, Geoffrey *The Randlords*, London 1985
Wheeler-Bennett, John W. *King George VI*, London 1958
Williams, Alpheus F. *Some Dreams Come True*, Cape Town 1948
Williams, Gardner, F. *The Diamond Mines of South Africa*, New York 1902
Wilmot, Chester *The Struggle for Europe*, London 1952
Wolff, Tatiana (trans. and ed.) *Pushkin and Literature*, introd. John Bayley,
   London 1986
Worger, William *South Africa's City of Diamonds*, London 1987

Yusupov, Felix *Lost Splendour*, London 1953

Ziegler, Philip *Mountbatten*, London 1985
   (ed.) *Personal Diary of Admiral Lord Louis Mountbatten 1943–1946*, London 1988
   (ed.) *From Shore to Shore: The Tour Diaries of Earl Mountbatten of Burma
      1953–1979*, London 1989
   King Edward VIII, London 1990
Zuckerman, Solly *From Apes to Warlords*, London 1978

Index

463

Index